GLAMOUR

TABLE OF CONTENTS

MUSIC BOX GIRL   by Sierra Simone   1

BEDTIME STORY   by Skye Warren   45

RIPPLES   by Aleatha Romig   87

ROYAL MATTRESS   by Nicola Rendell   185

IN A STRANGER'S BED   by Sophie Jordan   241

BROKEN HARP   by Nora Flite   293

RED HOT PURSUIT   by AL Jackson   351

KNOT   by Lili St Germain   431

MUSIC BOX GIRL

A Twelve Dancing Princesses Story

Sierra Simone

PROLOGUE
CAL

T HE POINTE SHOES were the first thing Cal noticed.

It wasn't that the shoes seemed strange on their own. It was just that they were wildly out of place wherever the girls brought them. Slung over their shoulders when they bought their trenta iced green teas at Starbucks. Spilling out of tote bags as they floated in and out of the library. Tossed on the thick green grass as they burst out of the studio and flung themselves tiredly on the ground, like so many gazelles at rest.

The second thing he'd noticed was that they weren't girls…not really. The youngest was just on the cusp of eighteen, and the oldest was nineteen. They were in that liminal space between girl and woman, a space made all the wider by their long, sleek bodies and barely-there curves, by their sheltered lives in Purkiss's cloister.

The third thing he'd noticed was that Purkiss was a dangerous prick, which was unfortunate, because in a very real sense right now, he was Cal's employer.

Cal tossed his binoculars onto the passenger seat and rubbed a tired hand over his face, feeling every week of his thirty-nine years. He'd been out late the night before chasing down a cheating husband, out even later the night before that to prove to an insurance company that one of their disability claims was spending his nights doing cash-only work for a chop shop up in Fredricksburg. He should've gotten some sleep before coming out to the ballet school, but Purkiss had hired him to find out where his students were going at night, and Cal was a firm believer that one couldn't find what was done during the night without understanding what was done during the day. Thirteen years in the Army and four years as a private investigator had turned that belief into a religion. Violence, crime and lies didn't come from nowhere; they were there on the horizon of hard-working, honest daylight, if only one knew where to look.

Which is why he'd spent the last three days watching the school and its dancers. Watching Purkiss bark at the ballerinas for every sin imaginable—bad turnout, weak legs, shallow arches, lazy, lazy, lazy. The dancers hated him. They never challenged him, never defended themselves, never acted sullen or sulky or hurt when he humiliated them, but they hated him, Cal knew. After his divorce, Cal had become something of an expert in the subtle art of hatred, and it was fairly easy to diagnose once you knew the signs. A glance over the shoulder when a back was turned. A flex of the fingers. A hard stare out the window.

It didn't matter how prestigious Purkiss's small school was or how many dancers found jobs in Washington or Boston or New York afterward, these girls were miserable. No wonder they were thoughtless with their pointe shoes. No wonder they snuck out of the dancers' house at night.

"They're going somewhere," Purkiss had told him that first day. "They come in the next morning haggard and slouching and not ready to dance...and their shoes!" His nostrils had flared then, anger shaking his short, slender frame. "Their shoes get *ruined*, absolutely *ruined*. It's a disgrace."

Cal had sat in the chair in front of Purkiss's desk, staring at the small white man in front of him. It was a trick he learned in Iraq—you stare long and hard and silent enough, and the other person cracks like glaze on an antique vase. Deeply and into a network of thousands of other cracks.

Purkiss had finally admitted his real worry. "Tamsin, the oldest. She's my daughter."

"Do you care what the other girls do? Or only her?"

Purkiss had scowled, but a scowl from an aging male dancer didn't frighten Cal in the least.

"She's an amazing dancer," Purkiss had said. "The best I've ever taught. She's auditioning for the ABT in two months. I can't afford for her to slip now."

Tamsin. Cal learned over the next few days that she was the one with pale hair and even paler skin. Gold and ivory. And when she danced, she closed her eyes, as if she could shut out the world around her. Like a music-box girl, twirling alone forever.

NIGHT ONE

CAL

LOUISA, LAEL, LING.
Daneice, Devorah, Nanami, Nina.
Ellie and Yasmine. Isabella and Mary Grace.
Tamsin.

Twelve girls. Twelve pairs of pointe shoes knotted and slung carelessly over shoulders as the dancers crawled one by one out of the second story window and onto a nearby tree branch. Cal had to respect their ability to sneak out undetected—even with his car windows rolled all the way down, the only noise that came from the dark house was the rustle of the tree branches as the girls crept along and dropped like silent fruit onto the grass below. They walked out past the school property and piled into two different cars, hybrids that made no engine noise until they turned off their street.

Cal put his car into drive and followed.

He had a plan, like he always did. He'd follow, get pictures, go home and sleep off this latest run of work. And then tomorrow he'd hand Purkiss the evidence, get his six hundred dollars, and move on to the next job. It wasn't much of a life, but it was about what a divorced ex-soldier could expect. He was lucky to have stable work, however lonely it was.

And it was lonely. In the Army, you were never alone, not really. There was always someone to keep watch with you, always someone else who couldn't sleep, always someone else squinting at the road alongside you looking for disturbed earth and foxholes. But there was some loneliness still. You missed your family, your friends, cold beer. You missed your own horizon, trees, snow, the Science Channel, 24-hour drugstores crammed with bright bags of junk food.

He'd stupidly thought coming home to his wife after his last tour would mean being cured of all kinds of lonely. How wrong he'd been; he'd never guessed that peculiar isolation of laying in bed next to a woman while remembering the pops and booms of desert guns, the scatter of bullets and the smell of gunpowder singed in the sun. The blood, the fear, the blood, the blood, the blood.

They'd told people they'd grown apart. But the truth had been that it was hard to keep a wife when Fallujah was your mistress. So his last tour hadn't been his last tour after all, and he signed up to go to Afghanistan instead.

Some kinds of loneliness were better than others.

The girls drove far out of Richmond, out into Goochland County where the horses and the rich people lived. Country roads were shit for tailing, so Cal had to stay farther behind than he'd like, following the unblinking red eyes of taillights through the bends and warps of the road, wondering where the fuck these ballerinas were headed. And then suddenly there were no taillights, just the trees in the dark, and Cal had to reverse to see what he'd missed: a narrow road turning sharply off the small highway, disappearing into the dark like a path into fairyland.

He killed his headlights, rolled down the windows again, and crept up the road. His eyes adjusted to the dark fast enough, to where he could see the individual trees and the black glint of the James River between their branches. The twist and rise of the road—

Awareness prickled on the back of his neck, and with a cold feeling in his gut, he realized he knew this place. It was different in the dark, different with the war ghosts in his mind, but the minute he cleared the rise and saw the sprawling, elegant profile of it, he knew.

Persepolis.

Shit.

He parked the car at the edge of the lot, killing the engine after confirming the two hybrids were indeed there. And sure enough, he could see the slender shadows of the girls down by the entrance of the building, gliding like swans into the door, the moonlight catching the shine of slipper-silk as they moved. And the idea of all those lithe bodies wearing their pointe shoes into Persepolis stirred up an uncomfortable amount of heat in his blood. The idea of Tamsin, long legs wrapped in ribbons, up on her toes and bent over a bench with her pussy exposed—shit. *Shit.*

She's nineteen, he thought angrily to himself. *A child. Stop it.*

But it was hard to stop. Especially with Persepolis in full view.

He rubbed at his forehead, trying to remember the plan, trying to ignore the blood flowing to his groin without his permission. The problem was that the plan had gotten a lot more complicated just now, because Persepolis wasn't the bar or house party he'd been expecting. Persepolis was the kind of place where people with lots of money and specific interests went to play. Whips and chains, that kind of shit. Cal had done a fair amount of work for them over the last four years, mostly background checks for new members, and so he knew very well what went on inside.

Which meant that he was going to have to tell Purkiss that his daughter was sneaking off at night to get beaten and fucked by strangers. Or maybe she was doing the beating. Either way, he didn't think Purkiss would take it well.

Still, he had a job to do and he could still follow the plan. Take a few pictures of the cars outside, go home and stroke himself in the shower thinking of how those pointe shoes would feel on his back as he buried his face in some young pussy.

Fuck.

Take those pictures and go home, Cal.

And yet he was getting out of the car. Walking down the winding path to the door without his camera. Nodding at the doorman who recognized him immediately. Stepping inside the wide windowed bar area where those not at play drank and laughed and talked.

Persepolis was too cautious to serve minors, which meant that the girls wouldn't be here. No, they'd be downstairs in the public playroom. Although, since they were far too young to be members, they must be guests, and there was a chance that whoever they were a guest of, he or she would have them in a private playroom.

Cal tried to ignore the knot of disappointment the thought tied in him. It had nothing to do with wanting to see those ballerinas fucking *en pointe*, those sleek, young bodies at work. Nothing to do with wanting to see Tamsin's pert tits or high, round ass.

Nothing to do with the thought of all twelve girls in one room, licking and twisting and rubbing.

Sure. Because he could lie to himself, but he couldn't lie to his cock. And his cock remembered exactly how long it'd been since it'd been inside a woman. Too fucking long.

He walked down the floating staircase into the airy concrete and glass playroom, taking care to stay in the shadows as he did. It wasn't hard—a woman was whipping a man on stage and the spotlights were on her, and darkness spilled in from outside like water. It was as he moved undetected around the back of the room that he saw them. Waiting by the stage in their shoes, literal dancers in the wings.

He took a seat.

The first show ended fast enough, applause and wolf whistles echoing through the room, and then a woman he recognized took the stage—Mistress Hell, a half-Persian Domme with an affinity for young women and riding crops. Cal had done her background check four years ago; in real life, she owned a pricey graphic design firm and volunteered twice a month at a food shelter. But at Persepolis she was Hell embodied, and God help the little submissives she took under her cruel wing.

And tonight, there appeared to be twelve of them.

The girls mounted the stage behind Mistress Hell. In the bright lights, a person could see every small curve and dip of their bodies underneath their thin leotards; Cal had to stifle a groan when he realized he could see the dark buttons of their nipples through the fabric. They'd added small tutus to their outfits, and when Mistress Hell snapped her fingers, they all dropped to their knees facing away from the crowd. She snapped again, and they dropped to their hands, on all fours now.

Another snap and they went down even farther, foreheads on the floor, tulle framing each perfect ass. It made for a spectacular sight, all those toned legs and asses in every shade of brown and black and beige, a rainbow of smooth skin raised over those delicately-laced pointe shoes, and Cal had to shift in his seat to allow for his thickening cock. He never thought he'd get off on this kind of shit, but as Mistress Hell began laying into them with a riding crop, he began to see the appeal. All that firm flesh, just offered up, getting flushed and angry under the crop. And—ah, fuck—the wet spots growing on the leotards as the girls got hot from it. They squealed and squirmed, wiggling at Mistress Hell until she'd give them the crop to rub against, and rub against it they would, like needy little kittens.

He wanted to be the one to rub them where they were wet, the one to make those tight asses glow with heat. He wanted to walk up and down the row of those ballerinas and take turns with each one of them. Lick them from clit to puckered hole. Fuck them, going from one to the other to the other, dipping inside every single cunt. He wanted to paint all their asses with his semen.

He ground the heel of his palm against his erection, desperate to relieve the ache there.

Shit, shit, shit. This was spinning out of control. He was *not* getting paid to jerk off to his employer's teenage daughter and her friends. He needed to get out of there.

Just as he stood up, Mistress Hell's show ended and the dancers rose gracefully and exited the stage. The lights to the playroom came on—the shows were over for the night. The rest of the playing would happen privately. And even though he hated himself for lingering to check, he couldn't stop the urge to *know*. Would they play more? Was Mistress Hell going to take them back to her room and make them lick her pussy? Would they split up amongst themselves and go with other members?

That seemed to be the case. Two or three girls with a man, a girl with a mistress, another girl with a master, three with a genderqueer Dominant named Jackson. By ones and twos and threes, they were all claimed by hungry club members and taken away, tulle and pointe shoes and all.

All except for Tamsin.

Tamsin stayed in the playroom until all of her friends were squired away to be fucked, and then she began to head for the staircase. Cal stepped into the shadows, cock still throbbing, and waited for her to pass by.

And then he followed her.

Up the stairs she went, through the bar, not pausing to say hello or glance at the river or anything. And then she walked through the front door. Cal gave it a moment and then followed.

Outside in the warm night air, Tamsin walked slowly down the path to the riverside, her head tilted back, as if she expected to catch raindrops on her tongue, only it wasn't raining. If Cal could have seen her, he knew her eyes would have been closed. It was the same way she danced, chin up, eyes closed, moving inside of a dream. It pulled at something inside him, that habit of hers. Empathy maybe. Nostalgia for the kind of loneliness the young feel, still so free of the jaded anger of the old.

She moved nearly as silently as him, but even in her pointe shoes he could hear the whisper of her tread. He'd learned to walk quietly in Fallujah, in heavy boots walking through rubble. It was easy to be quiet on a flat river path.

Finally, she stopped and sat on a bench and began to untie the ribbons around her legs.

A fucking shame.

He should go now, he knew that. But he also knew that he should have been gone forty minutes ago and yet he was still here, still unable to detach himself, still having dangerous kinds of thoughts.

She's nineteen. She's your client's daughter. You're a stranger to her.

It was her sigh that undid him, finally, and the way she slipped off her ballet shoes and cradled a foot in her hands. Even from the safe distance of several yards, he could see the tape and bandages holding her poor feet together. Jesus Christ. Was that what all their feet looked like under those sweet shoes?

Why he did it, he couldn't later recall, but he knew that sigh and the sight of that bruised and bloodied foot was part of it. But only part. The other part was submerged somewhere deep inside of him, a loneliness and a lust that had been denied for too fucking long.

"Tamsin," he said, stepping out of the shadows.

To her credit, she didn't jump at the sound of her name. She didn't act frightened. Cal had to wonder how many older men approached her in the dark if she was this casual about him being here. It was just the two of them on the riverside, and Persepolis was the only light and safety for miles. She should feel all kinds of unsafe and it worried him a little that she didn't. He kept his distance from her bench, kept his hands open and outward facing to show her that he meant no harm. That he wouldn't advance any closer.

"Who are you?" she asked curiously. Her voice was as dreamy as he'd thought it might be from watching her. Floaty and a little reserved, like she was in her own world. Like she was lost inside it with no one to show her the way out.

"Cal Dugan. Your father hired me."

She didn't seem surprised by that at all. "Of course he did," she murmured, looking back down at the river. "What for?"

"To follow you. To find out why you and your shoes look like shit in the morning."

She smiled at that, but only a little. "I should have guessed."

That surprised him. "Really? You should have?"

"My father only wants one thing from me—to see me become a principal dancer—and he'd do anything to see it happen. Have me followed. Threaten me. Take away things I love. I'm used to it."

She hugged her legs up to her chest, propping her battered feet on the seat of the bench. She leaned her head on her knees and looked at him, golden bun shimmering in the moonlight. She looked like a Degas painting, unreal and gauzily elegant. There was no approaching her, no reaching her dreamy soul through the paint. Forever untouchable.

"What will happen if he finds out about Persepolis?" Cal asked, even though he shouldn't. It was none of his business, and worse, the more he knew, the harder it would be to do his job. And he wasn't in a place where he could walk away from six hundred dollars and feel good about his month.

Tamsin lifted her shoulder in a gesture like a shrug, keeping her head on her knees. "He'll be angry," she said, voice blank.

It's none of your business, Cal, none of your business. Don't go there, don't even ask—

"Does he beat you?"

Cal didn't consent to the question leaving his mouth, it just did. But he suddenly needed to know, with gut-twisting urgency, whether Purkiss was hurting Tamsin. He couldn't afford to lose the money...but he didn't know if his conscience could afford six hundred dollars subsidized by this girl getting the shit kicked out of her by her teacher-dad.

Tamsin didn't answer the question, just unfolded her long limbs and stood, grabbing for her pointe shoes. "Don't worry about me," she said shortly. "I'll survive."

"Tamsin."

Her eyes flared in the dark and she stepped closer to him. In the daylight they were a soft gray, but now they were shimmering pools of silver. "Why are you so worried about it?"

Cal didn't have a ready answer for that. Only the truth. "I don't know."

She studied him for a moment longer, silver eyes scorching across his face and down his neck to his body and back up again. He was fit, he knew that much, but it had been a while since he cared what a woman thought of the way he looked. And so it was like a gift when she met his eyes again and her face was flushed.

"Goodbye, Cal," she said and left.

Cal watched her go with a clench in his chest that he hadn't felt in years. He would be back tomorrow night, he knew that much for certain, but what he didn't know was whether it was to do his fucking job or whether it was to screw this job altogether.

He only knew he couldn't wait to find out.

NIGHT TWO
TAMSIN

THEY WEREN'T IN a show tonight, but Mistress Hell had said they could come any night they wanted, and so they did. The night after a man named Cal Dugan stepped out of the darkness to speak to her, they decanted themselves from a bedroom window onto a wide tree branch, dropped to the ground and escaped to Persepolis.

The other girls chattered and gossiped—who did they want to see tonight, who did they want to fuck? She stayed silent through all of it. She didn't make it their business what she did at Persepolis, she didn't make it her business to know theirs. And she hadn't told them about Cal yet, even though he could bring hell raining down on their heads the moment he decided to do his job.

But she watched for him. As they crawled out of the window, as they drove, as they parked. She watched for him. She'd only gotten the barest sense of him in the moonlight, but it was enough to make it hard to shake the thought of him. He was older, forty maybe, and built like a fucking *wall*. Over six foot five, surely, with broad shoulders and wide swathes of muscle that his black T-shirt couldn't hide. He could have picked her up, tossed her over his shoulder and disappeared with her into the dark, and she wouldn't have been able to do anything about it.

It was shocking how inflaming that thought was.

His face, too—even hidden in the moonlight, there had been the stubbled edge of a proud jaw, the flash of eyes that spoke of experience and worldliness and knowledge—and all of that had been in his hard voice too. Everything about him screamed of the kinds of secrets she'd come to Persepolis to learn, only she hadn't felt half as terrified, half as wildly aroused at the sight of canes and cuffs as she had at the sight of Cal in the dark. *Cal* was the kind of dangerous she'd been craving, *Cal* was the kind of knowledge she was so desperate to know.

And when she'd woken up and the day went as it should, teaching the classes of younger dancers, her father yelling at her but no more than usual, she knew that Cal hadn't betrayed them.

Yet.

Persepolis was busy tonight—a high-profile Dom and sub were showing off tonight—and it was a Friday. The rich and powerful were out to play, and not for the first time, Tamsin sent up a prayer of thanks to whichever deity had seen fit to send Mistress Hell to their spring show. Whichever fit of attraction had compelled Hell to approach them and offer to introduce them to the club.

She supposed the line between kink and ballet was fairly blurry when you considered it. Pain and beauty in constant exchange. Entire lifestyles built on passion and discipline.

The girls flitted off the moment they stepped into the playroom, little wisps of sex on pointe shoes, caught by eager hands before they could drift very far. Tamsin herself, she decided to watch the show. She'd been back in a private playroom once or twice, and it'd never carried the taste of taboo she craved, not really. It all felt so...sedate. So safe. A leap with no risk of a fall. And so she was glad the other girls were happy enough here, but she didn't need to engage in disappointing liaisons night after night to know that she wasn't going to find what she was looking for.

"Back again?" a rough voice asked from behind her. It felt like that voice leaked into every crack in her armor; it blew in like cold, exhilarating rain.

She hadn't gotten to this point in her ballet studies to let her posture betray her for anything, and so she knew she remained perfectly composed as she turned to face him. In the indoor light, she could see him so much better than last night, and the effect it had on her was...disturbing. He had the kind of gold-infused skin that hinted at Latinx heritage, thick black hair trimmed short, military-style. His eyes were a dark green framed by thick, black lashes, framed by eyebrows that seemed permanently fixed in a suspicious furrow. His jaw was squared and dusted with dark stubble, his cheekbones and forehead were high, his nose the only imperfection in an otherwise perfect face. A crook at the bridge, like it had been broken.

But for some reason that twisted Tamsin up even more. Cal Dugan seemed like the kind of man who would take a punch to the nose and keep fighting, like the kind of man who would refuse to see a doctor about it. Like he'd drink half a bottle of whiskey, grab a mirror, and reset the broken nose himself. So different than the meticulously groomed ballerinos she danced with. So different even than the sleek suits that frequented Persepolis. This was a man who worked and fought with his hands.

And she wanted those hands on her.

"You didn't tell my father about last night," she said, skipping past his question and any of the other normal greetings. "Why?"

"You," he said simply. "I need you to tell me that you're going to be okay if I tell him, and you haven't yet."

And she wasn't going to. There was a difference between taking her father's blows and lying about them, and the closer to freedom she got, the clearer that line became. But still, that Cal cared, even as a casual stranger, about what happened to her felt foreign, exotic and enticing and *good*.

Cal studied her for a minute, then took her arm and led her without asking to a chair in the back. She expected him to offer the chair to her, but instead he sat and pulled her into his lap. Within an instant, she was enfolded in muscle and warmth and a heady masculine scent, wood smoke and skin.

"What are you doing?" she asked breathlessly.

"Enough people here know what I do for a living. It's going to raise questions if I'm here interrogating you, and neither of us are ready for that. We'll blend in better this way."

And they did blend in this way, just another couple getting ready for the show, anonymous in their pose of affection. But the upshot was that Tamsin couldn't restrain her body's reaction to Cal like this, not with so much warm, hard body pressed against hers.

The lights fell and the couple took the stage to applause, the Dom fastening his submissive wife to a St. Andrew's cross. Which was when Cal leaned forward and whispered in Tamsin's ear. "Now, what am I going to do with you?"

He meant about telling her father. She knew that, yet it was hard to remember with his lips at her ear and his warmth at her back. Hard to remember he didn't mean the kinds of dangerous, dark things she wanted him to mean.

"Whatever you like," she said, meaning that he should do his job or not—she didn't have any expectation of changing his mind. But the moment the words left her mouth, she knew they sounded much more breathless and eager than she intended.

"Is that so?" he murmured. A couple walking past glanced down at them, and Cal stroked a warm hand on the outside of her thigh to maintain the illusion that they were just a couple snuggling up for the show. She was only in a leotard, and it was bare skin he was touching, sending goose bumps rippling everywhere, everywhere, everywhere.

She was hardly able to stand it, the feeling of that calloused hand so possessive on her skin, the solid wall of his chest big enough that she could curl against it. Never had she felt like this, never had she imagined a man could be anything stronger or harder than the ones she'd already met. But those men barely qualified for the label of *man*, not after meeting Cal, who seemed like he'd already lived three lifetimes in the time it took most people to live half of one.

"You used to be a cop or something?" she asked. It was out of nowhere in terms of their conversation, but not of her thoughts—she had to know what made a man like him. What scars and horrors added up to the hulking mass of raw danger he was now.

"Soldier," he corrected, still stroking her leg. "Iraq and Afghanistan. Left a few years ago."

Suddenly she wanted more. More contact, more of his face and his voice. She twisted in his arms and he allowed her, watching her with that same expression of aloof suspicion that he watched everything with. She turned so that she was straddling him and facing him, her pointe shoes tucked delicately under her folded legs, her center resting directly against—*oh*.

He was hard.

He watched her face as she realized this, as her lips parted and her face flushed.

"Go on," he said, and there was a hint of lazy admiration in his voice. "Sit on it."

She hesitated. If she went any further, she was pushing this conversation past the casual—or whatever passed for casual in their situation—and into the territory of the sexual. She'd be admitting she wanted him. She'd be acknowledging that he wanted her.

Suddenly, there was nothing she wanted more than just that, to push them into something glittering and sweaty and raw. She sat on it—on him—

16

feeling the impossibly thick, impossibly long ridge of him flush against her center. Through the thin fabric of her leotard, she could feel every seam of his jeans, the line of his zipper, the exact width and heft of his penis. There was a part of her—a big part—that wanted to rub against it like she'd rubbed against Hell's riding crop last night. To grind down until she worked off some of this tension that he knotted inside her.

He seemed to read her mind. "Go ahead, princess. Make yourself feel good."

"It seems wrong," she said, even as she started swiveling her hips against him.

"This is a club full of wrong, sweetheart."

It was different, surely he saw that. "But you're old enough to be my father. That's bad to like."

A flash of teeth in the dim light. "Very fucking bad."

"And you could ruin my life if I didn't do as you said. It's wrong to like that you have that power over me."

His hands brushed along her waist, slowing to explore her navel through the leotard. "But you do like it?"

She couldn't explain it, she didn't even want to try. "I do," she admitted.

"You like bad things."

"I wanted…I've wanted bad things for a long time. But it's never felt bad here, just safe. Not until you."

She couldn't believe she was confessing all this and yet the thrill she felt when she saw Cal's stubbled jaw relax in understanding was worth it all.

"I think I get it now," he said, leaning back in the chair, as if to enjoy the view. He idly plucked at a nipple through her leotard, and she nearly had a heart attack. The pleasure shot to her center like a lightning bolt.

"Get what now?" she whispered.

He stared up at her. "Why you close your eyes when you dance."

That's not at all what she expected him to say, and she slowed the motion of her hips as he continued. "You close your eyes so you can pretend you're not alone."

Her breath caught.

"And," he said, his hands settling on her hips. "You close your eyes to dream that someone will take care of you." He flipped her around with those large hands, lifting her as if she weighed nothing. Settling her so she sat in his lap again, facing the stage, her legs open and hooked around the outside of his knees.

"And I bet you thought you'd be taken care of here," he said, one hand holding her hip steady as the other reached around to stroke along the lines of her inner thighs. "Isn't that right, princess? Find other people who liked the same kinds of wrong?"

She nodded. It was all she could manage. He was right, of course, so very right. If there was anything she thought Persepolis could promise, it was that there were people here just like her, lonely and hungry for the same things she wanted. But it was all so predictable here. Pain and bondage. No one cared about the grittier kinds of power exchange...like being spread open and touched by a man twice her age. Like fantasizing that he was *making* her do it or else he'd tell her father everything.

God, she was fucked up. But she already knew that. What she didn't guess was that there was a man like Cal around who would see it so clearly.

"Tell me," he said. "Tell me the kinds of wrong you are thinking about right now."

She squirmed in his lap but couldn't make the words come out.

"Don't worry," he said gently in her ear. A pair of blunt fingertips skated up her center, skimming across the fabric stretched over her pussy, and she tried to move closer to them, closer to the pressure, but they moved back to her thigh. "I'm going to take care of you, sweetheart. I promise. But first I need to know exactly the kinds of bad, wrong things my little ballerina is wanting."

So she told him. About the age difference and how it turned her on. Her blackmail fantasies. And more things too—how she wanted to be forced to crawl across the floor like a pet, how she wanted to look down and see a man's bare feet next to the pale pink of her ballet slippers, how much she wanted to watch him fuck her friends, every single cheap and tawdry way she wanted to be used and see others used around her. When she finished, she became aware of how much harder he was underneath her now, how the probes of her breasts and cunt had gotten harder, more insistent.

"You are so brave telling me such bad things," Cal whispered in her ear. "And brave girls get rewarded."

His fingers nudged along the crotch of her leotard, pushing underneath, and she almost came, she was that worked up, but then his fingers moved to her soaking wet folds, and she knew for sure she wasn't going to last long. His other hand moved to her breast, kneading the small curve of flesh as his other hand began exploring her in earnest now, dipping just inside her wet hole, rubbing up to her clit, which was swollen and hard.

"Oh, little ballerina," he groaned in her ear. "It's been so long since someone's taken care of you, hasn't it?"

"Yes." It came out as something like a whine.

His voice was soft when he asked, "How long, princess? Since you've had what you need?"

She tried to think. "I've fucked a couple people here at the club—"

"But that's not what we're talking about and you know it," he cut in. "How long since someone has given you *what you need?*"

And the honest answer to that was never. "They haven't," she said, her voice sounding unaccountably sad.

Cal *tsk*ed, big fingers starting to gently twist their way up inside her now. "What a fucking shame. But I'm almost grateful because—" his fingers slid in even deeper and she squirmed in his lap "—it means—" He slid up to the second knuckles and curled his fingers, driving pressure against her soft front wall. She gasped, her head dropping back onto his shoulder "—that you are starving for it right now."

And she was, oh fuck, yes she was. Starving like she hadn't eaten in days, empty like she'd been hollowed out and filled with air instead. "Please," she whimpered. "Please love me."

She didn't have to explain herself to him, she knew from the growl behind her and the way his hand cupped her possessively that he understood. He knew she didn't mean *love* like a feeling, like a commitment to a future, like red roses and musical greeting cards and dinners full of small talk. She meant *love* like a verb, a very specific verb. She meant *care for me, make me feel good, stay with me tonight.* She meant *come inside me, hold me so tight I can't breathe, touch me, touch me, touch me.*

"I'm gonna," he said into her ear. He twisted her nipple sharply through the leotard and she cried out. "And I'm not a fancy guy, sweetheart. You want me to stop, you say 'stop.' You want me to wait, say 'wait.' Got it?"

She nodded eagerly, ready to move past whatever barriers were keeping him from possessing her right now, and he seemed to feel the same way, because he shifted and his hand abandoned her breast. She wanted to pout at the lack of contact, but all attempts at pouting fled the moment she saw what he was reaching for in his back pocket.

A small folding knife.

She stared at it in the dim light, at the nicks and scrapes along the painted handle, wondering if he carried this knife while on deployment. If he'd ever used it to hurt someone.

Cal flicked the knife open with the ease born of lots of practice. "Don't," he said, "move."

She didn't.

She held completely still as the knife moved between her legs and the tip pricked carefully at the sensitive skin where thigh met cunt. And then his fingers withdrew, wrapped around the crotch of her leotard, and with a swift cut, her leotard was cut open.

The knife was folded, put away, and then Cal's fingers tugged her leotard up past her hips. She was fully exposed now, so exposed that all any stranger had to do was look at her and they'd see her nakedness. See the wet place where Cal's fingers were once again buried. See the hard points of her nipples through her leotard and the flush on her face and the tense lines of her thighs where she strained to hold them open.

"Someone might see," she said, and she wasn't sure if it was in a tone of protest or wonder.

"I want them to see," Cal answered. "I want them to see what a little deviant you are."

She tried to think of a response to that and she couldn't. His touch felt so good and the way he fingered her—slow curls inside coupled with the press of his palm on her clit—had her insensate. She was going to come soon. And hard.

"Let's play a game," he growled into her ear.

"Okay," she whispered.

"The game is that you have to do what I say, when I say it. And if you don't, I'll tell your father where you've been sneaking off to all these nights."

She shivered. It didn't take much imagination to recall the feeling of her father's blows. "Is...is the game real?"

Cal paused before answering. "Do you really want to know?"

No. It was fucked up for sure, but the very real threat of her father finding out made the whole thing feel so much more...delicious.

"No," she said, feeling certain of this one thing at least. "Don't tell me."

His hand withdrew from her folds again, and when she looked over at her shoulder at him, he was sucking her taste off his fingers, his eyes hooded. "You taste sweet, princess. Just like a little ballerina should. Let's see if you look that way too." And before she could protest—not that she would have anyway—she was pushed unceremoniously forward between his legs. He pushed her just fast enough for her to gasp, just slow enough that she could easily get her arms out in front of her and catch her weight.

It was a ridiculous position, all things considered—her hands flat on the floor, head hanging down, ass still secure in his lap. Thank God she was flexible enough to be comfortable like this. But then she felt his fingers run glancingly up her cunt to her ass and she realized this position wasn't ridiculous at all. It was decidedly and definitely humiliating—which made it perfect. Leaning all the way forward like this meant that her ass and pussy were open for Cal's viewing, and view them he did.

"Oh, your pussy looks so sweet too," he said. "Pink like your slippers."

"*Oh,*" she breathed as he took his thumbs and spread her folds. It was so fucking degrading, the air so cool on flesh that was usually hidden and protected.

"Don't squirm, sweetheart. You're letting me do whatever I want, re-member?"

"Yes, I remember," she managed from down by the floor.

A sharp smack on her ass. "Damn straight, you do." Then the thumbs returned, spreading her even more. "Like a pretty pink butterfly," Cal said with something between gruff wonder and lust. "I can't wait to fuck it."

"You're...you're going to fuck me?"

"Of course I am. I get to do anything I want with you. I've caught a little butterfly—I've caught you—and I'm not letting you go until I'm finished."

She shuddered at his words, at the wrongness, at the sharp feelings of desire they stirred up in her.

"That's right, sweetheart. You don't have a choice, not if you want me to behave. You be good for me, I'll be good for you, got it?

And then a thumb moved up higher, kneading gently at the little rosebud between her cheeks. "This is such a very pretty pink too," he murmured. "How good for me are you going to be tonight?"

She'd never done...*that*...never been with someone she trusted enough to do that, and yet the idea of doing it for the first time with a man like Cal was exciting on an order of magnitude she'd never felt before. She decided to be brave in their game too.

"I'll do anything you want," she said, and she didn't even have to work to make her voice pleading. "Just please don't tell my dad."

"That's what I like to hear," Cal grunted. A finger pushed back into her pussy, and he chucked darkly. "I knew you were a dirty one." And with strength she knew he had but was still shocking to feel, he wrapped his hands around her hips and raised her easily to his mouth.

"Oh God," she moaned. His tongue was so strong, his lips so firm. His sucks and licks so greedy. And then he left her cunt to trace wet circles around her anus, and her entire body shivered in filthy delight.

So wrong.

So, so wrong.

"You're going to let me inside you now," he demanded, and when she panted out an answering, "Yes," she thought that he'd take her right then and there in the chair. But he didn't. With an easy movement, he stood and slung her over his shoulder and carried her out of the public playroom.

"Where are we going?" she asked, lifting her head so she could try to get her bearings. They were in the hallway of private playrooms, dark wood doors leading off into private dens of sex.

"To the place where I'm going to fuck you," Cal said without inflection, producing a key from his pocket and unlocking a door.

"Are you a member here?" she asked.

"Not exactly. But I do enough work for them that it wasn't hard for me to get a room tonight." He opened the door, kicked it shut with his foot, and then dropped her unceremoniously on the massive king bed that dominated the room.

She stared at him from her new position on the bed, watching him stalk around the room, hitting lights, searching through drawers. "Are you looking for…" She didn't know if the word would insult him, but she said it anyway "…toys?"

He laughed at that, a low, dark laugh that curled her toes. "I don't need toys to play, sweetheart. I'm not a little boy."

No, he was not.

"I'm looking for condoms," he clarified, sliding open a drawer and finding a well organized stash. He selected one with two careful fingers and then turned to face her with that hard expression that turned her on so much. "Spread your legs so I can see you while I get ready."

She bit her lip and obeyed, daring to offer, "You don't have to, you know. Wear a condom."

His eyes had been on her cunt before that, but now they slid up to her face, and his handsome face looked almost…sad?

"Time out," he said. "Time out from the game." And then he sat on the bed next to her and pulled her hand into his giant one. The touch nearly made her tremble from its sheer gentleness; she couldn't remember the last time *anyone* had held her hand, except while dancing. She had the strange urge to press her face against his knuckles, to curve and coil around his hand and snuggle her face against it for weeks. And she had the even stranger feeling that he would allow her, that he would stroke her head until she fell asleep, that he would cover her with blankets and then wrap his large body around hers to keep her safe and warm the whole night through.

His other hand reached up to tuck a stray strand of hair behind her ear, and his fingers lingered there. "Are you on birth control?" he asked.

She shook her head slowly. "No, but my period hardly ever comes. I'm sure I can't get pregnant."

He gave her a rueful smile. "That's not good enough. You have an entire career in ballet ahead of you. I'm guessing a pregnancy now would ruin that."

She felt a childish need to defend herself, but he pressed a finger to her lips, his face growing stern again. "I'm not risking it, Tamsin. You are worth so much more than that. Game back on."

You are worth so much more than that.

It was stupid how much those words bit into her, got into her bloodstream and endocrine system and kicked hormones and hopes into high gear.

He released her hand with a squeeze and stood again, hiking his T-shirt up his back and pulling it off with the perfunctory grace of a long-term bachelor. Like he was used to undressing fast and easy, without thinking of how he'd look to anyone watching. It was fascinating to Tamsin; *everything* about how she moved was about how she would look doing it. Every step, every turn, every sweep of the hand…it was all for the audience, for the junction of music and soul and the Other.

But Cal—he just moved. Just got from Point A to Point B with a directness that had its own kind of beauty. And once his shirt was off, Tamsin found it hard to think about movement or aesthetics or anything else, because his body was magnificent. Incredible. Not just the hard, flat stomach or the broad chest or those mouthwatering lines that disappeared under his belt, but the hair and the scars and the *history* of it. He wore his experience and age on his skin, and it made Tamsin feel so soft and unspoiled and young. The contrast left her panting, wanting, craving.

Then he started working open his belt with one hand and she knew what craving *really* was. Craving was flipping over on her hands and knees to crawl to the edge of the bed for a better look. Craving was that tight, hot feeling in her cunt, that sharp puckering of her needy nipples, that sudden feeling of vacancy low in her core.

"I thought I told you to spread your legs," he said, noticing her rapt expression. "You want to make me happy or not?"

Oh, right. Yes. Shit.

She scrambled to be on her back once more, and he grunted again, this time in approval. He opened his pants and stepped out of them with the same efficiency as earlier, revealing a pair of black boxer briefs. And even before he pulled them off, she could see the head of his cock peeping over the waistline, looking swollen and angry.

She actually exhaled in shock when he pulled the briefs off, which earned her another pleased grunt. She couldn't help her reaction, though: Cal was big. Cal was very big. It only made sense given the size of the rest of him, but it still intimidated her to see the real length and girth of him, to see how it bobbed and swung under its own weight.

"You're big," she whispered.

Cal gave her a look. "And you're small."

For the first time since they started playing this game, Tamsin felt real hesitation. She wasn't a virgin and she wasn't a stranger to men, but Cal was something more. It wasn't just the thick cock now getting sheathed in shiny latex with a few practiced strokes; it was the thick cock *plus* him. Plus Cal and all his hardness and his experience.

Plus the game.

Make him happy.

Instinct sent her scooting up to the top of the bed as he approached, that shiny, blood-dark erection nodding between them as he walked to the bed.

"Nervous?" he asked.

"Yes," she said.

"Good."

He crawled onto the bed, crawled like a huge cat slinking closer to its prey, and grabbed her ribbon-wrapped ankles, yanking her farther down so he could cover her entire body with his own. Chest to leotard-covered chest, thigh to thigh, her silk slippers against the dark hair of his shins. He felt huge on top of her like this, not just long but wide and heavy, and she could feel the coiled strength in every fiber of him as he held the bulk of his weight on his arms.

She expected him to thrust into her, to spread her legs and push inside, but he didn't. He did something even more shocking.

He kissed her.

With his cock hard and pressing against her thigh, he brushed his lips over hers, starting at the corners of her mouth and working towards the middle. And when she parted her lips in surprise, he took advantage, sweeping his tongue in to taste hers, licking inside her mouth with abandon. His kisses swarmed her senses, a dazzling array of light and fluttering mixed with hard and possessive, and finally he reached a hand under her neck to tilt her head just right, and then his mouth slanted fully over hers, firm and demanding.

The erection against her felt hot and needy, grinding against her skin as Cal took his time with her mouth. He kissed her like it was his first kiss in years, like he hadn't had a woman underneath him in far too long, and he was determined to brutally savor every single second of this.

And indeed, when he pulled back to blink those dark green eyes at her, there was nothing but determination in his face. Nothing but more hunger around the kiss-swollen lines of his mouth.

"Am I making you happy so far?" she asked, daring to reach up and touch his jaw. The stubble scratched at her fingers, a scratch she felt everywhere, rasping through her fingertips and reverberating down her spine.

He stared at her, and his voice was surprisingly gentle when he said, "Yes, Tamsin. You're making me very happy."

The game wavered for a moment as they stared at each other, and Cal caught her hand on his cheek, bringing her fingers to his mouth to kiss. She gazed up at him as his lips caressed every knuckle, every flat and pad of her fingers. She didn't know how he could flip those switches inside himself, from degrading her to treasuring her, but she never wanted him to stop. It fascinated her, awakened something thrilling and alive. All her life she'd been treated like a china doll, a replica of her dead mother, a vehicle for her father's own wasted dreams. But Cal didn't look at her and see a ghost or a doll. He saw *her*.

Even as she had these thoughts, he seemed to come around to himself again, giving a hard shove against her thigh with his dick. "You say 'stop' if you want me to stop," he instructed her. And then he pinned both of her wrists above her head, put a knee between her thighs, and thrust inside.

It was an invasion, a forcing, but God, no invasion had ever felt this good. Like he was trying to wedge his body inside her, like all of him was pushing against the most delicate parts of her flesh, and everything in that moment, from the rough hair on his thighs to his weight on her chest to his huge hands trapping her wrists above her head, served to remind her how powerful he was, how big, how male.

It hurt, in the best way, the kind of stretch and push that she could feel everywhere—her inner thighs, her chest, the arches of her feet. With a grunt, he shoved in deeper, making her cry out and bow up against him.

"Yeah," he said, "like that." And he thrust again and again, hard and ungentle, his eyes searching her face for signs of pain or hesitation. He wouldn't see anything of the sort, Tamsin knew that for a fact, because she felt nothing of the sort. If she felt pain, it was only the kind that made her crave more. If she felt hesitation, it was only that she worried this would be over too fast, that Cal would empty himself and walk away and that would be the last time she ever felt so alive.

"I'll do whatever you want," she breathed up at him. "You can make me do anything."

"I know," he said with a dangerous glint in his eyes. "I know I can." He let go of her wrists and slid a hand under one of her thighs to raise it up to his hip, opening her up to deeper thrusts. His other hand he curled behind her neck, holding her head in place so he could brutalize her with more kisses, deep ones this time. He was pressing her into the mattress, a wall of hot muscle and firm flesh, and she used her newly freed hands to explore all of his body that she could reach. The furred expanse of his chest, the hard muscle of his back. The strong lines of his neck and shoulders.

"Wanna feel you come," he grunted, breaking away from her mouth. "How do I make you come?"

She felt strangely touched that he asked—none of the young men she'd been with had ever asked that. She was never fucking a boy her age again if this was what it was like to fuck an older man.

"My nipples," she said. "If you could suck—"

Before she'd finished, Cal had them both up and moving, and then she found herself in his lap, being impaled on his massive cock. Her head went back as she let out a long moan—this position pushed and stretched new places, and almost immediately she could feel the new tension curling around her womb, tugging at her lungs and spine.

Cal divested her of her leotard with the same perfunctory movements as he'd used to undress himself. And then before she could even adjust to being fully seated on him or to her new nakedness, his head was bent and a hot, wet mouth was closing over one aching nipple. He sucked and Tamsin arched to push her breast into his face. He bit and her toes curled. He moved to the other one, sucking and licking, his hands now on her back to hold her close to his face while he worked.

His stubble burned and scratched at her small breasts as she began moving her hips over him, struggling to breathe properly through the sensations crowding her nervous system. His thick length buried inside her, her clit against the hard muscle of his groin. The suction of his mouth and the chafe of his stubble. Each rock of her hips brought her closer and closer, but it was the demanding tugs of his mouth on her nipples that sent her over the edge. With a choked whimper, she came, the orgasm seeming too big to come from just inside her body. It felt like it came from everywhere, like the planets and the stars had realigned themselves just to ignite this thing.

"Fuck," Cal muttered, raising his face so he could watch hers as she fell apart. "Fucking hell, princess."

She was still shuddering with delight, still contracting around him. "Cal," she whispered, but that was it, that was all she had.

He waited until she was finished, holding her close and letting her work herself on his cock however she needed to make it through her climax. And then when her body finally, finally stilled, he murmured, "You come like you dance."

"How is that?" she said, burying her face in the strong curve of his neck.

"Like magic."

And then she was on her back again, him moving over her like a beast, rutting into her so hard and fast that a second orgasm stirred itself from the ashes of the first, biting into her with claws and teeth until she released with an agonized moan of ecstasy.

"Your dad gets angry about your shoes?" Cal asked breathlessly. Sweat was gathering in the furrows of his ridged belly, along his collarbone, sparkling on his neck. It enchanted Tamsin to see it, see the evidence of how all that muscle and sinew had gone to work to fuck her.

She nodded wordlessly, still trembling from her climax. Cal gave her a rare kind of grin—almost a smirk, almost playful—and then was pulling out of her. She sighed unhappily at the loss, but the sight that greeted her next froze any emotion but pleasure as he knelt on the bed by her feet and yanked off the condom in a rough, urgent move. And then he was jacking himself off, with hard vicious breaths pulling all the muscles of his stomach and rib into sharp detail and his ass taut with the effort as he fucked his hand.

"Tamsin," he said. Just that, like it was the only word he could remember, and then thick ropes of cum jetted out of his erection, spattering white filth all over her pointe shoes. White cum on pink silk. His entire body strained and tense, he milked himself empty, leaving her soiled and marked.

They both were still for a moment, their breathing the only sound in the room.

This was it, Tamsin thought with a crushing sense of horror. The moment it was all over and she had to go back to her music box life, spinning endlessly in front of cold, judging eyes.

But then Cal got off the bed, went to the drawer and rolled another condom onto his still hard-dick. He didn't bother to wipe down her feet and she didn't want him too. She wanted those shoes ruined beyond all hope.

"More?" she asked, reaching towards him.

"More," he agreed gruffly, and she spread her legs with a smile.

NIGHT THREE
CAL

H E COULDN'T SLEEP that night, or whatever was left of it when he finally packed a sated, sleepy Tamsin into her friend's car and then drove home himself. Having sex with Tamsin had clarified only one thing, and it was that he wanted to have sex with Tamsin again. *Love* her again, as she'd put it in her dreamy voice when she'd begged him to please love her, and he'd obliged the only way he'd ever known how. With skin and sighs and his arms wrapped around her until daybreak came to burn away the night.

To that end, he supposed it had clarified another thing: there was no way he could reveal the truth to Purkiss now. It was a complicated mix of protectiveness and attachment and conscience that Cal didn't care to examine too closely as he lay in his bed and watched the sun start creeping through his blinds. He'd told himself after his divorce that he was done with relationships for good, done with all their cryptic obligations and nuances of bitterness.

But he wasn't done with Tamsin. Not even close. And he couldn't deny that the thought excited him as much as it scared him.

Either way, it meant something needed to be done about Purkiss and this job. He slept for a few fitful hours, woke up to eat and make a couple phone calls, after which he showered and dressed.

Then he drove himself to Purkiss's ballet school.

THE CLUB WAS busy tonight, once again. A Saturday night in the warm summer heat; the rooms overflowed with people hungry for the kind of high they couldn't get anywhere else. Cal kept his eyes moving as he pushed his way through the crowded rooms, looking for any sign of pale gold hair or pink ballet shoes. He hadn't dared to go near the ballet school after ending things with Purkiss, since Cal's presence would only undo the lie he'd tried so carefully to spin. But it meant that he couldn't be sure the dancers would be here tonight. There was a chance, of course, but he couldn't be *sure*.

And there was nothing of Tamsin's presence, not even a sign of her friends, and for a moment, Cal allowed himself to register the ache of disappointment. The plumes of smoky worry that his plan hadn't worked and that, even now, Purkiss was venting his anger at his daughter.

He scoured the entire club—the private playrooms excepted—and then in a fit of moody indulgence he rarely allowed himself, ordered a shot of bourbon at the bar. He hoped the girls were safe from Purkiss, that his little scheme this morning had built shelter enough for them to hide in for as long as they needed. He hoped that one day he'd find Tamsin again, although he doubted it. Sometimes you met people that stirred you up like a storm and then you never saw them again. Life didn't owe anyone shit, and Cal Dugan of all people should know that by now.

"Rough night?" the bartender asked as he pushed the bourbon Cal's way. "Or not rough enough?"

"Something like that," Cal muttered, taking the drink in one swift motion and standing back up. He'd go home. There was no point in moping alone in the bar when he could mope alone at home for free.

A cool hand brushed his arm as he stood, and goose bumps raced up his skin as he tried to swallow down the hope that swelled in his throat like a balloon.

He turned to look down into Tamsin's exquisite face. It was like every feeling he'd ever had in thirty-nine years rushed through his blood and heated him up when he looked at her.

"Can we talk?" she asked in that floating, faraway voice, and Cal nodded mutely, all his words incinerated in the reality of her here, now, in front of him.

"I got a room," she said, taking his hand to lead him, and the shyness that colored her voice was almost too much to take. He wanted to cup her neck and kiss her until she whimpered, he wanted to cradle her in his arms and take her someplace far, far away from every care except taking the pleasure he wanted to give her.

All of this before his mind really registered her words and anticipation flipped in his belly.

He allowed her to lead him, her slender fingers wrapped in his large ones, through the crowd and down the hallway of private rooms. She let go of his hand to reach for the key, giving him a smile. "Mistress Hell let us have her room for the night."

Well then. Mistress Hell had been very busy today.

And *us?*

His suspicions were confirmed as the door swung up to reveal eleven ballerinas, all completely naked except for those maddening shoes. He felt their physical presence like a clench low in his groin, a heat of blood and tightness all along his dick.

"Girls, this is Cal," Tamsin said, like they were at a cocktail party. "Cal, this is Mary Grace, Louisa, Isabella, Lael, Yasmine, Ling, Ellie, Daneice, Nina, Devorah, and Nanami."

Each girl smiled or fluttered fingers or did a curtsey as they were introduced. It took every fiber of Cal's considerable self-control to keep his eyes on their faces. Not only because it felt polite, but because a fledgling sense of duty to Tamsin compelled him to make it clear he wasn't interested.

Even if that wasn't entirely true.

But Tamsin smiled. "Cal. It's okay. We're all here to say thank you."

He turned to Tamsin, since she was clothed and nominally his and therefore safe to look at. "You got my note?"

"Yes. And we are so thankful to you and Mistress Hell for fixing this."

He nodded. "Glad to hear it."

He was more than glad, but he didn't have the right words for his relief and his happiness and his fervent wish that…that something. He didn't even know what. He hadn't known when he called Hell this morning to ask her for help. He hadn't known when he stood in Purkiss's office and told the man that the girls were sneaking off to an influential ballet donor's house to use her private studio at night. And he hadn't known when he left Tamsin a short note in her tote bag explaining the lie—that Purkiss had bought it and that Hell was there to back up every part.

If he had to call it anything, he might call it a willful daydream. There was nothing more between him and Tamsin now, and yet he could not let go of this idea—this sweet illusion—that there might be. That she might look at his older, scarred body and see something she wanted more of.

"Cal," Tamsin said. "We want to thank you now."

"Okay," he said, trying to look at the rest of them without actually looking at them. "You're welcome."

One of the ballerinas—Ellie, maybe—giggled.

Tamsin came up to him and slid her hands up his chest, lacing her fingers around his neck. She went up easily on the toes of her shoes to do it, and the small act was so erotic that he had to close his eyes. The brush of her belly against the semi-hardness of his erection was undoing him, turning his cock to full stone.

"Tamsin," he said, opening his eyes. It was maybe a plea or an admission, but it wasn't a command. She had all the power tonight and she knew it.

"I want to play another game," she whispered.

"I don't want to play any kind of game that might—" he paused, not wanting to reveal too much of his own feelings. He couldn't say, *that might ruin anything between us.* There wasn't anything real between them. She was young and unattached and had her whole life ahead of her. She didn't need a washed-up soldier like him pestering her with unwanted advances.

She pressed her soft lips to his jaw, and he fought the urge to close his eyes again. "I want you to be with all of us. Please."

He kept his voice low, gazing down into her silver eyes. "It's not nothing, watching someone you've fucked fuck other people. There's no coming back from something like this."

"Good," she replied, kissing his jaw again. "I don't want there to be."

I'm afraid there won't be a future for us if I let it happen, was what he wanted to tell her. But he couldn't, couldn't bring the weight of his daydreams to bear against her, and yet he also couldn't consent to this. It was a stalemate.

Until, that is, Tamsin reached down and pressed a slender hand to his cock. Even through the thick denim of his jeans, there was no mistaking how hard he was. He pushed his hips into her touch with a low grunt, and she smiled.

"Come on, Cal," she coaxed. "You can say stop when you need to stop."

The idea of him needing saving from a bedroom full of agreeable ballerinas was ludicrous and almost pulled a smile onto his face. But not quite. He was still too preoccupied with Tamsin, despite the whispers and sighs of the waiting dancers around them.

"But I'm worried about you needing to stop," he told her quietly. "I'm worried about *you.*"

She wrinkled her nose. "Is this some kind of male thing where you think I won't get anything out of this? Or that my feelings will be hurt by seeing you fuck someone else?"

"No to the first," Cal answered. "And yes to the second. I know you wouldn't be here if you didn't think you'd get something out of this, but I would feel selfish if I agreed. Selfish and unthinking. I don't want to be that around you."

She ran her palm along his length, up and down, up and down, until he could hardly breathe. "This is fun for me," she said finally. "I like this. What I get out of it is the same thing I got out of last night. My feelings are only going to be hurt if you stop us from enjoying something we both want—just to be noble."

Noble. That was a word he hadn't used to describe himself in a very long time. Maybe ever. "Dammit, Tamsin, I'm not trying to be noble," he said, as if his rock-hard cock left any doubt about that. "I just want you to still like me after the night is over."

"Oh Cal," Tamsin murmured. She pulled away to look at him, and the loss of her touch on his dick had him nearly gnawing at his lip in agony. "I already so much more than like you."

Jesus. Her words bit him where he was vulnerable.

"Take a leap and trust me," she continued, still looking up into his eyes. "Join me in my dream."

It felt like that was all he'd ever wanted to do since the day he was born. He wrapped his hands around her jaw and pulled her face close to his. "Okay," he whispered. And then he kissed her, trying to pour every last feeling and fledgling hope into his kiss, so that she knew that she'd somehow become the most important person in his life over the course of a week. He couldn't tell her that, he couldn't act on it, he felt guilty even hoping around it. You didn't watch a girl through a camera lens and fall in love, you didn't play blackmail games with her and like it, you didn't fuck a girl once and wish for more unless you knew she wanted it too.

And yet.

He'd been kissing Tamsin so thoroughly and so deeply that he hadn't been aware of the other dancers inching closer until a hand brushed against his back. And another hand. And another. Too many hands. His entire body sang with hunger, but the knot in his chest necessitated that he refuse to respond. Instead he murmured against Tamsin's lips, "I don't want to hurt you."

"Trust me," she said.

And he took a deep breath and joined her in her dream.

✧   ✧   ✧

THE FIRST THING that happened was the kiss to his shoulder. He turned to see one of the ballerinas—Latinx, dark-eyed, Nina was her name—smiling up at him. It had been so long since he'd fucked a woman before Tamsin, and now the idea of fucking several women at once was almost laughable. Like he'd actually tripped and fallen into fairyland for real.

Tamsin stepped forward and took his hand, pressing it hard against Nina's small breast with its dark, erect nipple. "Don't be shy," Tamsin said to Cal. "We all want this. Do you?"

He did. Whichever that made him, man or monster, he wanted it.

Tamsin kissed him again, her tongue teasing at his lower lip until he opened to her, and then, with his hand still on Nina's breast, he slid his other hand around Tamsin's waist and pulled her tight against him.

"I want you close," he said against her mouth. "You be here with me, do it with me. Got it?"

She nodded, and he gave her a final rough kiss before he turned his attention to Nina. She purred as he thumbed her nipple and then lowered his mouth to her neck. She tasted different than Tamsin, who was all rose and delicacy. Nina was lavender, elegant, more grown-up smelling somehow, even though Tamsin was the oldest.

More like a woman.

And just as the thought breached his mind and sent a surge of blood to his already painful dick, hands were under his T-shirt, sliding warm and searching over the scars on his back, over the hair-dusted ridges of his belly.

"Off, off, off," a few of them chanted, pulling the cotton up over his head. He allowed this, allowed the giggling exploration of his back and chest after, the coos when they reached his scars, the *oohs* when they traced his muscles.

"With me," he told Tamsin, taking her hand and putting it to Nina's other breast, so that the two of them mirrored each other. A large bronze hand and a small white one, both flat against Nina's barely-there chest, both kneading and massaging and pressing. Nina moaned, her head lolling to the side, and Tamsin looked fascinated by the contrast and symmetry.

"With me," he repeated, and then bent to Nina's neck. Tamsin bent to the other side, and together they bit and licked until Nina was moaning against them. He guided Tamsin's hand down to where the naked ballerina was wet and waiting, and together he and Tamsin explored Nina's most secret place, rubbing her until she whimpered.

"You're hogging him," Ellie complained from somewhere beside him, and there was a resounding chorus of agreement. Before he could object—or indeed, even really understand what was happening—he was pushed and herded towards the large bed in the center of the room, herded with hands and shoulders and sighs. And then pushed so that he fell onto his back, an amused smile tugging at his mouth. It was like being attacked by a cluster of butterflies.

But he kept Tamsin close to him, so that she lay next to him on the bed, nestled against his side. He wanted this and he wanted her, and he didn't know how else to show her that he'd meant what he'd said. There wasn't a fucking Emily Post book about what to do in this situation.

The dancers came over them like a cloud. He found himself kissing a pretty black woman named Daneice, pulling her on top of him so that Tamsin could embrace her just as easily. The three of them shared a searing kiss, messy and breathy and wet, while hands started tugging at his belt. He hadn't felt someone else's hands on his belt since before his divorce, and for a minute he had to stop everything and just feel it. The novelty of being wanted as much he wanted in return. The now-unfamiliar feeling of different fingers fumbling on the buckle, yanking the leather through the loops. The slide of different skin under the waistband of his boxers. The grip of a different hand around his erection.

He groaned into Daneice's neck as an eager hand stroked him.

"You're so big," a ballerina cooed.

"So big," another echoed.

"I want to use him first!"

"I'll be next!"

"Oh fuck," he mumbled, feeling something wet and hot close over the hard tip of his cock. A mouth. A warm mouth with a fluttering tongue and soft lips. There were more giggles as he tried to lift his hips and push more of his shaft into that willing warmth, and then he felt other mouths. Pulling his jeans all the way off and kissing his thighs, working their way around his hips, nuzzling at the seams between his groin and his legs. More dancers came up on the bed, crowding around him and Tamsin and Daneice, their hands and lips everywhere.

He tugged at Tamsin's leotard, wanting it off, and she obeyed, even as she was just as busy kissing and squeezing and rubbing as he was. The mouth on his cock took him deeper and deeper, working him hard, until it was replaced by another mouth, and then another, and another.

Somehow, he worked his way up higher on the bed, making enough room for all thirteen of them to be arranged comfortably, if intimately, because there was no flesh not touching other flesh; the entire bed was a lacework of long, lithe limbs and smooth skin and silken pointe shoes. That pink silk was the only stitch of clothing any of them now wore, shocks of cool ribbons against all that hot skin.

There were too many kisses, too many hands, too many needy mouths and rubbing thighs to keep track of who was where and doing what, but Cal kept track of Tamsin beside him the whole time. *With me*, he'd said and he'd meant it.

With me, he said as Nanami rolled a condom down his dick. *With me*, as Mary Grace swung a leg over his torso and sank down his sheathed cock. *With me*, as he guided a pretty head between Tamsin's legs to make her feel good, as Devorah straddled his face and he held her hips as he sucked on her clit. *With me*, as they all fucked each other in a tangle of fingers and tongues. *With me, with me, with me.*

"We want you to ruin our shoes too," Lael said into Cal's ear. She was currently rubbing the swollen bud of Ling's clit as Ling rode him. He was getting close to the edge—Ling was the fourth ballerina to fuck him until she came—and Cal felt like he had no self-control left. His entire body was stretched tight, his toes digging into the sheets and his thighs so tense they ached. His cock almost hurting with the need to release.

Next to him, Tamsin had already come twice, once from riding his face, another time from Louisa's clever fingers. "Oh yes," she said, "you have to. Just like you did for me."

"Happy to," Cal said. "Might take more than one time though."

"I think we can make that happen," Lael purred, and then Ling came with a series of wracking shudders, her little mouth parted in an *O* of surprise. Cal gritted his teeth and endured the feeling with as much restraint as he could manage, but once she was finished, he gently lifted her away.

"Gonna come," he grunted, and with the same kind of grace and quickness they had on the stage, they arranged themselves in a little row on the bed. He managed to get to his knees and rip off the condom before it happened, and with a sharp wave of release, he emptied himself over several pairs of ballet slippers. With grunt after grunt as he stroked the semen out of his cock. He came so hard he could feel it in the soles of his feet and at the top of his scalp. And when he was finished, still-hard cock in hand, he saw that he'd only stained about half the shoes.

Which meant...

"More," Tamsin said firmly, pushing him back down on the bed and rolling another condom down his length after a few strokes to keep him at full mast. "You've still got more shoes to ruin."

And so he let the girl he'd started to care for guide pussy after pussy down on his cock, his face, his fingers. He fucked every girl in that room, more than once, he fucked them hard and soft, fast and slow, until the night grew old and blue at the edges, until they were all too sated and tired to do anything other than hum and snuggle and yawn.

And Cal ruined every single slipper they wore.

EPILOGUE
CAL

Two Months Later

CAL CAUGHT THE duffel bag easily and tossed it to the ground. He held up his hands to signal he was ready for more, and Tamsin leaned out of her window with her dance tote and dropped it down. That, plus a weekender bag and a pillow, and all of Tamsin's worldly possessions were ready to be packed away in Cal's car. He'd wanted nothing but this as early as eight weeks ago, the first weekend they'd met, but had respected her wish to stay until her successful audition with the American Ballet Theatre.

But finally, finally she was leaving, and instead of leaving on the train tomorrow like her father thought she was, she was sneaking out tonight with Cal. And he had one final surprise for her…if she wanted it.

Cal put her things in his car and came back to the window.

"Why don't you come up here?" she asked in a low voice. "One last time?"

He wordlessly started climbing the tree; he knew the way into Tamsin's room by heart now. Since their weekend at Persepolis, Cal had advised all the girls to stay in more often—Mistress Hell would protect them as much as she could, but a little caution would go a long way with a man like Purkiss. And they had cajoled and wheedled and touched him with butterfly hands to beg, and somehow he'd ended up agreeing to visit them on the nights they stayed in. They were insatiable, demanding, creative, and sweet, and after eight weeks of servicing all them, he understood Mistress Hell's fascination with the dancers. They were like gifts from the gods of fucking, come to earth.

And Tamsin…Tamsin most of all.

Cal had assumed what happened that first weekend had been some kind of adventure for them, an experiment of sorts, and that even if there'd been no lasting harm done to Tamsin's feelings, that it wouldn't happen again. He was used to women who didn't like to share after all, and he figured if a wife couldn't share her husband with war, then this young girl couldn't be expected to share him with eleven of her friends.

He'd deeply underestimated Tamsin. Tamsin and her obsessive craving for the wrong and the taboo in life. She loved nothing more than all of them playing together, she loved choreographing their orgies, debasing him and herself and everyone around them in delightful, ecstatic ways, and she came the hardest when she was the last one to fuck him. When she had him sweaty and raw and at the edge of his control. That's how she liked him best.

Tonight wasn't going to be elaborate or choreographed however. After he climbed up the tree and through the window, Tamsin nearly tackled him and pulled him to her pillow-less bed.

"I want it one last time here," she breathed, hands on his zipper. She was in a tiny little nightgown and leg warmers and—*Jesus*—no panties. He ran his hands up her thighs, playing with the place where the leg warmers met bare skin.

"Just you and me," he said, in a voice that brooked no argument. He loved fooling around with her friends—what red-blooded human wouldn't?—but right now, with his surprise burning a hole in his back pocket, he only wanted her. He'd play whatever dirty games she wanted, but at the end of the day, it was Tamsin who had his heart. Tamsin he'd move heaven and earth just to be near.

And he damn well had.

"Yes," she agreed, "just us." Her warm hands found his stiffening cock and pulled it out, rubbing it up and down. "Can't we do it without the condom?" she begged. "Just this once?"

"No," he said, even though it felt like *yes* was the only word he could remember.

"Mmm," she pouted, flipping up the hem of her nightgown to show off her pussy. She started rubbing the tip of him against her, getting it wet, slotting it inside her entrance and circling her hips and driving him mad.

"Just for a minute won't hurt," she said, batting her long, gold eyelashes up at him. "Just for a minute inside."

His arms were shaking where he held himself above her. "Just for a minute," he repeated. "No longer."

Her eyes lit up. "Really?"

"Shh." He put a hand over her mouth, because he wasn't sure he could do this without coming immediately, and he especially wouldn't be able to do it with Tamsin breathing naughty things in his ear. He closed his eyes and pushed inside.

There weren't words for how good her pussy felt. Wet and hot, tight like a fist. Every nerve ending in his penis felt electrified, every sensation was magnified, every inch farther was like a new revelation from God. She moaned under his hand as he stretched and filled her, and once he sunk in to the hilt, he carefully lowered himself onto her, chest to chest, letting his hand fall away from her mouth so he could kiss her. And kiss her and kiss her.

He couldn't wait to tell her, he decided. He wanted to tell her now, like this, when there was nothing separating them, no barrier, no distance, just the warm glide of them and their hearts beating so close.

"I'm moving to New York City," he whispered against her mouth. "I got a place."

Her lips parted underneath his, her hand reaching towards his face. "Really?" she asked, and her voice sounded so young then, so full of a hope and happiness that she hadn't yet learned how to hide.

"Really. I've got a key for you in my back pocket. It can be your place too, if you want."

"Yes," she breathed. "I want that. I've been so miserable thinking we wouldn't see each other as much as we wanted…"

"Remember what I said that night at Persepolis? *With me.* I want you with me, Tamsin, as long as you'll let me close."

"Yes," she said, kissing the corners of his mouth, his jaw. "I want to be with you always."

The words made him want to slump in relieved joy. "I like that you feel that way," he said gruffly, trying not to bother her with how much he felt. He still wanted her to be able to change her mind, leave him if she got unhappy or realized how old he was or met some other dancer that could better meet her needs. He didn't want to cage her, not his little music box girl, not when she was finally getting free.

Tamsin seemed to have other ideas. "Oh, you bear," she laughed. "I love you. And I know you love me. There's no need to be so stoic."

I love you.

"Tamsin," he groaned, burying his face into her neck. "I do love you. I love you too much, I think, than is good for you."

"There's no such thing as too much for me," she purred, biting his ear-lobe. "I think we've already proved that many times over."

With a low growl, he pulled out and reached for his wallet, rolling a condom on amid Tamsin's mewling protests. And then he grabbed the headboard with one hand, using his other to guide himself back inside her. With her heels at the small of his back, he thrust inside, deep and hard, wrapping both hands around the edge of the headboard now to drive in harder and harder and harder.

Soon they'd be in his car together, driving off to their new life. Soon she'd be in his bed every night that she wanted to be there. Soon they would see how far love could carry them as she danced and he worked and they had to fight off every problem that came with being in the real world.

But for now, he was happy to pretend he was still in fairyland, still inside the dream. And when Tamsin came and he came a moment later, filling his condom with heavy jerks and pulses, he murmured promises in her ear until they were both sweaty and still. *I love you* and *you're with me* and *I'll take care of you, princess, always, always, always.*

His promises were real, vows weighted with age and experience, and Tamsin seemed to wrap herself up in them like she wrapped herself up in his arms. "And we are going to live happily ever after," she murmured to him.

He smiled in the dark. "Ruined shoes and all."

THE END

About the Author

Sierra Simone is a USA Today Bestselling former librarian who spent too much time reading romance novels at the information desk. She lives with her husband and family in Kansas City.

Sign up for her newsletter to be notified of releases, books going on sale, events, and other news!

www.authorsierrasimone.com

BEDTIME STORY

A Sleeping Beauty Story

Skye Warren

ONE

The youngest fairy stepped forward and said, "The princess shall be the most beautiful woman in the world."

JESSICA

I SWIPE AT the tears on my cheeks, grateful for the pitch black outside. My eyes feel puffy, nose runny, but at least no one can see me like this. Yeah, that's good. One point for optimism, negative two thousand for the vortex of depression tugging at my toes.

Optimism. The secret weapon in a single mother's arsenal. Ky's running a temperature? That means extra cuddle time. The water bill's bigger than usual? We'll just have to make those last two hot dogs in the fridge last.

Then Ky's dad showed up outside our apartment.

I clench both hands on the steering wheel, so tight I can feel my heartbeat inside my fingers. That's okay, though. Optimism. I can make complete and utter terror look good.

A green highway sign flashes briefly in my headlights. *Provence.*

Working in a diner means I've heard a lot of random conversation, especially from people passing through. The name *Provence* registers as a small town outside Tanglewood. Which means I'm not nearly far enough away to be safe.

The truth is I'll never be far enough. Never really be safe.

So much for optimism.

Is the town big enough for me to hide? If only for the night?

I can't see past the twin domes of my headlight, the black tar texture visible despite the dark night. It had been an hour since I left Tanglewood city limits. I hoped to be farther by now.

Maybe I should have stopped to make better plans.

Should have booked a bus or even a plane. I couldn't risk it, not with Stefano outside my door, demanding to see his son. The moment the little bar in the test turned pink, my life changed. It stopped being about survival and became about something more. About a life for my child, free from danger, from violence. From fear.

Something fluttered in my chest, something like hope.

Stefano found the test in the trash can, and he had lost his shit. Beaten me so badly I was afraid I would miscarry. Then he kicked me out of the house. And even then, even clutching my stomach, my face bruised and bloody, it was a blessing.

A blessing, like the small child sleeping in the backseat.

At least he doesn't know how afraid I am right now, my heart thudding against my ribs, my sight blurring with adrenaline and exhaustion. He doesn't know how it feels to be hit, to be used, to be given as a gift by his own father. And if I have my way he never will.

The car jolts into the road, pulling a short scream from me.

Only a pothole.

I'm jumpy and way too tired to be driving. I check the rearview, but Ky's eyes are still closed. I hope he's dreaming about the dragons, like the light-up toy he clutches in his small fist. They're fierce. They don't need to pack up their belongings in the middle of the night and drive toward nowhere. They don't need to be afraid.

The bright side. There's *always* a bright side, no matter how dim.

Oh, I know. There are very few times in a girl's life when she could make this statement with complete certainty: things could not possibly get worse.

Red and blue lights flash in the mirrors, spilling light onto the windshield.

My heartbeat speeds up, almost frantic with its warning: danger, danger.

Oh God. Was he from Tanglewood? Had Stefano found me already? He had so many cops in his pocket. Why else would a cop pull me over? I wasn't speeding. The registration sticker might be a little old, bust he couldn't see that in the dark.

My stomach clenches—a hard ball of anxiety that rolls back and forth between *make a run for it* and *follow the rules*. Following the rules hasn't gotten me very far in this life. My finger throbs as if to remind me of exactly what rules had done.

Running won't work, not on this empty stretch of road that I don't recognize, with the needle closer to E than F. If the cop isn't dirty, he's not going to give up if I ignore him.

And if the cop *is* dirty, then I've already lost.

TWO

The second said, "She shall have a temper as sweet as an angel."

JESSICA

MY HANDS SHAKE as I steer the car to the shoulder. The cop pulls up behind me, the lights still spinning, throwing blue and red onto the worn cloth seats. I watch the driver's side door of the cop car, but it doesn't open. Seconds tick by, each one pushing the knife deeper. What if he's calling Stefano right now? I shouldn't be sitting here, waiting.

A wave of dizziness washes over me, turning my palms slick with sweat.

I don't think I can go on much longer, but God knows I can't stop. I'm in between the proverbial rock and hard place. The rock, a dangerous mob enforcer who thinks he owns me. And the hard place, a cop stepping out of his car and approaching my door.

"It's going to be okay," I whisper to Ky.

He's still asleep, and I'm the only one who needs reassurance right now.

I roll down the window and stare at a black belt and beige fabric.

A man leans down, one hand on the top of the car, the other shining a flashlight directly into the car, blinding me. All I can see is white. All I can taste is metal. I'm two seconds away from kicking the car into drive and pressing the pedal to the floor. It's not safe for Ky, but nothing is, definitely not a dirty cop working for the mob.

"Good evening, ma'am. License and registration."

In other circumstances, the honey-smooth drawl might have made me feel safe. Under these circumstances, on the run and exhausted to the bone, safety had taken a permanent vacation. Exactly where it had been most of my life.

I reach for the passenger side drawer, hoping he doesn't see my hand tremble. I find the little insurance slip—the cheapest kind that anyone sells. My license I pull from my purse. Then I hand them over, squinting into the light.

"May I ask why you pulled me over?"

There's a ninety-five percent chance that this will end in tragedy. That this cop is somehow connected to the Luski mafia. That even if he isn't, he'll run my papers which will somehow notify the cops who *are* connected to my ex.

But there's a five percent chance that I can play this right. That despite the odds I'll end up okay. That Ky will be safe. I've lived my life in that five percent.

He moves the flashlight to the paper, casting a demonic glow on his features. "You were driving erratically back there, Ms. Beck."

"I'm so sorry. I guess I'm a little sleepy. I'll stop at the next gas station and get some caffeine." And if he writes me a ticket I'll definitely be in the system, where Stefano's people can find me. "I promise to be more careful."

"Mason closes at ten every night."

The wheels in my tired brain turn slow and squeaky. "Who?"

A small upturn of his lips. "The owner of the gas station in this direction. He used to stay open until midnight, until Sherri had the baby. The next place isn't for fifty miles."

I was born in the Tanglewood county hospital, the eighth child in an unhappy home. All of us weeds coming up through the cracks—unwanted but unstoppable. I have never known anything other than the neon lights and exposed bricks of the city. Certainly every gas station is open twenty four hours, with metal bars on the windows and deals with the neighborhood gang to keep them from being held up too many times.

In all my eighteen years I've never seen such a long stretch of nothingness.

And in the middle of a black inky land there's him—a real life small town sheriff with a slow drawl and a twinkle in his brown eyes.

"Is there a motel nearby?" I won't get very far without gas.

Besides, nothing sounds better than a moderately clean bed.

"A motel? Lisa Renee would be offended to hear the word used to describe the Bed & Breakfast. She won't hear you say it, though. She's gone on a cruise to Alaska. Takes a trip every year during the slow season."

I can't imagine a place this wide open ever having a fast season.

"Do you think you could just let me go?"

That earns me a full-fledged smile, his teeth sharp white against the dark night. In my delirium he looks like some kind of prince, his sheriff's badge his shining armor and his black-and-white his honorable steed.

"No, ma'am. I wouldn't be doing my job if I let you keep weaving and bobbing on this back road." He tilts the flashlight to the side, casting a faint glow over the backseat without shining directly in Ky's face. "And it looks like you have a small passenger. Couldn't forgive myself if anything happened to him."

My stomach turns into a hard stone. "Then what can I do?"

His lips press together. He seems almost regretful as he looks back at his car and then to me. "What you can do is step out of the vehicle."

THREE

The third fairy said, "She shall have a wonderful grace in all she does or says."

JESSICA

FEAR HAS A flavor, like I've bitten into lip and drawn blood. Step out of the vehicle. That's what happens when you're in trouble. Big trouble. When things are about to get worse.

"Why?"

"I need to check you for alcohol consumption."

"I'm not drunk. I never drink." Which suddenly seemed like a travesty. Years of sobriety. Of careful planning and hiding, all turned to dust in one terrible evening.

"All the same, ma'am."

I press my hand to my forehead, as if the answer might be written on my skin. Somewhere close. Somewhere I can't see. I'm not worried about what he'll do if I fail an alcohol test. Even running on two hours of sleep I can walk in a straight line.

I'm more worried about what he'll do with me after that.

There are more corrupt cops on the city streets than clean ones. Even if he doesn't have ties to the Luskis he could touch me. He could use me. All while Ky sleeps peacefully in the backseat. I don't trust cops any more than he seems to trust sleepy drivers.

"You have to promise something."

His eyebrow quirks up. "It seems to me you aren't in a position to bargain."

"Swear that you won't touch me." I would floor the car before I got out, if he didn't agree to this. If he didn't make me believe in him this much.

Brown eyes seem to shine even in the darkness. That gaze skims over my body in the recesses of the car, seeming to take everything in. "I assume you're not carrying, Ms. Beck."

A shiver runs over my skin, whether from the cool night air or his piercing eyes. "I would never carry a gun, if that's what you mean."

"You'll have to excuse me if I'm a little cautious, considering the mark on your finger."

Every muscle in my body pulls taut.

I'm usually careful about keeping my hands hidden, but I must have slipped. Or he has a sharp eye. Either way he's seen the bleeding heart and the needle that runs through it, in black ink on the inside of my right forefinger.

Everyone affiliated with the Luskis has this mark somewhere on their bodies. Stefano has an elaborate tattoo covering his right hand, an anatomical heart with arteries dangling and spewing blood across his forearm, as if its been ripped from his body. The needle drawn straight up his middle finger. It's as beautiful as it is terrifying.

My tattoo is much smaller, much more crude. Because I'm not a lieutenant in the organization. I'm one of the girls they own.

At least I was until Stefano sent me away.

I curl my fingers around the steering wheel, staring into the abyss. "How do you know what it means?"

A low laugh. "Provence is about halfway between Tanglewood and Stillwater. We get a decent amount of drug trade coming through here. Weapons sometimes." He glances back at the sleeping child, as if moderating his words. "And worse."

Worse, meaning human trafficking. Humans like me. Like Ky would be.

No, Stefano would turn his son into a soldier. A cruel man, in his own image.

And that seems even worse.

"I'm not carrying," I say, my voice low with shame. Because even though I've never held a gun in my life, that's my heritage. An ancestry in violence and greed. "And I don't have any drugs. I only want to drive."

I open the car door, giving Ky one last look, praying he'll stay asleep for this.

The sheriff's hand doesn't go near his holstered weapon, but I imagine he could pull it out pretty fast, like one of those old-time western movies. I can feel his wariness, his watchfulness, as if I might be a drug runner with my baby in the backseat.

My sandal steps onto the pavement.

Which I'm surprised to realize isn't pavement at all. It roughened into dirt road, the sides delineated only by earth—no curb. The past summer had been particularly hot, and the overhead sun must have scorched the grass, leaving only crinkled chuff.

As the sheriff lowered the flashlight to the ground, I finally get a good look at him.

Wind-blown hair and slightly quirked lips. A broad chest and long legs. He looks like he could go to battle at four in the morning. Those brown eyes hold a thousand secrets.

Secrets like the tattoo on my finger and the pain it can bring.

Awareness hits me like a ton of childish bricks. My puffy eyes and runny nose would be very clear in the headlights from his patrol car. I had taken off my hoodie once we left the city limits, leaving only my thin tank top. Hours of driving without stop made me unsteady.

It looks bad, listing to the side like this. I can see how he might doubt my sobriety, but I'll prove him wrong. I've been stone cold sober since I turned fifteen, since I was born. Since Daddy gave me away like a gift, completing the promise made when I was born.

A modern-day curse.

FOUR

Then the spiteful old fairy's turn came. "When the princess turns of age, she shall prick her finger with a spindle, and she shall die!"

JESSICA

THE SHERIFF BENDS down and drags a stick through the dirt.

I feel my eyes widen. "You can't be serious. Where's the breathalyzer? I want to do that one. Don't worry about violating my right to privacy or anything."

His lips tilted, amused. "I appreciate the offer, but I wasn't trying to protect your privacy. We don't have one of those. This isn't Tanglewood, Ms. Beck."

My gaze slides to the lettering on the side of the cop car. *Sheriff* is written in large block letters. Hmm. Provence Police Department, the logo proclaimed. Definitely not in Tanglewood city limits, where the cops had way more than breathalyzers in every car. They had actual machine guns and tanks, ostensibly to handle riots even if everyone knew they're army surplus. Deals made in backrooms at the expense of the taxpayer—and the unsuspecting citizen the military gear would inevitably be used on. A war against its own people. That's all I knew about cops. The enemy. Not this man, leaning a hip against my rusty car, raising an eyebrow as he waited for me to walk the line he'd drawn by hand.

No, this definitely isn't Tanglewood.

"If you'll start from one end and walk to the other," he prompted.

I move to the end of the line. "Do I need to touch my nose?"

"Only if you want to," he drawled.

If it's optional I'm definitely not doing it. I'm pretty sure I look silly enough as it is, standing on the side of a back country road, afraid for my life but strangely exhilarated. As if I've been operating in the shadows for so many years. And in this moment, with night a heavy veil around us, I've woken up.

I hold my hands out in the air on either side. It just seems like the thing to do. I'm a tight-rope walker in one, two, three steps. When I leave the line behind, I turn my palms up and offer him a dry, "Tada."

I didn't mean it as an invitation, but it feels that way.

His gaze moves down my body, taking its sweet time and turning an inspection into a statement of interest. Heat flares in his eyes. I'm sure it's there, but the next second it's gone, replaced by that impersonal cop stare.

For the briefest moment, he definitely checked me out.

Did he like what he saw? A shiver ran down my body. I shouldn't care about that. It's just that it had been so long since I felt that kind of interest. Never, really.

The kind where she had a choice.

"You got a jacket in the car?" he asks.

The night breeze runs over my skin, making goosebumps. Not because it's cold. Because it's a tactile awareness of his gaze. I can't ever admit that to him. To anyone. Hell, I shouldn't even admit it to myself. And I'll let him bundle me in a down feather jacket if I don't have to explain the real source of her chills. Sexual awareness. A foreign feeling but undeniable.

Well, good thing I'm leaving here. And I'll be far, far away.

Never to return. I'll never have to see the sheriff again, and why does that suddenly seem worse than everything that came before? Like the worst tragedy in a sad story?

"Okay, I believe you," he says. "You're not drunk."

"Thank you."

"But you are unfit to drive. I can't ignore how you were driving earlier. More importantly, I can tell you're exhausted just from looking at you. It's a danger to the people around here. And it's a danger to you."

Blood rushes to my face, because what does he know about the danger to me? What does he know about fists and locks and being given as a gift before I could walk?

I wish I could be angry at him, but he's right.

It's something else that makes my cheeks hot. *Shame.*

Ky deserves better than this, even if I don't know how to give it to him. *Exhausted.* That's what the sheriff called me. Not only from driving for hours, from running tonight. I'm bone-deep tired. Soul-deep tired.

"I understand." I swallow hard, more deflated by this one moment than I was for years of pain and powerlessness. This moment seems to cut deeper than all of them, standing in front of this man who is so far above me. "I'll sleep it off in my car until daylight, and then we'll go."

"I'm afraid I can't let you do that either." The drawl shrank under the serious, almost regretful tone.

That old anxiety resurfaces—mistrust of anyone with a badge, of anyone with a dick. "Why not? I wouldn't be endangering anyone that way."

"Well, there's no way I could trust you to stay put unless I also stayed out here all night, which I'd rather not do. Then there's the fact that leaving you out here and defenseless wouldn't be safe for you."

"Do you have any ideas, then? Because I'm fresh out."

"Is there someone who can come pick you two up?"

FIVE

At this all the guests trembled, and many of them began to weep. The king and queen wept loudest of all. For a curse like this could not be broken.

JESSICA

M Y SLEEP-STARVED MIND turns the question over like it's completely new. Like I've never before wondered if anyone could help me. First my mother had failed me. Then my father. God, every person who looked the other way on the sidewalk when a teenage girl cowered beside a man old enough to be her father had failed me.

That was the way the old Jessica saw the world.

Then the little window on the pregnancy test showed positive, and everything changed. This was my fresh start. Ky had a real chance at life. And I learned to look on the bright side.

Like the fact that I can take care of myself and him. Usually.

Loneliness rises like acid. "No."

Crickets serenade us in the pause that followed. The sheriff doesn't look like he's coming up with an idea. He looks like he's trying to talk himself out of one.

Finally he says, "You can sleep at the police station."

My mouth falls open. "You're putting me under arrest?"

"Absolutely not," he said smoothly.

"Would I be sleeping a cell?"

After a pause, "Yes."

"So let me get this straight. You want to take me, in your police car, to the police station, where I'll spend the night in jail. How is this different from being arrested?"

He cocks his head. "Less paperwork?" At my small noise of protest, he looks apologetic. But unrelenting. "The cot is very comfortable, I've been told."

"Oh great, well if the *cot* is comfortable…"

"We do it all the time when someone has a little too much to drink at the bar in town. They can't drive home so they sleep it off."

I can't believe how wrong I had been, not only fifteen minutes ago. Immediately wrong. I thought things couldn't get worse? I'm going to jail. My optimism was well and truly deflated, punctured by a handsome sheriff and a country road that last for eternity.

"And what about Ky? He's going to be under arrest? He's six months old!"

"He won't be under arrest." The sheriff's brown eyes soften. "His name is Ky? Does it stand for something?"

His interest makes my heart swell with pride, a maternal instinct that overwhelms self-preservation. "It's not short for anything. Only Ky. I wanted to honor my mother, Makenna."

To honor the woman she could have been if she hadn't been beaten down to the mere shadow of a woman by the time I was born. This is how they kept us docile, generation after generation of girls broken before they were even women.

The sheriff takes a step toward my car, looking at Ky through the back window. "He's a handsome boy. I'm sure she's proud."

Sometimes it's a relief that she died before I could be sent away as a gift, fourteen years old and crying like a child. What would she think of me being a mother? What would she think of me running to keep Ky safe? Would she be proud? "I like to think so."

Recognition flashes over his face, grief for a woman he didn't know. "I'm sorry."

I manage a pained smile, tears pricking my eyes. At least it's dark enough that he can't see my lower lip trembling, my breath shuddering in and out of my chest.

"I'm not arresting anyone," he says gently. "It's just a safe place for you to rest."

Something clicks into place inside me, as if I've been waiting for this offer my whole life. A sad little jail in a country town shouldn't be anyone's idea of paradise, but I've been afraid for so long. A safe place to rest sounds like heaven.

"Okay," I whisper.

"Why don't you grab what you need from your bags? I can move the carseat over."

I pull the baby bag from the backseat, then move aside so he can unhook the carseat. He does so with a quiet efficiency that has me raising my eyebrows.

"I have three nieces," he says when he sees my face.

And he does handle the carseat like a pro, lifting the heavy weight with ease, using his free hand to keep the base steady while he circles my car to his. I watch him lean into the backseat of his patrol car, latching the seat into place and measuring out the bands so that it fits securely.

The beige fabric of his uniform slacks pulls taut over his ass and thighs, revealing strength and leanness in one package. Shock rises inside me, swift as a flood. I'm checking him out. That's what I'm doing right now—checking out the man who's not-arresting me.

I can't remember the last time I checked someone out.

I can't remember *ever* checking someone out.

My sexuality was stolen from me a long time ago. Before I became a mother. Before I had even become a woman. Men were always things to be feared. Monsters that sometimes had nice smiles, which only made them scarier.

And in the middle of nowhere I had found something other than fear.

I found desire.

SIX

The wise young fairy came from behind the curtain and said: "Your daughter shall not die. I cannot undo what my elder sister has done; the princess shall indeed prick her finger with the spindle, but she shall not die. She shall fall into sleep that will last a hundred years. At the end of that time, a prince will find her and awaken her."

JESSICA

*F*INN. THAT'S HIS NAME.

He stands back from the door and gestures me inside. I would want to sit next to Ky no matter what, so it shouldn't feel like I'm under arrest. Probably I would be handcuffed if that were happening. But I can't quite step inside. The glass divider and handle-less doors might be the straw that breaks my emotional state's back.

I'd be trapped back here, unable to leave until he let me out.

"Wait," I say, my throat thick with fear. It doesn't have that much to do with him. It's about me, and the all the ways I've been trapped before. "What if you're not a cop at all? What if you're a serial killer and this is some sort of death contraption you're using to lure me in?"

I follow his gaze inside the police car, where condensation hugs a large Styrofoam cup and an array of crackling equipment crowds like barnacles to the dashboard. If this is a kidnapping, it's a pretty elaborate one. And if he planned to kill me he could have done so on this deserted road without anyone seeing a thing.

So I feel a little silly, as the blatant accusation hands in the air between us, until I see his face. For the first time, his reserved expression cracks. I bask in the approval that shines there, like I'm seeing the sun for the first time. No one else has protected me.

No one else even wanted me to be safe.

He nods toward the baby bag slung over her shoulder. "Do you have a cell phone? Call 911 and they'll confirm my identity."

"911? That seems a little… excessive." Not to mention, a pretty good way to alert Stefano about their location. That call would definitely be recorded.

"Your safety qualifies as an emergency, Ms. Beck," he said, and I believe he's law enforcement officer for sure. He has the voice, sort of gruff and condescending at the same time.

It makes me wonder uses that tone in the bedroom, if he ever lectures on the perils of sexual dissatisfaction. *Your need to climax qualifies as an emergency, Ms. Beck.*

And it did qualify as an emergency. Suddenly. Shockingly.

How could I have given birth without having one?

I don't doubt him in this moment, but I already started this. He watches me expectantly, so I make a show of getting out my phone. "Give me the number for your precinct," I say.

His eyebrows raise, but he gives it to me in that low, authoritative voice.

I press each number carefully as he says it, feeling something tight in my stomach that has nothing to do with fear or pain. Something about him giving me commands and me following them. Something primal.

My forefinger hovers over the Send button.

His eyes become hooded, a challenge and a command all at once.

It's a game of chicken between his lids and my finger—which one would drop first.

Well, he asked for it. I press the button and wait while it rings.

"Provence PD. Bridget speaking."

"Hi… Bridget. This might sound silly, but do you happen to know if Sheriff—"

And here I realize I don't even know how name. I was about to get in the car with him, without knowing his name. *I checked out his ass, without knowing his name.*

"Locke. Sheriff Finnegan Locke," he says, and inexplicably the sound of his name, spoken with a husky twang made my insides melt. He sounds like a man in the middle of sex, a man close to climax, and oh god why am I imagining how his face would look, all taut and pained, arrested with the sweetest agony?

I've never thought a man looked sexy that way, rutting and sweating and grunting. I've only ever seen Stefano that way, but it's something I never want to see again.

It would be different with Finn. I know that as surely as I know that he won't hurt me.

"Yes, he's Sheriff Finnegan Locke. Can you confirm that he's on patrol?"

A snort over the line. "Finn? Yeah, he's around here somewhere. Causing trouble, I suppose." And then, rather shockingly, she shouts over the phone. "Finn, you sonuvabitch. Why are you bothering this nice girl?"

I jerk the phone away from her ear, wincing a little.

Then cautiously pull it back. "Um," I say, "I'm not sure he heard you."

Finn's eyes dance with laughter, which means he knows my ear is ringing and why. I like him better this way, his brown eyes bright with laughter. It softens up his whole face, makes him look even more handsome, which I do need to be thinking about at all.

"Well, you tell that man to get his ass back here," Bridget says. "His burger was delivered two hours ago. Nothing more disgusting than cold fries. Tell him that for me, will you?"

I close my eyes, trying to hold in a laugh. And that's the greatest accomplishment of all, that I could find anything amusing on this night. "Bridget says dinner's waiting."

Finn shrugs, his lips twitching. "Had a protein bar on the road. Besides, the fries are probably cold."

"Right," I say into the phone. "Thank you for your assistance."

"Don't let him give you any trouble. He's a good man, but you know, ever since the accident, he's had a stick is so far up his—"

"Great, thanks, bye." The words come out in a rush as I end the call. I run my eyes over his body, as if checking for injuries. "You were in an accident?"

A shadow passes over his face, wiping away any trace of softness. "No."

Message received. We won't talk about his past.

Does that agreement extend to my past?

I grant him a regal nod. "Okay, Sheriff. Take me to jail."

SEVEN

And so the curse came true, leaving the princess to sleep for a hundred years, her coffin made of glass, a thick wood with thorns grown up around the castle.

FINN

RUN MY hand over my face, hoping to wake up myself up.

It's only a thirty minute drive to the station, but coming at the end of a ten hour shift, it feels longer. Or maybe that's the sleepy vibes from the woman behind me.

When we got about a mile away from her car, she went out like a light, snoozing as peacefully as her baby. I'm glad I caught her before she'd wrapped that broken little car around a tree trunk.

Something about her sleep seemed to call to me, making me want to wrap myself around her, use my body as a shield. To protect her, the instinct stronger and more primal than I felt for ordinary people.

The cruiser slides through the inky black night.

This is my favorite time to patrol, when everyone's tucked safely in their homes, when I don't have to wear a fake smile lest anyone worry I was going to fall apart again.

A glimmer of that old panic hit me when I saw the swerving tail lights in the distance. I flashed back in time to when I saw a car careening toward me instead of away. I hadn't been a cop then. Just a guy out for a night on the town, with a woman in the passenger seat, no fucking clue what would happen next.

A squeal of tires and a horrifying crunch of metal is all I remember after that.

Of course, Jessica wasn't a drunk driver. Only a drowsy one.

A scared one too.

I recognized that lost look, as if she didn't know where to go, as if she didn't think there was any place left, because I felt that way after the accident. I still felt that way, at times, but I kept on pushing, kept on faking it, because I didn't know how to do anything else.

And then there's the little boy, the one with adorable footy socks and a new carseat, fully stocked in baby supplies even while the mother wore faded jeans and shadows under her eyes.

Jessica slid sideways in the backseat, leaning on the carseat as if protecting the child even in sleep. Who are they running from? The father, probably. The thought made his blood run hot.

Her head dipped to the side, giving me a flash of her face lit by moonlight in the rearview mirror. Dusky eyebrows that hide ocean-blue eyes. Lips that are full and pink and begging to be kissed. These days I mostly avoid human touch, especially the female kind. But there's something about this night, so expansive, so isolating. So very random that one woman, years ago, died on this road, and this one safe and alive—and comforting when I believed myself beyond comfort.

I pull into the parking lot behind the station, relieved to see Bridget's dirt-spattered truck still here. Her shift ends when mine does, but she tended to wait until I return before leaving. It's her way of looking after me—the whole town did that, as if the depression that held me captive after the accident is still after me and would one day catch up. And maybe they were right.

I circle the car and open the door. Resolutely ignoring the soft skin of her arm or the snuffling sound she makes, I nudge her away from the carseat. I unlatch it and pull it from the car, along with the baby bag.

Bridget meets me at the back entrance of the station, her eyes worried. "Look at the poor dear. She didn't mention she had a baby with her."

"I don't think she wants to be found," I say, keeping my voice low.

Sadness flickers over Bridget's face. "You know my lips are sealed. We don't have to file an official report. Here give me that child. I'll see if his diaper's wet."

Bridget raised three grown men, so I trust her to take care of the child. And she also survived a true asshole of a husband until he went too far. Beaten and bloodied, she took his hunting rifle down and shot him. Self defense, of course.

I return to the patrol car to find Jessica still asleep. God, she must be exhausted.

Bridget would probably take good care of her, too, but Jessica's stuck with me. Reaching inside I unbuckle her seatbelt and carefully lift her slight weight from the car. Slamming the door shut with my foot, I head inside, carefully not thinking about why I hesitated to wake her, not thinking at all about how good it felt to have a woman in my arms after so long alone.

I carry Jessica through the station and into the single cell. I lay her down on the cot, keeping my eyes averted, as if even a dressed woman on a bed is a sexual tableau.

With her it is.

She's a beautiful woman—stunning despite her tiredness. Her disarray and shadowed eyes give her a tragic look, stirring something deep inside me, making me want to find a white horse just so I could ride in and save her. It's goddamned ironic.

I figured out a long time ago that I can't save anyone.

EIGHT

A great many changes take place in a hundred years. The story of the sleeping princess was almost forgotten. And then one day a prince came upon the castle.

FINN

IN MY OFFICE I lean back in the chair and run a hand over my face. I need a decent night's sleep. Possibly inside a freezer so that I could get my body back to the cool, unaffected way it had been. And I definitely shouldn't go back into that jail cell.

Bridget appears at the door, arms crossed. "Where'd you find those two?"

"Out on the road," I say blandly. "Falling asleep at the wheel. Where's the baby?"

She gives me a measuring look, but I can't take offense—whatever weakness she sees in me is real. "I changed his diaper, fed him a bottle that was already prepared and ready. Then tucked him back into his carseat, where he promptly fell asleep. I put him next to her bed."

I try to act disinterested, casual, as if I ask for favors all the time instead of never. "Can you spend the night here tonight? I imagine they'll sleep straight through. I'll come back and take her to her car in the morning."

One look at her expression tells me I'm screwed. "I am far too old for a sleepover. And you are far too old to run away from a pretty girl."

"She doesn't trust men."

Her eyebrow raises. "Any particular reason for that?"

"Probably more than one. There's a heart-and-needle tattoo on her finger. She's affiliated with Luskis. Owned by them, more like, considering how they treat women."

Bridget blows out a breath. "She didn't seem so afraid of you when she called. When she got into the back of your car and let you bring her here."

"Didn't give her much of a choice."

"Well, these old bones do not need to sleep in a cot."

I try another tack, disturbed by the idea of sleeping under the same roof as Jessica. "Usually the boarders we get from the pub are men. It would be better if a woman stayed with her."

"What are you going to do, have sex with her?"

Oh good, my continued celibacy is an actual joke now. I think it's funny too, in a way that makes me want to laugh, then smash my head into the wall repeatedly.

I raise an eyebrow that I hope is appropriately stern. "Are you finished?"

She grins. "Finished and heading home. You can watch her. It's like I told Henry. You bring the puppy home, you clean the piss off the floor."

"I think she's potty trained. I'm almost positive about that."

"Well, you're going to find out, because I'm leaving. Don't forget to lock up behind me."

With a sigh of resignation, I follow her to the back door and waved her off.

She works hard enough that I'm not going to insist on it, even though I'm technically the boss. And I don't think she needs the money. It's something she does to get out of the house. There are bad memories there, but she refuses to leave. Says there are too many good ones.

Is that how Jessica feels about Ky? She might be running from the Luskis, but she seems to take incredible care of that little boy. She would have kept going until they were on the other side of the world, but the body can't last as long as the will.

I find myself checking on them, the baby asleep in his carseat, Jessica curled up in the same position as I left her. The soft fabric of her tank top has shifted slightly, revealing a thin strip of pale skin above her jeans. She's wearing flip flops, which probably aren't the most comfortable to sleep in. I should take them off. Should tuck her under the blanket.

That would require touching her, though, if only briefly.

And that's not a good idea.

So I turn the heat up a few degrees and return to the office.

As Bridget pointed out, I don't have sex. Not even if a woman comes on to me, which happens more than it should for a man who avoids company. My bad reputation is some kind of draw, no matter what my badge says now. That's how I recognized the Luskis mark, not even from my experience as sheriff. There had been drugs and women and guns. I broke the law, completely unafraid of the danger it might bring.

In the end it wasn't my business deals that had ruined everything. Only a random drunk driver. I found no joy in life after that, none in sex or drugs. I cleaned myself up, became a cop and then the sheriff. Women liked that kind of thing, the bad boy who had changed his ways, as if they could be part of my reformation.

Or maybe turn me bad again, as if my blind adherence to the badge is a jail of ice, as if they could free me with a hot body. But the ice isn't around me, it's under me, supporting me, and if it cracks, there will be nothing to do but fall back into the biting waters that had claimed me once before.

Even though Jessica's beautiful and tempting, I'll avoid her.

Soon, bright and early, she'll drive away from this town, from me. Not tomorrow morning, like she thinks. I send a couple inquiries out to his old contacts in Tanglewood to figure out exactly who the hell's after her and where to find him. If that means fighting the criminal underworld I had once been part of, then that's what I'll do.

I'm going to protect her, but then she'll leave.

There's a twinge of regret inside me, of wondering what could have been, but it's for the best. I'll return to my solitary existence, and she'll find some place new.

Some place she wouldn't have to be afraid.

In the cell beside hers, I pull off my uniform shirt and my belt. Wearing only slacks and my sleeveless undershirt, I glare at the cot with distaste. Exactly like the one in her cell, it has a thin pad on metal slats. Worse, it was slim and short, so while Jessica fit perfectly, my feet fall off the end and my shoulder rests on the cold edge of the frame.

I close my eyes, attempting to sleep, but all I can see are Jessica's lips, full and tempting. They parted, when she fell asleep in the back of his patrol car. Aside from the many things I want to do with that mouth, the pink intrigues me. What other parts of her share that color?

And now I'm hard. Great.

NINE

The young prince began to force his way through the thick wood. The stiff branches gave way for him, then closed again, allowing no one else into the castle.

JESSICA

I WAKE UP disoriented.

It's pitch black, without even the red glow of her alarm clock or the blue stars from Ky's turtle light. My back aches, my neck is sore. My eyes feel puffy like I've been crying. My lids are heavy, threatening to drag me back into slumber.

But something woke me, and I need to know what.

Is Ky awake? I don't hear him crying.

Shifting slightly, my hands fumble along a rough sheet to a sharp metal edge. It comes back to me, then. Coming home from work at the diner, picking up Ky from his sitter. Then hearing the banging on the door.

Stefano had been drunk and angry. Which is business as usual for him.

I held Ky's body against my chest, huddled in the closet, praying he would go away. And then he did, but it was too late. I knew that we wouldn't be safe there. Whether he wanted me in his bed again or whether he was interested in raising Ky to be like him, we had to go.

As soon as Stefano left I packed what I could into the trunk and left.

The carseat sits beside the bed, Ky kicking in his sleep, his little brow wrinkled. I touch my hand to his forehead, and it smooths out beneath my fingers.

Forcing myself out of the cot, I kneel in front of Ky and check his diaper. Not too wet, but I change him often so he doesn't get a rash. So I lay out the plastic mat onto the cot and pull the sleeping baby from his seat.

He wakes only briefly as I change him, his eyes cloudy with sleep. His small hand captures a lock of my hair, tugging until I gently pry his fingers apart.

"No pulling," I whisper with a small smile.

He gives me a mystified look, as if he's trying to understand.

"I love you," I tell him.

He gives me a toothless grin.

My heart gives a kick. I bend down and press my lips to his soft forehead. When I pull back his eyes flutter closed. Before I even have the new diaper fastened he's sound asleep.

I could bring him onto the cot with me, but the padded carseat is probably more comfortable. And definitely more secure, once I buckle him in.

A muffled sound comes through the wall.

That must have been what woke me. It came again, along with a skip in my heartbeat, that universal recognition of distress, of danger, the intrinsic pull to soothe I didn't even know I had before I became a mother.

I glance back at Ky, uncertain. Should I leave him?

He sleeps peacefully, with that completely lost expression, as if he's far away in some baby dreamworld with unlimited milk and rainbows. I pick up the heavy seat by its handle.

The barred door to my cell lay open, just slightly, like a parent might do for a child, in case she called out in her sleep or got scared. But it isn't me or Ky crying out out for help.

I slip into the hallway, a little unsteady on my feet, following the restless sounds to the cell next door. The barred door is also ajar and I take that as permission to enter. I only want to check on him—whoever it was, though I knew it was Finn.

Sheriff Finnegan Locke, sprawled on a cot, muttering in his sleep.

Most people look peaceful while sleeping, more relaxed than when they're awake. He's just the opposite. Earlier he wore a perpetual half-smile, as if the whole world amused him, when he could be bothered to care.

Now his forehead is furrowed, a low sound of distress coming from deep in his throat. The contrast startles me, distracting enough that I'm already at his bedside, setting the carseat on the floor, shushing Finn back to calm before I realize what I'm doing.

His skin feels clammy under my fingertips, his hair damp with sweat. His voice sounds raw, and I wonder how long he's crying out, how often he does this at night. He quiets beneath my soothing touch, his movements slowing, his face smoothing out.

I don't want to let the nightmares come back, so I keep running my fingers along his forehead, his temple, even the bristle of his jaw. I swallow hard, realizing that I enjoy this—touching him, comforting him. I don't consider myself an overly nurturing person. I love Ky, but that's the extent of my maternal side. Then again, the way I feel about Finn isn't maternal. It's something else, something just as deep and infinitely more scary.

My eyelids droop in sleepiness, and I force myself away from him.

I would have picked up the carseat, would have left the room, but my gaze lands on a grey felt blanket. I pull it over him, and the wind from the fabric ruffles a lock of dark hair across his forehead.

He stirs, blinking up at me with those soulful brown eyes. "Jessica?"

It's the first time he's spoken my name, and in that hoarse and sleep-thickened drawl, it may be the sexiest thing I've ever heard. Feeling as though I've been caught, I whisper, "Hey."

His eyes sharpen, coming to alertness. "Are you okay? Is Ky—"

"Shh, no. We're both fine. I just heard something."

He glances at the sleeping baby, his expression relaxing a fraction. "I woke you up?"

"It's okay. No big deal."

"Shit." Propped on one elbow, he runs a hand over his face. "Sorry."

"I just heard you moving around in here and wanted to see if you were okay."

"Yeah. Of course," he says absently, like he knows it's more than *moving around*. He's the one who had to live his nightmare. "What about you? You need something? A drink of water?"

I shake my head *no* even though I do need something. How quickly he turned from his need to mine. It seems so ingrained in him, a habit now. Maybe it comes from serving people in his job, maybe from something else. *Maybe from the accident, whatever that means.*

I have needs aplenty, the need to talk to someone about Stefano, the need to get away from him once and for all, the need to make sure Ky would be safe a powerful ache. And springing from somewhere deep—a need to connect with another adult, more than just serving someone coffee at the diner or sharing a cute story about Ky with one of the other waitresses. A need to be with another person, a man, a need to be a woman.

73

Not something I've ever needed before but so very real right now.

I need to touch and be touched, to know that my worth isn't down the drain alongside the rest of my sad little life in Tanglewood. But I can't bother him with that. He's my jailer and my caretaker, not my lover. He doesn't need to be bothered with this, with me.

He catches my wrist as I move to leave, so quick I can only gasp.

"Stay," he murmurs.

TEN

The prince came to a chamber of gold, where he saw upon a bed the fairest sight one ever beheld—a young princess who looked as if she had just fallen asleep.

JESSICA

THIS WAS THE part where I should leave. Where I should tell this man, who's clearly good down to his bones, that I'm bad news. Where I ignore everything but survival, because that's the only way I've survived this long. Instead he asks me to stay, and I do.

If Stefano were to find me here, if Finn were to confront him…

Regardless of what I want or wish for, the only thing I can do is run. The only thing I can trust is isolation. But what happens when people are together, really together, when they become intimate in a way beyond bodies hurting one another? I never knew, even though I should, and like a dense fog, it kept me apart.

But drunk on sleeplessness and a shimmering sense of wonder, I see things clearly. If I'm wrong, if I make a fool of myself with him, it would be okay. He would make it okay.

So there's no way I can ignore his raw request for my company or the tremor in my own body that whispered—*yes, I want that too, stay with me.* No way I can leave now, not until morning.

"I'll stay," I say softly.

He curses softly. "No, you should go. I'm still half-asleep right now and my self-control isn't what it should be. I'm about two seconds from acting inappropriately. I mean, really inappropriately."

My nose scrunches. That would normally be enough to send me running, but the truth is that I wouldn't mind inappropriate behavior right now.

Being desired feels a lot better than being afraid.

He blows out a breath, sitting up in the cot. "And I think most of all, the

Town Council would *really* mind the dirty thoughts the Sheriff is currently having about his prisoner. Yeah, they would not appreciate that at all."

"I thought you said I wasn't under arrest."

"I'm hereby placing you under arrest. You have the right to remain silent. Now go back to bed."

Instead of listening I climb onto the cot beside him. "This is exactly my problem, every time. You're just like every other guy. You ask me on a date and then you just… you just *arrest* me."

His lips quirked. "Happens to you often, does it?"

All the time. All the time I'm left with the dark shame of being not good enough, of being the girl with a man banging on her apartment door, drunk and angry, instead of a man who loved her. I swallow hard, turning away so he can't see my tears.

"Hey." This time when he catches my wrist, it's light, tentative, barely a touch. "I'm sorry. I'm an asshole, really. If it's any consolation, I know I am."

"Why would that console me?"

"We don't need to talk about me. Let's talk about you. You can tell me why you were driving like a bat out of hell out of Tanglewood. It'll be better than *not* sleeping on these damn cots, especially when the night is so…"

The night was so very something, I know exactly what he means, and lying on a hard cot in a lonely jail cell by myself is too depressing. Sitting on a hard cot beside a self-confessed ass is marginally better. Even if he is a cop.

I settle in, connected to him only by the felt blanket we share.

"He's a cop," I say, though that short sentence can't possibly express everything.

He seems to understand anyway, his body stiffening beside me. "Jesus."

"A dirty cop. I'm sure you're shocked about that. I'm sure you thought a man scared me bad enough to fly out of the city like a bat out of hell is just a nice upstanding law enforcement officer." I meant to sound relaxed, but my voice got high pitched at the end—then broke.

"That's terrible," he says, his voice low.

"We were together. I lived with him. It wasn't exactly…" Consensual. "But I just couldn't see a way out. Then I missed my period. And another one."

I glance at him, but he already knows where it's going. The proof of that is five feet away, sleeping soundly. Deep breath. "Stefano didn't want anything to do with a baby. I thought he would do something drastic. Beat me until I lost the baby. Maybe drug me and take me to a clinic. In the end he threw me out. It was such… God, it was such a relief."

Fury flashes in those brown eyes, so different from the soft way he looked at me a few minutes ago, different even from the careful casualness on the road. "What did you do?"

"I didn't have any money, but I had a few friends leftover from school. People who understood why I couldn't keep in contact, why I had to drop out—"

"Wait. How old were you when this Stefano fucker took you?"

The word *fucker* startles me, but not as much as the word *took*. There are other ways he could have said it, ways other people would have said it. How old was I when we started dating? How old was I when I moved in with him?

Finn seems to understand the subtext, but then he did recognize the tattoo.

That's exactly what happened. I was gifted by my father. Taken by Stefano.

"Fourteen."

Finn sucks in a breath. "Jessica, how old are you now?"

"I'm eighteen now, okay? So don't worry."

"Don't worry. You want me not to worry about you, when you're admitting that you were essentially trafficked as a girl, that you were abused and battered and—"

"Stop please," I say, wincing at those words. They land like stones on my skin. "I'm not excusing what happened. I'm not saying it was okay, only that I survived."

"Yes," he says, the admission coming gravely. "You did."

"And I want to stay that way."

"I'm going to help you, Jessica."

"You don't understand. Stefano, the people he knows, they're dangerous."

He makes a small sound. "Do you know what I did before I became a cop?"

"You were a boy scout?"

"I told drugs. Occasionally I helped run guns."

My insides turn cold. I scoot away from him on the thin mattress.

"You're a dirty cop."

"No, beautiful. That was before. Before the accident."

By degrees I feel myself relax. "What happened?"

"I was driving on this road, the same one where I found you. Running guns for this asshole who paid a lot of money not to ask questions. I had a woman in the car with me. It was only…" He looks almost ashamed. "Only sex between us. Only money. I picked her up in a bar in Tanglewood, determined to have a good time."

My stomach clenches. Stefano's work is incredibly dangerous, so much so that it became my dream. That he would one day wind up dead. That he would never come home.

"Did someone take the guns?"

A humorless laugh. "No. That would have made sense, at least. Instead it was a drunk driver. He hit us from the side. Of course I wasn't wearing my seatbelt, so I flew through the windshield, landed on pavement."

"Oh my God."

"That ended up saving my life. The woman was trapped inside. Unconscious, I can only hope. Because all those guns—they caught fire. Exploded. The whole car, gone. Right there in the street."

The pain in his voice draws grooves inside me, a kind of shared memory I won't ever forget. Not his fear or his injuries in that moment, but for the woman.

"I'm sorry."

"Don't be," he says sharply. "I don't deserve a damn thing."

"You didn't mean for her to be hurt."

"I didn't even know her name."

There's a hollow in my chest, whether from what I hoped this man would be or from his own shame. "I'm still sorry," I say softly.

"Yeah," he says, his voice rough. "I'm sorry too."

"And then you became a cop?"

"Took a while. Woke up in a hospital outside the city, the cops asking a lot of questions. There was a time it looked like I wouldn't walk again, definitely not run far and run fast enough to pass the physical. But I had to do something with my life, something useful, or I couldn't see any point to living it."

The difference struck me, then. How Stefano had become a cop to have power, so that he could live above the law. And how Finn had become a cop for the opposite reasons.

"Is that why you're alone?" I ask.

I don't just mean whether he's in a relationship. There's an air of loneliness around him. I recognize it because it's the same one I carry with me.

He makes a rough sound. "I like people just fine. I just don't want to get too close."

"I don't know how to be close," I admit.

He's quiet a moment, looking pensive. "We make quite a pair, you and I."

"But we're okay. We're going to be okay." Optimism. I would have to find enough for both of us. "We don't need to get close to enjoy each other's company."

"We don't?" He sounded skeptical, but also slightly interested.

"No sex either," I add quickly.

He gives me that faint smile, the one I recognize from the road. "Of course not."

"We can play a game."

"Unfortunately I left my monopoly board at home."

"Something without a board or any parts. Like I Spy." It's something I play with Ky, even though I have to play both parts. Mostly it's just me pointing out things and naming them. Having a grown up to play the game with actually *does* sound fun.

He raises his eyebrows. "I spy something dark."

The whole cell is dark. "You were the kid in class who heckled the teacher, weren't you? Okay, smarty pants, you name a game we can play."

"Truth or dare." He says it like a challenge, like we're already playing.

"No dares. The only point of that is to get naked, and we already decided not to do that."

"Did we decide that?"

"I'm deciding it now."

"Fine," he says. "Only truth."

"And I get to ask first, since I already told you everything about my life."

He inclines his head in a gracious nod. "Go ahead. I'm an open book."

"Ha! I very much doubt that."

Finn seems casual enough when he pulls you over on the side of a deserted country road, with his quips and his detached amusement, but I've seen him pant in a nightmare, heard the desolation in his voice when he spoke of the things he no longer let himself do.

I want to know so many things about him, everything really. Each new bit of information I learn about him feels like a bead, one strung after the other. *He's a good man, but you know, ever since the accident, he's had a stick is so far up his—*

I know why he became a cop, but not why he became a criminal.

"Who was your father?"

First there's surprise. It flashes in his eyes, lightning quick. Then thunder rolls across his face, dark and ominous. "You're a smart little thing, aren't you?"

I close my mouth, feeling guilty and defensive all at once. The question sprang half-formed from my lips, spurred by a growing curiosity about this man. I never meant to anger him—or hurt him.

"Never mind," I say quickly. "It's none of my business."

The storm cleared as quickly as it came, smoothed out into nonchalance so pure it couldn't be real. "No, it's okay. Fair question."

"Hey." I put a hand on his arm. "I'm serious. We can play something else. The quiet game. That's a good one. I play it sometimes with Ky, but fair warning, I'm pretty good at it. He always loses. Possibly because he doesn't understand the rules."

Plus there's less chance of me putting my foot in my mouth that way.

The corner of his mouth kicks up. "My father did the same thing I did. Only with less hesitation about killing if someone got in the way. Here's the truly ridiculous part, I actually felt like a pretty decent guy, that I only ran drugs instead of people, that I mostly paid the girls I took with me and made them come when we had sex. Yeah, I'm a great fucking guy."

My stomach clenches. He has so much remorse inside him, it's impossible for me to hate him. Or maybe it's because I grew up on the same streets as he did. I know that he actually *was* a great guy by those standards. And then he made himself even better.

"I'm sorry." Sorry I brought it up. Sorry I had brought all this back for him with my middle-of-the-night escape from the city.

He continues as if he didn't hear her. "The people of Provence. They didn't trust me at first, which was smart of them. And then after a while, they did trust me. Bridget, she's always trying to set me up. She says it's time for me to stop punishing myself, but that's the thing. I have moved on. This is what it looks like, steady, quiet."

Bleak. And lonely. And heartbreaking. "I think it's for you to decide. What you want, what makes you happy."

"What makes you happy, Jessica?"

Unaccountably, this. Sitting in the dark with a kind stranger, spilling secrets I don't even want to remember. The warmth of his arm under my hand, the solidness of his body beside mine.

He sounded a bit lost when he asked the question, looked a bit forlorn there in the shadows, and that seemed all wrong. I don't know how to console him, but I can give him my company. He doesn't have to be lonely tonight. And I don't either.

I pat his shoulder. "Come on."

He stares blankly but allows me to tug him down on the cot. I lay at his side, my arm slung over his chest to keep me from rolling backwards. Heat lingers in my body, leftover desire, but our touch is pure comfort.

"I'm afraid," I whisper in the dark.

"Go to sleep, beautiful. I'll watch over you."

The determination in his voice is proof enough that we'll be safe. If only for these few precious hours in a jail in the middle of nowhere—safe. A precious gift. Relief from a curse placed a long time ago.

Now I know what intimacy would be like, deeper than physical. Our worry, our sadness wells together, and we hold one another, adrift. There's no cure for shame or for grief but time, nothing to do but wait, and for tonight we would float together.

ELEVEN

The prince knelt beside her and awakened her with a kiss. And the enchantment was broken.

FINN

I EMERGE FROM sleep, but only barely.

Faint orange light dances through the shadows, as if I'm underwater, at the bottom of an ocean. I feel sluggish but also warm and cocooned and I don't want to wake up, because it will end this. I don't even know what *this* is, only that it's fleeting.

Managing to crack one eye open, I check that the baby is asleep.

Then I close my eyes and focus on my other senses.

A sweet feminine smell manages to somehow be sleepy and sexy at the same time. How long has it been since I've had a woman beside me? So long, too long since I felt the cushiony softness against his own hardness, and fuck, I'm rock hard.

I don't feel worried though, not this time. Just relieved.

Relieved to feel like a man again, a man fully alive, one who gets morning wood and uses it with the soft, sleepy woman next to him. She makes little snuffling noises of almost-awake as I shift her in my arms, as I position my body above hers.

And then—thank you, Jesus—she pulls me down closer, harder, touching me everywhere. I push my knee between hers in question; she parts hers in answer.

I hitch between her legs, so damned comfortable I could spend forever, just there, the aching ridge of my cock against the heat of her sex, my body cradled within hers. She moans, surprise cutting that sound short when I bend my head and put my lips to her neck. So soft, so sweet. She bucks against me, jerkily, as if she can't help it, as if I dragged her half-willing into the madness I'm living in, where everything was heat and sex and the blessed

82

feel of skin on skin, and I don't have to think, didn't have to mourn or pretend.

Only this, only lips beneath mine, and hips beneath mine, and soft, plush skin in my hands to mold and to caress. I find her nipple through silky fabric, rubbing it gently with my thumb. It hardens, and a deep sense of possession forms inside me.

Mine. This body is mine. *This woman is mine.*

I might go crazy with needing to be inside her, but something holds me back. Some sense that it would break the spell, that maybe she would turn to ash in my hands if I dare to push for more or even look, and so I hold myself suspended in torment, savoring every second.

But I can't hold out, not with her little pants against my neck or her not-so-gentle hands scrabbling at my back. I rock against her, incensed and senseless. She shuddered beneath me in a small, early climax and it's too much. Too fucking sexy to bear.

I freeze that way, suspended on ice, my body rigid with denial.

"Jessica?" I ask, my voice hoarse.

I need her to do more than take me, to accept this. I need her to want it as badly as I do. Because I won't accept only one night with her. Not if I'm going to be inside her.

Her eyes opened wide, as if I surprised her.

As if maybe she'd been in a dream all this time, while I touched her, while she orgasms, her pussy warm and wet through our clothes, my dick aching to be inside.

She pushed at me, and I let her up.

Her hair was tangled on one side and sticking up on the other. Her shirt clung to her body in the wrong places, wrinkled from sleep and my hands. She was glorious.

Blue eyes blazed with anger and arousal. "What are you doing to me?"

I used to be good with women, smooth enough I could find a new one every night at the bar. And now here I am, trying to convince a woman who had just orgasmed against my cock to let me do it again. Not only once. Forever. Again and again.

"Do you want me to leave?"

Very smooth, Locke. I'm sure she'll swoon with that kind of smooth talking.

The anger fades from her expression, leaving only sadness. "No. Of course not."

Realization is a cold ball in my stomach, and I pull away from her. I sit on the edge of the cot, unwilling to leave her until I'm sure she's okay. Not that I'm much help. "You're saying that because you think you owe me. Because you think I'm asking for payment."

Doubt flickers in her eyes. "It's not… you."

I can't help the sardonic, humorless laugh that escapes me. "It's not me, it's you? I'm the one who came two seconds away from fucking you while you slept."

She touches my arm, and it's all I can do not to flinch away. "It's just that's how men have been for me. Always demanding something. And I've never wanted it."

Then I can't help it. Her words hit me like a blow. I recoil, physically, standing so that I can get some space from her and the terrible truth of this. Of course she's terrified of men. She has the mark of the Luski mafia on her finger. I don't know what they did to her, but I know they love violence. She would have seen her share of it, would have experienced it at the hands of terrible men.

Men like me, apparently. *And I've never wanted it.*

"Fuck," I say, running a hand through my hair. "I'm sorry."

"Until now," she says, kneeling on the cot, looking more like a sex goddess than she has any right to look in a jail cell. "You made me want it. I thought you could feel it."

Her cheeks flush as if she's embarrassed to even talk about her orgasm. As if she's embarrassed that she even had one. *Oh fuck.* "Was that your first?"

She looks away, ashamed. "You know I've had sex before. I have Ky."

I take two long steps back to her, tilting her chin up so that I can see those beautiful blue eyes. There's so much pain inside them, it almost hurts to look, but I can't stop. "Your first climax. Was that your first time?"

"Yes," she whispers, eyes wide, unblinking.

Jesus.

My high walls, my careful distance melt to nothing, leaving me exposed. Every desire and every hope. If she can twist me up this much in one night, I can't imagine what prolonged exposure might do. I would self-combust.

Or have sex with her, which seemed possibly worse and so much better all at once.

"Stay," I say roughly, my voice gravel against concrete.

Her blue eyes flash with worry. With longing. "What about Ky?"

Did he think he would want her without her child? "He can live in my house. It's big and empty. And there's a room in particular that would look great painted blue."

She sucks in a breath. "You don't know how much I want that. How much I want to have a regular life. How much I want *you*. But I can't stop running."

Because she experienced more pain and subjugation than any woman should have to. Which meant I should leave her alone. Not send her on her way with only that shitty car. I should give her money and safe passage so that she could start a new life—free from the hard cocks and hungry eyes of men who would want her, men like me.

I should really let her go.

"I'll keep you safe here," I say instead.

She opens her mouth to tell me about the dangers. And I would hear them. Then I would fucking vanquish every last one of them. But first I need to do something. I've needed to do it since I first saw her sleepy blue eyes and beautiful face staring up from her car window.

I kiss her, a light brush, my lips against hers.

Like a question, asking her to stay with the words I haven't yet spoken aloud. She's wound up so tight, full of worry and fear, and I want to make her feel safe, to caress her body until she turns into a puddle of need and incoherent begging.

She makes me crazy, and once upon a time I sought that out, wanting to feel wild and on edge. Not for a long time, though. These past years had been about isolation. About driving down dark country roads alone. And all along, I was looking for her.

Without even knowing it, looking for her.

Her lips are swollen, her skin flushed. She's so incredibly sensual that it makes my body ache. At least it would if I could look away from her eyes. They blaze as bright and as blue as a new day, full of hope. She's radiant like this.

"Morning," she murmurs.

"Good morning, beautiful," I say, leaning in for another kiss.

THE END

THANK YOU!

THANK YOU for reading Bedtime Story, the sexy modern retelling of Sleeping Beauty. I hope you loved Finn and Jessica as well as sweet little Ky!

You can meet Jessica and Ky where they were first introduced in the Masterpiece duet, starting with USA Today bestseller THE KING, which is available now. *A trailer park princess. The son of a criminal king. We don't belong together, but I'm caught in a twisted game...*

And be sure to sign up for my VIP reader list to get new release alerts and more!

RIPPLES

A Prince and the Pauper Story

Aleatha Romig

"Just as ripples spread out when a single pebble is dropped into water, the actions of individuals can have far-reaching effects."

~Dalai Lama

Author's Note

The multifaceted concept of *The Prince and the Pauper* by Mark Twain has always fascinated me in a fairy tale sort of way. The premise of the story is that at one time or another, the idea, dream, or fantasy of almost every person is to live as someone else. Whether for an hour or a lifetime, most people imagine stepping outside the box that is their life.

In a fairy tale, this phenomenon would occur with the help of magic, but in many adaptations of this story, as well as the original, the transformation takes place through circumstance and chance.

The second allure of *The Prince and the Pauper* is the revelation that no one is truly free—whether prince or pauper. Every life has chains. Most are metaphoric and bind us in place by responsibility and expectation. The life that others envy or that looks free often isn't. In each individual's life, the chains are what differ.

In most adaptations of this story, the final outcome is a better understanding of and appreciation for life—something that can only come through the life-altering experience. It just so happens that sometimes that journey can be more sinister than anyone expects.

A GLANCE INTO THE FUTURE

Intuition will tell the thinking mind where to look next.
~ Jonas Salk

"DADDY, I WANT to introduce you to my fiancé."

Natalie's father's brown eyes darkened as he gazed upon the man at his daughter's side. Even at his age, her father was an intimidating and formidable man in all matters, personal as well as business. Retirement was but a word not fully in his repertoire. He'd built his family's castles and riches from nothing. He'd be involved in their success until he took his last breath.

That didn't mean he was an absentee father. On the contrary, he was omnipresent—as he was in all things.

This greeting, after Natalie's disappearance, was personal and difficult to accept, leaving him and his wife uncharacteristically unnerved. The young woman making the introduction was their beautiful baby, their second daughter, the one for whom the world held fewer expectations. He, however, had plans for her—expectations and dreams—as did her mother, none that included the man at her side.

Natalie's course may not have been as defined as her older siblings, but their stories were for another time. This was Natalie's.

Her father's shoulders broadened and neck stiffened. Before Natalie could say anything, her mother's petite hand landed upon her father's sleeve. The diamond ring on her mother's finger glittered with dancing rainbow prisms as her touch gently reminded Natalie's father that this was their cherished princess and apparently, her chosen prince. It was not the time for her father to assert his dominance.

Yet he knew that this wasn't the way it was meant to be.

It wasn't the future they had planned for their baby girl.

Her father's question formed—a demand to know how this union happened. It teetered on the tip of his tongue while at the same time his wife's grasp tightened, pleading for his understanding, if only momentarily. It was truly her gift, the ability to calm the seas without uttering a word.

In the short time that all their gazes locked, the answers to her father's questions and more lurked in the shadows of the present and past. There was more to this man—the one with the audacity to have his hand on Natalie's back—than there appeared. There was a darkness that was all too familiar.

Her father let out a long breath and offered his hand. His handshake was not to be interpreted as a white flag. Natalie's father didn't surrender.

As their grips tightened, her father stared knowingly into the eyes of evil. They weren't hard to recognize. He'd seen them often enough in the mirror.

One day the secrets may be revealed; however, some things are better left behind closed doors. Because the truth will reveal that despite the best efforts to keep his baby girl safe, it was her father's doing that set her fate into motion.

CHAPTER ONE

BEFORE THE FUTURE AND AFTER THE PAST

*When you have expectations, you are setting yourself up for
disappointment.*

\- Ryan Reynolds

THE DREARY OVERCAST sky settled around the buildings, obscuring their
height as the car slowly made its way through Boston traffic. The holiday
break was here. Soon Natalie would be faced with the truth of her reality. All
of her father's money couldn't propitiate the cause any longer. Her time at
Harvard was done.

She'd managed to keep the news from both of her parents, but soon
they'd hear it, and as it should, it would come from her. In today's world, it
was a miracle that they hadn't already heard, either from the gossip-hungry
leeches on social media or from the registrar's office. Of course, there were
rules about confidentiality for adult students, but when it came to her father,
rules were at his discretion.

She'd practiced her speech a hundred ways yet nothing sounded right.
She still didn't know how she would tell them—or especially him—that she'd
failed. No matter what she said, her fourth semester as a Harvard student
wouldn't happen. She wasn't her father nor even her siblings. The world of
business and all that it entailed may be in her genes, but it wasn't in her heart.
It never had been.

Maybe she was more like her mother.

Life beyond the walls of expectancy was where Natalie's dreams could be
found, a sliver of time where she could be herself—no one's daughter or
sister, and perhaps not even a woman she yet knew. There was more out in
the world than she'd seen. There were people with the freedom to make their
own choices and forge their own trails based upon their desires.

She had desires, ones that she couldn't articulate as if they were an unknown part of her, ones yet to be revealed. The frequency of these thoughts had increased to the point that in her mind they'd moved from ideas to wants to insatiable cravings.

As her classes focused more upon the major her father had chosen for her, her ability to concentrate waned until she couldn't find the ambition. It was lost. Instead of seeking help, she gave in to the inevitable, and now her time at Harvard was done.

Natalie gasped as the car skidded, the wheels swerving on the slushy street. As she reached out and her body lunged forward, the seatbelt tugged her backward. It was a metaphor for her life: any attempt at freedom would be met with a gentle but firm reminder that her bubble served the purpose of safety. She had a designated place. It was where she was to stay.

"I'm sorry, miss," the older driver said as his eyes remained steadfast on the road and traffic. "The roads are getting worse."

She didn't respond. The roads weren't her concern. Currently, her flight to Munich and then onto Nice, as well as the conversation awaiting her once she arrived, topped her list.

Beyond the windows, the snow-lined sidewalks provided a simple strip of wet, salt-covered concrete. The pedestrians huddled beneath their hats and coats as Natalie imagined the crunch crackling under their boots. It wasn't difficult. The floorboard beside her feet was white with pellets.

"Miss, your mother made your reservations. Your first flight leaves in an hour and a half. This traffic isn't helping. I have your passport and boarding passes. You're TSA PreCheck, but you'll still need to hurry. For international travel, they recommend…"

Hurry. What if she didn't? What if she missed her flight?

Her psychology professor may surmise that missing her flight had been Natalie's plan all along. It was the reason she purposely delayed packing and wasn't ready when her car arrived. A less analytical observer would say she was delayed because she'd spent the majority of her time saying goodbye to her friends, classmates, and roommates.

They knew what her family didn't.

Natalie also knew that her mother would be devastated if Nat missed their family time. Nat's choices seemed unfair: go on holiday and disappoint, or not attend and do the same. Either way, the stress of her failure would be another addition to Nat's growing list of her parents' disappointments.

She thought of her mother. Seemingly fragile yet strong, soft-spoken and yet always heard. Her mother was as different from Natalie's powerful father as day was from night, and despite that, in her own way, her mother was the true force.

Natalie gave that more thought. If that were the case—that her mother was the force—then why was Natalie on her way to Christmas in France? Her mother detested the cold.

Since leaving the campus, the soft, cool mist beyond the windows had morphed, first becoming pinging ice and then snowflakes the size of quarters. Each transformation further eclipsed the afternoon sun. Even the twinkling lights on the trees lining the streets failed to fill her with the holiday spirit.

If only she could go somewhere else.

Natalie contemplated her packing. She didn't have gifts. A sweatshirt from the campus bookstore saying *Harvard Parent* no longer seemed appropriate. That was fine; there were plenty of shopping opportunities in Nice.

Nat rubbed her gloved hands as her body shivered. This deep-seated chill wouldn't go away. It was more than her present—it was going to be her future. A chateau in France, even the South of France, may be a few degrees warmer than Boston but most likely equally as dreary. Usually, as was her mother's preference, family holidays were spent in the sunshine. What had disrupted the normal plans and why was Natalie on her way to France instead of a tropical location?

If she'd taken the time to talk to either of her parents for more than a few minutes here and there, she might know. Then again, she also might have blurted out the truth of her failing grades. Avoidance seemed the best answer until it was no longer possible.

"Miss? You're very quiet. Is everything all right?"

"No, not really."

"Don't worry about your flight. When you were delayed at the campus, I called the airline. They won't leave without you."

"Of course they won't. My parents?" Natalie asked.

"They're already in France. They flew privately…"

It was how she was supposed to travel. However, being the youngest had advantages. There wasn't much she couldn't convince her father to do or give. She told him she didn't want to fly privately, so she wasn't. The real truth was that she didn't want to fly to France at all.

The driver continued, "I'm sure you know that your brother…"

Yes, her brother. She'd read something online recently about his amazing feats in the European markets. Years ago, political changes allowed her father a foothold in the EU that according to the article, her brother has recently capitalized upon. Like father, like son.

Truly, Natalie's older sister's accomplishments were no less impressive than their brother's, though her story contained an interesting, if not scandalous footnote. It was something the family never mentioned.

"I'm sorry," Natalie said. "I'm sure I was already told, but will everyone be there?"

"Everyone? Your family will all be there. If that's what you're asking."

More ears to hear her announcement and more eyes to convey her father's disappointment.

The car eased to a stop under the covered entrance before the Boston airport. The driver rushed from his seat and opened her door. Cool air replaced the warmth. She stepped onto the curb.

At least the falling snow was blocked by the roof, even if the cold wind was not. The older gentleman handed Natalie an envelope, her family name embossed in the corner. "Your boarding pass and passport, Miss Natalie. Hurry through security. I'll check your luggage."

"Thank you, Jamison."

"Miss, I know you expected Mr. Roach. He had some business to attend, but will meet your plane in Nice."

Another person to look at her with relentless dissatisfaction.

Taking another step, Natalie squinted. Beyond the covered drive, beyond the signs of different airlines, the ground was quickly becoming covered with a blanket of white. "Do you think they'll delay the flight?" she asked.

"No, miss. They know your father is waiting."

CHAPTER TWO

Coincidence is the word we use when we can't see the levers and pulleys.

~ Emma Bull

"**Y**OU MADE IT," the man in seat 2B said as he stood, allowing Natalie to move past him to her seat beside the window.

"Why, yes," Natalie sighed more than said, shoving her carry-on bag into the overhead compartment and making a brief assessment of her travel companion. "Even with PreCheck, the security lines were unreal." Settling into her seat, she looked up. Since the man was still standing, she couldn't see his face. Instead, she started with his long legs and moved upward to his trim waist, firm torso, and broad shoulders. She liked the view, even contemplating that perhaps the flight wouldn't be as bad as she'd expected—until he sat and spoke again.

With his jaw clenched, his words came out harshly. "Why wouldn't you expect that? You should have allowed for the delay. It's the holiday travel time. In a few more minutes, they'll be closing the door. Do you realize that you could have missed the flight?"

His crass tone and cool eyes took her aback. It was as if he were reprimanding her. "Excuse me, do I know you?"

At once, his stern demeanor melted, taking the ice from his eyes and raising his cheeks as a smile bloomed. He lifted his hand. "We haven't been formally introduced. I'm Dexter, Dexter Smithers."

Years of manners were impossible to forget, even with this man's unusually stern introduction. Slowly, Natalie extended her hand and they shook. His grip was firm and warm, a nice contrast to the temperature outside. "Nice to meet you. I'm Natalie. My friends call me Nat."

"My friends call me Dex," he said, "but to be honest, I hate it."

She laughed. Maybe the flight wouldn't be so bad.

As he buckled his seatbelt, she stole a sideways glance. Now that Dexter's expression had softened, he definitely looked like the type of man she would consider handsome. Probably a few years older than she, with dark blond hair that covered the tips of his ears and blue-green eyes, he had a sexy, suave Norwegian look. When she first arrived, she'd rushed past him so quickly that she couldn't be sure of his height, but based on the fact that he'd tilted his head within the cabin to stand and the way he filled the first-class seat, he was easily over six feet.

Natalie found taller men more attractive. She'd inherited her father's height—towering over her mother—topping off at nearly five feet nine inches. Being a fan of high heels, she thought tall men made the best arm candy.

A loud noise drew her attention to the window. The deicer truck was farther back, shooting something hot against the wing. The snowy air filled with steam as a loud hiss permeated the cabin. "I really hate this. I wish they'd just postpone the flight instead of taking all of these precautions. I don't feel safe."

"Safety is simply a matter of trust. No one is ever really safe. There is always someone else with more power. Besides, postponing wouldn't do. My plans have been in place for too long."

She took a deep breath, momentarily closed her eyes, and leaned back against the soft seat. "I guess I need to trust the airlines. They wouldn't take off if it were dangerous, right?"

"Danger, now that's another concern altogether. It implies harm."

"Your plans?" she asked, her eyes now open as she spoke, hoping to shake the strange feeling brewing beneath her skin. She rubbed the arms of her sweater, taming the goose bumps materializing underneath. "Are they for the holiday?"

"The holiday? No, my plans are for much longer than a few weeks."

"Really? Do you live in Europe?"

His lips quirked upward. "Not permanently, but with the isolation, it seemed like the perfect place to begin. Wouldn't you agree?"

His words left her uneasy. Instead of concentrating on them, Natalie thought back over her various travels. "I've found Europe to be magical—the castles and history."

"Tell me, Natalie." He leaned closer. "I'd like to get to know you better before I call you Nat..."

She swallowed, her mouth suddenly feeling dry.

Where is the attendant?

As Dexter spoke, she scanned the cabin, fighting the restlessness coming to life somewhere below her consciousness. There was something about this man that put her on edge. Something about the intensity of his stare, as if he could call her *Nat*, as if he somehow knew more about her than she did about him. But that was silly. She'd never seen him before, never met him.

Her imagination was playing tricks. With her concern over facing her parents, flunking out of Harvard, and the cold temperatures in France, she hadn't been sleeping well. This agitation was all part of the stress. If only she could get away from it all instead of flying into the lion's den of her parents' rented home.

"Did you hear me? Are you listening?" His scolding tone pulled her from her thoughts.

"No, I'm sorry. I think my mind was wandering. Have you seen the attendant?"

"I asked you if you believe in magic." When she didn't answer, he continued. "You said that Europe is magical."

"Not literally," she scoffed. "Not as in wizards, witches, spells, and wishes. If those were real, I'd be going somewhere other than France to spend the holiday with my family." She looked around the cabin.

"Where would you be going?"

"Tell me, kind sir, are you my fairy godmother, or should I say father? Are you here to grant my wishes?"

He lifted his hand and pushed the button near the overhead lights. Within seconds a woman in a blue blouse and skirt with the airline's emblem on her name pin materialized. "Sir, do you need anything?"

"Yes." He turned to Natalie. "What was it that you needed?"

"Um, a glass of water. Thank you."

The attendant nodded and with a quick pivot hurried toward the hidden area beyond the seats and before the cockpit.

"You didn't need to do that. I was late getting to my seat. That's why she didn't come by. I'm sure she's upset that we're throwing off her schedule." The sound of beeps turned her attention outside the window to where the deicer truck had begun to back away. "We're probably about ready to take off."

Dexter shook his head. "I've never gotten out of Logan without at least a twenty-minute taxi. Sometimes it seems as though we're driving instead of flying. Besides, you asked for the attendant. It was your wish."

Within seconds the woman was back with a plastic cup filled with ice water and a napkin. Reaching for the drink, Natalie thanked the attendant and turned to Dexter. "It was my wish and you granted it? So you are my fairy godfather?"

He took the napkin dangling from her fingertips, ran the soft white paper over his palm, before placing it on the armrest between them. "I'm too young to be your father. Go ahead and drink your water. As for the rest, it's a long flight and many hours before we reach our destination." He leaned back.

From Natalie's view, she caught Dexter Smithers's profile—his protruding brow, high cheekbones, and chiseled jaw as well as the concentration in his stare. The way the muscles in his neck and cheeks flexed as if he were clenching his teeth, as if he were mulling over some serious matter that required his utmost concentration. Despite his lighter complexion and coloring, the look was hauntingly familiar, a focused expression she'd witnessed many times.

After she took a swallow of her water, the plane began to move. She turned his way. Dexter's eyes were open, yet she had the feeling he wasn't seeing what was visible—the back of the seats in front of them, the small screen, and pocket of traveling supplies reserved for overseas flights.

"Is everything all right?" she asked.

He turned her way. With the cabin lights now dimmed, his eyes were darker than before, more aqua blue, the shade that grows darker in the ocean's depths. "I was thinking about what you said. You mentioned history."

"Yes, I've always found European history interesting. American, not so much."

"So things that happened in your own country, even closer to home, don't interest you?"

Natalie shrugged. "Not as much as the royals and dynasties of the past."

"I've found the old adage to be true."

"Which one is that?"

"Those who don't learn from history are destined to repeat it."

CHAPTER THREE

Neither comprehension nor learning can take place in an atmosphere of anxiety.

~ Rose Kennedy

TRAVELING EAST AS Natalie was doing, away from the sun and into the future, caused the loss of time. Hours disappeared with each mile in the figurative rearview mirror and with each kilometer through the windshield. Different units of measurement couldn't explain the phenomenon. The time in Boston and Munich was never the same. Hours were forever lost, fading into obscurity like the faint cloud of exhaust left in the plane's wake.

Caught within the confines of her first-class cabin, in seat 2A, time accelerated. Nat's body may only have aged six hours, yet the clock ticked faster, progressing twelve hours. As she left Boston behind, reality, too, slipped away.

Natalie watched what happened around her, touched, tasted, and even smelled it. She was never alone. She had help, ever-present, omnipresent assistance. With each tick of that clock, Dexter became more attentive as her comprehension lessened. His hand covered hers reassuringly. He helped her order her meals, even ordering wine.

Natalie wasn't old enough to drink, not legally, in the United States. That didn't mean she never had. She'd had the occasional glass of wine at family dinners and parties. She'd attended parties at school. Yes, even Harvard had those kinds of parties.

Even so, she'd never over-imbibed. She'd seen friends stumble and slur their words. She'd helped some back to their apartment and put them to bed. She'd even assisted with the obligatory ponytail hold. Yet she'd never been the one who lost time, never been the one to wake and ask what she'd done. After all, while her parents were complacent about certain things, other things were unforgivable.

An unforgivable sin was impairing appearance. There were always people watching. A person was never completely alone. That was true of fellow students with phones that could instantly transmit a picture over social networks reaching hundreds, thousands, or more people. That was also true of fake-news organizations that would jump on the story depicting the youngest daughter of a renowned businessman behaving poorly in public. It was even true in her own home. The cameras were for security, but surveillance never stopped.

It always was. Natalie's mother accepted it. Her siblings had done their part to fight it, but it continued. Like the rising and setting of the sun, it was beyond her reach.

Why fight what you cannot change?

That was something her mother told her more than once, something Natalie had taken to heart. It was what it was—learn to accept it. Perhaps it's the reason she accepted her failure at Harvard. Could she have changed it?

As they approached Munich, nearly seven hours after leaving Boston, Natalie couldn't answer that question. It wasn't the only question she was incapable of answering. Simple equations, her favorite color, the name of her first pet...

Basically, everything was slightly beyond her comprehension and thoroughly beyond her articulation. All of the information was just out of reach...as if she were watching instead of participating.

After helping her back to their seats from the bathroom, Dexter reached for her boots from under the seat ahead of them. "Nat, it's time to get ready to disembark."

The boots sitting in her lap were hers; she recognized them. Why were they in her lap?

"I-I..."

He shook his head disapprovingly. "Dear, don't tell me that little bit of wine still has you this confused even after your rest?"

Dear? Rest?

Her eyes narrowed. "I-I don't know you." The words were thick and her tongue sticky.

"Sir, is everything all right?"

It was the woman in blue. Maybe she could help Natalie understand. Yet before Natalie could speak, Dexter spoke. Nat couldn't make out their words though their lips were moving. The woman smiled and nodded. Nat turned to Dexter; he was doing the same.

The woman leaned down to Natalie. "Congratulations. You're a lucky woman. I'd be celebrating too."

Natalie's head shook but words didn't form. Not at the necessary rate for conversation. One person spoke and then the other. Long pauses made for uncomfortable silence.

Finally, when Dexter squeezed her hand, Natalie thought to smile—wordless communication. It worked. The woman left.

Wait, was that what she wanted?

"Let me help you," Dexter said, lifting her legs over the center armrest until both of her bootie-covered feet were in his lap. Tenderly, he removed each paper covering, the ones provided by the airlines, and slipped each foot into her black boots. Once they were zipped, he gently placed her feet back upon the floor.

"Thank you," she managed, "…but why?"

"Let me get your bag in case you want to freshen up."

She remembered his blue-green eyes, long legs, and smile. She liked it when the smile reached his eyes. Why did that matter?

Dexter opened her messenger bag, the one she always used for traveling, and ruffled inside. She wanted to stop him, to remind him about privacy, yet the connection was still missing. The words were in her head but they wouldn't move to her tongue.

Suddenly, a passport was in her hands, opened to the page with her picture.

He leaned close and spoke, his volume low with a tone that bid her attention. "I know you aren't feeling like yourself. That's all right. Look at this." He tapped the information within the small folder. When she looked down, he went on, "We don't have much time. Listen closely and do as I say. Customs should be easy, but they might ask you a question or two. I'll explain that the combination of alcohol and sleep deprivation has you confused, but it's important to know your name."

She blinked, making the words come into focus. "My-my name is Natalie—"

"Your name is Nellie Smithers."

She shook her head again. "No, Natalie—"

"Nellie Smithers." His timbre slowed. "Say it."

"Why?"

He didn't answer, only repeating the name she didn't know, each time slower than the last. She tried to block him out, looking closer at the passport in her hand. It was her picture, but it wasn't her passport picture. This picture couldn't be more than a month or two old. Where did it come from? The picture in *her* passport was taken four years ago, when her childhood passport had expired. In the picture in her hand, she's her current age with long brown hair and big green eyes.

Though their personalities couldn't be more different, Natalie was the spitting image of her older sister, if her sister had green eyes. Instead, her sister had inherited their father's brown ones. Nat always thought they made her sister appear stronger, a more formidable force like their father. That wasn't what her dad said. When he looked at Nat, he'd say that she—his baby—was the perfect combination of light and dark.

Her mom and her dad.

"No…I have a flight to…" She tried to remember where she was going. It was somewhere cold. Her parents were already there. And her brother. No doubt her sister was coming. "…to…I'm going to…" Her eyelids were heavy, so heavy.

Hadn't she slept? She thought she remembered sleeping.

"Nellie—"

"No, Natalie!" She spoke too loud, too drawn out. People would stare.

Dexter smiled. "That's right, dear. I'll take care of it all."

He'd take care of what? Why was he happy? She'd said Natalie. Quietly, she said the name again, more of a whisper to herself rather than to him. "Nat-lie."

It didn't sound right. She licked her lips. The *T* was soft, though consonants are rarely soft. It wasn't coming out as two syllables.

"Naalie…"

No that wasn't right.

It was then she noticed her left hand, the rings.

Dexter must have seen her lift her hand because he helped her, raising it higher until the combination of diamonds and gold was right in front of her. "I'm so happy that you like it."

It's a strange sensation when an aircraft begins to slow. Tons of metal, hundreds of people, the weight exceeding anyone's imagination, suddenly decelerating its forward thrust, hanging precariously in the air as if at that moment the aircraft could drop to the earth. It's a frightening sensation—the passengers unable to change the deadly trajectory.

That was the sensation Natalie experienced, a free-fall from a mile high, her stomach in knots. Perspiration dotted her skin, her palms moistened, and the breakfast she couldn't recall eating pushed upward. "I-I'm going...sick..."

Dexter's lips quirked upward; even his eyes lightened. "No, dear, you won't. I made sure of that. The anti-nausea component of your little cocktail won't allow it."

"C-cocktail?"

"Why yes, we're about to land in Munich. You're old enough to drink there. In Germany, it's sixteen for beer and wine. It's eighteen for spirits. The laws are the same at our final destination. Though I must say, as your husband, I'll need to keep a close eye on your intake. It does seem as though you have a rather low tolerance."

There was too much in his speech, so much to decipher.

"Destination?" Her chest clenched. "M-my mom...France."

"Yes, it's interesting that she's who you mention. Of course, one day we'll visit. Keeping us from your family isn't my goal. I doubt our visit will be in France. You won't be ready. Besides, they're only renting that chateau. I'd love to visit their island. I'm sure it's beautiful. But first, don't you think we should get to know one another better?" His hand splayed over her thigh, the heat transcending the material of her tight jeans. "My dear wife."

CHAPTER FOUR

*Acceptance doesn't mean resignation; it means understanding that
something is what it is and that there's got to be a way through it.*

~ Michael J. Fox

WITH EACH SECOND that Natalie stared, unsure what to say, Dexter's hold intensified until the tips of his fingers blanched with the depth of their grip. Pain ached deep below her skin.

Dropping the passport, she clawed at his unmoving hand. "Stop. Y-you're hurting me." The sentence came faster, the pain returning her ability to speak, yet through clenched teeth, the words were barely audible.

Dexter's hand didn't move. The pressure neither lessened nor increased. His words, however, were clear and concise, knives cutting through the plane's rumbling. "On this plane, with the roar of the engines, our conversation is private. Remember to keep it that way when we're off the plane." His fingers dug deeper.

Natalie gasped, biting her lip to keep from screaming. "Please."

Again, the pressure leveled. With each assertion, she prayed that he wouldn't make it worse. She could bear it as long as there wasn't more.

"Tell me your name," he demanded.

She tried to remember. Everything was still foggy. The answer was in the passport. Not the real answer, but the one that would bring her relief. The small folder was now wedged beside her leg where she'd dropped it.

Dare she let go of his hand to look?

Before she was able, Dexter snatched the passport with his other hand. The one on her thigh never twitched or wavered in its mission.

"I-I can't remember," she admitted.

Dexter's head slowly shook. His fingers dug harder into the jeans, into her leg.

Tears prickled to life behind her eyes.

"No," he growled, a low rumbling hiss. "That won't do. We have customs soon and a car to secure."

"But…I have another flight."

"Don't be silly. Europe is too beautiful, and what did you call it? Oh, I remember…magical. It's too magical to miss seeing the countryside."

"I don't understand," Natalie replied, keenly aware that somehow she'd grown tolerant to the pain his hand continued to inflict.

"Your name?"

Her eyes closed to her silent plea and then opened.

Europe wasn't magical, or at least its airspace wasn't. This man—the one she barely knew—was still before her. She'd wished him away. She wished she'd done as her parents wanted and flown privately. She wished she'd never met him, but there he was. Deep ocean-aqua eyes, growing darker and deeper by the moment, staring back. Not staring—demanding. His fingers continued to dig, probing into her skin.

As her breaths hastened, Natalie moved her eyes from side to side, looking…searching. The couple on the other side of the aisle was too interested in one another to notice what was happening. The attendant walked back and forth, seemingly unaware. The people in the seats in front of them spoke, but she couldn't hear what they said. That meant that those near them couldn't hear Dexter either.

No longer prickling, tears teetered on her lids as she asked the questions churning in her stomach, knotting her insides. "Why are you doing this? Are you going to hurt me?"

Dexter's chest expanded and contracted as he leaned even closer.

This man was bigger than she remembered. Wider, stronger. He dominated her vision.

His eyes scanned to where his fingers grasped her thigh and back. "The *why* can wait. Tell me, am I hurting you now?"

If she weren't watching his firm lips, she might not have heard his question, but she was watching. Her thoughts were once again forming words and her brain was functioning. Synapses were firing. It wasn't at full speed, but it was there.

Her neck straightened as she answered, "Not as much as at first."

"Explain."

"At first, it might have been shock, but now the intensity…I don't know…" An unwanted tear escaped to her cheek, revealing her lie.

He *was* hurting her.

Still not releasing her thigh, Dexter wiped the tear with a satisfied grin. "The thing is, Nellie, I've slowly increased my hold. Your ability to accept what I'm giving you excites me more than you know."

What the hell? He had? Nellie?

Before she could form a question, he continued, "Will I hurt you? I'm leaving my mark. I plan to leave more. The intensity, your ability to handle what I give, is at your discretion as are your responses and your honesty. Tell me, what's your name?"

She remembered. He'd said it. "Nellie…Nellie…" The twisting in her stomach tightened. If only she could get sick, she'd vomit all over him. But he'd planned for that. What else had he planned?

"Go on."

Her heart beat like a drum, pounding out a signal that no one but she heard. "My name is Nellie Smithers." When he didn't respond, she added, "Please."

"Please, what? My dear wife, what are you asking?"

Only her eyes moved, looking down again at the blanched tips of his fingers.

"In the future, we'll work on using words, but for now that will do." His smile widened as his grip loosened.

As it did, pain shot through her thigh, worse than with his grasp. She lunged forward with a whimper, feverishly rubbing the material of her jeans.

"Yes, you see," he calmly explained, "the sensation of blood returning to starved tissues can be more painful than the pressure itself." He paused, pursing his lips in contemplation. "Consider that food for thought. Be careful what you ask. There'll be times that I'll be more than happy to oblige." His head tilted. "And other times when you must trust that I know best."

Who the hell?

Natalie's eyes widened. The world was becoming clearer though it still didn't make sense. "If it's money, my dad—"

"Don't be so naïve."

The blood running through her veins chilled as she considered her options. "I can scream. I won't let you do this."

"Do what, my wife?"

"I'm not your wife."

"Au contraire, every form of identification you possess states that you are. Who do you think will be believed, an inebriated woman or her sober husband?"

Natalie frantically pulled the bag from the floor, the one he'd given her earlier from the upper compartment, the one containing the fake passport. Where was her real one? She dug and dug through her things. Her heart raced quicker with each unsuccessful search. No other passport. No boarding pass for her next flight. Even her phone was missing. "Where...?"

And then she remembered her driver's license. It would prove her identity, even containing her Iowa address. A sigh escaped her lips as her fingers brushed the small leather clutch stowed in the bottom of the larger bag. Surely, he hadn't known about that. It was her golden ticket, the one to her freedom and safety.

Dexter didn't speak as she opened the small purse.

Nellie Smithers. Nellie Smithers.

Her ID. Each plastic card. Everything down to the Amex Platinum card her father had given her, had that name.

"How?"

"I realize it was premature, and one day I'll change the first name. I rather like Nat—my little bug—and soon we'll be better acquainted. In the meantime, this will help our cause."

"No, *I* got on this plane, me, not Nellie Smithers. The airlines will have record. My father will—"

His finger touched her lips. "If you think for even a moment that I haven't thought of that—of everything—you underestimate me." He roughly rubbed his fingers over her bruised thigh, eliciting Nat's small wince. "I look forward to more underestimating."

At that moment, the attendant appeared with hot cloths.

Ever the gentleman, Dexter reached for one, unfurled the roll of material, allowing the steam to escape, and handed it to Nat with a smile. "I wouldn't want it to burn you."

She took the cloth.

"Miss, I hope you're feeling better," the attendant said.

Natalie looked from her to Dexter. Silence settled as the beating of her heart increased. A second and another passed.

Finally, Dexter prompted, "Tell her how you're feeling, dear."

Natalie slowly raked her teeth over her lower lip as her gaze moved between the deep ocean eyes silently warning her to the woman's kind face. Nat took a deep breath. It wouldn't help to make her case in the sky. She needed to wait until there was someone who could help. "I'm feeling much better, thank you."

"Don't worry about it, honey," the woman said. "The altitude and alcohol...your new husband took good care of you. You're in good hands." She winked. "He said you hadn't eaten with all the excitement. It's a combination we often see.

"And as we promised him, your secret is safe with us. Newlyweds and all. Besides, everyone else was so preoccupied in their own world...don't you worry, no one noticed."

Natalie's stomach sank. She wasn't sure if this was good or not. Appearances were taught to her from an early age. However, if she'd been noticed...

"That was very good," Dexter said once the attendant was gone. The light was once again in his gaze. "I can either reward you for being a good girl, or slip you more of your new favorite cocktail if you plan to misbehave."

Her lips came together. The hairs on the back of her neck prickled with his patronizing tone and condescending words. She wasn't a little girl to be praised or punished. She also didn't like the effects of the drug: the lack of control, the queasy detachment.

"The choice is yours," he continued. "Customs will go much smoother if you're coherent. I'm also prepared to handle it if you're not."

She ran her palm over her tender thigh as the landing announcement spilled from the overhead speakers.

He lifted her hand and brushed his lips over her knuckles before holding it and rubbing her skin. "You're very beautiful, Nat. I've watched and waited. I've had this day planned for a very long time."

"My friends call me that. We're not friends."

The caress of the top of her hand stopped. His thumb pressed. The bones beneath were fragile, like matchsticks easily snapped. Before the pressure became too much, he spoke, "You're mine now. And you're right: we're more than friends. Aren't we, my little bug? That's what I'll call you until you earn back your name."

"Stop..." She tried to pull back her hand, but his hold stayed steadfast.

"I have no doubt you'll do it. You'll earn your name as well as mine. I have the utmost faith. You have your father's determination and your mother's submission. It's a fiery combination that I can't wait to explore."

"What do you know about my parents?"

"Everything."

Natalie shook her head as the ring on her left hand caught her attention. It was a large diamond lifted high on white-gold prongs; the band below it was simple. She yearned to take them off and throw them away. In the pit of her stomach, she knew that these rings didn't signify love and commitment, but a collar of ownership.

She hadn't been for sale nor could she be owned. Yet the way Dexter spoke to her was as if he knew otherwise.

"They're not real," Dexter said, releasing her other hand.

"They aren't?"

"No, bug. You'll need to earn that too. And let me tell you, the real ones are spectacular."

"Stop calling me that."

"What would you like me to call you?" he asked with a new unsettling gleam in his eyes.

Her stomach pinched. "My name."

"Go on. Tell me again what that is."

She took a deep breath as another tear escaped and slid down her cheek.

Getting off the plane and avoiding his cocktail were her two immediate goals. Though there was a small part of her that felt a rush from what was happening, the smarter part was telling her to run. Appeasing him would help. She was in control of her answer. Not him. Once they were on solid ground, she'd figure out a plan.

"I'm waiting." His fingertips tapped the armrest, pinkie to forefinger, once, twice. "You should know, I don't like to wait."

"My name is Nellie Smithers."

CHAPTER FIVE

Things are not always as they seem; the first appearance deceives many.

~ Phaedrus

A S DEXTER AND Natalie slowly progressed through the customs line, his hand remained in the small of her back, a constant reminder of his presence and expectations. On the surface, they appeared the happy yet weary couple. The reality was more ominous. She concentrated on standing, stepping, and taking in the world around her. The drugs—the so-called cocktail he'd given her—weren't completely out of her system. The effects lingered. Speech was back and, according to him, mobility had never been fully lost. It was how he was able to convince the attendant of her intoxication.

Before they left the plane, Dexter explained the effects of his chosen combination of drugs: lower inhibitions, eliminate awareness, and increase obedience. In a deep, soothing voice, the tone that if others heard would sound comforting, he went on. His words contrasted his timbre, but only Natalie was privy to those.

"But, my bug..."

With the crook of his finger, he gently caressed the line of her jaw, burning her with his touch and branding her with his mark. It took all of her willpower not to pull away.

He continued as the plane taxied to the gate, "It's truly a wonderful concoction. No one in the cabin questioned your sincerity."

"I-I don't remember."

"Of course you don't. That's the problem. If I gave you more for customs, you'd comply with my every command. Honestly, it would make this easier on me." He shrugged. "Maybe even on you. But easy isn't as fun or as thrilling." His hand gripped hers, swallowing it in his girth. "The way you answered the

attendant earned you this privilege. Don't disappoint me."

A madman was threatening her and taking her away from her family. He'd already admitted—and demonstrated—he was willing to hurt her.

She repeated his word, as her neck straightened, "Privilege?"

"Why, yes. If I gave you more of your cocktail, you wouldn't remember what's about to happen. How you willingly obeyed, willingly walked to your destiny." *The aquamarine irises glittered. "I want you to remember that this was your free will. Don't you want that, too?"*

"Bug." His voice, accompanied by a nudge, brought her back to the large room, the line, and the people.

Reluctantly, she moved, keeping their place in line. With each passing moment, coherency improved. High above, the ceiling was dotted with darkened globes—cameras—recording their movement. Every now and then, she'd look up, hoping that her picture would be recorded. She may have earned this *privilege* as he called it, but this was her chance to end this bizarre abduction before it could go further.

With the necessary forms in the breast pocket of his jacket, Dexter was never more than a few inches away. She hadn't seen what he'd written, only heard his warnings.

He expected obedience. But she couldn't. If she did as he'd said, there was no hope. The person in the booth was her hope. He or she had to believe Natalie when she said her real name, not the one Dexter wanted.

Nellie Smithers.

The name was in her head and on the tip of her tongue. Dexter had made her repeat it, even write it on a paper napkin as they descended airspace. Surprisingly, the signature she wrote resembled the one on the fake passport and the New York driver's license. He also made her say her birth date. At first, she hadn't noticed the subtle alteration: one month and one year different than her real one. Similar, yet changed.

That was how he'd ordered her wine.

By the time their dinner arrived, the world was fuzzy. Natalie had initially assumed that international flights allowed her to drink at twenty; however, a flight's age limitation was based upon the country of origin. It was her falsified ID that gave Dexter the ability to ply her with alcohol as well as his *cocktail.*

Step by step, they moved forward. She'd simply nod as he spoke, having difficulty concentrating. She had questions, ones she couldn't ask, but important ones nevertheless.

When was her connecting flight scheduled to leave Munich? Her absence on that flight would set off alarms. After all, she wasn't just *any* passenger: her father was waiting for her arrival. That was what Jamison had told her.

And Phil.

Jamison had said that Phil would be meeting her at the airport. The dread she'd felt at disappointing him with her grades was forgotten. He'd been with her family her entire life. He may be in their employment, but he felt more like an uncle.

And then there were her real uncle and aunt and cousins...

"With your recent change of plans, you would have gone through customs here."

She jumped, startled by the way Dexter spoke, close to her ear.

"What?"

"You're making it a point to look at the cameras. Your presence here will neither be considered odd nor unusual."

Nat took a breath and spoke in a low voice. "No. I shouldn't be in customs until France. I don't want my plans to change."

"My bug, that's no longer an option." He nodded toward one of the custom booths. "See that woman, barely more than a girl really, the one who just passed this checkpoint?"

Natalie saw her. She was young, tall, and slender. Her dark hair was pulled back into a ponytail that flowed through the back of a cap. Her clothes were expensive yet average: jeans, boots, a dark green top covered by a light brown sweater. Just before the woman disappeared into the crowd, Natalie noticed her bag: it was one identical to the bag she carried.

And the cap...Natalie wasn't wearing it, but she had one exactly the same.

Suddenly, the room grew warmer and her skin prickled.

Nat's mouth dried as her knees grew weak. "Why? Why did you point her out?"

"I thought you were smarter than that. You're disappointing me."

There were only a few more passengers ahead of them before they would reach the front of the line. The tears returned as she swallowed the bubbling bile. "She's me?"

"Now there's something you probably didn't expect to say. Who expects to see herself walk away and disappear into a crowd?

"Technically, no, she isn't you. You are you. However, the identity you may be contemplating telling to the man or woman we approach in one of those booths has been cleared to enter Germany. The name you had when you boarded is already officially in Munich. That woman has her—or should I say your—old passport, your boarding pass, all your information." Dexter pressed the small of her back, forcing her to take a few more steps, moving with the line. "The government officials won't believe you if you claim to be her."

Nat's heart thundered as the room teetered. What would happen if she fainted?

"Do you know the kind of mental facilities they have in Germany?" Dexter asked. "Not exactly as luxurious as the resort where your mother stayed."

She looked up to his face, her mouth agape, as her already-twisted stomach formed another knot. "How do you...?"

Her mother's episode had been ages ago, after her sister was born and before her brother. It was part of the family history no one mentioned. *The time before* was how it was referenced. By all Nat's accounts, there was no need to bring any of it up. Throughout all of Nat's life, her mother was steady and stable, kind and loving. The story Nat had been told was that a traumatic event, combined with an injury she'd suffered in an earlier accident, had sent her mother into what the professionals called *a break with reality.*

What would happen to her mother if Nat disappeared? Could it send her back?

Dexter continued to whisper, "I can't help you if they take you away."

Help me?

Studying his expression, Nat assessed her captor. Could she simply outrun him? He was tall, taller than she, possibly as tall as her father, and he was a large man—not fat by any means but solid and hard. Those same adjectives could be used to describe his expression. Solid and hard, as if he were discussing the weather, not her mother's mental health or her own. "But if I disappear, my mom..."

"You won't," he said reassuringly, tenderly rubbing her lower back, his large hand beneath her sweater, yet above her top. To the casual observer, it was a kind, encouraging gesture. "Don't worry, bug. Behave as we've discussed and the other *you* will send your parents a planned text message. You won't disappear. You simply decided that Munich was as far as you would travel and changed your flight."

"Why would I do that?"

They were nearly at the front of the line.

"Which do you think would be easier for your mother? Her baby girl missing the Christmas holiday because she's embarrassed about her failing grades or her baby girl in a foreign mental hospital after a breakdown brought on by the same thing?"

How did Dexter know about her grades? She hadn't even told her parents. Neither her sister, Nichol, nor her brother, Nate, knew. "I-I…"

"Come, dear," Dexter said, tugging her hand, "it's our turn. Nellie Smithers," he reminded softly as they approached the booth.

CHAPTER SIX

Our lives are defined by opportunities, even the ones we miss.
~ F. Scott Fitzgerald

"REASON FOR YOUR visit?" the man with a heavy German accent asked as he scanned the passport barcodes over a light and looked from the small documents to their faces.

Dexter answered, offering their forms and then quickly encasing Natalie's hand in his own. He confidently explained, with just the right amount of detail to sound convincing, that he and his new wife were on holiday—a delayed honeymoon, something about her passport coming with her new name, about castles, snow, and magic. With each word, the gravity of the situation settled around them with the doom of a suffocating cloud—the opposite of his answers—invisible to everyone but her, imprisoning her body and soul as it dazed her vision and stole her rebuttal.

His words sounded innocent and benign. No one but Natalie heard the reality. His speech was a malignant cancer gnawing at her insides and consuming her future.

Though she tried to listen, her thoughts centered on his threat, the one where he said she'd be thought insane. Her mind recalled stories of foreign mental institutions, conjuring images of bleak, lonely rooms with a single cot and no window. She didn't want to believe him.

Mental health didn't hold the stigma it had when her mother was diagnosed. During the last quarter-century, science and medicine had made significant progress, especially in the field of traumatic brain injuries. That was the contributing factor to her mother's episode. It wouldn't be a factor for Nat. She hadn't had an accident. Instead, if she were misdiagnosed, they'd only assume her to be crazy—a family trait.

She wasn't crazy. Neither was her mother. This was all ridiculous. Germany was a modern industrialized country with top-notch doctors who aided in cutting-edge research. This wasn't a third-world country. There were US military installations. The US embassy…

She was a US citizen. A kernel of hope sprouted to life. The officials *would* help her. She just needed to make her case.

It wasn't until Dexter nudged her shoulder that she remembered she was part of the farce occurring around her, assigned with the task of perpetuating his story.

"Time difference and a few glasses of wine," Dexter said to the man, with a laugh.

His chuckle rang with mocked joviality through the air, yet his eyes spoke louder, demanding her obedience. Her heart accelerated—what was normally one beat became two, if not three. The increased blood flow lacked the required oxygen, making her lightheaded. Maybe if she'd taken the cocktail, this wouldn't hurt as much.

"Mrs. Smithers," the agent asked, "what's your occupation?"

"M-my occupation?" That wasn't a question she'd anticipated.

"Yes, ma'am."

Dexter hadn't prepared her for this query. "I'm a student…I was."

Dexter wrapped his arm around her shoulders. "I suppose that now makes her a wife."

The agent nodded, looking from one to the other. Finally, he asked, "Do either of you have anything to declare?"

Nat began to open her lips to declare her real name. But the agent hadn't asked her name. Why?

He already knew it—the wrong one. He'd addressed her with it, and she'd answered.

Before her words formed, the agent stamped each passport and pushed the folders across the counter. When Dexter reached for their documentation, the agent nodded. "Enjoy your stay." He turned toward the crowd. "Next."

Next.

Next.

The word rang in Nat's ears as Dexter escorted her into the crowd. A puppeteer was what he was—able to control her simply with pressure upon her back—pulling strings and moving levers. Passing through a large archway, they entered another cavernous room that reminded her of the train or bus stations in big US cities: Grand Central Station in New York, or perhaps

Union Station in Chicago. Sounds echoed off the domed ceiling and tiled floor. Though attached to a modern airport, it felt as though they'd stepped into the country's past, into history.

Silently, he led her to a bench where she sat, dejectedly doing as the puppet master commanded. The crowd and commotion faded into a mist of despondency. Voices and faces disappeared. Her hand went to her chest as her breathing labored. Could the mist be poisonous? Or was this debilitating pain physical? Wasn't she too young for a heart attack?

Why wouldn't her lungs fill?

The answer stared her in the face with eyes as cold as the ocean's depths.

His plan was in motion. Stepping away from the booth was her final mistake, her opportunity to stop this—whatever it was—from happening. Her eyes went to the direction from which they'd come as her mind tried desperately to comprehend her dire situation.

Natalie blinked once and then again. Air slowly filled her lungs. Like a fading computer screen, the fog dissipated as the world came back into focus. There were people and noise. She turned toward her captor as he put his phone into the inside pocket of his jacket. If he'd spoken, she hadn't heard.

"Did you call her...me?" Natalie asked.

He kissed the top of her head. "Nothing for you to worry about."

"But my parents, will she text them?"

Natalie hadn't been thrilled about the chateau, but now that it was gone, she wanted it. She couldn't stop the tears as she imagined the scene: waking Christmas morning, the chateau beautifully festive for her mother loved decorations, her father's deep laugh and mother's approving gaze as they all sipped coffee around the tree. Other people may be there, but through it all, Nat could count on her immediate family. From the moment she arrived, her siblings, Nichol and Nate, would tease her about being the baby. She wasn't just her parents' baby, but theirs too. And now...

Tears blurred the noisy crowd.

Dexter stood and reached for her hand. The scene she'd created was gone. She was back in the hands of this...man.

"No tears, bug. Not yet. Save those for me."

Icy chills scurried up her spine with the tiny feet of a million mice. *Save her tears for him? What the hell?* And then there was his nickname. She wasn't a bug. The moniker grated her nerves, yet she needed to pick her battles, another of her mother's sayings.

Outside, the wind whipped around them, blowing her hair and chilling her skin. A car was waiting. As they approached, Dexter spoke to a uniformed man in German—another thundering blow. Natalie couldn't ask for help if she wanted to. While she was fluent in both French and English and knew enough Spanish to get by, speaking German was outside her capability.

Dexter opened the passenger side door and gallantly gestured for her to enter.

With her hand on the top of the door, her steps stuttered. She took one last look at the crowd, the bustling world around her, as the cool breeze prickled her moist eyes. Where was she going?

"Your coach awaits you for our magical adventure."

There weren't words capable of expressing her thoughts. Instead, with a deep sigh, she got into the car, settling into the cold seat. After Dexter positioned himself behind the wheel, he offered her a water bottle. She'd watched him buy it, watched his every move. She didn't trust him, not one bit. If she weren't so thirsty, she wouldn't consider drinking what he offered, but she was.

Hesitantly, she opened the cap and sipped, barely enough to wet her parched lips.

With a huff, Dexter took the bottle from her hand, placed it to his lips, and took a long draw. His Adam's apple bobbed as nearly a quarter of the liquid disappeared. Handing it back, he asked, "There, does that make you feel better?"

It did…until it didn't.

He'd taken a drink from it with his lips—his mouth. The small sip she'd consumed percolated within her stomach. It was silly. She wasn't the baby her family made her out to be. She was twenty years old, despite the falsified date on her bogus identifications. She knew what was coming. Drinking from the same bottle would be the least of her concerns or of their connection. Yet if she could fight, she would.

As if reading her mind, Dexter retrieved the water bottle and offered her another. "Here, this one is without my germs. Remember, bug, we'll soon be sharing more than a bottle of water; there won't be a place my lips won't touch."

"My luggage?" she asked, after taking a drink from the new bottle, trying to think of anything but his unappreciated and completely unnecessary verbal confirmation.

"Your layover was long enough. The *other you* will retrieve it. The real you doesn't need it."

She pulled her sweater tighter around her shoulders and tugged the cuffs over her fingers. Beyond the windows the sky was gray and over the ground was a dusting of snow. "I need my coat. It's in my suitcase."

Dexter hit a few buttons on the dashboard, bringing the heat to life, and then shimmied out of his sports jacket. "Here you go."

Tentatively, she reached for the wool sports jacket. Instead of putting it on, she laid it over herself like a blanket. All at once, his scent—masculine with spicy cologne—filled her senses, mixing with the dread of the future. It was a new concoction bubbling in her gut and challenging her sanity.

"Where are we going?" she asked, needing her bearings if she were to plan her escape. As she waited for his answer, warm air flowed from the car's vents. It didn't only fill the air but surrounded her. Had he turned the heater on in her seat? Her eyelids grew heavy. And then she remembered his phone was in his jacket. Maybe she could somehow use it…

The thought slipped away.

He hadn't answered her earlier question. She tried again. "Where…?"

With her inability to complete the question, the realization hit: the cocktail must have been in the second water bottle. She wanted to call him out but she couldn't. Thoughts disappeared, no longer making it to her lips as she submitted to the warmth and his scent. The world went dark.

CHAPTER SEVEN

The irrationality of a thing is no argument against its existence, rather a condition of it.

~ Nietzsche

NATALIE AWAKENED WITH a start. She was in the moment where dreams collide with reality at the intersection of consciousness and unconsciousness, where memories linger only to be blown away, the end of one and beginning of the other, the flash where connections blur and lines fade away.

Cold and damp.

So cold.

She huddled closer, tighter within herself, her knees at her chest as she hugged her arms nearer. Heat was the element she craved, yet her body was without.

Every muscle ached as if she'd been maintaining this position for too long. It wasn't only her arms and legs that hurt; her stomach also cried out. Its need wasn't for warmth but for food. Audible grumblings of hunger echoed off the empty walls.

Where was she and why was she cold and hungry?

Blindly she reached for a blanket, a sheet, anything. Her cool fingertips met a scratchy surface.

Crash! The sound of reality and dreams smashing together.

Natalie's eyes squeezed tighter as memories appeared behind her lids. If she didn't look—didn't see—perhaps nothing would be real. Yet in her heart, she knew that she hadn't dreamt or even had a nightmare. The deep ache in her bruised thigh confirmed the reality—flashes of recollections on the plane, in the car, and in a room—she'd lived it.

Her eyes sprang open as she quickly scooted to a sitting position. Her knees still pressed against her breasts, and her arms now hugged her legs. She moved across the rough bedding until her back collided with something hard.

Behind her, at the side of the bed where she'd slept, was a cool painted concrete wall. Like the mattress where she'd lain, its texture scratched her skin.

Her *skin*.

Natalie ran her palm over her bare leg, one and then the other, both. Goose bumps peppered her body, not only her legs but her arms and torso too. Her nipples beaded. Everything—all of her skin, of her body—was exposed. Her clothes were gone.

Her teeth chattered and body trembled as she unsuccessfully fought the urge to cry. This couldn't be happening. It couldn't be real.

As occurs in dim light, her eyes adjusted, allowing her prison to materialize.

There wasn't much to see.

The same dull white walls, four of them, created a box—perhaps more of a rectangle than a square. The ceiling was high and painted the same white as the walls, devoid of color. She searched for a light or even a bare bulb. The dimmed illumination that allowed her to see didn't come from electricity but from a narrow strip of glass high upon one wall. It was a window, but not one that would open. Even if it did, it was too high to reach and too small for her to fit through. As she stared, the distortions in the pane caught her attention. The glass was reinforced and leaded, the kind of window found in renovated ancient castles to keep invaders out or prisoners in.

The only interruptions in the sameness of the walls were two doorways. One was covered with a solid wooden door, closed and painted to match the monotony of the room. She didn't need to check to see if it were locked. The absence of a handle told her that it only opened from the other side. The other doorway appeared open, simply a frame with no door.

A quick flash.

She blinked.

Had she imagined it? She scanned each surface, searching for its source.

Again.

It didn't last longer than a millisecond.

Like the walls, the tiny flash was devoid of color, so quick and insignificant that if she blinked at the same second, she would have missed it. Shivering upon the makeshift bed, she waited and counted.

Twenty-two seconds.

If the room were brighter, she wouldn't have noticed it. Nevertheless, she did.

She counted again.

Twenty-two seconds later, it flashed again.

The flash came from a small knob fitted snuggly into the window sill. Well disguised, it could pass for a blemish in the trim. However, imperfections didn't flash. It was a camera and meant that she was being watched.

Another person may not have known, but Natalie grew up with surveillance as part of her life. It hadn't bothered her before. Then again, before, she'd been clothed.

She was now sitting. She couldn't pretend to still be asleep. Her empty stomach twisted. Dexter would know she was awake. Would he be coming to her? Was he asleep? What time was it?

Did she dare look in the other room?

Again, her stomach complained.

She clawed at the bed in the dimness, hoping for a blanket, sheet, or even the mattress covering, something in which to wrap her body. But there was nothing, only a cot with a single scratchy mattress.

Turning from the window—from the camera—she used her arms and hands to cover her breasts and core. It wasn't much, as she hurried toward the open doorway.

Once within, she fumbled along the wall for a switch and in the air for a string. Nat found none. This room was darker with no window, only the dim light trickling in from the room with the bed.

As her eyes continued to adapt, the second room came into focus: a simple yet efficient bathroom. Everything was white, reflecting light and helping her see. Straight ahead upon a pedestal was a sink, to one side, a toilet, and to the other side, an old iron clawfoot tub. Above the tub, mounted on the wall was a showerhead. Reaching in the darkness, she searched for a curtain, one to contain the shower's spray.

Rings rattled upon a track, higher than her head, but the curtain was gone. Natalie sunk to her knees and crawled about the cold floor, searching for towels, a robe, or anything. Back on her feet, her hands splayed over the walls. An empty towel bar beside the toilet and an empty hook near the doorway were all she found.

Thankfully, there was toilet paper, but it would take the entire roll to cover her, and then what if he wouldn't replace it?

How could she even rationalize his thoughts? These were the doings of a madman. She wasn't crazy. He was.

Again, her stomach grumbled.

Did he plan on starving her?

Natalie reached for the handle on the sink. Air and moisture sputtered, and then water began flowing. Using her hands, she cupped the cold liquid and brought it to her lips. The stench of sulfur filling her nose was worse than the musty aroma of her cement cell. Without drinking, she opened her hands and allowed the water to splash into the sink and disappear down the drain.

Perhaps at least, she could make it warm. That would help.

There were two handles. Natalie turned the handle on the left of the faucet as far as it would turn. As she waited for the temperature to change, she took care of other business. Her hand stilled as she began to wipe.

Had he touched her...there? Obviously, he'd taken her clothes. Had he raped her?

Memories were fuzzy at best. She recalled floating or being carried. Though she was cold—chilled to the bone—and her muscles ached from trying to keep herself warm—too long rigid and contracted—she didn't feel injured or sullied beyond her nakedness.

When she'd boarded the plane to Nice, Natalie had been a virgin. Surely, she'd know if she weren't any longer.

Forgetting about the camera, she carried the toilet paper into the light and sighed. There was no blood. She'd heard there would be blood.

Natalie wasn't completely without sexual knowledge. She'd dated boys in Iowa. They'd kissed and petted, but even with the biggest football star, she had a figurative wall around her, protecting her from going too far. No one dared be the boy to look her father in the eye after taking her virginity.

At Harvard, it was different, yet the same. Though her father's reputation held no boundaries, it was Natalie who didn't want to cross that line. It was she who didn't want to face not only her father but also her mother until the man who earned her hymen was also the one who earned her heart.

Some would consider it old-fashioned.

Maybe it was seeing her parents' devotion to one another. She wanted what they had. They'd overcome more obstacles than she even knew, and through it all, they loved one another unconditionally. They had the kind of love that survived life's trials and came out stronger.

Tears returned. Will she ever see her parents again? Can their marriage survive the tragedy of losing their daughter?

The ache in her chest grew larger, bubbling out with an audible sob.

Throwing the toilet paper in the water, she grabbed another piece and wiped her eyes. As it all swirled in the darkness and disappeared down the drain, she straightened her neck. She would survive this ordeal. Somehow, some way, she'd make it back to them.

Reaching for the running water, she expected heat. The reality was a few degrees above ice, reawakening her chill. Beside the handle was a small bar of soap. As she washed her hands, she turned off the one handle and tried the other.

A buzz or whistle sounded—shrill yet short. Had it come from the pipes? Natalie tried to listen, to hear it again. Like the light of the camera, would it recur?

With each passing second, the sound stayed away; only her beating heart thumped in her ears. However, to her delight, the water warmed. To her cooled skin, the liquid heat was heaven. On any other day, in any other place, combined with the stench, it would be unacceptable. Today, in this hell, the slight rise in temperature was the best thing she'd found. Forgetting everything else, she stood still, allowing the warmth to run through her fingers and return her circulation. As her hands warmed, she splashed some on her face. Even though she couldn't dry it, the water took away something—cleansed her as well as restoring something, bringing her back a small sense of normalcy.

When the warmth began to fade and she turned off the faucet, a shadow passed over her, chilling her skin. Was it simply a figurative cold to the loss of her warmed water? Had she imagined it?

Though there was no mirror above the sink—only more wall, the same as the rest—she lifted her face. Even without the reflection, Natalie knew. Standing taller, she braced herself as the hairs on her bare skin came to attention like small soldiers ready to fight.

What she'd endured so far was only the prelude. The battle was about to begin.

"Turn around, bug. We have rules to discuss."

CHAPTER EIGHT

Of all the animals, man is the only one that is cruel. He is the only one
that inflicts pain for the pleasure of doing it.

~ Mark Twain

D EXTER'S COMMAND HUNG in the musty air.
       Paralyzing fear: it's mentioned in books and seen in movies. A thing
of fiction until it was real…so real that even blinking seemed impossible.
Involuntary movement commenced. The trembling from earlier returned,
causing Natalie's hands to visibly shake. It was when her knees began to
knock that she managed to reach out to the sink, an anchor to keep her from
falling.

"Rule number one…" His tenor slowed. "I don't repeat myself."

Natalie had never been fully nude in front of a man—even those she'd
dated. She wasn't a prude; she was merely twenty.

"May…" Her voice cracked, the word stuck in her throat, barely a croak.
She cleared her throat, still facing the wall as her fingers gripped the edge of
the sink. "Please, may I have something to wear?"

His shoes upon the cool, hard floor echoed, each step reverberating louder and louder as he came nearer. When he stopped, she looked down. On
either side of her bare feet were shoes—boots with rounded toes. She thought
they were the same ones he'd worn on the plane, but she couldn't be sure.

His body, merely inches behind her, radiated warmth, the temperature
she craved. Yet his proximity did little to reassure her.

Dexter's hands moved up and down, feathering her arms, a conduit of
electricity springing the small hairs to life, similar to the effect of rubbing a
balloon. "You're cold."

It wasn't a question. There was no sympathy to his statement. It simply
was.

"Yes."

He leaned closer. His coffee-flavored breath reawakened her hunger while also caressing her neck and shoulder in warmth. "Tell me, bug, how you can get warm."

Each word weighed a ton until her head dropped forward, unable to bear the load. Tears filled her eyes. "I-I don't know what you want."

Dexter took a step back. "Rule number two. Disobedience will always be punished. If I tell you to turn, turn. If I tell you to answer me, answer me."

Her shoulders quaked. If there were a door on the bathroom, she'd close it. It wouldn't really be an escape, but it would give her space. And then she realized...the door. The one he entered.

Quickly she spun and raced forward. As soon as she neared the barrier, she saw the error of her ways. She was naked in the better lit room, and the door was shut, locked, still with no way to be opened. However, that couldn't be true. Dexter was with her. He wouldn't lock himself in, would he?

"You have a great ass," he said, running a hand over her skin. "Show me what else I want to see."

"Don't, please." Natalie shook her head. "You saw me—everything. You had to see. Who took off my clothes?"

He barely touched her shoulder, encouraging her to turn.

Flinching away, she spun, her loose hair landing upon her shoulders. With a steely expression, she faced him. What difference did it make? He'd obviously undressed her.

Silence prevailed as only his eyes moved up and down her body. Like his touch, his gaze was fire—a scalding hot poker raking her skin. Finally, he spoke. "Legs shoulder-width apart."

Her eyes squinted in the dim light, as if seeing him clearer would give meaning to his words. "What?"

Dexter lunged forward.

Natalie gasped.

His hard body stopped inches away from hers as her chin became locked in his iron grip. Pulling her gaze to his, he said, "I'm running out of patience." The ocean of his eyes was deep and murky. "I've waited for you to wake. I've waited for you to turn and show me what's mine. I won't wait again. Don't ask me to repeat myself. You heard my instructions."

When he didn't release her chin, she slowly repositioned her feet, moving one and then the other.

"Hands at your sides, palms away from your thighs."

She had reached up to his hold upon her chin, trying unsuccessfully to loosen his grip. It took conscious effort to make her hands obey, to untangle her grasp from his, lower her arms, and turn her palms out.

"Shoulders back and breasts out." He made a show of stepping back and admiring her breasts. "I like them. They're not large, but oh, the possibilities are limitless."

Her eyes closed.

When he released her chin, it began to fall forward.

"No." He lifted it. "You're a proud woman. I don't intend to change that."

She audibly exhaled at the absurdity of his statement.

Dexter grabbed her hair and yanked it backward, causing her to wince. "Don't do that. Don't make assumptions. Don't assume that I'm debasing you to make you less. When this part of our journey is complete, you'll be more than you ever imagined." Releasing her hair, he took a step back.

"Before I entered this room there was a noise, a buzzing sound. Did you hear it?"

"Yes." She'd thought it was the pipes.

"When you hear that sound…" He tapped the floor with the toe of his boot. "…you'll stand here, facing the door, offering yourself." His gaze narrowed. "Do you need me to make an X?"

"No." She wanted to make an X—on his chest and use it as a bull's-eye.

"You'll stand as you are right now. Legs parted so I can see your pretty pussy. Chest out, so I can watch your nipples bead. Hands at your side, surrendering yourself to me, and most importantly, your shoulders back and chin high. Do you know why?"

A tear fell from her eye. "No."

He stepped closer, caressing her jawline as he'd done on the plane. "Because you may be my bug, my Nat, but you're no one else's. You're a queen, no longer your daddy's spoiled princess. A queen who'll learn to appreciate the spoils of life. That understanding will give you a regal comprehension that others will see and respect." His smile widened. "And a queen bows to only one person." He walked around her, daring her to move from the position. One circle and then another. "Tell me, my queen, to whom do you bow?"

The answer was obvious; it was right there. But Dexter Smithers wasn't her king. He never would be.

When she didn't answer, he pushed her down, commanding her new position. "On your knees."

The concrete floor bit into her knees. She fell forward, her hands extended, when all at once her head was yanked back by a fistful of her hair.

"No. Get off your hands. You aren't crawling, not this time. Kneeling is like standing, only lower. You'll assume the correct position."

The tears fell faster. "I don't know—"

Crouching down on his haunches, he secured her head back until their gazes focused upon only one another. "Have you knelt before another man?"

"No." The word was choked with tears of both pain and humiliation.

"Never put a cock in your mouth?"

She shook her head. "No." More tears.

"That's it, bug…" He leaned forward and kissed her cheek, tasting the salty emotion. "…you saved the tears for me. I'm expecting many more." He licked his lips. "They're so good. Now, as with standing, knees spread…" He released her hair and using the toe of his boot eased her legs apart. "Back straight, sit back on your heels with your toes as your support."

Without instructions, she rested her arms at her side and turned her palms up.

"Very good. Now tell me, which is a more comfortable position, standing or kneeling?"

She swallowed. "Standing. The floor is hard."

"You didn't turn when I told you. Where will you be the next time I enter?"

"Standing where you said…" Her heart ached, but the words came easily. "…how you said."

Dexter nodded. "Good girl, but no. In the future, but not next time."

Her eyes opened wide.

"I promised you punishment. This is it. You'll remain as you are." He looked up at the window, at the camera. "You already know that I can watch you. Don't move, shift, or so much as readjust your pretty pink pussy. If you do, your next punishment will be worse, and the next one even worse, until it's your blood I'm tasting instead of your tears."

Her entire body clenched. He couldn't possibly mean what he was saying. The concrete dug into her knees as her toes bent uncomfortably. She couldn't imagine staying this way. "How long?"

Her stomach again rumbled.

Dexter smiled as he stood. "I almost forgot."

The buzz filled the air as he walked behind her. She was facing the bed, but the warm air entering the room told her the door was open and that it was warmer beyond the doorway. If only she could turn and look, but just as quickly, Dexter was back, carrying a tray.

"I'd planned to discuss so much more, all my expectations and rules for our relationship. I'd planned to do that over coffee and pastries. They really do make amazing baked goods here. The Sachertorte is my favorite." He removed the cloth napkin, uncovering a tray.

The aroma of coffee and rum-infused cake replaced the musty air. Like Pavlov's dog, her mouth watered.

Dexter set the tray on the bed, turned over one of the cups and poured rich, warm coffee from the decanter. Bringing the cup to his lips, he hummed. "It's too hot, but the mug feels nice and warm." He sat the mug on the tray. The plate was filled with Sachertorte, a famous Austrian cake.

Did that mean they were in Austria? Or did they serve that in Germany?

Natalie couldn't think as her lips parted in a silent plea and her fingers ached to touch the warmth of the cup.

"I had plans, bug. Plans that you decided weren't to your liking. Plans you sabotaged by disobeying." He poured the second mug. "This would have been yours." He shrugged. "I suppose technically it still is."

Her heart raced. Yes, even coffee would help her hunger.

He placed the full mug on the tray. "Good girls get rewards. Bad girls are punished. Don't move and don't even think about touching this tray. You didn't earn it."

The tears were back again.

What could he do that would be worse? Whatever it was, it couldn't be as bad as starving on the cold floor, could it?

Dexter stood. "Whatever you're thinking, I promise your imagination can't begin to conjure the possibilities." He leaned down and kissed the top of her hair. "Don't test me. Bugs can be squished." He ground the toe of his boot into the floor and then moved it toward her knees, spreading them even wider, exposing her core and causing her thighs to ache. "I'll be watching."

And then there was another buzz, a gust of warm air, and the closing of the door.

This can't be happening. This can't be real.

Her eyes closed. Perhaps she could forget about the tray, but it was impossible while the scrumptious aroma surrounded her. Seeing it within her reach was a sick kind of torture. With each passing minute, her toes ached more and more. Even her thighs called out in pain.

Perhaps it was hunger, perhaps the effect of the drug, but as time passed, her head began to bob, to fall forward, as her eyes fought to stay open. Each time it fell, she'd pull it back. Through it all, her shoulders screamed out. No longer could she feel her extremities. The tingly sensation had passed; now there was only heavy nothingness.

Natalie didn't know how long she'd been there. There was no way to measure time.

She assessed the clues. The light through the window was now brighter. The coffee was no longer warm as no steam came from the dark, rich liquid. Though she hadn't drunk, her bladder again felt full.

And then it happened. The buzz sounded.

Dexter was back.

CHAPTER NINE

Some things are so unexpected that no one is prepared for them.

~ Leo Rosten

NATALIE TALKED TO herself throughout this punishment or whatever it was—Dexter's power trip. She didn't do it audibly: he could see so it was possible he could also hear. She spoke in her mind. It helped her stay awake as she convinced herself she could do whatever she needed to do to survive. She could fight his ice with ice, his commands head-on, until she found herself on the other side of the door, back in the sunlight, and then she'd run.

No matter where he had her, what country, there had to be a US embassy. Her father was wealthy and influential. He had friends and business associates all over the world. He would move heaven and hell for her. Of that, she had no doubt.

Natalie wouldn't be forgotten or allowed to disappear simply because she supposedly decided not to meet her family. No matter who that other woman was, Dexter's plan was flawed. Natalie's immediate family may be in Nice, but that didn't mean that her father didn't have people all over the world. The abrupt change in plans would serve as a red flag signaling Phil's people to track the other Natalie. Once they discovered that she was an imposter, it would be all over the international channels: Natalie Rawlings was missing.

As time passed and her extremities lost feeling, she'd tried to come up with Dexter's motivation. Since she was sitting—no, make that kneeling—on a concrete floor in basically a dungeon, naked, the sexual component was obvious, but there had to be more. It didn't take a genius to figure out that the *more* was money. Anthony and Claire Rawlings's daughter was a valuable commodity.

All of her life her parents had preached caution and safety. The cameras and bodyguards seemed second nature while at the same time overkill. She'd never in twenty years seen or felt a threat. Had there been some and Phil's team had thwarted them? Had everyone in her father's world kept the specifics away from her to protect her?

What had that false sense of security cost her?

She recalled times when she'd pondered a life away from the watchful eyes of her father's security. It wasn't that the security bothered her. Knowing she was watched hadn't changed her plans or behavior, because it always was. Yet there'd been a part of her that longed for a simpler life than living up to the standard set by Nichol.

Getting away from the Rawlings expectations had sounded like a dream. If this was it, the reality was a nightmare. The realization created more tears. Each one burnt a trail down her cheeks, dripping off her jaw and landing in a warm, salty splash on her cold breasts. Each tear took a piece of her soul until the pieces begged for glue—for a way to come back together.

Her hope was her knowledge and confidence in her family. They would never hesitate to monetarily pay for her return. It was her goal to convince Dexter that they'd pay more if she were returned unharmed—unsoiled, so to speak.

Buzz.

Natalie's chin snapped upward. Despite her crying, her tears were now dry and nose had ceased to run. Her plan was in place. She'd had her breakdown. Now it was time to appear strong and indifferent, the same way he appeared. If Dexter wanted to believe she would play his sick game, she'd let him.

Still facing the bed and the tray of untouched food and drink, Natalie couldn't see what was happening behind her, only hear. There were footsteps and wheels.

Wheels? Did she hear wheels moving over the hard floor, like a cart?

If only she could turn, but she refused to give him another reason to retaliate. Instead, her mind filled with possibilities. She pictured the carts used by the staff at the estate in Iowa that brought food to the dining room or to the suites. There were the carts used in hotels when room service was summoned. Each of her thoughts had a common denominator—food.

Her stomach had surpassed grumbling, giving up as it had grown accustomed to emptiness. That was, until the new sounds revived it: a pang and softer rumble murmured in the damp, musty air.

She closed her eyes and tried to summon non-food alternatives. There were the carts the maids used at the estate as well as in hotels, ones with bedding and supplies. That possibility even excited her. A towel for the bath or a sheet for the bed. Such simple needs.

Natalie pushed down her expectations. If she didn't hope, Dexter couldn't disappoint. She feared that would be worse than more punishment.

As each second ticked by, marked by the tap of his shoes upon the concrete, she began to wonder if he planned to talk, to acknowledge her obedience—anything. The anticipation of what may occur brought her tired, aching body back to life, restoring the circulation and bringing needles to her veins. The new rush created a painful and prickling sensation.

Natalie stifled a cry, biting her lower lip, careful to stay silent and vowing to keep secret her suffering. And then Dexter changed the rules by giving her what she feared most—hope.

The door shut with a thud. Before she could fathom that he'd left her again, Natalie wobbled as the heat enveloped her.

His lips came close to her neck as he wrapped the blanket around her shoulders. "I'm very proud of you, my bug." He kissed her hair.

It wasn't just a blanket. It was warm like the cloths on the airplane or a garment recently removed from a heated dryer. The plush heat tingled her cold skin. The circulation that had resumed, generated by anticipation, now sprinted to life. The temperature was heaven. Its consequences were hell. Pleasure and pain. Natalie didn't know which was the cause of her tears.

Dexter crouched beside her, wrapped the blanket tighter. And then with his hands on her shoulders, he asked if she could stand.

Natalie stared.

There was something different in his gaze.

"Bug, answer me."

She tried to reach up. Her arms were dead weight, lifting them only a few inches took all her strength. Her legs were nothing more than noodled pincushions. It was as if her bones had lost their rigidity. She shook her head. "I-I don't think so."

What would he say? Would he be upset?

Dexter nodded and stood. Her heart sank. Would he leave her there?

After removing the tray from the bed and placing it on the floor, in one swoop he reached down and lifted Natalie from the floor, pulling her into his arms as if she weighed nothing.

Nat cried out as her toes and legs exploded in pain. It was worse than any cramp or charley horse she'd ever experienced. Gritting her teeth, she buried her face against his broad chest.

She hadn't meant to find comfort in his attention, but she did. His shirt smelled like fresh air—clean and cool, so unlike her surroundings—while his cologne added just the right amount of musk and spice.

With her cradled in his arms, Dexter sat upon the bed.

She didn't know what to say or do. This wasn't the same man who'd made her kneel for hours on end. It was, but it wasn't. In her deprived state, her thoughts couldn't keep up.

"Tell me," Dexter said.

Natalie looked up to his face. There was something different in his tone as well as his stare. Maybe it was hunger making Natalie delusional. She couldn't be sure, but for some reason she wanted to answer. "My toes…" Her eyes closed, her lashes dampened with tears. "My legs…"

"They hurt?"

Natalie nodded.

Balancing her on his lap and against his chest, Dexter reached for her foot and his large hand squeezed.

Pain shot up her leg. Natalie screamed, louder than before.

"No, bug," he said soothingly. "It'll get better. Give it a minute."

Biting her lip, she watched as he massaged one foot and then the other. He was right: the prickling subsided and before she knew it, they felt better.

"Remember my saying that the rush of blood to starved tissues can be more painful than the pressure?"

She nodded.

"That's what happened." He kissed her forehead. "I didn't think you'd make it. I really didn't. You're so much stronger than I realized."

His words flowed through her, providing the same effect as the blanket. She didn't want to like pleasing this man, but she did. She enjoyed this tone, the way he held her and wiped her cheeks. And then he placed her upon the edge of the mattress and stood. All at once, she was hit with the startling realization that she didn't want him to leave. She didn't want to be left alone again, even with the blanket.

"Dexter? Are you going?"

When he turned, his lips parted. There was something new in his gaze: shock or surprise. She was too sore and hungry to understand.

He dropped to one knee and placed his hand over her blanket-covered leg. "Say that again." His command wasn't urgent, more of a request.

"I-I'm sorry if I shouldn't..." This was all so new. She didn't know what she was supposed to say.

Caressing her blanket-covered thigh, he explained, "No, just say what you said, exactly as you said it. I want to hear it again."

"Are you going?"

His head shook. "My name. You said my name."

"Dexter?"

"It's the first time you've said it."

She blinked. "It was?"

Again, his knuckle ran the length of her jaw. "Yes, bug. And I like hearing it from your lips."

"Are you leaving again?"

"No, not yet." He reached for her hands. "Now can you stand?"

The feeling was back in her legs. Gingerly, she shifted her weight to her feet and rose. Her legs quivered and her feet were heavy, but his grasp of her hands gave her the extra needed leverage. Like a newborn deer, she stood unsteadily.

"How do you feel?" he asked.

"Sore, but I can stand."

"And walk?"

Natalie nodded.

Dexter tilted his head toward the bathroom. "Go do whatever you need to do. I'll give you privacy. When you come back out, we'll have the talk we didn't have this morning."

She tugged the blanket around her, but after only a step, she stopped. "May I..." It felt strange to ask for such a mundane thing. Dexter said they'd discuss the rules, but they hadn't. She wanted to be sure she wouldn't upset him. She'd do whatever was necessary to avoid the cement floor. "...may I keep the blanket...around me?"

He nodded. "I think for now...you earned it."

"Thank you." Nat hurried toward the bathroom as too many different emotions fought for supremacy.

Somehow, after everything, it was gratitude that prevailed.

Her mind told her she was being ridiculous. Grateful for a blanket? Yet she was. She could cover herself in the bathroom. She could keep it wrapped around her while they talked. Yesterday, she would have told herself it was silly to be thankful for a blanket. That was before.

Today, her life was different.

CHAPTER TEN

The best way to find out if you can trust somebody is to trust them.

~ Ernest Hemingway

NATALIE CAME TO a stop, standing unmoving in the bathroom's doorframe while contemplating the possibility that Dexter had been right and she was delusional. Hunger and stress can be triggering factors. Sleep deprivation is another. She'd slept, but more accurately, she'd been drugged. Wasn't that different?

"Come and sit," he said, turning and catching her stare.

Tentatively, she moved forward, the blanket snug around her.

In the brief time she'd been in the bathroom, he'd set up a small round folding table with two chairs. The cart she'd heard before was now in the room. Two covered dishes, a decanter, and a large glass bottle of water were upon it.

Natalie eased into the chair he pulled out.

"This is still," he said, pointing to the water. "I can bring sparkling next time, if you prefer."

She shook her head. "I like still, thank you."

Definitely delusional, having a surreal conversation discussing water as if she weren't wearing a blanket and at Dexter's mercy.

He placed the dishes upon the table. The cake from earlier was gone. In its place were large grilled sandwiches that emitted the most amazing aroma. A side salad of leafy greens and vegetables sat beside it on the plate.

When she began to reach for the sandwich, he stopped her. "Not yet. Patience."

Dejectedly, she placed her hand on her lap. Would he again tease her with food and then not allow her to eat?

Dexter placed a mug on the table and poured from the decanter. It wasn't the dark, rich coffee aroma she'd anticipated; instead, the liquid was lighter in color. The steam filled the air with a familiar scent. Before she could decipher the flavor, Dexter spoke.

"Ginger tea. It should help your muscles."

"Thank you."

He took the other seat and scanned their meal.

"Tell me, bug. What do you want?"

Closing her eyes, she pressed her lips together and compiled. Her list was simple and yet comprehensive: her life back, freedom, outside, her family, sunlight, clothes, a shower…

The movement of the other chair caused her eyes to open. Dexter was no longer across the table, he was directly in front of her, his face in hers. She gasped.

"Don't hesitate." His harsher tone was more commanding. "When I ask you a question, don't overthink. Answer immediately or lose the opportunity until I feel generous again."

"To eat. I want to eat." It was the obtainable goal. There were bigger wishes she wanted granted, but at this second, as her hands shook with hunger, food was paramount. She scanned the table. She also wanted the ginger tea.

It had never been her favorite flavor, yet she knew the Chinese believed it to have healing qualities. While her legs were better, the muscles were tight. "And drink, tea…please," she added.

Slowly, his chest expanded and contracted and nostrils flared. It was obvious that he was thinking, contemplating. She just didn't know what he'd decide.

How does one predict the moves of a madman?

"No more warnings," he said. "Keep rule number one in mind."

"You don't repeat yourself," she said, remembering his rule.

Her breathing stalled as he tugged the top of the blanket, lowering it from up around her neck to below her collarbone and lower still. Natalie's eyes closed. She wanted to stop him, to scream or reach up and scratch his hand, but she knew that none of that was within her power. When she opened her eyes, in her current seated position with Dexter standing, she couldn't help but notice his arousal. As his hand lingered, her skin chilled.

His gaze swept from her chest to her face and back again. The blanket was now as low as the swell of her breasts. His warm finger traced her skin, dipping between her round globes along the hem of the blanket. She was no more exposed than she would be in a scooped blouse, yet it felt as if she were once again naked.

Dexter lifted her chin until their gazes met. "What will you do to earn your meal?"

Everything within her froze. Her blood forgot to flow.

"Please, Dexter." She purposely used his name, hoping for the effect from before. "I know that isn't an answer to your question but I don't know what I can do." It was a truthful answer. She didn't want to offer more than he'd accept, nor did she want to offer less and lose her second chance at a meal.

Again, he traced the scoop of the blanket. "Lower it," he said. "Keep your breasts exposed for me, and then you may choose one thing from the table."

She scanned the feast. Sandwiches and salad weren't by definition a feast, but to her they were. What difference would it make if she removed the blanket? He'd seen her totally nude. She took a breath. With trembling fingers, she reached for the edge of the blanket.

Her eyes focused on the plate. She didn't want one thing. She wanted it all. "One?"

"Rule number one."

Natalie nodded. He wouldn't repeat himself. He'd said *one* thing.

She wondered if she removed the entire blanket, could she earn more than one item? With a ragged breath, she opened the blanket, leaving it draped over her shoulders with her chest exposed. The cool air made her nipples harden.

A deep murmur resonated from Dexter's throat. Pushing the material over her shoulders, he left the rest bunched around her waist. "Now touch them."

Touch them?

In his tone, she heard his meaning. Dexter didn't want her to just touch them; he wanted her to touch them as she would alone in her darkened bedroom.

Again, she lifted her hands.

His eyes stayed glued to her movement as she kneaded both breasts, pushing them up and twisting her hard nipples until her breasts grew heavy and engorged. As she caressed and teased, it was impossible not to notice that his erection grew, straining against the zipper of his jeans.

How long did he expect this to go on?

Her skin warmed under her own touch and lips parted as she startled herself with a small, unexpected whimper. Was her body's response from her own ministrations or from the lustful gleam in his blue-green eyes? While his erection scared her, there was more, something new and erotic in what they were doing. A strange tenseness formed between her legs, causing her inside muscles to clench.

Surely, she wasn't turned on by this man.

Finally, he spoke, his voice weighted with lust. "You've earned two things from the table." He turned and went back to his chair.

Natalie let out the breath she'd been holding.

"What do you choose?" he asked.

"The tea and the sandwich." She didn't hesitate, didn't overthink.

Dexter poured water for himself and nodded.

Taking that as his sign, Natalie hurriedly dove in.

Never had anything tasted as delicious. The bread was heavenly, grilled to the perfect crispness. Between the slices, the vegetables were sautéed and pasted together with rich white cheese. With each bite, the flavors exploded in her mouth. The blanket he'd moved off her shoulders, fully exposing her breasts, was forgotten. Chewing and swallowing monopolized her thoughts while the warmth of the mug gave her hands needed heat.

Dexter watched silently as she ate her sandwich and drank her ginger tea. He watched everything, not only her breasts, but also the way she sipped the tea, wiped her lips, even the way she chewed. His gaze was omnipresent. Once the sandwich was gone, he asked, "Wouldn't you like some water? It wouldn't be good for you to dehydrate. Besides, there was only one cup of tea."

Natalie did want water, but she was beginning to understand that everything came with a price.

"May I have water?"

He poured the clear liquid into her glass.

When she didn't reach for it, he grinned. "Good girl, bug. I was right about you. You're a quick learner. Are you ready to learn what you must do to earn that water?"

Though dread flooded her veins, the food gave her strength. "Yes."

"This time, your job is simple. It's not your body, although you'll soon offer me more than a view of your tits."

Offer? Did that mean he wouldn't take?

Before she could give it much thought, he told her what he wanted. "Your mind."

CHAPTER ELEVEN

It is hard to fight an enemy who has outposts in your head.
~ Sally Kempton

"MY MIND?" NATALIE asked.

"Tell me what I want to know, and you'll earn water. Tell me enough and I'll even leave you a bottle. The water from the pipes isn't fit for consumption. I'd hate for you to get sick."

But you'll kidnap, freeze, and starve me to death? Instead of saying that, Natalie nodded.

"Go ahead," he prompted, "take a sip."

As she lifted the glass to her lips she remembered his cocktail from the plane. Her hand stalled. "Did you…is this…?"

"Does it contain the drugs I gave you before?"

Her parched lips came together as she silently agreed.

"Will you believe me?"

It was a good question. She shouldn't. "I don't know. I suppose I have no choice."

"Yet you'd ask. You hesitated. Why?"

She did as he said, answering honestly and not overthinking her response. "Because I didn't like it. I didn't like the way it made me feel."

Dexter nodded. "That water isn't drugged. Go ahead and take a drink."

Obeying, she was rewarded with a clear, clean, and refreshing drink. Each swallow lubricated her tongue and throat in a way the tea hadn't. How long had it been since she'd had water? She wasn't sure how long she'd been asleep, and then there were the hours spent on the floor.

Natalie didn't want to stop drinking. Dexter had said *one* drink. Perhaps if she never stopped swallowing, it would still be one. Her mind told her to put the glass down, but she couldn't. It tasted too good. Now that her body had food, this was the other element to life.

The realization hit her: no matter how strange her life had become, she wanted life. She wanted to live.

Finally, she put the empty glass down, scared to look across the table at what she might see. Instead of anger, Dexter's laugh echoed throughout the small room. "My bug was thirsty. Now then, I allowed you your reward before you did your part. It's time. Tell me what you're thinking."

"What I'm thinking?"

He moved his head back and forth. "If I wanted a parrot, I would have taken one. I took you, a thinking, breathing, sexy, smart woman. I took you, bug. You're now mine. Tell me how you feel. How…" He gestured about the white room. "…this makes you feel and your thoughts from the time you woke until now."

It was a tall order. Exposing her breasts was easier than her thoughts.

Don't overthink. That was what he'd told her.

"I'm scared."

"Go on."

"I was hungry. That's better." She looked around the room, suddenly realizing it resembled the images she'd conjured in her mind about foreign mental institutions. She wasn't the one who was crazy. No. That person was sitting across the table from her, his arms folded over his wide chest, assessing her and her exposed breasts. "I'm embarrassed and quite honestly, humiliated."

"Why?"

She fidgeted with the blanket on her lap. "I'm sitting here without a top. It should be rather obvious."

"You're mine. I'm keeping you. That means every part of you, bug. There's nothing that should embarrass you. Baring yourself to me shouldn't be embarrassing."

"But it is," she answered too quickly. "I don't know you, and regardless of what you say, I don't belong to you. I'm not your bug." She shook her head. "I really hate that, too. It's patronizing."

His blue-green eyes lightened with amusement. "Well, that won't stop. I like it. And as I told you, you'll earn your name back."

Earn. Why was everything earned?

"Now tell me," he went on, "what proof do you need to understand that you do belong to me, that you are mine? Would a bill of sale make it better?

A contract? I can have one drawn up, but essentially a marriage license is the same thing. The one we have now isn't real. But one day."

When she didn't respond, he continued, "How about my intimate knowledge of your sexy body? Will that prove that you're mine? For example, the way your pussy clenches even when you're unconscious?"

Natalie gasped, squeezing her legs together. "Did you…?"

"Did I…what? Fuck you?"

She didn't respond as tears filled her eyes. If only she could cover all of her with the blanket, her face and her head, and of course, her breasts.

"No," Dexter answered, "I didn't. I want the first time that I'm inside you to be something we both remember. As much as I wanted to…" He uncrossed his arms and leaned forward. "…and I still want to—I didn't."

A lone tear trickled down her cheek. "Thank you."

More gratitude for things that should never be gifts: a blanket, food, and her purity. And then she remembered his words. "But you said you know how…how I clench?"

"One taste. I'm a man and you're a beautiful woman. One day you'll want me to taste you, to bury my face in your cunt until you scream my name. It was only one taste."

Her head fell forward as more tears flowed.

"Bug?"

Her head snapped up. "Violated!"

Dexter's gaze darkened. "I didn't violate you."

"You asked me how I feel. There, that's it. Violated."

"You were not. I could have. You were right there." His large hand slapped the table. Plates and glasses jumped as silverware clanked and water sloshed. His expression hardened. "I could do it right now. Who's going to stop me? Not you. Not anyone.

"You need to get that through your head. You're now mine to do with as I want. Even knowing that you're mine—at my disposal at any time—I respected you enough to remove your clothes, taste your lips, kiss your soft skin, and yes, take one small taste of your warm pussy.

"Do you know what you did?"

She shook her head. She didn't want to know. The meal she'd eaten along with the tea and water were churning faster by the second. "No."

"You instantly became wet. Did I want to be inside you with my fingers, tongue, or cock? Yes, but I didn't. I'm not sure what other assholes you've been with, but when I do those things, it'll be with your consent and for your pleasure."

Her neck straightened. "None." She wasn't sure why she'd told him—why it slipped out—but she had, and she couldn't take it back.

"None," Dexter repeated her word slowly as the realization hit him. "None, no one?"

She shook her head.

"You've never been with a man?" He stood, the astonishment overtaking his whole demeanor. "Answer me, damn it."

"No! No assholes in my past, no good guys either." *You're the only asshole.*

Dexter ran his hand over his face and paced a small circle. "Fuck. Fuck." He turned her way. "No, you're lying. You're twenty years old. High school…college?"

"So because I never slept with a man, there's something wrong? Fine, there is. And I want to keep it that way." Tired of this discussion, she pulled the blanket back over her shoulders and tucked it around her chin, covering her breasts. "I'm not lying. I'm also done with the sandwich. Leave the water, if I've given you what you wanted or if you've *taken* it. If you're not satisfied, don't leave it. Whatever. I'm done."

He yanked her to her feet, holding her shoulders at arm's length. "You're not in a position to dismiss me—ever. We're done when I say we're done." His eyes were now the deepest ocean depth. "Do not fucking lie. Are you a virgin?"

She lifted her chin. "I was when I woke yesterday."

"One fucking taste, a kiss to your sweet, wet lips. I didn't…how the fuck would I know?"

Indignation rang as her volume increased. "I don't know, you could have asked or let me tell you. There are more possibilities than drugging and kidnapping me!"

She didn't see his hand until it was too late. Her cheek stung as tears filled her eyes.

Dexter took a step back. "Don't make me do that again."

Make him? What could she possibly say? He'd just hit her, actually slapped her.

Dexter's tone hardened. "Respect. I gave it to you by not fucking you when I could—which includes right now, too. You give it to me. That was your last outburst. The next one will be met with a harsher reply.”

Harsher than a slap?

She straightened her shoulders, ignoring the tears flowing down her cheeks. “Yes. I’m a virgin. And if you want the money my father will pay to get me back, you’ll return me to him that way.”

Dexter took another step back, increasing the distance between them and rubbing his hand over the stubble on his chin. “You have this all wrong. I’m not holding you for ransom. Not everyone is after your daddy’s money. I have plenty of my own.

“You’re here for one reason: because you’re mine. We’re meant to be together. I’m not returning you.” He turned a small circle. The muscles in his neck tensed as his jaw clenched. “Now, bug, we’re done. Drop the blanket.”

Her eyes widened.

He tilted his head toward the floor, the spot where she’d knelt. “Stand in position—unless you’d rather kneel.” His blue-green eyes shone her way, daring her to disobey.

With her heart beating faster, she dropped the blanket and made her way to where he’d pointed. Biting her lip, she did as he’d said: feet, shoulder-distance apart, shoulders back, arms at her side, palms out, and lastly, chin up. The cold chill returned, tracking up her body from the hard floor all the way to her scalp.

As if she were no longer there, Dexter worked, putting the food back on the cart as well as the table and chairs. Once the room was clear, he turned. His gaze moved up her body, lingering momentarily on her pussy and then her breasts. When their eyes met, he said, “A virgin.” He shook his head. “I guess I do know how to pick them.”

Natalie momentarily closed her eyes.

“I’ll leave the blanket and the rest of the water. Don’t move until the door is shut. When I return be exactly as you are now. For the rest of the day, my two rules are simple. First, no touching or pleasuring yourself. Don’t think that you can in the bathroom. There’s a camera in there too. And do not bathe. We’ll discuss that on my next visit.”

He walked closer until the musk of his cologne filled her senses and the warmth radiating from his chest rippled over her bare skin. “Tell me, have you? Touched yourself? Made yourself come?”

Heat sparked in her cheeks. Not only there, a flicker of flame heated her core with an embarrassing rush of warmth.

"Please, Dexter."

His grin grew. "Oh, you have. I can tell. It's permissible to think about it. Think about how much better it will be with a man, one who knows how to please you." His knuckle caressed her jaw. "That's it, bug, imagine. Just do not touch." He stepped back. "Can you behave?"

"Yes."

"For the record, I said you should never feel embarrassed, and I meant it. I'm glad to know you've touched yourself. I can tell the idea turns you on. Your cheeks are pink and I smell your arousal." He laughed. "What I didn't say is that I wouldn't humiliate you. I will. Because I enjoy it. I'll also exalt you. You can plan on me doing both. Just remember, it'll only be me who'll debase you, only I'll see you broken, because only I can put you back together.

"You're my bug, but more importantly, you're also my queen. No one else will ever see or know what we do alone."

Her breathing deepened at his statement. It wasn't a threat, but a promise.

And then he was gone.

Natalie's shoulders relaxed as the door shut. She rushed to the blanket lying on the floor.

The man was certifiably nuts. And how dare he tell her not to touch herself? She hadn't planned on it. But now, the seed was planted…

CHAPTER TWELVE

Once you consent to some concession, you can never cancel it and put things back the way they are.

~ Howard Hughes

DAYS LOST MEANING as time passed into weeks. If Natalie were a missing person, she hadn't heard. She hadn't heard anything about anything, except from Dexter.

She'd boarded the plane in Boston on a Friday in mid-December. It had been before Christmas and her sister's birthday. She'd tried to keep track of time, but days and nights intertwined. Sometimes when Dexter arrived with breakfast, it was still dark through the small window. Some days it never seemed to get fully light. Other times, their day would end, and the light would persist.

After a few days, she earned artificial lighting. At first, she hadn't seen the source. It was a rope-type light hidden high above in the seam between the wall and ceiling that only Dexter could control. Though the room was still stark, the light helped her spirit.

Everything in Natalie's life came with a price, the value determined by Dexter. Whether it was towels for the bathroom, washcloths, soft sheets, or even a pillow for the bed, only he could assign their worth. Sometimes it was an act of submission or obedience. Other times, a thought or a feeling, verbally shared. Sometimes it was memories. Every question asked must receive a truthful answer. Recalling memories was the most difficult and emotionally taxing. The bigger the sacrifice, the greater the reward.

While sometimes it felt otherwise, everything was also Natalie's choice. She could opt not to give the price Dexter determined. That too would be met by consequences. Which did she want: the reward or the punishment? In all things, the final decision was hers.

A mortifying change in Natalie's life was bathing. Due to his rule about self-gratification, taking a bath wasn't allowed to be done in private. It wasn't enough that she knew Dexter could watch via cameras: he insisted on being present. At first, he physically bathed her as if she were a toddler in need of assistance. When it was his hand that wielded the sponge or cloth, she was rewarded with rich-smelling bath salts, soaps, shampoo, and conditioner. And then after he'd dry her—all of her—he'd instruct her to lie on the mattress and he'd cover her skin in velvety lotions. The scents varied, but their presence permeated the musty air, creating a pleasant cloud.

Though Dexter claimed she was his, that she belonged to him, Natalie didn't really know him. His touch made her uneasy. Subconsciously, she'd tense.

Nothing remained subconscious—nothing. Dexter required her thoughts and feelings on everything he did, that she made him do, and on every reward or punishment.

"Tell me how it felt when I slapped you."

"It hurt." The answer was honest and not overthought.

"No, bug." Dexter touched her chest, the spot between her breasts where her heart metaphorically resided. "How did it *feel?*"

The talking was worse than the actions.

It was one thing to be made to stand in a corner for hours, like a rebellious child. It was another to describe the humiliation. It was one thing to be required to crawl to his feet and sit like a pet between his knees, another to admit that the shame made her wet.

Without a mirror, she couldn't see her face, but she could see the bruises that often discolored her skin. The first one on her thigh had faded, but others had materialized. Some were felt more than seen, such as those that sometimes made sitting difficult. Others resulted from restraints or the hard floor.

After Natalie confessed that she didn't like being bathed, Dexter stopped. Since he'd listened, she should have been happy. Yet she wasn't. From that time forward, the soap he brought to her each day for her bath was abrasive and strong-smelling. The water without the bath salts reeked of sulfur and dried her skin. The shampoo barely lathered, and of course, the lotions ceased to appear. Natalie was now free to bathe herself—with his supervision—but her honesty came with a price.

Over the weeks, her life became a predictable routine. Sometimes she'd wake before he arrived with her breakfast, other times she was asleep. No matter, she quickly learned the sound of his arrival, and after a few slow-to-rise mornings that resulted in his desired punishment, Natalie always stood as she'd been instructed, presenting herself for his entry.

After breakfast was exercise time. There weren't many options in a 12-by-8-foot room. Dexter's requirement was that she continued to move. Walk, dance, run in place, do jumping jacks, or sit-ups, the choice was hers, but standing still or sitting or lying upon the bed—the only furniture that remained permanently in her room—was forbidden. This activity continued nonstop and lasted until he arrived with her lunch. Though she had no way to tell the time, she knew it varied. Some days, exercise went on and on until continuing to pace took the last of her energy.

Meals were earned, never to be expected. Usually she sat with Dexter at the small table. Sometimes she was permitted the covering of her blanket, other times not. If he were feeling particularly dominant, she ate on the floor, at his feet, her food coming from his fingers. She soon learned that the number of chairs at the table was the deciding factor. As she stood in his desired position, her breathing would quicken if the door shut with only one chair in place.

It meant her walking for the day was done. On all fours, she'd approach his feet.

Between lunch and dinner was what Dexter referred to as *his time*. It was when Natalie's job—her ability to earn a reward—was contingent upon his pleasure and often her humiliation. He'd remind her that only he could do these things to her, only he could mark her skin and debase her. The world would see her as his queen, but first, she needed to please her king.

As the weeks passed, her virginity stayed intact.

It wasn't that he didn't touch her; he did. His fingers and hands roamed her face, neck, and collarbone. She'd stand or lie—whatever position he requested—as her breasts, tummy, and behind were pleased or punished. He saw all of her, yet he never breached her vagina.

The inattention to that particular area, combined with his actions and dominating presence, awakened her arousal, creating a desire for things she'd never before considered. Erotic, sensual needs monopolized her thoughts.

Where at first she'd thought of her parents and family, over time, it happened less and less. It wasn't because she didn't care about them, but that they lost their relevance. Dexter was in control of every facet of her life.

He was her god and her devil. His presence and approval infiltrated even her dreams.

At night, her hands would ache to give herself relief. When he'd first forbidden her self-pleasure, she'd thought it would be the easiest rule to keep. Now, it was nearly impossible. There were even times that her hands wandered in her sleep. Quickly, she'd awaken and move them within sight of the cameras, scared she'd lose the bedding she'd earned, with merely one rub of her clit.

Masturbating had never dwelled within her thoughts, but when she was alone with the memories of his most recent *Dexter-time*, the need was almost too great not to face. She recalled the way her hands had been outstretched and tied to the bed's metal frame. How her knees were bent beneath her and a bar had been positioned, attached to her ankles and also bound to the bed. How he'd verbally described his view.

Tears dampened her pillow at the memory. It was mortifying enough to know she'd been on display, her ass in the air and her most private parts exposed, but when that was accompanied by her own body's betrayal, a glistening essence leaking down her thighs, it added to her agony.

Bathing was next on the schedule after *Dexter-time* and then dinner.

After dinner, there were minutes or hours before the lights went out. That time was spent either alone or in Dexter's presence. That was up to him, his schedule, and his responsibilities.

Natalie didn't know what he did when he wasn't with her. She knew nothing about anything beyond the door. All that could be seen from her designated place, the place where she was to stand when he entered or exited—assuming she wasn't bound or being punished—was a gray hallway, the opposite wall made of concrete blocks.

Wherever Dexter went or whatever he did, he was clean and smelled of fresh air and spicy musk whenever he entered her room. Wherever he spent his time away from her, it wasn't in a dingy cement room. Despite the things he did to her, she found herself missing him when he was gone. Maybe he'd been right. Maybe she was insane. Who would actually want this man's presence?

The only true measure of time came with her period. She'd always been regular: every four weeks like clockwork. Telling him wasn't necessary: she'd awakened with the realization.

Of all the humiliations she'd endured, this wasn't one. While she anticipated his anger over the soiled sheets and even perhaps demoralizing words, she hadn't expected his understanding. Feminine hygiene products appeared and her schedule lightened. Natalie wanted to tell him that she wasn't ill. It wasn't like needing a pass to be excused from gym class. Yet the reprieve was welcomed.

His only demand was that she inform him when it was complete.

That had been over a week ago, and now lunch was done. Since her return to their regular schedule, *Dexter-time* had taken on new vigor, as if during the reprieve he'd conjured new ways to let her earn the kindness he'd already paid to her.

With Natalie bent over the foot of the bed, the metal frame bruising her hipbones and her face upon the mattress, Dexter ran his hand over her behind. His large palm warmed her skin as his touch roamed, teasing the edges of her core. Each day she fidgeted more, wanting the violation she'd previously feared. He spread her essence over her thighs, wordlessly acknowledging her arousal.

Natalie whimpered against the soft bedcovering. Tears of unsatisfied need pooled upon the comforter. She gasped for breath, her dissatisfaction coming as a sob.

"Talk to me, bug."

Sometimes it was easier to talk when he had her in these positions. She couldn't see his deep ocean eyes or decipher his thoughts. She was free to talk without witnessing the consequences. "O-okay."

"Tell me what you're feeling."

She hated that question most of all. Instead of answering the way she always did, admitting her embarrassment, she threw caution to the wind. "Frustrated."

His hand stilled on her ass. "About?"

She shifted her footing. "Me. I'm so confused." When he didn't respond, she added, "I've never felt this way before."

"This way?" It was Dexter's turn to parrot.

Her core clenched. "I need...I want to come." She was a virgin, not a nun. She knew the relief brought on by an orgasm. Though her cheeks caught fire with her confession, there was also relief.

"How?" he asked.

"How?"

Dexter leaned near to her tearstained face. "How do you want to come? My fingers, tongue, or cock?"

The latter scared her, but the first two sounded doable. He's kissed and licked the rest of her body. Though at first she hadn't liked it, now she did. It meant the pain was over and he was making it better.

Natalie swallowed and stared into his turbulent eyes. The waters were rough. Would she survive the storm? She didn't know. Either way, it was time to face it. "I'll consent to your wishes, my king. And there's one other thing…" Her heart raced.

"Tell me."

"When it's time…will you…" The words were hard to say, to admit, yet they were sincere. She wanted him to be pleased with her.

"Bug, will I what? Will I hurt you?"

For some unknown reason, that hadn't crossed her mind. She shook her head. "No, Dexter. I trust you to do what's best. I was wondering if you'd help me bathe?"

Chapter Thirteen

People grow through experience if they meet life honestly and courageously. This is how character is built.

~ Eleanor Roosevelt

"TILT YOUR HEAD back."

Natalie did as Dexter said, supporting herself with her arms as warm, clear water flowed over her hair. Coconut permeated the air, surrounding them in the scent of sunshine as Dexter retrieved another pan of water from the sink.

She watched as he stood, turning his back toward her.

With his shirt off to keep it from getting wet, she watched the only part of his body she'd seen: his wide chest, thick muscular arms, and toned torso. She'd been nude ever since she arrived, and yet she'd never seen more of him. The disparity suddenly filled her thoughts.

She'd never seen any man naked. She'd seen pictures, but never of an erection. She'd felt his against her, through his jeans. Natalie knew how hard he could become when he rubbed himself over her, but through his clothes, she couldn't gauge anything else.

It had been over two weeks since she'd asked him to let her come. By the time it happened, she'd done more than ask. Her body and words begged for relief.

At first, he'd used his mouth. She would say it was his tongue, but as the memories tightened her core, she knew it was more. With her positioned over his face, he described his view. If he'd meant to embarrass her, it hadn't worked. Instead, his words turned her on, primed and ready for what would come next.

But she wasn't ready.

What Dexter did with his mouth lifted her higher than anything she'd ever done to herself. Sucking and nipping, he'd worked her into a frenzy until she was no longer conscious of her actions. Holding the headboard, she writhed as her hips rocked and breasts heaved. The tension within her built until she was sure something within her would break. She'd never been wound so tightly. Just as she thought it would happen—that her orgasm was imminent—Dexter told her to stop, that they were done.

Stop? She could barely comprehend his command.

She didn't want to stop. Her body begged to disobey. She'd willingly take his punishment, if she could just have more of what his mouth could provide. The scene came back.

With her knees on either side of his face, she stared down into his eyes. His lips glistened with her essence as her pussy sat inches from his chin.

"You heard me. Don't make me repeat it."

If he repeated himself, she would be punished. But she wasn't thinking straight. "Please, Dexter. I-I'm so close."

His shiny lips smiled. "I know. I think you can wait a little longer."

Her entire body shook with need. "I can't."

His large hands splayed over her hips as he lifted her off him and onto the bed.

"Did I...?" She didn't know how this worked. He'd been the one to direct her position. Maybe she was supposed to have done something else. "Did I do something wrong?"

"No, bug." He kissed her cheek, leaving her own scent on her skin. "You're perfect."

"Then what happened?"

"It's time for your bath."

Her bath? Now?

Submerged in the sweet scent of lilacs, he offered her the relief she'd wanted. The price was her speech. She needed to tell him how it felt to ride his mouth, how his tongue, lips, and teeth had felt on her core. And how it made her feel when it ended without resolution.

Natalie's description was simplistic and honest. It felt good and when he stopped, she was heartbroken.

"And now, do you still want to come?"

"Yes," she answered too quickly. She didn't wait for him to tell her the price; she knew she'd pay whatever he wanted. "I'll do anything."

His grin widened. "Anything is a big promise."

Her breasts heaved in the warm water. It was the first sweet-smelling bath she'd had in a month. The water was even warmer as the silky salts coated her skin. "Anything," she repeated.

Dexter took her hand and helped her stand. In the clawfoot tub, she was nearly his height, but not quite. Doing as he led, she stepped to the floor and stood with her hands on the side of the tub with her back toward him. Water slid from her skin, pooling near her feet.

Even the cool air didn't dampen the heat of his touch as his fingers roamed her body, tweaking her nipples and moving down to her need.

Natalie shifted as the pressure within her rekindled, stronger than before.

"Talk to me," he commanded.

"Please, Dexter, touch me."

His lips found her neck. "Don't let go of the tub."

She nodded. Words had become difficult to form. His kisses continued stoking the flames of the fire inside her. Through his jeans, his erection pressed against her behind. Over and over his lips roamed. No longer foreign, they left a trail of hot coals as she craved more of his touch.

When his nips became bites, she screamed out, "Please…"

"Who do you belong to, Nat?"

He'd said her name. It was almost too much.

"You," she panted. "I'm all yours."

"Who's your king?"

"You, Dexter."

"Who do you kneel for?"

"Only you."

Her legs shook as his fingers found her folds. She gasped as one, and then two digits slid inside her. Just as she had with his mouth, she rode his hand, bouncing on the balls of her feet to the rhythm he established. He stoked the fire he'd started, fanning the flames hotter than before. It was as he found her clit that his deep voice confirmed her answer.

"Mine, you're my Natalie."

The world spun as she cried out. Fireworks detonated as relief exploded through her system. The pleasure was so intense that it teetered on pain. Her fingers blanched as she rode out the orgasm, her skin covered in perspiration as she came harder than she ever had. Her swollen clit ached as her insides spasmed. Her legs quivered and face fell forward. And then his hands were gone. The sound of his zipper brought her back to reality.

Her breath caught in her chest. Now that she'd come, the idea of him being *inside her was terrifying. Yet she'd promised anything.*

"Dexter?"

Her hands trembled on the edge of the tub.

"Don't turn around."

She closed her eyes. He'd given her what she wanted; now it was time to pay.

As she braced herself for his cock, the bathroom filled with Dexter's moans. His breathing hastened. Yet he wasn't inside her.

Natalie longed to turn around, to see what she only heard. Her mind filled with the erotic image of him pumping his erection. She was certain that was what she heard, and then a deep roar vibrated off the walls as warm liquid splashed over her ass and back. It continued as the warmth dripped down her legs.

Nearly two months ago, she'd tensed at his touch. Now his cum coated her skin and all she could do was imagine what it would be like to have seen his hard cock. And then the zipper signaled the end of his pleasure.

"Give me your hand."

He hadn't told her to turn around, so she didn't. She lifted her right hand as he directed her back into the tub.

"One more time," Dexter said, telling Natalie to lean her head back as he again poured warm water. The memories of that day made her nipples bead as she concentrated on the muscles in his arms, the way they flexed as he rinsed the conditioner from her hair.

Usually, she had her hair trimmed every six weeks. It was overdue, but Dexter liked the way it flowed over her shoulders. Sometimes he'd even braid it. The first time he'd done it, she found the attention intimate. Now when he did it, as with the placing of only one chair, the action frightened and shockingly excited her. It signaled the beginning of a particularly taxing *Dexter-time*, one that would leave her skin moist with perspiration and possibly bruised.

Today's *Dexter-time* had been a braid day. After he'd secured the end, he directed her to the bed. Like a lamb off to slaughter, she willingly obeyed. Whatever he had planned wouldn't be as bad as it could be if she fought. She'd learned that lesson early in their relationship.

It was funny that in her thoughts she described what they had that way— a relationship. That reasoning helped her cope with the reality.

Once her hands were bound above her head, he removed clamps from his pocket and showed them to her. Lying in the palm of his hand, the shiny silver contraptions looked innocent enough, but she knew the truth.

"Nipples or clit?" he asked.

Her pulse increased. She'd never had a clamp on her clit. What would that feel like? How badly would it hurt when he placed it, and worse, when he removed it?

Dexter's head shook. "You had a choice."

"Nipples," she answered.

He kissed her nose. "You hesitated. You were overthinking. Tell me what you were thinking." As he spoke he tweaked her nipples, twisting and teasing as they morphed to hard points.

"I was thinking…" It was hard to concentrate as he worked her body, kissing and sucking as her breasts grew heavy. "…about what you said…about the blood coming back."

"How painful it can be?"

"Yes. I don't want to use the clamps anywhere."

"But I do, bug." He hadn't used her name since that one afternoon. "And it's all about pleasing me. You know that I enjoy your pain as much as your pleasure."

She tugged on her wrist restraints. It wasn't like she thought she had a choice. "Oh…ouch…." She bit her lip to keep her words from spilling out. Tears filled her eyes as he tightened the clamp around one engorged nipple.

"That's it." He leaned down and kissed the tear away. "Your tears are nearly as sweet as your pussy." He secured the second clamp.

Natalie had learned that if she ignored the pressure, concentrated on something else, the initial pain would subside…until he removed them. He spread her legs, tightening her insides. Maybe he'd let her come. She could concentrate on that.

"No!" Her hips bucked and screams echoed as the clamp tightened over her clit.

Dexter's lips kissed her folds. "You hesitated. You lost your choice."

And then his fingers were inside her, working her pussy, bringing more circulation to her clit. The closer the orgasm, the more painful the third clamp became.

How could something feel so good and hurt so much?

"Please, Dexter, don't make me come."

"But you like to come."

Even in the tub, the memory brought moisture back to between her legs. And then Dexter ran his hands over her wet breasts, causing her to flinch.

"Are they still sore?" he asked, pinching the bruised nipple.

"Yes," she whimpered.

"How's your clit?"

"It still hurts too." She couldn't believe how easily it had become to talk to him, to answer his questions.

"Tell me your thoughts."

"Before I was remembering today, I was thinking about the time you came behind me."

His eyes widened. "You were?"

She nodded.

"Go on."

"You've let me come so many times since then, yet you only did that one time. Can I...?" She suddenly felt unsure.

"Can you what?"

"Can I help you?"

She waited and watched. Though his eyes grew a deeper shade of ocean blue, Dexter didn't answer. She'd almost forgotten her offer by the time he helped her from the tub, tenderly dried her body, and after directing her to the mattress, coated her skin with lotion. She became transfixed on the man above her. With each aromatic application, his muscled torso flexed, making the indentations of his abs more defined. His large hands—the ones that could cause both pain and pleasure—gently caressed her tender body. At times like this, witnessing his restrained power, Natalie understood what his words never uttered: it took more strength for him to control his actions than to wield a crop or cause her tears.

There was something in that realization: the knowledge that she could give him an outlet for both, taking his bite and allowing him to make it better with a kiss, caused her heart to swell. Maybe she was going crazy.

"How, bug?"

Dexter didn't need to say more. She knew what he was asking. How was she willing to help him?

"I've never seen a man...I know we're going to have sex. I think I'm ready, but first, can I touch it?"

"So only your hands?"

She shrugged. "And maybe my mouth."

Dexter groaned. "It's time for your dinner."

"Maybe this once, we can eat later?"

He stood. "Off the bed, Nat. Kneel for your king."

CHAPTER FOURTEEN

Being deeply loved by someone gives you strength, while loving someone deeply gives you courage.

~ Lao Tzu

NATALIE SCURRIED FROM the bed to the floor. The anticipation building inside her camouflaged the hard surface beneath her knees. She didn't notice the concrete as her breasts heaved and she sat back on her bent toes with her hands at her side.

Had she given up hope of ever leaving this room? She didn't know. What Natalie had come to realize was that her life as she had known it no longer existed. The turmoil over classes and meeting everyone else's expectations was a thing of the past. Keeping up appearances and pleasing everyone didn't matter. Those pressures had been chains holding her in a box designed by her birth, family, and social status. As strange as her existence was now, it was simpler and surprisingly freer.

Natalie now had one priority. He was currently observing her every move.

Her breath stilled as Dexter walked around her, once and then again. He gathered her damp hair and secured it at the top of her head with a tie.

Natalie exhaled. He hadn't braided it.

Again, he was in front of her. "Go ahead, open my jeans."

She reached up, and as she unsnapped his jeans, her tongue darted to her suddenly dry lips. Everything about this was scary and exciting. Through veiled lashes she looked up as she reached for the zipper. When he nodded, she lowered it. Beneath his jeans, his briefs were black and silky.

"Keep going."

Her throat dried as she tugged his jeans to his thighs. She'd never before so much as seen his thighs. Did all men's thighs look as powerful? Her heart raced as she reached for the band of his briefs. The large bulge of his erection was in front of her. What would it look like?

Dexter stopped her hands. "Nat, I'm going to come, either in your mouth or on you. Do you realize that?"

"I want you to. I want to be the one who makes that happen, like you are for me."

"Fuck," he breathed the word more than he said it.

With more confidence than she truly felt, she lowered the band. Her eyes opened wide as his penis sprang forward. Natalie gasped. "It's so big." She looked up to him. "I-I...inside me?"

Dexter petted her hair. "Not today, bug. Today, kiss it."

With her heart hammering loudly in her chest, she leaned forward, familiarizing herself with the only man to have her. His musky scent, the way the skin of his thick shaft stretched. His hair—there—was coarse. Her lips came forward and puckered as they contacted the tight skin. Despite its hardness, the surface was velvety soft.

"Now your hands."

It took both of them as she wrapped her fingers around him. Beneath her grasp his cock thickened, growing even larger. The tip glistened as pre-cum leaked from a slit.

Up and down her hands moved, faster and faster. More cum oozed down his cock, creating a slick medium that allowed her hands to slide as she pumped.

"Suck it, bug."

She opened her lips wide and pushed her tongue to the base of her mouth. The flavor was musky and salty, like nothing she'd tasted. Keeping her hands around the length, she lowered her mouth until she couldn't take any more.

"Fuck, that feels so good."

It was the encouragement she needed. She was doing this. Sucking his cock was like accepting his pain. It was what he expected, but unlike his pain, this didn't hurt. It was empowering. And then he took that away.

His hand found the ponytail he'd styled. Gripping it tighter, he dictated the movement of her head. No longer in control, she fought the urge to gag as his length reached the back of her throat. Her eyes began to water and nostrils flared. It wasn't the same kind of pain as that brought on by a crop to her sensitive skin, yet it created the same fear. Would she survive?

Her skin prickled as her jaw ached and lungs fought for air. She was at his mercy, and then he released her briefly, only to begin again. Soon they fell into a rhythm allowing her to breathe. She forgot the ache of her jaw as he pumped faster and faster. No longer was she sucking; she simply existed as a channel for his pleasure. The realization dampened her core. His grip upon her hair tightened until all at once his breathing quickened and his thrusts became more forceful and erratic.

Like other times with Dexter, this would leave Nat bruised. It wasn't something she questioned. She'd take whatever he offered—his wrath or his cum—if it made him happy. And then it happened: warm liquid spurted in her mouth. Her bruised lips tightened around his penis. There was so much of it as his cock shuddered and more and more filled her mouth.

"Swallow."

Of course she obeyed. Gulp after gulp until all that remained was his still-hard cock.

He pulled it back.

Her eyes were filled with tears, yet her shoulders were straight.

"Fuck, Nat, that was fantastic."

Her battered lips smiled.

Dexter helped her stand. Her toes were tingly, yet she hadn't been aware of anything but him. He pulled her close as his lips found hers. A kiss, a real kiss. His tongue gently teased her lips.

He'd kissed her many times—her skin, her hair, her tears. This was different. They were kissing each other.

Natalie moaned and core pinched as her body melted toward his.

Dexter stepped back and reached for his shirt.

Her heart sank, knowing he was going to leave her alone.

She wanted to ask when he'd be back, if he was getting her dinner, if she'd done okay. But she knew the routine. Dejectedly, she turned toward the door and took her position.

His shirt came over her shoulders, hanging to her thighs. He eased her arms through the sleeves and rolled them up. Button by button, he closed the front.

Dexter smiled. "That looks good on you."

It was better than any ball gown she'd ever worn and more precious than anything she'd ever possessed. "I-I may wear it?"

He nodded with a grin. "Yes, bug, you may wear it. I'll be back."

Though he was gone, her heart swelled as his fragrance remained.

The days and weeks that followed blended together. She'd had another period. That was her most accurate tell of time.

Dexter-time changed. Not only did he explore her body, but she also explored his. There was still both pleasure and pain, yet she was allowed to touch him as they conversed more. No longer only answering his questions, she discussed her life, regrets, and dreams with him. One afternoon, straddling his hips, Natalie ran her hands over his firm chest. The beat of his heart thudded under her palms as her core clenched at the sensation of his erection nudging her behind.

Nat looked him in the eye. "I'm ready."

No longer turbulent, his eyes glistened like the rays of sun over the ocean's waters. "Once we do this, there's no going back."

"I know."

"You said you were waiting."

Nat nodded. "I was waiting until the man who earned my body also held my heart."

"And…"

"And, Dexter, I'm yours. You have all of me. That means my heart too. You've had all of my body except my virginity. Like the rest of me, it belongs to you too." Her face flushed. "I mean, it's up to you, but if you want it, it's yours."

His neck and chest flexed as he leaned up until their lips met. And then he lifted her off him and onto the mattress and reached for his jeans.

Natalie's heart clenched. "A-are you leaving?"

He handed her his shirt—the one she now wore as a dress. "No, Nat, you're not losing your virginity in this room. I took your innocence here; your gift deserves more."

Suddenly faint, she could barely breathe as her circulation quickened. "You're going to let me leave?"

"Bug, you're never leaving me." He caressed her jaw as she buttoned the shirt. "I'm going to take you to a real bed. It's time to remember how a princess lives, but now you're no longer a spoiled princess. You've come a long way, my queen."

He reached for her hand while at the same time he pushed something in his pocket. The buzz sounded and door opened. Her bare feet barely kept up as he pulled her down the concrete block hallway. "There's no one else here now, so no one will see you."

Others? There had been other people in this house, or whatever it was? She'd never heard anyone. *Had they heard her screams?*

At the end of the hall was a door. Even if she'd gotten out of the room, she would have needed another key to exit the hallway. When the door opened, she had the sensation of a movie her mother loved. Suddenly, she was Dorothy opening the door of her small home to the magical world of Oz. No longer black and white, everything had color. So much color.

Ornate carpets and rich textures replaced the yellow brick road. Her feet stilled upon the soft, plush surface. There were lush leather sofas, bookshelves filled with colorful spines of books, and a wall of electronics.

It was sensory overload as he led her through the large house. It seemed as big as her home in Iowa, but they weren't in Iowa. On the first floor, she gasped at the windows—real windows revealing the world he'd kept hidden from her. A thick blanket of white covered large trees and open lawns like the inside of a snow globe.

She wanted to ask where they were, but it was all too much.

Step by step, he led her up a grand staircase to the second floor. His large hand holding hers gave her the strength to keep moving. No longer damp and cold, the air was fresh and warm. The floor beneath their feet wasn't concrete but polished wood.

Dexter opened a tall wooden door at the end of one hallway to a sitting room. Beyond, he opened the second door. Her blood stilled. This was where it would happen. It was a bedroom easily four times the size of the room where she had been held. Heck, her room was about the size of the giant bed.

"Dexter?"

He dropped her hand and began to undo the buttons on the front of her shirt. "Natalie, I've waited for this."

She swallowed and nodded.

He leaned down, kissing her hair, neck, collarbone, and breasts.

Her eyes closed, relishing the sensation as his lips sent electricity straight to her core. And then he stopped. When her eyes opened, he was on his knees.

"Nat, you're my queen."

"Dexter?" She didn't know what to do. It felt wrong to have him kneel. That was her job.

He brought her hand to his lips. "You're everything I've ever imagined. You said that I have your heart. Natalie, you have mine. You've had it since before we met."

"I don't understand."

"I know you don't. Just remember that I love you—not despite everything, but because of everything. That's why what we're about to do is right. It's always been right."

"You love me?"

"Forever and always." He stood, scooping her into his arms, and carried her toward the bed.

Before he set her down, she reached up and wrapped her arms around his neck. "I'm scared." He'd made her give him her mind and honesty. It only seemed right now.

"I know, bug. I know. This isn't about pain."

"But you like that."

He nodded. "I do. I also like bringing you pleasure."

After a long kiss, Dexter threw back the blankets, revealing softer sheets than she'd slept on in months. He gently laid her on the bed.

Their eyes stayed fixed on one another as he removed his clothes. She marveled at his body, that this handsome, powerful man was the man who loved her. The hardness of his muscles and the gleam of his gaze mesmerized her. By the time he climbed onto the bed, her desire almost exceeded her fear.

Dexter removed the shirt from her shoulders. Moving slowly, tentatively, he touched and caressed her folds and clit, his teeth nipping her skin until her wanton need surpassed reservation. Her breasts heaved as he finally eased over her.

And then with his rigid cock teasing her entrance, he stilled.

"Dexter?"

"I'm never letting you go."

She shifted her hips, ready for him to take her. "Please, Dexter."

"What, my little bug?"

"Please, never let me go...I don't know what I'd do without you."

"That's one lesson you don't need to learn."

She sighed as her hips continued to fidget in anticipation. "I'm all yours.

Please take me." Her back arched as he worked inside her tight channel. And then as she grew accustomed to the pressure, he gave one hard thrust. Natalie cried out as pain overtook the pleasure.

"Nat, that was it." His voice was tender, soothing. "Relax, let me make it better." He kissed away her tears.

Natalie tried to do as he said—to relax. She trusted him to do as he promised and make it better. That was what he did. Whether it was her aching legs from kneeling, sore ass after a spanking, or her nipples after the clamps. He made everything better.

In and out he moved. The pain disappeared as her body came to life.

Grasping the soft sheets as the pleasure built, she called out the name of the only man to have all of her. Dexter Smithers was the only man to give her everything she never knew she wanted. With their bodies now one, they climbed higher and higher until together they shattered, and he filled both her body and her heart to overflowing.

CHAPTER FIFTEEN

Just when I think I have learned the way to live, life changes.

~ Hugh Prather

NATALIE'S PRISON CELL changed, but not her routine. Dexter's suite was now where she lived. Since the outer sitting room required clothes, he had an entire wardrobe delivered. It seemed unnecessary. There were more clothes than she'd wear in a semester—when she used to go to classes, events, and parties. There were sweaters, coats, and boots, yet she hadn't been outside since she arrived. Her world was limited to Dexter and the occasional staff member. The latter was the reason for clothes.

Dexter no longer delivered her meals, though he was usually present when they arrived. There were multiple household staff who came and went, all speaking German. They always spoke respectfully, addressing her as Frau Natalie. As Dexter's queen, she was the woman of the house. If they questioned why she rarely left the suite, she wasn't aware of it. Though over time she learned a few words, to explain how she'd come to live in this exquisite villa high in the mountains in Austria was impossible. She couldn't even come up with that story in English.

Behind the second door, in the room with the large bed, Dexter's shirts were all she was allowed to wear. The wardrobe he'd purchased included lingerie in all colors, textures, and lengths. Those were only worn upon request and usually meant the night would involve very little sleep. Truthfully, Nat didn't mind; it changed up her routine. And no matter how Dexter would elicit her tears, pleasure was always within reach.

There was another room attached to the master suite that contained exercise equipment. Instead of jogging in place, she now had a treadmill and weight machines. There was always something to keep her busy and her mind focused on him. That didn't mean she didn't think about the life she once had—about her family. She did. There'd been times she hadn't loved her life as the Rawlings princess, but now that it was gone, she had mixed feelings.

Though her calendar was still her menstruation chart, she knew she'd missed so much. December was more than Christmas in the Rawlings household. Their holiday would have included celebrating Nichol's birthday and her parent's celebration of their first wedding, as well as Christmas. February was both her father's and brother's birthdays. Her mom liked to plan something special. If her family had celebrated, Natalie missed it.

According to Nat's speculations, spring was near. Their altitude wouldn't allow for the greens of Iowa. Snow still covered the grounds. From the windows of the suite, no other homes could be seen. She literally believed at times she was confined to the snow globe of her first impression.

The suite she shared with Dexter had walls of shelves filled with books, the old kind with paper and spines. It was more than she'd had in what she referred to as *her room*. Though there was nothing to connect her to life beyond her snow globe, the books became her salvation. After breakfast, exercise, lunch, *Dexter-time*, and bath, which now often happened with Dexter in a spacious glass shower, Natalie had some time in the afternoon and evenings to herself. Those were the occasions where she'd disappear into the pages of fiction. It was a better alternative than remembering those she'd left behind.

With time, Nat was allowed to join Dexter in other areas of the house. If the staff were present, it was another reason to wear clothes. However, she was never alone. Those outings always included him. She still didn't know what he did for a living, but on the first floor, he had a large office with many computer screens. It was something about stocks, margins, options…she should have paid better attention to her classes at Harvard.

It was late one night as they lay together in bed that Dexter's words smashed Nat's snow globe and glass shards littered her world. "We've been gone for months. I need to be back in the United States."

Her heart raced. "Are you going to leave me here alone?"

He pulled her warm, naked body closer until her head rested upon his shoulder. "No, bug. I'm never leaving you, remember? But we'll need to fly."

She lifted her head. "Please, Dexter. No cocktail."

His eyes closed as he exhaled. "I remember you saying you didn't want it. I'm conflicted. I have it ready for you. I don't know…you haven't shown me that you'll behave and not leave me, given the chance."

"I won't," she answered quickly.

"Oh, bug. I believe you mean that now, but it'll be different when given the opportunity. In the States, communication will be easy. You could even be recognized."

Recognized? Would she be? Now that she lived in a suite with mirrors, she wondered if she looked the same as she had. Her reflection somehow seemed different. She wasn't the same girl who'd boarded the plane in Boston.

Besides, what did the world know? Would she want people to know who she'd become, that she enjoyed the way Dexter treated her…even when she didn't? That by making himself her entire world, he'd given her new purpose and a sense of being loved, not as a child or sibling, but as a woman?

Natalie shook her head. "Please, Dexter. I don't want to feel the way that cocktail made me feel. I don't like being out of control."

"You have no control."

It was a simple statement, yet accurate. She nodded. "I'd rather give it to you willingly than unconsciously."

"I know. But remember, you have to trust me."

"I do. I trust you. I also remember that I'm your queen. What we do behind closed doors is our business, no one else's." Her heart ached, but the words were true. "I'd never want others to know that Natalie Rawlings kneels for hours or welcomes your punishment, that what you do to me makes me wet and wanting. It's true, you know it is. I'll continue to do it—for you and for me—but it's no one else's business."

"What about your family's? What's their business?"

Natalie sat up, suddenly chilled as her old and new life collided.

Dexter followed her up and again wrapped her in his embrace. Tears she didn't expect cascaded down her cheeks.

"Shhh," he soothed. "Nat, it's something we both have to address if we're back in the States."

"What can I even say to them? I disappeared." She hiccupped. "I moved on."

"You didn't."

"What do you mean?"

"I told you to trust me. I wanted you. Now you're mine. I told you in the very beginning that I wasn't trying to remove you from your family or the other way around. We just needed time alone before we added them to the mix."

Natalie's skin prickled as a myriad of emotions flooded her system.

Dexter eased from the bed. "Don't leave the bed, bug. I'll show you something that'll help you understand."

Nearly an hour later, Natalie looked up from the tablet, her eyes red and swollen. From what she'd read, she hadn't missed a thing. On every milestone, holiday, and birthday *Natalie* had communicated with her family. She'd sent pictures of landmarks with long-winded emails explaining her need to find herself after the debacle that was her college experience.

There were responses from both her father and mother. Though at first their words reflected their disappointment, with time, they both forgave, claiming they wanted nothing more than her return. Even her siblings corresponded. Not surprisingly, Nichol was more critical; however, like their parents, they both wanted her return.

"Why?" It was the only question she could form.

"For you. For them."

She scrolled. The emails dated back to the day after her flight.

"This wasn't for me…" Her volume rose. "…or them. It was for you!"

Dexter's eyes darkened.

"You did it so they wouldn't look for me." She met his gaze, knowing that she should apologize for raising her voice, but she couldn't. His actions may have saved her relationship with her family, but they also stopped the worldwide search she'd at one time prayed for.

Her shoulders straightened as she braced for his retaliation.

What would be the price for her outburst?

"Yes," he said calmly. "It was for me, to give us time. It was also for you." When she didn't respond, he stood. "Nat." He pointed to the floor.

Setting the tablet on the bed, her heart rate accelerated. Despite the fact they'd made love only an hour ago, her core dampened as she slid to the floor and knelt at Dexter's feet.

"Tell me what should happen, what your outburst should cost."

Her pussy clenched and breasts throbbed. This shouldn't bring her body to life. His threatening tone shouldn't make her as excited as she was frightened, but it did.

Natalie leaned forward until her face was near the floor and kissed the tops of his feet. Sitting back up, she replied, "I'll take your punishment, my king. I was wrong. I should thank you for what you did. I guess it scares me. I want to see them. I miss them, but I don't want to lose you."

He reached for her shoulders and lifted her to standing. "You won't lose me. I won't lose you." He lifted her chin. "Your family will see you for the queen you've become, not the spoiled princess you once were. While you were away from them, you received a tremendous gift. You went without to learn to appreciate. What do you say?"

"Thank you, Dexter, for my gift."

"Now, turn around, bug. Hands on the bed, feet apart. My belt will remind you who you're talking to and that outbursts are unacceptable."

Her core clenched as she obeyed. Biting her lip to keep her smile at bay, she turned her face back over her shoulder until their gazes met. With veiled eyes, she asked, "Not your hand?"

Dexter ran his hand over her ass, dipping his fingers between her wet folds. "No, my queen. You like my hand on your ass too much. This needs to teach you a lesson."

Chapter Sixteen

The greatest gift that you can give to others is the gift of unconditional love and acceptance.

~ Brian Tracy

Natalie's heart raced as Dexter pulled the silver Jaguar XF through the iron gates of the Rawlings estate. They were both dressed for the occasion. It seemed odd to be so formal. Natalie had gone months without clothes; to be wearing a long gown, heels, and makeup with her hair styled added to her unease. She did find comfort in how handsome Dexter was in his tuxedo. This wasn't a large gathering. There would only be the four of them, but it was the Rawlings estate.

Dexter's deep-ocean hued stare served as her reminder. She'd done as he said and avoided the cocktail on their transatlantic flight. This trip, however, was on a private plane, the way he usually traveled. Still there were attendants and TSA. Truthfully, it hadn't been difficult to play the role of his queen—it wasn't a role. He was her fiancé and she now had the real ring to prove it. He was also much more: her king, tormentor, and savior.

Dexter Smithers was her everything. She was his. It was the way they both wanted it to be.

The last few weeks had been spent adjusting to his estate in Vermont. Like the home in Austria, it was secluded and luxurious. While her freedoms grew, she found comfort and sanctuary in their private space and his approval. Their home was similar to the world in which she'd been raised to live, but now she'd learned to appreciate it as the queen.

The queen who bowed only to her king.

His hand reached across the console and squeezed hers. "You've done well on the telephone calls. It's time to face them." Every call, every word, had been said in Dexter's presence. The first time she heard her mother's voice was the hardest. Natalie's stomach pinched, knowing that in a few moments she'd see her.

The large white house appeared as the trees parted. It was beautiful and stately, the house her father had built for his queen. It was where her childhood was spent, but it was no longer her home. That was in Vermont.

Dexter and Natalie walked hand in hand up the front stairs. When the front door opened, Nat expected to see the familiar face of one of the staff. She didn't.

"Natalie!" Claire called as she raced forward and wrapped her daughter in her arms. When her mother finally pulled back, her emerald-green eyes were full of tears. To Natalie, her mother never aged, as beautiful today as the pictures of her when her parents first married. "Thank God. I've missed you so much."

Claire held tightly to Nat's hand as she turned to the man beside her daughter. "Hello, you must be Dexter Smithers."

He bowed his head respectfully. "Yes, ma'am. It's nice to meet you, Mrs. Rawlings."

Claire's cheeks rose. "That's rather formal from the man who stole my daughter's heart. Please, my name is Claire."

During their telephone calls, Nat explained how during her adventure of self-discovery, she'd met Dexter. At first, he'd helped her, staying with her and keeping her safe. With time, their relationship grew. Dexter was now the man she loved, the one she was engaged to marry. In reality, her stories were true. It was just their adventures that varied.

As they all stepped inside, three set of eyes turned to the dominating footsteps of Nat's father entering the foyer. Dropping her mother's hand and stepping away from Dexter's possessive touch upon her lower back, Natalie ran to him and wrapped her arms around his neck. Without hesitation, he embraced her.

"Daddy."

"My little Nat. You had us all very worried." Even at his age, his deep voice summoned respect while commanding any situation.

She reached for her father's hand and led him back to where Dexter and her mom stood. Stepping close to Dexter, she said, "Daddy, I want to introduce you to my fiancé."

Her father's shoulders broadened and neck stiffened. Before Natalie could say anything, her mother's petite hand landed upon her father's sleeve.

As Claire's diamond ring glittered and prisms of rainbows danced, her touch served as a gentle reminder that this was not the time for Anthony Rawlings to assert his dominance.

Her father let out a long breath and offered his hand. "Hello, son. It's good to finally meet you." The address was a statement of Anthony's position and age, not a term of endearment. This battle wasn't over. Anthony Rawlings didn't surrender.

"Sir," Dexter said.

"My husband, Nat's father…Mr. Rawlings," Claire said, introducing the two men. "Tony, this is Dexter."

"Dexter Smithers," Dexter repeated.

Tony's dark eyes narrowed. "Relation to Jonas?"

Surely he knew the truth. Anthony Rawlings would have known after the first time he saw Dexter's name. If he didn't know on sight, a search by his security would have been conducted and within moments the dots connected.

There was no reason for Dexter to deny it. "Yes, sir, his son."

"We lost touch. I didn't know he had a son."

"Second wife. Only child, a little later in life. My father's no longer with us."

"I'm sorry to hear that," Tony said.

Natalie watched and listened as her father and Dexter spoke. She'd never heard about Dexter's family. She'd spoken about hers, but he'd never offered. Yet in merely seconds, her dad had shed more light than Dexter had offered in nearly five months.

"Dexter, can we offer you a drink before dinner?" Claire asked.

"Thank you, I'm not much of a drinker."

Tony nodded toward an archway. "Cognac. It's a man's drink."

As they all started walking toward the den, Claire reached for Natalie's hand. "If you gentlemen will excuse us for a moment, I have a few things upstairs for Nat." She smiled. "Your Christmas gift."

Natalie looked to Dexter. She wasn't supposed to leave his side or speak out of his sight. He'd made the rules crystal clear. The panic may have shown in her gaze until he grinned and kissed her cheek. "Hurry back."

As they walked up the stairs, Claire chatted about Natalie, how beautiful she looked, how handsome Dexter was…she asked about the sights Natalie had visited…and then they reached her parents' room and Claire shut the door.

Her mother's emerald eyes no longer shone. There was darkness in their depths that stung Natalie more than a slap to her cheek. Somehow, in this brief span of time, her mother knew. She knew Nat's secrets... knew what happened behind closed doors.

"Is he good to you?" Claire asked.

Natalie shifted, finding it difficult to keep her mother's gaze. "He can be, Mom. He really can."

Claire's eyes closed as her face momentarily fell forward. When she looked back up, Natalie's eyes were wet. Claire wrapped her daughter in her arms. "Tell me if you love him."

"I do. I can't explain it. Please don't ask me to."

"I don't need to ask. I understand."

Natalie's head shook. "I don't think you do. It's not like you and Dad."

Taking a step back, Claire sighed. "Oh, my baby. Some day when you have children, you'll understand the struggle. Parents are complicated. We play such a vital role in our children's lives. Sometimes we keep secrets hidden to protect, but it seems that it doesn't always protect; it leaves the door open, an invitation to those who wait."

"I'm not sure what you're talking about."

"Does he value your feelings and opinions?"

It was a strange question, yet Nat answered. "He wants them. He's always asking me to tell him how I feel and what I'm thinking."

Claire smiled. "That took your father longer."

"Mom?"

"I love you, Natalie Rawlings. I always will."

"I know, Mom. I love you, too."

"Your father does too. We also love one another."

Natalie slapped her hands against her side as she let out an exasperated breath. "I know. I always thought I wanted what you have, but then with Dexter..."

Claire reached for her daughter's hand and led her to a small sofa where they sat. "When I found a man I loved more than life itself and whose love for me was overwhelming, I was alone. I didn't have my mother. I'm not unhappy with the final result, but let me just say that the journey would've been easier if I wouldn't have made it alone. I know you aren't ready to hear or say more. I can see it in your eyes. They're mine. They always have been, different from Nate's and so much different from Nichol's. Natalie, you are me."

"I'm not…" A tear trickled from her freshly painted eyes as her words faded away.

"You are. The question I asked—if he's good to you—was the same question your Uncle John asked me a long time ago. You answered it exactly as I did."

"Mom?"

"No matter what I need to do," Claire said, "I want you *and Dexter* to know that I won't judge you. I won't lose my baby or her babies. Your father will be more difficult, but leave him to me. Please promise me that no matter what the future holds, no matter your last name, you'll always be a Rawlings."

"I don't know about my name. Dexter and I haven't discussed…"

Claire smiled. "I don't mean your legal name. You have a man in your life. One who consumes your thoughts, one who takes up most of the room in your heart, but, baby, there's always room for more. I know, because there was a time I believed your father was my everything. It's not that he wasn't or isn't. It's that each time I learned that there was a baby inside me, my heart grew. The same will happen for you. I'm just asking that you also keep a spot for us—for your family and especially for me. No matter what, I'll be there."

Natalie leaned into her mother's embrace. "I love you, Mom."

After their hug, Claire rose and walked to a bookshelf, reaching for a small box with a ribbon. She came back and handed it to Natalie. "Merry belated Christmas."

Nat's eyes watered as she opened the hinged box to the delicate necklace. "It's like yours and Nichol's necklaces." A small pearl sat nestled in a white-gold X.

"It is. I'm not sure why we never had one made for you before. But when you weren't at Christmas, I realized how much the necklace means to me and to your sister. Your father and I gave your great-grandmother's necklace to Nichol when she was young. It was your dad who surprised me by having one remade for me. It's more special that I can even articulate."

Claire smiled as she touched Nat's hand. "Yours and mine are identical; they're replicas. That doesn't make them less than Nichol's. It makes ours the same, like us. I can see it in your eyes and hear it in your voice. Natalie, you're no longer our baby."

"I'm not."

"You're a beautiful woman and always know that we're proud of you."

Nat's cheeks filled with pink as her heart swelled. "Thank you, Mom. I was afraid that after Harvard—"

Claire squeezed her hand. "Sometimes life takes a detour and gives us an opportunity to live a life different than we ever imagined. Are you happy with where yours took you?"

"Yes."

"Then that's all that matters. I have another gift for you, but right now, let's go back downstairs. I think it might be beneficial to keep your father and Dexter supervised."

CHAPTER SEVENTEEN

Acceptance of what has happened is the first step to overcoming the
consequences…

~ William James

A FEW WEEKS later, back in Vermont, Dexter entered their master bedroom suite.

Wearing only one of his shirts, Natalie rose and met her fiancé at the door.

Dexter kissed her hair. "What have you been doing this evening?"

She looked at him through veiled eyes. "Reading."

Reading didn't require a submissive gaze. Something wasn't as it appeared. His eyes went to the sofa where she'd been seated. His neck tensed, the muscles becoming rigid as his gaze landed upon the book she'd been reading. "Where did you get that?"

"My mother."

"Your mother?"

Natalie went to the sofa and lifted the old book. The pages were yellow and the spine was marred with the scars of multiple readings. On the cover was the title: *My Life as It Didn't Appear.*

"Your mother gave you that?"

Natalie nodded.

"Why?"

She shrugged. "I guess she decided I wasn't a baby who needed to be protected anymore. She thought it was time I knew the truth."

The book, *My Life as It Didn't Appear,* dictated by Claire Nichols Rawlings and penned by Meredith Banks, detailed Claire Nichols's meeting and first marriage to Anthony Rawlings. Upon its publication, it had been an instant bestseller. Through years of legal wrangling, which concluded over fifteen years ago, the Rawlings attorneys successfully had it removed from sale and circulation. The world forgot, ceasing to obsess over old news. There were more important stories. And through it all, somehow, Nat's parents had managed to keep its existence, as well as its contents, hidden from their baby girl.

"And how does it make you feel about your dad?" Dexter asked.

"You know what it's about?"

"Bug."

Her entire body stiffened. He'd asked her a question. Instead of answering, she'd replied with a question. Natalie quickly re-spoke, "No different."

"How can you say that?"

"How can I not?" Natalie replied. "And before you reprimand me, that *is* an answer. I don't feel differently. Why would I?"

Dexter led her to the sofa and they sat. "What do you mean?"

"How could I think less of him when I love you?"

It took Dexter a minute, but then he let go of her hand and went to the bookcase. Behind a false panel—one that she didn't know existed—Dexter brought out a copy of the same book.

Natalie shook her head as she reached for it. "How?"

"I found it among my father's things when he died." Dexter opened the cover and pulled out a yellowed piece of paper. "And this."

Natalie silently read. It wasn't legal, no binding contract. It was simply an agreement between college friends. They'd begun a company: CSR – Company Smithers Rawlings. Together they vowed to make it great, uniting their families and lives forever.

"What happened?" Nat asked.

"After a few years your dad bought my dad out. It was very amicable. Mr. Rawlings paid my father a generous sum. They both went on to do very well. It was the part about keeping the families united that got me thinking. Then I read the book and looked into the Rawlings family. That was when I knew…"

Natalie laid the book on the sofa and fell to her knees. Her bare core clenched as she scooted between his spread legs. Looking up, she spoke. "It was when you knew I belonged to you."

"Yes, bug. That we belonged together. I knew what I wanted, what I needed. And after watching you for a while, I knew in my heart that you were born to be my queen."

"But my dad…" It wasn't easy for her to read the things her father had done to her mother. It was even more difficult to say them. "…she awoke to luxury?"

"Is that a question?"

"I think it is."

"I didn't use your mother's story as a guide. It simply gave me an idea of how you'd respond. Think about it. Your mother came from a simple life. Your father gave her what she'd never experienced."

Natalie nodded. "A detour. I came from wealth—from everything."

"And did you appreciate it?"

"No, not really. It just was. I didn't question it. I appreciate it more now."

Dexter kissed her hair. "I love you, Nat. Do you think that one day you'd want to write down our story for our daughter to read?"

Her cheeks warmed. "No, I'd rather keep it in my heart. But if one day I think she needs to hear it, I'll share."

"You will?"

"I will. It helps to know that there isn't anything wrong with me. I'm not the only one to experience these feelings."

"What feelings?"

"Love so overpowering it consumes me. An irrational yet intoxicating need to both please you and make you happy that supersedes all else, even my own safety."

"No. Your safety was never and will never be in question. I told you that safety is a matter of trust. Do you trust me?"

"I do." After all of the things he'd done and all that she willingly accepted, how could she not?

"Danger," Dexter went on, "is something else. However, eliciting your tears doesn't put you in danger. It's never to *harm* you. It's to *hurt* you. There's a difference. What we do is controlled pain, learning how much you can handle, how much you're willing to sacrifice for me. It's seeing my marks on your skin and hearing your cries. That doesn't make me want to harm you, but to worship you."

Nat nodded. "I understand. After a few weeks in that room, I found myself anxious for your arrival while at the same time scared. I feared I was going crazy. I mean, I shouldn't have wanted what I knew you'd do." She looked at the book. "Now I know that I'm not crazy. Like my mom has said: *it is what it is. Don't fight what you can't change.* Now it makes more sense.

"It's what we enjoy behind closed doors. And that's okay." She smiled. "You asked what I'd sacrifice. For you, my king, anything. I'd move naked into a simple room in our basement if you desired."

Dexter's eyes shone as he reached for the buttons lining the front of her shirt-dress. "I think I like having you here in our room, naked and on your knees."

"I love you," she said as she leaned back on her bent toes, shifting to his desired position.

After he'd opened her shirt-dress, he looked down to her spread legs. "Are you wet, my queen?"

"Yes."

"What will you do to earn the right to come?"

Her heart hammered within her chest as her thighs glistened. "Like everything else, that decision is yours. I willing give you control. As always, my answer is anything."

"Forever and always."

THE END

FOR MORE...

If you haven't read the beginning of this story…if this was your first introduction to Tony and Claire Rawlings or maybe you began their story, but didn't complete it, it's not too late.

The Consequences series is five full-length books: Consequences, Truth, Convicted, Revealed, and Beyond the Consequences. For more insight into Tony Rawlings, after the series has been read, there are two companions: Behind His Eyes Consequences and Behind His Eyes Truth. Book one, Consequences, is free on all channels.

Thank you for reading Natalie and Dexter's Prince and the Pauper story, Ripples, a story where physical chains are more freeing than figurative ones, and in finding a new life, the princess becomes the queen.

I hope you enjoyed the consequences…

LINK to Consequences series on all platforms:

www.aleatharomig.com/consequences-series

.

ROYAL MATTRESS

A Princess and the Pea Story

Nicola Rendell

"True story."

– Hans Christian Andersen, *The Princess and the Pea*

1

DAVE

BEFORE I START, I need to put one thing out there: I was born Ivan Alexander Hallsett Ratislav Stefanik IV, Exiled Prince of Greater Moravia and Lower Bohemia. But for fuck's sake, call me Dave.

Five years ago, I was living just far enough outside Newark that it didn't feel like I was anywhere near Newark. I'd bought and renovated an estate halfway between Montclair and Falls River. It was ten acres, with a long driveway and rolling hills. When I first saw it, the real estate agent called it *palatial.* Exactly.

But the house and name aside, I was otherwise pretty much an ordinary guy from New Jersey. I liked my coffee black and my Jets games close until the second half of the fourth quarter. I paid for my Beemer in cash, and I had all my bills on autopay. I mowed my own lawn, because who the hell doesn't like riding a John Deere, but I had a service do my laundry because doing laundry is dead-ass in the middle of the category of *life is too goddamned short.*

Not to be an ass about it, but for a guy in my late thirties, I felt like I was a pretty good catch. I could hang with those militant fanatics at CrossFit if I had to. I could run a half marathon without getting totally winded. I took a lot of hard looks in the mirror and thought, *Solid.* Not like some fairy-tale prince or whatever, but not bad. Good head of hair, strong jaw, respectable abs.

And doing *just fine* on the money front.

Unlike the Ivan Alexanders I through III, who burned through the family "fortune" like a god-awful Fourth of July mishap in a bone-dry national forest, I had no choice but to make my own way in the world. So I did. After I got my MBA, I decided I'd focus on what I'd decided was the only sure thing after death and taxes.

Mattresses.

Yeah, yeah, I know. You thought I was going to say food-delivery apps or drones or some shit. But no, mattresses. *Everybody* needs a mattress. A good mattress, though. Not one of those cheap, springy pieces of shit that jabs you in the spleen all night long. I got into the game before Tempur-Pedic and Posturepedic and the rest. Royal Mattress was the first: I zeroed in on the luxury mattress market, and wouldn't you know it? It worked. Like pennies from pillow-top heaven, the money rolled in. I had everything I could ever want. Cars, houses, vacations, a killer stock portfolio. A regulation-sized pool table. I was thinking about buying a yacht. But there was one thing I *didn't* have: the most important thing of all.

Someone to share it with.

I had shit luck with women, and I always had. Truly, epically, comically bad luck. The kind of shit luck that my buddies laughed about until they cried into their beers. *Fuck, remember the time that woman put a flaming empty popcorn bag of dog shit on your porch?* Hideously bad. The thing was, I had an old-fashioned belief in *the one.* I really believed, in my gut, that somewhere out there, there was a woman who needed me as much as I needed her. I really thought that when I met her, I'd *know.* I believed we would be two parts of a whole. I once knew a guy from Mexico who said that down there they say *two halves of the same orange.* I felt it in my bones. I was waiting for her, the other half of my orange. She'd make everything fall into place.

I looked for her everywhere. I kept my mind open. I didn't pull some douchebag move about only liking skinny blondes or some shit. No way. I figured she could be anybody—the sparkle had to be inside someone, and all I had to do was keep looking. So I became a serial first-dater. I went out with a kind-hearted nurse. A red-lipped gold digger. Two different socialist vegans. Women with rhinestones stuck into their nail polish and who said things like, *"Totes awesome!"* A librarian. A preschool teacher. A lady who specialized in some rare fern fossil found only on the eastern slope of Colorado. I ran the whole gamut. But *the one* wasn't anywhere to be found.

Part of it, of course, was totally my fault. Who the fuck walks into the ocean and says, "I'm looking for a fish, but I don't know what kind of fish. All I know is, *not that fish.*" Or maybe only idiots believe in orange halves. But what I did know was it wasn't *all* my fault. The other part had nothing to do with me, but it was something I'd inherited. And no, I'm not talking about my name.

I'm talking about Grandma Katrina.

Unlike me, who had about as much interest in claiming my "hereditary title" as picking up a medication-resistant skin infection at the gym, Grandma Katrina was *into* it. Her online poker handle was BaronessStefanik. When she met someone for the first time, she'd hold her hand out, palm down and wrist bent. Totally Queen of England. She was old-school exiled royalty from irrelevant dissolved non-nations. (There are more of us than you'd think. Seriously.) But Grandma Katrina was also a goddamned unicorn in the world of "where'd-you-say-you're-from?" royal families. She was one part Serbo-Croat-Moravian-Bohemian princess, one part card-carrying Wiccan, and a 100%-devoted gold-level member of Ancestry.com. And she was absolutely determined to see me married before she "drop-kicked the bottle of Smirnoff." Her words, not mine.

One wintry Sunday night, when she was over at my house for dinner, I studied her in the way people study statues and paintings and the wreckage of non-fatal car accidents. She'd outlived two husbands, both my parents, and an African gray parrot named Franz Ferdinand. Fucking told you. Unicorn. Nobody, including me, had any idea how old she was. Somewhere between 80 and 119. Strong as an ox, whip smart, no filter at all, and no patience for bullshit whatsoever.

At that moment, she was hunched over the iPad I bought her, with a phone book beside her, scanning the names. Around her neck, on a long piece of pink yarn, she wore a glass God's Eye that she bought on her retirement cruise to Greece. In addition to being a practicing Wiccan—so help you God if you stumbled into her bedroom unannounced—she had a seriously unnerving interest in grassroots revolutionary movements. That night she was wearing her favorite hoodie, with Che Guevara's face on the front. She believed that the only way to reclaim the lands formerly known as "Greater Moravia and Lower Bohemia," but now known as, you know, the Balkans, was by a carefully planned royal coup. Like I said, *into it.*

Outside, the wind whistled against the double-paned windows. I poured myself a scotch and looked out into the blowing snow. I heard the sound of Grandma putting a line through something in the phone book with her stubby golf pencil, which made me suspect she was up to no good again. Then she hammered out some letters into the iPad and gasped.

"Honey buns! Look!" Grandma said. "This lady…" She peered over her bifocals at the phone book. "This Julie Dubrovnik. She could be just the one. That name checks out, and look at all these *leaves!*" Grandma held up her iPad to show off the family tree of yet another woman whom I'd never met and had no plans to meet.

"Christ. Not this again."

"Yes, this again! How are we going to retake our lands without an heir and a spare?"

I doubled my scotch and ran my hand down my jaw, scraping my stubble, extra thick because it was a Sunday. "I'm not dating a woman you picked at random and who might be my distant cousin. We've *been through this.*"

"Shh! This one might still be single. And she's cute! Kinda. Maybe a big forehead and a gummy smile, but that's okay." Grandma scrolled through Google, using her ergonomic stylus to flip through the search results. "Goddamn it. No. Married! *Why are they all married?*"

The timer dinged behind me, and I crouched down to look at the roast in the oven. If there was one thing Grandma loved more than revolution and trying to match me up with total strangers, it was a roast leg of lamb. I grabbed the thermometer and stuck it in the thickest part of the roast and then shut the oven door. As I watched the temperature climb out of *rare* and head toward *medium,* I told her, "You need a new hobby, Grams. I'll buy you a Segway. Fuck, I'll buy you a Tesla. Just knock this off."

Grandma broke her bifocals in two at the magnet in the nose, and each half flopped down like glass ears onto Che Guevara's portrait, making a weird Mr. Potato Head thing happen. "I'm telling you, you're a natural! Bribery, honey! That's the key! Long may he reign!"

I gave her an only half-joking glare. "Listen, Baroness…"

Completely unfazed, she snapped her bifocals back together, went back to her phone book, and crossed off Julie Dubrovnik.

Using silicone hot pads, I pulled the roast from the oven and put it on a rack to cool. Then I tented it with a piece of foil while I listened to Grandma pound out the name of yet another unsuspecting stranger into Ancestry.com. And not for the first time, I thought, *Maybe I should buy her another parrot.*

Grandma didn't live with me. She lived about ten miles away, in a 55-and-over retirement community where everybody did water aerobics together and where all the widows flirted shamelessly with widowers over games of Cards Against Humanity. No shit. I saw it with my own eyes. She absolutely loved it there. They called her Hurricane, as in Hurricane Katrina. Fucking perfect.

She came over every Sunday for lamb, and that Sunday was no exception in spite of the weather. "No way is some pansy-assed winter storm named Lola gonna stop me from practicing my God-given right as a Moravian princess. Give me lamb, or give me death!" But as I turned off the oven and started dealing with the salad, I realized Winter Storm Lola might not be just *a storm.* The conditions outside were fucking awful, and then there was even more proof of something out of the ordinary happening: On the muted TV was Grandma's other obsession—The Weather Channel. A red bar flashed across the bottom that said, STATE OF EMERGENCY / TRAVEL BAN / SHELTER IN PLACE ORDER FOR THE FOLLOWING COUNTIES: PASSAIC, BERGEN, MORRIS, HUDSON, UNION, ESSEX…

"Turn that up, would you?" I asked her.

"How do you feel about cougars?"

"Christ." I ditched my hot pads and grabbed the remote to turn up the volume. The weather guy, who looked weirdly like Al Roker and yet weirdly not, read from a printout. "We've just received word from the National Weather Service that Winter Storm Lola has been upgraded to a major blizzard, but that's not all." On the screen flashed a new version of the radar map that had been repeating on a loop all night. The regular rotation seemed to…stall out, almost. Like it was running into an invisible wall. All the clouds and precipitation behind the line smashed into the invisible space. I'd never seen anything like it. And believe me, thanks to Grandma, I knew my shit when it came to weather.

Not-Al-Roker could barely contain his excitement and was actually clasping his hands together, just about one move away from *Here's the church, here's the steeple.* "Blizzard Lola is currently experiencing a rare weather phenomenon, known as explosive cyclogenesis. For those armchair weathermen out there, *bombogenesis.* Some of you may remember the storm that inspired *The Perfect Storm,* and Blizzard Lola is behaving in very much the same way. However, because conditions are so cold, we are looking not at nine to ten inches of rain, but instead ninety to one hundred *inches* of snow."

Grandma looked up from her iPad with her stylus perched in midair. "Holy shitballs," she said as the map shifted from a swirl of blue and white to what looked like a mess of finger paint flung onto the screen with a motherfucking vengeance. But all of it seemed focused on one county in particular.

Not-Al-Roker zoomed in on the graphic, and I saw that the eye of the storm hovered just about *exactly* on top of my property.

The weatherman put one hand to his forehead, because now, even *he* seemed worried. And then he looked straight into the camera and said, "Hold on tight, Essex County. It's going to be one hell of a night."

Holy shitballs, indeed.

2

LISA

THE SNOW WAS coming down so hard that my headlights made me snow-blind and I had to pull over. I maneuvered my Wagoneer off to the side of the road and brought it to a stop. Rubbing the fog from my window with my mitten, I peered out onto the deserted, rural country road. It looked like one of those sorts of places where people from Hollywood would come to film a headless horseman scene. The trees were gnarled together over the top of the road in an arch, and the road snaked in a spooky, old-fashioned way. But that wasn't slowing down the storm. The snow was coming from everywhere, and the wind was so intense that gust after gust shook my Jeep on its axles, same as if a whole line of eighteen-wheelers were passing me at eighty miles an hour. The road, already thick with new-fallen snow, shimmered in my headlights as snow snakes curled into the lights from the dark.

From my purse, my phone started to make a noise that it had never made before—a *raa-raa-raa* warning sound accompanied by a violent buzz. Like an Amber Alert, but more urgent. Tugging off my mitten with my teeth, I grabbed the phone from my bag. On the lock screen was a red-bordered warning from the National Weather Service, telling all travelers in PASSAIC, BERGEN, MORRIS, HUDSON, UNION, and ESSEX to "cease all travel and await help from the New Jersey National Guard."

Awaiting help wasn't my jam, but I also had no clue where I was. The day had started normally enough—at a bakers and candy-makers trade show in Philadelphia. And yes, of *course,* I knew there was a storm, but I also knew that weathermen in the Northeast sometimes got a little…*excited* about storms, which then fizzled out with all the glory of a soggy taco collapsing on a plate. So I'd hedged my bets and gotten on the highway after the show, heading home to Providence with a pounding headache from sampling so many kinds of frosting.

But I'd seriously misjudged Winter Storm Lola. A slowly disintegrating wet taco, she was not.

I'd gotten on this road because the highways were almost impassable, but I soon found out that the side roads were even worse, and there I was in *Sleepy Hollow*. Opening up my map, I unpinched my fingers over the dot where I was. And saw I was smack dab in the middle of the mess. The map was blinking red, too—slightly pixelated on one side because my signal was so weak. My battery was, as usual, a thin strip of red. Plunging my hand into my purse, I pulled out my spare battery and plugged it into my phone, turning it on with a freezing finger.

Dead.

A new set of alerts popped up. I saw the phrase *snowfall at nine to ten inches an hour* and also some word I'd never seen before, *bombogenesis*.

I dropped my phone in my lap and looked out at the flakes. The wind made an eerie whistle through the trees, and at the end of the branch-tunnel I saw that the sky along the horizon was a strange pinkish color. It looked like I was heading for a different planet. And here I was, stuck in a 1997 Jeep Wagoneer with a dying cell phone, half a bottle of water, and nothing but... I looked in my purse again. A snack pack of almonds to eat. And a smooshed Tootsie Roll.

I knew that I was, in a word, screwed. But suddenly I remembered that ages ago, I'd picked up one of those chargers that plugs into the lighter. I dug around in the glove box, through a stack of insurance cards—I never knew if I should throw them out or not—and found it. A little bright green thing shaped like an open frog's mouth that I'd gotten at a gas station.

I plugged it into the lighter and hooked up my phone, praying that the lightning icon would appear in the corner of my screen. I jostled the plug, I blew into the lighter, I revved the engine.

Nothing.

I rubbed my fingers along the wooly edge of my hat on my forehead, the itchy strip where the yarn touched my bare skin. I was already freezing—my Jeep had never been very dependable, even in simple matters like *heat*. The snow was coming down at nine inches an hour. And the temperature was dropping.

Two words: *totally screwed.*

But there was no way in hell I was just going to sit there and wait for help. There was no way I was just going to bide my time and hope someone found me before I got buried. There was no way in the world I was about to *shelter in place*. So I put my Wagoneer in drive and got back on the road, heading north toward the glow of Newark. I cut my lights to give myself half a chance of seeing where I was going, and it helped a lot. The flakes no longer blinded me, and I made some good progress, keeping my eyes on the edge of the road and gripping the wheel at nine and three, like an old lady driving home from bingo. I could do it, I knew I could do it. All I had to do was keep moving, and one way or another, I'd get out of this thing. All I had to do was stay on the road, take it slow, and I'd make it out of this spooky, desolate place. But then I saw maybe it wasn't so desolate. Out of the corner of my eye, something caught my attention. It was a big stone pillar with a mailbox set in the middle. My heart leapt. It meant I wasn't all alone out here—that mailbox meant that there had to be a house nearby. And judging from the stonework, a big one. A fancy one. Maybe one that would take me in for the night before I got buried under ten feet of snow and Blizzard Lola turned me into a pudding pop.

While I was distracted by the mailbox, my Jeep hit something, and the whole cab rose and fell. Instinctively, I turned my lights back on, and my view was nothing but a wall of white. But then, through the snow emerged something dark. And craggy. And getting bigger every instant. It was a huge tree trunk coming straight at me. I slammed on my brakes.

And then everything went black.

3

DAVE

A KNOCKING WOKE me. I sat up in bed and listened. At first, all I heard was the roar of the storm and the whistle of the wind through the forest, but then there it was again. *Thump-thump...thump.* My first instinct was that one of the shutters had come loose and was banging on a window downstairs. But then I heard the doorbell.

I jumped out of bed, put on my flannel pajama pants and then hustled down the steps. I wasn't concerned about waking Grandma Katrina—she'd been out cold for three hours, and without her hearing aids in she was stone-deaf, a fact she often used to her advantage when someone started talking about something she didn't want to hear. So I wasn't worried about waking her—all my attention was, instead, focused on whoever the hell was at my door in the middle of the worst blizzard in New Jersey's history. From the landing, I could see a shadow outside. Without an instant of hesitation, I switched off the security system and flung open the door.

A blast of cold air and blowing snow pelted my bare chest. When it cleared, I saw that there was someone there—I knew immediately it had to be a woman from her height, barely taller than my shoulders. She was bundled up in a big puffy parka, with fur around the hood. I couldn't make out her face because it was in shadow from the porch light. "I'm so sorry to bother you," she said, her voice weak and raspy, "But I was in an accident and..."

She took one step toward me, but it was as if her knees went out from under her, and she began to fall. I reached out for her, catching her before she fainted to the floor. I hooked my arms around her body just in time, and though she'd begun to sink to her knees, I had her. I scooped her up and carried her inside, slamming the door shut with my shoulder, one arm under her shoulders and the other under her knees, newlywed style. But it was dark, and I still couldn't make out her face. What I knew for sure, from the feel of her hips on my bare arm, was that she was frozen damn near solid. I carried her into the living room and laid her on the big leather couch in front of the fireplace. Her boots and pants were crusted in snow, and clumps of ice stuck to her leggings all the way up to her thighs. The fire I'd lit earlier was still burning, low but bright, and when I unsnapped her hood, I finally saw her face.

She was *stunning*. Her cheeks were a raw, tender red from the wind, and her nose, too. But that just made her somehow even *more* beautiful. I put my fingers to her neck and felt for a pulse, just to be sure she was still with me. Her heartbeat was steady but not very strong. She was shivering hard, and I noticed that the curly tendrils near the nape of her neck were damp. I pulled off her hat and found that her lovely dark brown hair was damp with sweat and melted snow. I pieced it together in an instant—she must have gotten in a wreck and trekked through the storm for help. But it was below zero and dropping. She'd slogged through at least a mile of snow, so she'd gotten sweaty in spite of the cold. Somehow, I flashed back to some survival show I'd seen once. *It's not the cold that'll kill you. It's the sweat.*

I turned on the reading lamp on the side table and saw then that there was a thin trickle of blood from a cut on her forehead. As gently as I could, I checked to see if there was any more damage. The cut was surrounded by a bump, like maybe she'd smacked her head on a steering wheel. Not a windshield though, I guessed. The damage wasn't bad enough to have been caused by a pane of glass, and thank God for that.

Crouching beside her, I pulled her up to sitting, supporting her with my arm. I unzipped her parka and pulled one sleeve off and then the other. She slumped against my body, and by keeping her close to me, I was able to get the parka all the way off. Underneath, she was in a gray hoodie, with what looked like… I squinted. A cupcake on the front? Definitely a cupcake, and under that a logo that said:

PRINCESS PASTRIES

Gently, I laid her back down and positioned a pillow behind her head. I'd never been so grateful that I hired an interior designer. Since I'd moved in, I'd cursed all the damned throw pillows, but now they came in handy. When I was sure that her head was supported, I pulled off her snow-crusted boots and put them aside. I grabbed a blanket from the back of the couch and another from the wingback by the fireplace, wrapping her up tight. When I did, I noticed that her hoodie was damp with sweat, too, and her shivers were getting more and more violent.

Fuck.

I stood up and thought about what the hell to do next. I wasn't a guy who'd had a shitload of experience with extreme weather situations—like I said, I'm from motherfucking Newark—but I knew I had to get her warmed up, and fast. I put three more logs on the fire, and a couple of Firestarter sticks just to get it all roaring as quickly as possible. With the increased amount of light, I could see she was actually starting to turn blue around the lips.

Fucking fuck, fuck, fuck.

Getting an ambulance to come was out of the question in this weather, and asking Google about hypothermia would eat up time she didn't have to spare. I knew there was only one thing I could do in that moment, only one thing that I could do fast enough to make a difference. I had to get her out of her damp, cold clothes before it was too late. I had to get her warmed up. In order to save her life, I was going to have to undress her.

I busted ass back up to my bedroom and turned on my closet light. I grabbed two of my hoodies and one pair of flannel pajama pants. I snagged a pair of socks and the heavy down comforter off my bed. Then I bolted back down the stairs.

She was still unconscious on the couch. I pulled off the throw blankets, taking a deep breath as I considered where to start. I peeled off her wet socks first, revealing a pair of small, delicate, and ice-cold feet. Next, I pulled off her pants, doing my goddamned best to disregard the lacy panties, the creamy white thighs, the small birthmark on the side of her left leg, and the smoothness of her skin. I tossed her snow-caked leggings aside and pulled my spare PJ bottoms onto her. She was swimming in them, tiny compared to me, but still—it was something. I cinched up the tie and then put a pair of my athletic socks on her, giving her feet a couple of rubs to warm them up with friction.

I wrapped her bottom half in the comforter, bracing her limp body with my hand to her back. I unzipped her hoodie and then pulled her slightly sweaty thermal shirt off over her head. Underneath, she was in a light pink bra, and for one second I thought, *You can't take that off, man. You gotta leave it. She's a total stranger. You can't be taking off her goddamned lingerie, you douchebag.* But as I had her up against my chest, I could feel that even *that* was damp with sweat, the slightly padded cups wet and cold. So I fucking bit the bullet. I held her close, unhooked her bra at the clasp on her back, and cradled her in my arms, pulling it away from her without tipping her body backward. I didn't look at her breasts, even though I could have, because that was way the fuck over the line.

But god*damn,* was she beautiful. The light from the fire sent long shadows over her face, over her full lips. I pulled her right up against me and rubbed her back to warm her up. Using my free hand, I grabbed one of my hoodies and put it on her. I didn't bother with putting her arms through the sleeves. There was no time for that. As I zipped it up, I did see her breasts, but I willed myself to ignore how full they were and how perfect and the very faint tan line that was still there, probably left over from summer. I took the second hoodie and wrapped that around her, too, zipping it up all the way to the delicate hollow of her neck. Her head slumped back limply as I laid her back down gently on the throw pillows. She looked like a little girl, almost, wearing my too-big clothes. Tiny and frail and well and truly in the danger zone. Still, she shivered, an unconscious and involuntary chatter that made her teeth clack against each other.

I pulled the comforter up to her neck and tucked it in around her sides, wrapping her hourglass figure in the blanket, jamming my hand under her body to envelop her in a tight cocoon. But then, standing there over her, I knew there was one more thing I could do. There was one more way to warm her up: with my own body heat. If she woke up while I was holding her, she might freak the fuck out. But at least she'd be warm. Angry and weirded out she might be, but at least she'd be alive.

Untucking the blanket, I made a gap for myself next to her. Keeping her facing the roaring fire, I climbed over her, with one knee to the sofa cushions so that I was straddling her. Then I slipped in behind her, almost pushing her to the edge of the couch—it was hardly big enough for the two of us together. But it was good enough, and as I enveloped her with my body, I nestled my face against her sweet-smelling hair. I used all my size and weight to do what she couldn't, and I willed all my body temperature into hers. I pulled the comforter around us both; I pulled her hips into mine, aware of her curves—so feminine, so perfect—underneath the loose flannel pants. I focused on her breathing, which was regular but shallow, and I felt wave after wave of shivers tear through her. I slipped my arm out from the comforter to turn off the lamp above us, plunging us into just firelight. Moving a lock of her hair aside, I held her as close as I'd held anybody in years. Crisscrossing my arms in front of her chest, I watched the flames and held her tight to reassure her, even in her unconsciousness, that she was safe and that I would look after her. And then I prayed like hell that she was going to be okay.

4

LISA

BLINKING HARD, I opened my eyes and tried to get my bearings. I felt disoriented and confused at first. I was lying on my side, on a couch, and in front of me, there was a huge roaring fire in a big stone fireplace. A real fire, too, with real logs that popped and hissed. I looked around. The room was vast, two stories high at least, with built-in bookcases lining the walls and thick Oriental carpets on the floor. Outside the windows on either side of the fireplace, the storm still raged, and snowdrifts were a quarter of the way up the big panes. But I was warm and calm and peaceful. And in addition to the comforting woodsy smell of the fire, there was something that smelled like…a man. Soap, or cologne. Or both.

That was when I realized I wasn't alone. There was someone on the couch with me. I turned my head to get a look and caught sight of a strong, manly sideburn. Full, sexy lips. Startled, I turned back to face the fire. I realized it had to be the man who answered the door—I had vague, blurry memories of a bare chest and a pair of flannel pajama pants—but I was so delirious by the time I got here, I hardly remembered that at all. It was just a fuzzy, dreamlike streak. I remembered only the utter, overpowering relief that someone, *anyone,* answered when I knocked. I must have fainted, and now here I was.

He was holding me very close, his body right against mine, spooning me. He was huge and warm and, judging from his regular breathing, the comforting and strong breaths, absolutely *sound asleep.* In a heap on the floor, I saw my parka and my clothes. My boots. And, oh God, my bra.

For just one instant, I felt a rush of panic. But then I made myself think it through. After I fainted—first time ever!—he must have… I went through the paces. Unpeeled my leggings from my legs, unzipped my sweatshirt, taken off my tank top. Lord. But I knew why he'd done it—to get me out of my cold, wet clothes. I looked down at my chest to see what I was wearing. One, no, *two* hoodies. But my arms were against my bare body. I wiggled my toes and felt that I was wearing socks, but they were much too big for me. And I also felt an unfamiliar waistband high on my stomach. I worked one of my legs free from the comforter and saw the bottom hem of a pair of men's pajama pants.

Oh.

Ever so slowly, I tried to sit up, but he had me in a bear hug, and I couldn't shift him. His arms were massive, and the hand pressed to my chest was attached to a huge, muscular forearm.

Gosh.

His left arm was underneath my head, and I was nestled down against it, the crook of my neck on his bicep. His left hand was hanging off the couch, relaxed and open. With no wedding ring. I let myself be vaguely conscious of the feel of his hips against mine, and what might be his… I shimmied my tush just half an inch. Yes. Midnight wood.

Lordy.

All of which together meant I wasn't just warm now. I was actually *really* hot. He was like a furnace behind me, and then there was the fire warming me from the front. I tried to wriggle free, but as I did, I shifted his arm just enough to wake him up. He inhaled hard and fast, like he was startled. "Holy shit," he said. "You're awake."

I found my eyes sort of flitting upward, to the huge darkly stained wooden beams that ran in parallel lines across the ceiling, like maybe I could get some guidance on this from above. What kind of conversation was I going to start with this man, this stranger who was *spooning* me in the middle of the night? *Hello, thank you for saving me. Thank you for taking off my clothes. By the way, my name is Lisa. And you're super-duper sexy.* "Yes, hi."

As he shifted, my head rolled off his arm, and he let me go free, moving his hand away from where he'd been gripping me so tightly, even as he slept. I slipped my legs out from under the comforter and sat up. And then I turned to face him.

He was *perfect.*

He got up on one elbow, with the light of the fire sending golden rays onto his Adam's apple, and his stubble, and his absolutely beautiful face. Thick, dark brown hair, cut close on the sides and longer on top. He was friendly in the eyes, with long eyelashes and heavy eyebrows. And he was studying me so carefully, so caringly, that a quick blush flooded my cheeks. "You sure you're okay?"

"Oh yes, I'm…just…" I began trying to stick my arms through the sleeves of the hoodies I was wrapped in, because I honestly just didn't know what else to do. I don't think anybody in my life had ever looked at me with so much worry or so much tenderness—and certainly never a perfect stranger. It knocked all my small talk right out of my head, and I was left with a rather unfortunate unfiltered honesty: "… I'm just really *hot*."

Good work, Lisa. Top marks.

But he wasn't bothered and looked absolutely relieved. "Well, thank God for that," he said, sitting beside me, his huge thigh pressing against the side of my comparatively much smaller one. I noticed our pants were sort of matchy-matchy, like two versions of the same plaid. I was definitely wearing his clothes. Not his girlfriend's or his sister's or—God forbid—his out-of-town wife's. Nope. These were his pants I was swimming in. They were so huge that my feet disappeared under the bottoms. I lifted up my big toe and snagged the hem, pulling it tight because the other side was pinned under my heel. He reached across me and unzipped the top hoodie, slipping it from my shoulders.

He closed his eyes. "I won't look," he said, smiling a little and unzipping the next hoodie just enough for me to let it slip down off my shoulders and find the sleeves with my hands.

"I think it's a bit late for that," I said, with a laugh sneaking up on me.

"Desperate times," he said, clearly trying to keep down a laugh himself. He was a gentleman about it, though. He didn't look, not until I'd gotten myself zipped back up, now with both my arms fully operational.

He reached across me and switched on a lamp. "I'm Dave," he said, extending a huge hand to shake mine.

There was something so sweet about it. My clothes in a heap on the floor, me in his PJs, and him introducing himself like we were meeting for the first time on a blind date, and not at all like he'd just saved my life by undressing me. I extended my hand, too. His palm was warm, his fingers girthy, his whole presence very…*swoony*. "I'm Lisa."

"It's really good to meet you. And I'll bet you're hungry."

Oh my God. My kind of man. Saved my life and his first thought was of…snacks? "Starving." I smiled at him, almost overwhelmed with gratitude. "And thank you for helping me. Really. I'm sorry that I woke you up."

He clicked his tongue and put a firm hand on my thigh. And then winked! Actually winked! "I'm *glad* you woke me up, and I'm so fucking relieved you're all right."

5

DAVE

I SPREAD A thick layer of peanut butter on two slices of bread and said, "I'd make you a hot toddy if I had any idea what the hell that was."

"Oh, I know what it is," she said, waggling her eyebrows. The light from the pantry was on and one of the under-cabinet lights as well. She really was just fucking *beautiful,* even swallowed up by my pants and with my hoodie hanging on her like a tent. "Got some bourbon, honey, and a lemon?" she asked.

"Copy that." I set down the peanut-buttery knife and got all the fixings for her.

"Can I?" She looked up at the rectangular pot rack over the huge island in the middle of the kitchen. She reached up and put one finger on a small saucepan.

"All yours."

Coming up on her tiptoes and reaching up for the pan, she gave me a perfect view of her belly button and the soft, bare skin of her stomach. Man, oh fucking man. "And I need two mugs."

I got those for her, too, but I grabbed the good ones—the ones that matched, the ones Grandma told probably-bullshit stories about. As much as I liked the idea of her lips on a Royal Mattress mug, that mouth of hers was way more suited to fine china than the sort of promo shit people got for free with an extended warranty.

I could tell that having something to do made her feel less awkward, which I totally understood. The situation was pretty much once in a lifetime—I was certain it wasn't every Sunday night that a stranger stripped her naked and got under the covers with her.

Fuck me.

But she'd rolled with it like a champ, totally graceful under fire. She took a knife from the block and a cutting board from a hook. She sliced the lemon in half and squeezed it into the mugs, followed by bourbon and a drizzle of honey. Then she filled the saucepan halfway with water and turned on the stove. She was mesmerizing—the way she moved, the curve of her throat, the thought that underneath my hoodie were her bare breasts. To stop myself from standing there with my mouth hanging open, I went back to the sandwiches, covering the empty halves with grape jelly.

Then I heard her hiss with pain, and I glanced at her. She was holding her hand to her forehead. "Lemon juice on my fingers. Shit."

I grabbed a washcloth, dampened it under the faucet, and then turned on a second light to get a better look. "You're lucky this wasn't worse," I told her as I tried to clean away the lemon juice on the small but angry red line, crusted with blood. "Normally, head wounds bleed a lot."

"I think I was already freezing to death when it happened, so there's that," she said, wincing as I dabbed.

"I've never had anybody faint into my arms before," I told her, just to break the ice a bit.

"Gosh, I don't think I've ever fainted. Maybe once when I was a kid, but not since."

Small smudges of her blood soaked into the washcloth, but I was careful not to push too hard. "That okay? Still stinging?"

She shook her head a little. "That's much better. Thanks," she said, almost shy now. Like she didn't like all this fussing over her.

But *I* liked it. A whole fucking lot. "So, what happened?" I asked as I arranged the sandwiches on two plates.

"Stupid Lola!" she said, pointing at the storm. She was so animated, it kind of took my breath away. I'd gotten so used to women who were poised and controlled and whose every movement seemed like it was practiced in the mirror. But not her. She was just...*her*. Lisa, with her makeup smudged and her hair a mess. Cute as a button. "Totally hoodwinked me. I had no idea it would be this bad." Lisa glanced out of the kitchen window. "Bombogeneroisis or whatever."

I looked out the window, too. One of the pine trees in the distance was damn near bent double. "You drive off the road?"

She nodded as she took a huge bite of her sandwich. And when I say huge, I mean, *huge*. Stuffed her face with it. Not a delicate nibble, hell no. A huge, glad-to-be-alive bite. So goddamned awesome. Then she pointed toward the front of the house and said something that sounded like, "Hecked my beep."

I took an equally big bite of my sandwich and watched her carefully as she chewed. I studied her every fucking move, every shift of her dimples, every shy blink. She was laughing and trying hard to swallow so she could talk, but she was jumping the gun. She'd just have to wait it out, and in that long, silent moment, I found myself standing slightly closer to her than was totally polite. But I couldn't help it. She was like a magnet, and I liked watching her suffer—watching her be a good girl and not talk with her mouth full. Thanks to the peanut butter and white bread, clearly stuck to the roof of her mouth, I got a chance to really study her. Her freckles, the curls around her face from where she'd gotten hot under the covers with me before. Christ.

"Wrecked my Jeep!" she clarified, when she'd gotten free of the vise grip of the Jif.

"Seemed like you walked quite a ways. You were caked with snow." I tucked a quarter of my sandwich into my mouth.

She nodded hard and turned off the simmering water. She poured half into each mug. "I went to your neighbor's first…"

"Big, white place? Spanish tile roof? Looks like a gigantic Taco Bell?" I asked, wiping my mouth with my palm.

Lisa giggled softly. "That's the spot!"

"He's in the Bahamas."

"Clearly," she said, stirring the toddies. "It was confusing because I could see the light from your porch, but then I lost it behind the hill, so I just assumed it was coming from his place. Which it wasn't. So then I had to go back down his driveway and up the hill, and that's how I found you."

The thing was, in spite of the fact that she called it a *driveway,* I knew how far that meant. I jogged my own "driveway" all the time. It was at least two miles, all by itself. So then double that and add whatever she had to walk on the road. "Fuck. That's a hell of a hike."

Lisa nodded. She handed me a steaming mug, and the sharp bourbon and lemon scent filled the air. A sudden yawn snuck up on her, and she shielded her mouth with her hand. When she opened her eyes, they sparkled by the light of the hood over the range. "I really am sorry about this. I don't want to impose. I'm sure the storm will be over soon. I'll be gone before you know it."

Two thoughts ran through my head at the same damned time: *I'm not so sure about that,* and *I fucking hope not.* The snow was piling up, and the idea of her getting stuck at my house? Sounded pretty damned great to me. I looked her up and down, and I made sure to make *a thing* of it. I allowed her to feel my eyes on her, just long enough to let her know how she was making me feel already. "You're welcome for as long as you want to stay," I told her, and *clink* went our mugs.

6

DAVE

AFTER WE FINISHED our drinks, I led Lisa to my favorite of the guest rooms, which—bonus—was on my side of the house, on the opposite end of the mansion from Grandma. One thing I wanted to avoid, at all costs, was Lisa getting turned around in the dark of the night, flipping on the bathroom light, and finding herself faced with Grandma's teeth in a glass. She'd been through enough already.

"This is really nice…" Lisa said, trailing off as she lightly touched the end of the big mahogany bed frame with her fingertips. She turned to me and blinked. "…*So* fancy. I've never been inside a house this beautiful."

You're making it a fuckload more beautiful. "The bed is super comfortable," I told her, turning on the light switch on one of the side tables. "And it adjusts." I didn't give her the whole goddamned showroom shtick, but I raised and lowered the knee rest and a few things like that. I opened the cabinet under the TV and grabbed a few bottles of water for her and put them on her bedside table.

"Thank you," she said again, with her eyes twinkling with heavy yawn tears. One of them tumbled out and spilled down her windburned cheek. And every fiber in my being said, *Wipe it off for her. Touch her. Do it.*

But I didn't. I kept my shit together and played the gentleman. "There's a spare toothbrush and everything you might need in the bathroom. But if you're missing anything, just let me know. I'm sure we have it here somewhere. I'll just be down the hallway. Fourth door on the right. I'll leave my door open. You're sure your head is okay?"

It was like the question startled her, like she'd forgotten, and her fingers moved gingerly up to the cut at her hairline. She winced as she touched the wound, and my goddamned heart dropped. "I think so. It's sore, but I'm all right."

I wasn't so sure, though. I took a few steps closer and stood in front of her, holding her by the shoulders. What I meant to do, of course, was check to make sure her pupils weren't different sizes, to make sure there was no obvious sign of a concussion. I wasn't exactly an EMT, but I'd played soccer long enough to know a thing or two about what a mild head injury looked like, or worse. But instead of actually checking her pupils, I got totally lost in her eyes. They were this deep green, with brownish flecks at the edges, and one tiny darker fleck inside the outer rim of the left one, giving her the most mesmerizing asymmetry.

She pressed her lips together. "Do I get the all clear? Dr. Dave?"

"I've got no idea what I'm looking for, to tell you the truth." *But you are so fucking pretty.*

Something between a honk and a snort shot out of her nose. Fucking adorable. Cute, pretty, sweet, and in my pajama pants. "Me neither. But I think I'm okay."

"You need an Advil?"

"I'm good."

"They're in the medicine cabinet. And Tylenol. And some fresh soap."

She nodded and looked like she was going to giggle. "You're pretty cute, you know? For a guy in a mansion."

Awwww, fuck.

Before I literally couldn't pull myself away—ever seen a magnet get too close to another one and actually become airborne?—I let her go and stepped back.

But her hand snuck out and grabbed mine. It was like a fucking earthquake inside me, like some deep need was coming to the surface. Her thumb was pressing into my palm, her small fingers on the back of my hand. "Really. Thank you so much. I'd never have survived if you didn't answer the door."

"I think you'd have been fine."

"Own it, Dave. You're a hero." She lifted her shoulder, which made my hoodie slip off her bare skin just enough to give an eighties vibe to the whole scene, Christ almighty. "No shame in that."

Yeah, see, this woman was hitting the spot every goddamned which way. All it would have taken was one lunge, and I could have shown her exactly what she was doing to me. But I didn't. My birth certificate didn't say *Prince of Lower Moravia* for nothing. "Have a good rest. Come get me if you need me."

"Okay," Lisa said and let my hand go, smiling. With soft footsteps on the thick carpet, she made her way over to the bed and flopped down on the thick, down comforter. The comforter, the feather bed, the sheets, and the duvet almost swallowed her up, but not completely. I could still see the line of her breasts through my hoodie, and her adorable feet dangling off the side, with my socks—far too big for her—hanging off her, too. "This is amazing. I feel like I'm on a cloud." She kicked her legs and then raised her arms, flopping them back behind her like a snow angel. She reached for the controller and then elevated the top half of the bed so she could see me. "I love this!" she said as she lowered herself back down flat again.

"That's the idea," I told her as I switched off the main light and stepped out into the hallway.

"Dave," she said, poking her head up from the pillows.

Holy fuck. Yes. This. Goddamn it, yes. "Yeah?"

"Thank you again."

It wasn't what I wanted, but it'd have to do. "Sweet dreams."

✧ ✧ ✧

THIS TIME, IT wasn't a thumping that woke me up but a raging goddamned hard-on. The sexiest women I'd ever seen in my life was less than fifty yards from me, in my house, probably half naked now because I'd kicked up the heat and because she was underneath a whole stack of feather duvets. I turned over in my bed and listened to the wind howl, and listened too for any sound from down the hallway. Her punching her pillow, her adjusting her comfort zones, her adjusting the lumbar support so that her hips would be at exactly the right angle to… *Fuck.*

I sat up, drained my glass of water and then headed into the master bathroom to take a piss. The storm was still raging, even worse than before. I grabbed my phone and looked at the weather alerts, all of them stacked on top of one another, just minutes apart. I even saw a news alert that said the National Guard would be arriving in the morning, to help "extricate the citizens of Essex County." But that wasn't really what worried me at all. Thanks to my grandma's Depression-era habit of hoarding all the essentials for some always-looming catastrophe, I'd had a huge generator installed. My basement had not two but three chest freezers and enough gallons of water to see us through an actual nuclear winter. We'd be fine. But what I was less sure about was Lisa. And that head wound. I'd gotten lost in her eyes before, and I hadn't even really checked her pupils. Which was, technically, her fault. But I couldn't really blame her for having eyes that made a guy forget everything he was doing.

So I looked it up on my phone, *Symptoms of concussion.* The usual array of super serious shit topped the list—vomiting, hallucinations, bleeding from the ears—Christ almighty. But then some less common but still scary-as-hell possibilities: Recurring unconsciousness. Irregular breathing. Seizures. And WebMD was clear about it, *Those suffering from suspected concussion should be woken every three hours.* Looking at the time, I realized it was almost exactly three hours at that moment. I'd left her at 11:30. Now, it was just about half past two. I raked my hand through my hair and thought about it for about one millisecond. I should check on her—I should *definitely* check on her.

Forcing my hard-on to relent and adjusting my package so I wasn't coming at her with the flagpole at full staff, I walked down the hallway and listened outside her door. I had left it cracked, and she hadn't shut it all the way. I pushed it open an inch and listened for her breathing or for the sounds of her shifting on the sheets. I didn't hear anything, so I opened it a bit wider. And there she was, like Sleeping Beauty herself, surrounded by fluffy pillows and the down comforters, with the eerie storm glow from outside lighting up her profile.

I watched her breathing to see if it was regular and normal, but I just couldn't tell from where I was standing. Advancing with careful steps farther into her room, I found myself beside her bed looking down at her. Much to my relief, her breathing was regular. And fuck me, she was even smiling a little. Like my hand wasn't even attached to my body, like I was fucking dreaming, I moved a lock of her hair away from her forehead. She moaned and turned toward my hand, nudging me with her cheek and nestling farther into the covers.

"Lisa," I whispered.

She stirred but didn't open her eyes. Her pretty eyebrows furrowed together, though, like I was interrupting a dream and she was annoyed about it.

"Lisa, wake up," I whispered again.

This time, she made this cute little whine, like I'd imagine she would when her alarm clock woke her. She rolled over in a huff and stuffed her face into the pillows. She was probably thirty or thirty-five, but right then, she was every bit as spoiled as a sleepy teenager, and I fucking *loved* it. But still, she slept.

I placed one hand on her shoulder and shifted her onto her back. I leaned in closer to get a look at the wound, to make sure it wasn't bleeding again. It wasn't, but her face was so damned beautiful, so peaceful, so sweet, that suddenly I just found myself bending over her. I was drawn to her like that; she was just so *irresistible.* As I got closer, I could smell a faint scent, something like strawberries, possibly. Or flowers. Or strawberries and flowers together. I couldn't put my finger on it exactly, but whatever it was, it was seriously crazy-making. And before I knew what I was doing, I brought my face down to hers, and I was pressing my lips to her forehead.

Which was, of course, exactly the moment when she woke up. "Oh, fuck, what is going on?" she gasped, jerking away from me and giving me a startled shove like any normal human being would when they found a guy hovering over them in the middle of the night.

Smooth, you weirdo. Smooth. "Sorry. I was checking for a concussion. I had a bad feeling and… Sorry." *Just keep on digging, asshat.* I stepped back like I'd been tased. What an *idiot.* Kissing some total stranger on the forehead while she slept? Telling her I was checking for a concussion? I'd be lucky if I got out of this thing with only a restraining order to show for it. I rubbed my stubble with my hand and looked away. "Jesus, I really am sorry. That was totally out of line. I don't know what I was thinking."

Such total bullshit. I knew exactly what I was thinking. About her. And me. And how badly I wanted her. About how her body felt against mine when we were curled up on the couch, about how relieved I felt when the violent shivers shifted to regular, calm breathing. About how *good* she felt there tucked up against me. With me. I wanted her then, and I wanted her even more now. It was really that simple.

Lisa sat up in bed, her hair in a loose ponytail. "It's okay."

"Sorry, I'll let you sleep," I said and began to walk away.

But before I could get more than a step away, her hand left the comforter and she reached out for me. It was awkward—she grabbed my first two fingers like a little kid might have—but it was enough to get me to stop cold. Then her grip shifted to something way more adult, and she flattened her palm up against mine, pivoting her wrist so we could have been on either side of a pane of glass in prison. In that moment, I swear to God I could hear the grandfather clock a whole story away going tick-tock, tick-tock.

Moment of truth. Now or never.

But I wasn't going to push. Fuck knows I'd pretty much pushed my luck to the limit already.

"It really is okay, Dave. I'm glad you came to check on me."

"Yeah?"

"Oh yeah," she said with a smile in her voice. I don't know how I could hear it, but I could. I could hear her smiling, even though I couldn't see her. So I took my chance. I bit the bullet for the second time that night; I shifted my fingers slightly and knitted our hands together. My grip tightened, but hers tightened even more. It absolutely did. For a minute, I let myself get caught up in the size of her hands against mine. She wasn't some shrinking violet—she was strong enough to hike four miles in the worst weather I'd ever seen—but still delicate. So much the opposite of me, really. In size, and the softness of her skin, and the tenderness of her touch.

"Please don't tell me you've got some boyfriend worried sick about you," I said. "Because I'd be fucking wrecked."

She laughed softly through her nose. "No, I don't."

"Or a husband."

"Not that either."

"Or a girlfriend. Or a wife."

"Or that," she said, laughing a bit more. "You're sweet. But, no, there's nobody. Not even a dog. I work too much for any of that."

I wished I didn't understand that, but I absolutely did. "Good. That you don't have anybody. Not that you work too much." *Hear that sound? That's the hole you're in, getting bigger.*

But Lisa was either still half asleep or infinitely patient with my BS. "Well…maybe," she said softly, "we shouldn't think about work."

God*damn it.* It was happening. "Agreed. But I've got something else we should think about."

"Do you?" she said, and her left eyebrow arched just a fucking millimeter.

I moved the pad of my thumb down her lip. "Yeah. I do."

Still holding my hand tight, she moved the comforter back to make some space for me. "Come on. Get in."

When she pulled the sheets off of her body, I actually growled. She wasn't in my pajamas anymore, but instead, in her lacy panties, a shock of pink against the white sheets.

Seeing that made something inside me go crazy for her. Up until that moment, I'd managed to resist her somehow, to ignore the thing that had to happen—but then I saw those bare hips and the curve of that ass and her inner thighs, and I was fucking powerless to stop myself. The need to have her took over—so simple, so basic, so exactly right. I didn't listen to logic; I didn't listen to rules. Instead, while it sounded like the world was ending outside her window, I listened to my cock. I got on top of her, my knees on either side of her body, and took her other hand in mine. I pinned her hands back onto the sheets, on either side of her head. I leaned in and nudged her cheek with my nose and dragged my stubble against her cheek. Yeah, flowers. Yeah, strawberries. Yeah, *everything*.

"I think you were kissing me when I woke up."

"I was," I told her, letting her feel my weight, making her understand what she was in for. "Just on the forehead, though. Not like I wanted."

Lisa nodded, her hair shifting. "I think you should do it again. For real."

"Oh yeah? You want me to kiss you?" Now my hard-on, which had been *raging,* was becoming almost unbearable. I shifted my hips, and my cock emerged from the opening in my pants. I let the head of my cock slide along the lacy edge at the top of her panties, moving toward her belly button.

"I do."

"Kissing you isn't all I'm going to do," I told her.

And how did she answer me? There, pinned underneath me, so fucking sexy I couldn't even see straight?

She pressed her hips into me, bit her lip, and said, "I sure hope not."

Fuck.

7

LISA

A ND DID HE *ever* kiss me. He did this thing, like when I startled him
awake on the couch, where he'd inhale hard and hold his breath like he
was savoring me. But I was savoring him, too, savoring every single thing
about him because he kissed…with passion and aggression and not one
instant of hesitation. If it were a fairy tale, I'd have said he kissed like a
prince.

But, really, he kissed like a *boss.*

He kissed with his whole body, too, and I could feel how hard he was,
and how huge, when he pressed into my stomach. I made a move to try to
reach out for him, to touch him, but he wouldn't let me—he just gripped my
hands in his, pressing them farther into the downy, fluffy, luxurious mattress,
and I felt him smile into the kiss.

It wasn't like me to do this, to get in bed with a man I'd only just met.
But I was just so drawn to him and so glad to be alive and so utterly floored
that this gorgeous man, this boss-kissing, hip-driving, hunk of a man was the
one whom I'd fainted into, that I found myself utterly swept away by it all.
And for the first time in my life, I just let that happen. I didn't question it or
get self-conscious about it. I just went with it.

And it was absolutely magical.

"Tell me what you want," he said as he pulled away from the kiss finally,
letting me catch my breath.

"You. This," I said, trying to show him as best I could from my delight-
fully compromised position underneath him.

"Say it."

"I want you…"

"Where?"

"You know where."

"Say it, Lisa," he said, all gruff and aggressive.

"Inside me."

"That's what I want to hear." He let my hands go free and came up to kneeling on either side of me. Automatically, my hand moved to his waistband, my fingers trailing along that silky map. The treasure trail was absolutely perfect. Not too much, not too little. Not wimpy, not bear-like. Just…billboard-perfect.

"Me first," he said, crawling down my body and taking the zipper of his Jets hoodie between his front teeth. Because it was so loose on me, he couldn't get a good grip. But I held the zipper steady, and tooth by tooth, he undid me.

"Jesus, you're beautiful," he said, sliding his hand down my body—and not being gentle about it either. I reached through the gap in his PJs and parted the seam of his boxers until I found him. *All* of him. Boss. Total boss.

Again, he growled, a deep, chesty rumble I found totally intoxicating. "I like that," I told him. "I didn't think you'd be a growler."

"No?" he said, watching me as I slipped his cock free from his pants, groaning as I ran my fingertips softly over the shaft.

"I thought you'd be more polite."

He laughed, and it made his abs ripple. *Dear lord above.* "I'm a lot of things, but polite isn't one of them." His eyes flashed at me, and then he gathered a mouthful of saliva, letting it run down onto my palm and his shaft, and even onto my thigh. I pulled on the lacy elastic top of my panties and then let it come back down onto his cock. I loved the look of that delicate lace against his throbbing veins. The perfect pairing.

The noise he made was like he'd just burned himself. "Fuck, that's hot…"

It really, really was. I sat up so I could get a better look. The lace was just below the head, and the delicate fabric accentuated how big he really was. But he didn't let me savor it for long. He planted his hand on the mattress and climbed off of me, hooking the waistband of his boxers and his pajama bottoms in one smooth movement. Everything fell to the floor at once. And there he was, in all his holy-shit glory.

"Are you for real?" I asked, staring at him. Huge, absolutely freaking huge.

"Are *you* for real?" he asked, climbing on top of me again. He pulled his hoodie off me, balling it up and tossing it off into the darkened corner of the room. I made a move to wriggle out of my panties, but he grabbed my hand hard. "Those stay exactly where they are."

Working his length with one hand, he moved my panties aside with the other, and then he positioned himself at my opening.

"Fuck, you're so wet," he said, moving one finger over me and up to the edge of my clit. He didn't go right for the center, bless him, but instead made a very focused circle around it. Exactly the right way, exactly the way I liked. This guy knew what he was doing.

And what he was doing was *me*.

"Oh God..." I said, with my face halfway into the pillows.

"Look at me," he said, sudden and greedy.

I turned my face toward him, and we locked eyes. He brought one hand up to my jaw, almost pinching my cheeks. Dominant and dreamy and all the very best things. "You ready?" he asked.

As I nodded, I pressed my jaw into his palm, and his grip softened. He moved a lock of my hair aside. And then he pressed into me, making a wave of *yes* roll right through me.

8

DAVE

S HE FELT SO goddamned good that no matter how hard I fucked her, I wanted more. I bent her legs back, gripping the underside of each silky, curvy thigh and digging my fingers into her flesh. I pushed her knees to her shoulders so I could get inside her as deeply as her body would let me.

She was noisy, and she was a biter, and I fucking loved it. As I drove into her, so hard that the mahogany bed *whump-whumped* against the wall, she sank her teeth into my shoulder and let out this primal, gorgeous, fearsome roar.

"I thought *you'd* be more polite," I said into her ear, giving her some of her own medicine.

But she was too far gone to sass me back. She just bit down harder, making me feel like my balls would burst.

There was something about her that made me insane—pure chemistry, no logic, just *need*. For everything I gave her, she matched me. Every thrust of my cock was met by a moan, or a bite, or a hella-hot squeeze from the inside out. If she was going down, I knew she was going to take me with her.

I caged her in with my arms and licked a long line along the edge of her ear, nipping the lobe hard enough to make her know I wasn't fucking around. When she felt the pain, she bore down on my cock with her pussy. It surprised me and sent a bolt of the most basic need straight down into my balls and back again. It also, in a way, pissed me off—I was running this goddamned show, and yet I nibble her ear and she damn near pushes me off the orgasm cliff? Fuck no. Fuck *no*.

Without warning her, I pulled out of her, climbed off her, and flipped her facedown onto the mattress. She squealed, and I watched her toes curl. I hooked my forearm around her hips and brought her up onto her knees. Her face was in the mattress, and her ass was in the air. Fucking perfect. "Touch yourself," I told her as I plunged back inside her. "I need to feel you come on me. Just like this."

She made a part-moan, part-laugh into the sheets. "I like your style, you know that?"

Wham, I gave it to her again, so hard that it flattened her. "Same here," I said, deep and dark into her ear. Again, I yanked her onto her knees and kept my forearm at that perfect bend in her body. She reached up and ran her fingers down the back of my head, just a tickle that intensified everything I was feeling already.

I got her back up on her knees and moved my fingers to her clit, staying buried deep inside her, giving it to her over and over again until she whacked the mattress with her palm. Like a goddamned wrestler, tapping out.

"Too much?"

"Just give me a minnnn...oh, *shit,*" she said as I sped up on her clit.

I didn't give her a minute—I didn't even give her a second. I fucked her slow and worked her clit fast. And that's when it happened. She gripped the sheets and buried her face into a pillow and came so hard I thought she'd bring the mansion down. Most beautiful thing I'd ever seen in my life, and I was the one making it happen. To hell with being a prince. She made me feel like a king.

As the contractions of her orgasm rippled up my cock, I realized that if I wanted to keep at it, I was the one who was going to need to tap out for one second. But then I thought, *Fuck it. You only live once.* "I need to come inside you. Tell me that's okay."

She was so lost in it, she couldn't answer. But she reached out, grabbed my hand, and squeezed as she nodded into the sheets.

The memory of her trembling and helpless earlier flashed back to me. But now, she wasn't helpless. She was exactly the opposite. She was a fucking goddess, and I didn't stand a goddamned chance. As I exploded into her, as I made her mine for what I knew would be only the first of many, many times, I saw her thighs quiver as a second wave of her orgasm hit her. She was trembling again.

Fuck yeah, she was.

9

LISA

I WOKE UP to a cup of steaming coffee on the bedside table, along with a little pitcher of cream and a few cubes of brown sugar. I sat up in the cozy warm bed and dropped a cube of sugar into the cup, along with half the cream. I stirred it with a small silver spoon and then scooched down into the warm bedclothes.

"You up?" I heard Dave ask as he came into the room.

"I could get used to this," I said as I snuggled in deeper.

He walked toward the bed, smiling wide. "You sleep okay?" He stood beside me and checked the cut on my head and then smoothed my hair with his strong fingers. It was doubly sweet because he was a little bit unsure about it, like he'd never really done it before.

I nodded as I sipped the coffee, which was perfectly yummy. And also surprisingly familiar. I inhaled deeply, and I tasted the coffee. There was no doubt about it. "Are these…Dunkin' Donuts beans?"

"Hell yeah," Dave said, sitting down on the bed.

"Hazelnut?"

He gave me a manly flick of his chin. "One of the best things," he said as his eyes moved up and down my body, as if to say *But not as good as all this.*

No *kidding.* His hand edged up my leg, strong and sure right through the down and fluff. "Last night, Lisa…" He whistled quietly and rubbed his temples. "I mean… *Jesus.* Never in my life."

I nodded at him again, this time unblinking. I silently ran through the words that might be adequate to describe it—earthshaking, mind-blowing, oh-God-oh-God-oh-God—but none of them was even close to enough. There I was, all warm and comfy, so happy and so surprised by all this that I felt like the heroine in some fantasy—all I could do was nod and smile at him. And plop a second cube into my cup. "I *know.*"

Dave winked again and stood up. "I washed your clothes because I wanted to make sure they were dry. They'll be out of the dryer in…" He checked the massive, fancy watch on his huge wrist. "Just a few minutes."

"And you do laundry?"

"Not usually. But you're the exception."

Oh-God-oh-God-oh-God. I set my coffee on the bedside table and flopped back into the pillows. "By the way, this mattress is fantastic." I squeezed my buns and got a respectable bounce going. "I don't think I've ever slept so well."

And then for some reason, Dave laughed. "Glad to hear it. Come on down when you're ready. I'll leave your clothes in here, and then I'll make you something to eat. How do you feel about bacon?"

"Like maybe you're my knight in shining armor."

"Attagirl," he said, and I heard him head down the hallway.

Coffee in bed. Fresh laundry. Bacon. Best sex of my life. I rolled over into the comforter to wrap myself in a burrito and then went crazy with kicky-legs.

✧   ✧   ✧

MUCH TO MY surprise, though, when I came downstairs freshly showered, warm, and comfy—led to the kitchen by the smell of bacon and feeling decidedly like a bloodhound on the trail—I realized that Dave and I weren't alone in this great big house. Seated at the kitchen table was a very, *very* ancient lady, with a huge mug next to her emblazoned with the words IDRIS ELBA'S BATHWATER. Next to that was a red aerosol container of whipped cream. I was well behind her, on the far end of the kitchen, and she hadn't seen me. She was reading something on her iPad and had a phone book next to her. She had the font on her iPad set so big that even from where I was, I could almost make out the words. And also, possibly, leaves? Whatever it was, she was intensely focused. Without looking up from what she was reading, she shook up the whipped cream, filled the mug to overflowing, and then proceeded to dig into the white fluff with a soup spoon.

In the oven was a jelly roll pan with rows of thick-cut bacon sputtering away. Next to the stove, in a bowl, were a few uncracked eggs waiting to be scrambled. Expecting to see Dave around the corner, I stepped softly into the kitchen and said, "Good morning?"

"Oh Jesus!" screeched the old woman, her arms flying up and sending the can of whipped cream tumbling to the wooden floor with a *ping-ping-ping*. "Who the hell are you?"

"Lisa," I said, smiling and clutching my mug like a protective shield. Dave wasn't anywhere to be seen, but the old lady was approaching with purposeful shuffles of her slippers. She was peering at me, holding the frames of her glittery purple bifocals, her gnarled fingers vaguely reminiscent of eagle talons. Vaguely, though. Not like *exactly* like that. But close. "I'm Lisa."

"And I'm Grandma. Just that. Like Cher. Grandma," she said, still eyeing at me and inching closer. She leaned toward me and sort of…sniffed. But I was pretty sure she wasn't sniffing the bacon—she was sniffing *me*. I noticed her sweatshirt had someone who looked *a lot* like Vladimir Lenin silk-screened on the front, but it was pretty faded out, so I couldn't be sure. She held up a skinny, big-knuckled finger. "Where'd you come from?"

Suddenly, it occurred to me that she probably heard me last night—I had a feeling I screamed the house down, and I grimaced at the memory and clapped my eyes shut.

I felt a cold finger press into my cheek. "Why are you doing that? Last time I saw someone with their face that way, they had end-stage tetanus. It was in El Salvador in 1979. Bad business."

I dropped the grimace and summoned my best impression of the traffic girl on the local news—pure sweetness, pure smiles, even in the face of a twenty-car pileup and a three-hour delay. Nothing to worry about, folks. Nope. "I live in Rhode Island. I crashed my car last night in the storm. Your…grandson? Dave? He helped me."

Grandma nodded and did the sniffing thing again. "No, I mean, where did you *come* from? Originally, honey! Where are your people from?"

My people? I felt like I was in some unused scene from *The Godfather*. "Um…outside Detroit."

Grandma grumbled. She inched closer to me, and I got the very definite sense she was assessing something about my jawline. Or my hairline. Or both. "Name?"

"Lisa!" I said, this time louder, like I sometimes had to do when I brought cupcakes to the nursing home for Christmas. I figured she hadn't heard me the first time, so I went at it with guns blazing. "I'm Lisa! Leeees-ahhhh!"

"Stop shouting, honey!" she hollered back, waving her iPad stylus in my face. Without dropping her voice, she added, "Before Detroit, where were your people?"

"Oh! Baltimore!"

"Christ! I mean, your heritage! You've got a kinda bohunk nose. Know what that means?"

I hadn't the faintest. I automatically moved my hand to the bridge of my nose, though, because I wasn't sure how a word like *bohunk* could be anything but bad.

"Never mind the schnoz!" she shouted again and hobbled back to the kitchen table and took a seat in front of an iPad. "Name! First and last!"

"Lisa…Smith?" I said tentatively.

"Unclear about *Smith*? Why does that sound like a question?"

"*Smith!*" I said, this time with much more certainty.

Grandma turned to me, making Lenin's face contort like some psyche-delic video montage in a David Bowie music video. "You're shitting me."

"Umm, no?" I said.

"Middle name!"

"Anne."

Grandma slapped her sweat pants with her liver-spotted fists. "Lisa Anne Smith? That's worse than Jane Doe! What am I gonna do with that?"

I looked at her iPad. And the God's Eye over Lenin's face. And the row of mood rings on her fingers. "What were you planning on doing with it?"

"Looking for royal heritage, honey! But with a name like Lisa Anne Smith, fuck it. And Dave wonders why I resort to the phone book." To demonstrate this, she flipped one of the tissue-thin pages with such fury that she tore it clean in half. Apparently, it wasn't the first time, because she produced a roll of Scotch tape from her sweatshirt and went to work repairing it immediately.

But before I could ask her what I wanted to ask, which was, of course, *Hang on one sec, did you just say "royal heritage"?* Dave came around the corner, and I watched his gaze bounce from me to Grandma and back again. He put two fingers against his temple and shook his head at the floor. "Lisa, meet Grandma."

"We've met!" Grandma bellowed. "Girl's got a name like a placeholder ID in a half-priced TJ Maxx wallet." With that, Dave moved *both* hands to his head, like he was in an ad for Excedrin, as Grandma went on, "Lisa Anne Smith! Christ!"

Dave looked up at the ceiling and shook his head and then refocused on me. We had a sort of tender, quiet moment, in which his eyes said, *So sorry about my insane relative.* I waved it off and took a sip of my coffee. I shook my head and mouthed, *It's fine!* He guided me over to the far end of the kitchen, which was absolutely enormous. I hadn't really realized it last night, not in the half-light and focused as I'd been on making hot toddies. But now I noticed, and I saw that on one counter there was a special marble top for rolling out dough. *Be still my beating heart.*

Turning on the stove with one hand, he expertly cracked the eggs into a bowl with the other. "Sorry about that. There's coffee in the pot, if you'd like some more."

From the other end of the room, Grandma leered at me. My initial thought about her talon-hands wasn't totally off the mark. Only, less like an eagle and more like…a molting falcon. I whispered to Dave, "Did she say *royal heritage*?"

"I mean, it's not…" Dave glanced at me and then set to scrambling the eggs with a fork.

"Wait…" I stared at him. "Are you famous?"

"No, no," he gasped. "Exiled, like five generations ago. The opposite of famous. It's so totally mundane. Not worth mentioning, really." He sprinkled some salt into the eggs and then cracked some pepper from an antique silver grinder, which had something that looked *a lot* like a family crest carved into the front.

What was happening to me? Was this a dream? Was I actually still unconscious in my Jeep on the side of the road, clutching my frog charger and waiting for the National Guard? "Are you a prince or something?"

He stopped scrambling the eggs and stared at me. "I sell mattresses. That's pretty much the most interesting thing about me."

I glanced around the kitchen, at the rows of heavy-bottomed copper saucepans hanging neatly from the rack above. At the matching set of chef's-quality chopping knives in a block. At the walk-in pantry and the enormous Sub-Zero refrigerator. "I had no idea mattress sales paid this well."

"I don't *sell* them, really. I own a company. I'm in mattresses." Dave opened a nearby cabinet and handed me a mug. A swirly, fancy logo wrapped around the ceramic front.

ROYAL MATTRESS
Sleep like a queen.
You deserve it.

"Oh my God," I said, giving him a shove on his rock-solid upper arm. "You're the Royal Mattress guy! You were in *People* magazine!"

Dave waved it off. "That was totally a PR thing. I had no idea I was going to be on that list."

"Pfffft!" I shoved him again, and he mock-stumbled, as if I were way above his weight class. He glanced at me for one second and then looked away again. But now I really was a bloodhound on the trail, and it had nothing to do with bacon. "Most eligible bachelors, yada yada yada? And no wonder the bed was so comfy!"

But then I noticed he was actually blushing. A rosy glow was reddening his rugged cheeks, and he couldn't even face me. He really was just so stinking adorable. And handsome. And wearing an apron and scrambling me eggs while a dozen pieces of bacon cooked in the oven. "Seriously, though, are you royalty? Are you…a prince?"

He gave me a stare to say *stop it.* "I'm about as much a prince as you are a princess."

I noticed his eyes on the logo on my hoodie. A cupcake with a frosting tiara. Feeling a bit embarrassed—it seemed somehow ridiculous, given that I was talking to an actual prince—I clapped my hand to it. I was suddenly very self-conscious about my little bakery, named after every girl's fantasy. But in truth, I was just barely scraping by. As if there was any doubt, I knew it then for sure—I was way, *way* out of my league. My efforts to hide my logo had made it so I'd inadvertently perked up my girls from below, giving him an accentuated view of my cleavage, and I clapped my free hand over that. I was clutching my chest like I was having a heart attack, and I might as well have been. "I'm no princess."

He gave me the up-and-down again, and not just zeroing in on my cleavage either, but lingering on my lips and my throat. He glanced over at his grandma and snuck a little grab of my ass when she was looking away. And Dave said into my ear, "I wouldn't be so sure about that," as he sprinkled some cheese into the eggs.

✦　✦　✦

JUST AS DAVE was turning off the burner, the lights flickered. For one startling second, everything went silent—all the appliances going dead at once sounded like a sound effect from a cartoon—but as quickly as everything had gone quiet, it whirred back to life again. "Goddamn it," Dave growled, carefully arranging my omelet on my plate and adding a few strips of bacon to the side, along with a sliced orange. *Goodness.* He popped a slice of bacon into his mouth and wiped his hands off on a dish towel. "You stay here. I'll go make sure the generator is ready to go." As he moved away, he left me with a perfect view of You-Know-Who, spraying some whipped cream directly into her mouth.

"I'm a good shoveler!" I added, not at all halfheartedly as Grandma shook the container, making the pellet inside sound *a lot* like a ricocheting BB.

"No way am I letting you go out there," Dave said, and off he went toward some far corner of the house, where surely there were shiny cars in a row in an immaculate garage.

Which, of course, left me alone with Grandma. I wasn't sure what to compare it to, really—maybe being left unexpectedly with a surprisingly dangerous animal at the zoo. And so, as if I were in a cage at the zoo, I moved slowly. *Very* slowly. *Do not disturb the ostrich.* At first, I thought she didn't realize we were alone, but when the triple beep of the security system announced Dave had opened the door, she sprang to life mid-thought like someone had just plugged *her* back into the wall. "To hell with Baltimore! I'm talking old country! I want percentages! Irish? Scottish? Austro-Hungarian?"

Though I admired them, I just wasn't able to dice my family history into slices of a pie chart—*50% Italian, 25% Swedish, 7.5% Finnish, 1.25% Cherokee...* "As far as I know, I'm just good old-fashioned, Apple-Pie American," I said, jamming a piece of bacon into my mouth to stay busy.

"American! Bullshit! That's a continent, not a nation!" She unfolded herself from her chair and made a new approach, stylus extended. "Anybody every mention Moravia? Anybody have an almost superhuman knack for cooking lamb? Anybody do weird things like get a daily newspaper in Slovenian while saying they were from Austria?" Inexplicably, she put both *Slovenian* and *Austrian* in air quotes and then went on, "Because that—" she tapped her hooked nose and pointed at my slightly curved one "—is a dead giveaway for *something!*"

I shook my head and shoveled in a mouthful of eggs, which were *delicious.* "No, no, and no."

"Anybody ever plan a coup? Active or passive? Anybody ever sketch out the downfall of an existing government on a paper napkin?"

I choked on my eggs and shook my head, pressing my palm into my mouth. "No to that, too."

"Your heritage sounds like Yawnsville, hon."

"Pretty much," I said, with my mouth still half full.

Grandma ripped open a packet of hot cocoa and filled up her mug partway with the boiling water spigot on the faucet. "Mmmm."

"I was adopted," I told her. "So what I know about my adoptive parents has nothing to do with..." Now it was my turn to give some scare quotes. "...*my people.*"

She narrowed her rheumy eyes at me and fished a tiny sad marshmallow out of Idris Elba's bathwater. "Adopted," Grandma repeated, slowly chewing the marshmallow. "So, you could be from...anywhere?"

I nodded vehemently, feeling delighted that I was probably out of the running for a full-on royal heritage examination. *Is there a test for royalty? Is it like witches? Is she going to put me in the tub and see if I float?* Grandma sighed and dabbed at her nose with a tissue that she produced from inside her sweatshirt sleeve. Desperate for a subject change, I opted to steer clear of Lenin and pointed at her mug. "I'm a fan, too. You know there's a new season of *Luther* coming soon? Might even be out now. I could check online if you wanted."

"I do love me some Idris," Grandma said wistfully, staring longingly at nothing in particular, it seemed, somewhere in the middle distance. "What a hunk of man he is. Why they didn't cast him as Bond, I'll just never know. Fools!"

"And how," I agreed, thinking to myself, *But he's got nothing on your grandson!*

Grandma did look tempted by my offer about *Luther*, but just as quickly as she looked lured, she redoubled and shook her head. "No, honey. I can't be watching television this early in the day. It'll put me into a stupor like an epileptic dachshund. How do you feel about board games?"

The truth was, *Not awesome.* For the life of me, I could never win a round of Monopoly, and no matter how many times someone tried to teach me chess, it never stuck. But in that moment, I felt better about board games than whatever other plans Grandma seemed to have on tap. Like putting my hair into a potion or something. We were up to our eyeballs in snow, and I figured we'd have to do *something* to pass the time. "Sounds good to me."

"Excellent," Grandma said. She shuffled off to an antique hutch at the far end of the kitchen and crouched down to open a cabinet. She made pained noises as she did and gripped one knee.

"Here, let me help you," I said, putting down my coffee and going to help her. I knelt and put my hand to her bony back. The air smelled strongly of baby powder, mixed up with Bengay.

"No need, honey! I got it right here," she said, standing up and beaming. "Maybe we can ask the powers that be about your heritage!"

She gave the box in her hands a shake. And that's when I saw it.

A Ouija board.

Oh no.

10

DAVE

IN MY WHOLE life, I'd never seen snow like that. Heavy as concrete and with drifts past the tops of the garage doors. I got out the shovel and the snow blower and got to work, yard by painstaking yard. I had no sense of how long it took me to clear a path from the garage to the generator shed, but by the time I got back inside, I saw that shit had taken a *serious* turn for the worse.

Grandma was standing next to Lisa, with her wrinkly hand on Lisa's smooth forehead, while on television played reruns of *Unsolved Mysteries*. Lisa stared at me, blinking hard. "Oh, Dave! *There* you are," she squeaked. "Hi! Hello!"

Christ. "Gram, you're freaking her out."

"No, we're all good!" Lisa said, her voice high-pitched and panicked and sounding exactly the opposite of *all good*. "Took us a while to get a…signal?" With this, Grandma nodded slowly, and Lisa looked back at me with even *more* panic. "But so far, we've discovered a man named Stand With Knife is buried underneath the house, and a lady named Jane Gunderson killed her second husband with a cast-iron pan in the kitchen in 1899." Lisa blinked hard and raised her feet onto anxiously pointed tiptoes beneath her bent knees. "The more you know!"

"But not a goddamned peep about you, honey bunny!" Grandma roared, making a frustrated alphabet soup with the planchette.

Lisa scrunched her eyes shut and sucked in a breath from between gritted teeth. "Never know what's coming up next! Third time might be the charm!"

I had to hand it to her. Not every woman could stumble into an alternate reality with so much grace, and I felt somehow proud that, even though I'd only known her a little while, I could read right between her lines to hear her say, *Oh my God, help me!* I mean, it wasn't exactly hard to figure out, but still.

I liked the secret language.

After a couple of long strides, I was prying the planchette out of Grandma Katrina's hands. "Prude!" she snarled. "No sense of occasion! None!"

"I think you might need a nap," I told Grandma, looking her in the cataract-clouded eyes.

"*You* need a nap! And a shave!" Grandma said.

I widened my eyes. *Listen, Baroness…*

There was a flicker of laughter at the corner of Grandma's mouth. Hell on wheels. "Fine! All right, fine," she said and snatched up her iPad. As she padded away, barely picking her slippers up off the wood floors, I heard the ding-ding of an app, followed by her asking, "Okay, Google! How do you test for royalty?"

Lisa snort-snickered as she boxed up the Ouija board, minus the planchette. I took Lisa by the hand and led her into the kitchen. "She's intense," she said, ruffling up her hair with her fingers. "I like her. But holy moly!"

I totally got that. As a preemptive measure, I put the planchette on the top shelf of the glasses cabinet, too high for Grandma to reach it even with her mechanical arm. "Did she freak you out too badly?"

Lisa ruffled her hair a bit more. "Naw, nothing a few sessions with my therapist and some hypnosis won't fix." She was totally deadpan. Absolutely killed me.

"I'll pay for it," I said without cracking a smile.

"Big shot."

And then we both dissolved into hushed laughter. But all kidding aside, I was a bit worried about her. I was pretty sure Lisa had never been accosted by some old lady who wanted to ask her a thousand questions about her bloodline, for God's sake. "You sure you're good?" I asked.

Lisa gave me a little smile and then made some hair-smoothing moves like she was putting herself back together. Finally, she blew out a long breath and nodded. After that, she seemed to have totally regained her composure and was somehow even prettier than I'd remembered her from an hour before.

"You hungry?"

"Always."

"My kind of woman, but I'm not talking about lunch."

"My kind of *man!*"

I wrapped my arm around Lisa's waist and pulled her into the walk-in pantry. I pressed her up against the shelf full of pasta sauces and oils and vinegars. "Full disclosure, Grandma doesn't actually live with me. In case you were worried about that."

A tickled smile started to show on Lisa's face. "And why would I be worried about that?"

"Don't know." I dropped my voice. "But maybe because when you come, it's like a fucking earthquake. I'll bet you made the needles shift at the USGS."

Lisa tried to shove me, but I didn't budge, and instead, I just pressed my chest back into her hands, crowding her up against a row of chutneys that I got in a gift basket from my investment banker. Lisa said, "She really is a piece of work. I just don't know why she wants to figure out my *heritage*."

I couldn't help myself and moved my hand around behind her ass. I gave it a squeeze, and Lisa moaned, then pushed her hips into my thighs. "She wants to get me married off, that's why."

Sizing me up carefully, she shifted her puckered lips to the side. "Is that so?"

Nodding at her, I bent down, nudging her cheek with my nose. I crowded her space a little more, and the glass jars shifted behind her. "But I'd rather find *the one* myself."

I hoisted her up on one of the pantry shelves, and a box of crackers tumbled to the ground, followed by a bag of pasta. Lisa reached up and hooked her arms around me. "And how do you plan to do that?" she asked as she hooked her ankles around my ass and raised her eyebrow.

Goddamn it, what a pistol. Perfect in every way. "One step at a time," I told her and then put her down to give her a piggyback ride up to my bedroom.

✧   ✧   ✧

WHEN WE GOT to the master suite, I let her slide off of me onto the bed and then went down onto my knees between her legs. I hooked my fingertips over the waistband of her leggings and pulled them down. No panties now—God bless this motherfucking blizzard.

"Won't she wake up?" Lisa whispered, propping herself on her elbows and glancing at the door, which I'd closed and locked.

"She's out cold, at least until midafternoon, and she couldn't hear us anyway. She's in a different wing."

Lisa's eyes flashed with that word, *wing,* and her gaze moved around the master suite, darting from the ceiling to the long silk drapes to the leather sofa on the other side of the room and up and down the posts of my bed. "This place is really amazing."

"You know what else is amazing?" I brought my tongue to her clit, tracing the edges and tasting her for the first time so far. "*This.*"

She moaned up at the ceiling, and I pushed her thighs open wider. I got a little obsessed with the idea of my cum still inside her from last night—fucking dirty, fucking lewd—but I let myself go there. Her smell was the trip wire, her taste the fuse. I'd seen it last night, and I had the bite marks to prove it. She was sweet as frosting on the surface, but underneath was a whole different story. As I sank down deeper, giving her more of my tongue, her fingertips moved softly through my hair. Her toes curled below me, gripping the rail of the bed frame.

I slid my first two fingers into her, and her body bucked off the mattress, her ass squeezed tight. I worked her clit slow and firm and eased her back into submission. Inside my pants, I was rock hard. Wiping my mouth on her thigh, I grazed that soft skin with my stubble. "I'm going to make you come like this, and then I'm going to get inside you, where I'm going to come again. And again. We clear?"

Her grip on my hair tightened. She lifted her face to meet my stare, and she said, "Crystal."

"But I need you to be *a little* bit quieter than last night." I dragged her ass closer to the end of the mattress, the seam of the edge making a line in that perfect flesh. "Because I don't want any interruptions."

Lisa pursed her lips, holding back a laugh. "Sorry."

"Don't you dare fucking apologize," I said and got back to business.

11

LISA

HAVING TO BE quiet was…*the best thing ever.* It intensified everything, not being able to let it out. After he spooned me right through a nap and back, I tottered to the master bathroom. I felt like a newborn foal on a nature show—like my legs didn't work right at all. He'd made me come so hard that my knees were actually knocking together. I braced myself on the edge of the sink and looked at his reflection, him watching me from the bed. His eyes moved down to my bare ass, and he shook his head. Smug. Satisfied. And *totally* entitled. I spun to get a look, and there, in glorious pink welts, was his handprint.

He rolled out of bed and followed me into the bathroom. Just as he was about to close the door, though, we heard a clattering of pans from downstairs.

Dave pinched the bridge of his nose. "I love her, but I'd *really* rather that we'd ended up here snowed in, just the two of us." He pressed into me from behind so that the marble edge of the countertop made a cold line against my thighs. "Because there's a pool table in the basement, and I *really* have to see this body on that felt."

With *that* thought making me shudder—fingers tangled in rope pockets, on my knees, goodness *gracious*—I turned to face him. "Dave, I need to be straight with you. I don't usually do things like this. Actually, I *never* do things like this. I've got a three-date minimum before things move to the bedroom."

Dave didn't seem fazed by this at all. "Wait. So you don't usually find yourself in the middle of a once-in-a-century natural disaster, stumble into a stranger's house, and have the best sex of your life?"

Little did he know that the most exciting date I'd had recently was a round of speed dating cut short by a restaurant kitchen fire. *Smoking hot!*

"Not since George W. was in office. And even then, it was only a tropical storm."

He snickered and pressed his still half-hard cock into my belly button. "Me neither, actually. I have the shittiest luck with women. It's like a sitcom."

Out of nowhere, I got a flash of jealousy. Him. With other women. I didn't like it. No, I did not. But I didn't have a claim on him, I knew that. How silly. How ridiculous. That a man like this, with a mattress empire and an estate, would want anything to do with little old me.

Except, before I could make some self-deprecating crack to let him off the hook, Dave said, "Listen, I don't want to go too far toward the Ouija board side of things, but I gotta tell you, Lisa..." He dug his hands into my ass more aggressively, and I watched his thick eyebrows shift into a serious line. "Maybe it's crazy, but I really just...*like you.* And I want to see where this goes."

Seven thousand butterflies took off in unison in my stomach. I raised my eyes to him, and he hoisted me up onto the countertop. "You do?"

"Fuck yeah, I do. Don't you feel it? The sparks?"

Sparks! Please. I could feel it in the heat between us and every time he touched me, but *sparks* wasn't even close. "More like a fire at a fireworks warehouse."

"You're goddamned right about that. So, what do you say? You want to set fire to this and see what happens?" He gave me another thrust. "Because I don't think we can fuck like we do without getting..." His eyes moved over my face. "Attached."

This man. He was over the top. He was clearly a die-hard romantic. He was also lovely and respectful and made a mean scrambled egg. He did things to me in bed that I didn't even know were possible. *And* he was some sort of prince!

"I'm not opposed to attached," I whispered, so overpowered by the moment that even my voice was unsteady.

"Good. And I love my grandma, but I don't give two shits about where you come from. I just want to get to know you. And fuck you senseless every chance I get. How does that sound..." He lifted my chin so he was looking me in the eye. "...princess?"

If he hadn't had me perched on the countertop, I think my knees would've gone straight out from under me then. "Pretty much perfect."

"Good girl," he said, tipping me back for a kiss.

But before I got lost in him all over again, I stopped him. "I'm determined to win her over, Dave. I won't let a lady in a Lenin hoodie scare me away."

"I've got no fucking doubt about that at all."

✧   ✧   ✧

WE CAME DOWNSTAIRS to find Dave's grandma on the sofa, with a hilariously huge bowl of popcorn in her lap and her mug of whipped cream nearby. On the big flat-screen television, Idris Elba as DCI John Luther was strolling through the wet streets of London with his hands jammed into his blazer pockets. I glanced at Dave, with his dimples and his brawn and his kind eyes, right then looking in the refrigerator and scratching his stubble thoughtfully and considering what looked like a whole roasting chicken for dinner. I glanced at Idris, still with his hands in his pockets and strolling along. Dave put the chicken on a cutting board and looped an apron over his head. Sorry, Idris. No comparison. Not to me.

"Honey! You were right!" Grandma said. "New season!" She smacked the sofa next to her, signaling for me to come take a seat. I glanced at Dave, and after sizing up the situation—appearing to scan for, I don't know what, a stack of tarot cards and *Witchcraft for Dummies*, probably—he gave me a reassuring look to say, *Yeah, go ahead.* "You want coffee? Tea? Something stronger?"

"Ooh," I said, taking a peek at the clock. "Can we drink at two p.m.?"

"All's fair in love and storms," Dave said, patting my ass. "Two hot toddies, coming up."

"Remember how I made them?"

Dave clicked his tongue against his teeth. "I watched your every move."

Heavens.

I made my way into the huge living area off the kitchen and took my place next to Grandma on the sofa. She thrust a fuzzy throw blanket into my arms and nudged an ottoman toward my feet. Then she offered me the popcorn and grabbed a remote, licking butter from her fingers. She pressed something, and the blinds went down on the row of huge picture windows. Instant home theatre. See also, *awesome.*

"Listen, honey," Grandma said, "Didn't mean to scare you earlier. I get a little carried away."

She didn't look at me when she said it. I felt like we were two cops on patrol, both looking out of the windshield as we cruised along.

"That's okay."

"It's just that he's my only little prince. His folks are gone, only child. Same old story."

Turning, I watched Dave in the kitchen, where he was crushing some garlic. He wiped the knife off on a dish towel and programmed something into the oven, giving me a perfect view of his yummy buns.

As if he could feel me looking at him, he met my stare and winked. He made a bottoms-up gesture and pointed at the stove, and then he gave me a single finger in the air to say, *Coming right up.*

A bony elbow jabbed me in the side. "You listening, hon?"

"Sorry. What was that?"

She passed the whole container of whipped cream to me, her eyes locked on me. Like a test. I considered the can and thought about going to get a spoon or a bowl or something. But, what the hell. When in Rome. I squirted a big dollop onto my tongue, and Grandma hooted. "I just want to make sure you're the right kind of girl."

I swallowed my mouthful of sweet cream. "I don't want to be rude…"

"Pffft. You say *rude,* I say *no bullshit.* Potato, potahto."

I handed the whipped cream back to her. "But I don't know him at all. We haven't even been out to eat together. What if he's a…I don't know…loud chewer? A slurper? A skimpy tipper? Maybe's not good enough for *me*," I said, totally joking. In my periphery, I saw him trussing up a chicken like he was on a cooking show. *Way too good for me, way too good.*

She snapped apart her bifocals and began cleaning them with her sweat-shirt, nodding somewhat sadly at the lenses. "He does slurp sometimes, but he always tips twenty-five percent. He's my person, honey. We're blood-bound. I want to see him happy."

"I understand that. I really do. But this isn't anything serious. We just met." As soon as I said it, I knew that was a lie. It might be really early, but I could feel it: the excitement, the hope, the connection. It was never too soon to feel that.

"When you've been around as long as me, you know which way the love-winds are blowing. He's roasting you a chicken, isn't he?" She raised a painted eyebrow, as if to say *roasted meats equal love.* "But I'll stop with the Ouija. I'll just let nature take its course."

"Promise? Because you really freaked me out!"

She chortled and then put a bony hand on my forearm and squeezed. Then she turned up the volume as Luther stepped into a grisly crime scene. "Promise," she said.

"And I promise I won't go breaking his heart," I whispered.

"Good enough for me," Grandma whispered back.

I settled down into the couch a little deeper, making sure there was room next to me for Dave, if and when he came to join us. I scooted closer to Grandma, and the smell of Bengay got slightly stronger.

But as I got comfy, I felt something poking into me from underneath. I scooted my tush side to side—there was definitely something there. Something large and hard. Thinking it had to be another remote, I took my feet from the ottoman and crouched down next to the sofa. I stuck my hand under my seat cushion, where I found…a cue ball.

I looked at Grandma, and Grandma looked at me, for just one fleeting instant, before she went back to *Luther* and shoved an enormous handful of popcorn into her mouth. I took the ball out from under my seat and put it on the sofa next to her. Grandma played totally dumb and didn't even look at it.

"Okay, Google," she'd said earlier. *"How do you test for royalty?"*

I considered the situation. No way. This woman couldn't possibly have gone completely fairy tale on me. Insanity. Madness. And yet…

Sure enough, as I plunged my hand back under the sofa, I found more round items—one of those big balls of rubber bands, a round lip balm container, and finally… I peered at the strange little something between my fingertips.

"Is this a pea?" I whispered.

She didn't answer right away, but instead waited for a gap in the dialogue and whispered back, "Wasabi edamame." And beamed.

THE END

THANK YOU

Thank you for reading ROYAL MATTRESS
by Nicola Rendell!

nicolarendell.com

Facebook:

www.facebook.com/AuthorNRendell

Twitter:

www.twitter.com/AuthorNRendell

IG:

www.instagram.com/cute_chameleon

Reader Group:

www.nicolarendell.com/reader-group

Newsletter:

http://eepurl.com/b9h7pn

IN A STRANGER'S BED

A Goldilocks Story

Sophie Jordan

Once upon a time Goldilocks became lost in the forest. She walked and
walked until she came upon a house…

T HE BUS WAS gone.

It took several moments to comprehend. Thea scanned the beautiful landscape. The green hills and mountains beyond. The navy blue skyline. Nature at its purest form. And no bus. She rotated in a small circle, searching for it as if it might suddenly materialize. Nope. Still no bus.

She was well and truly alone in the Highlands of Scotland.

In the distance, she heard a sheep bleat. It was a pitiful little sound that echoed precisely how pathetic she felt in this moment.

The wind swept over her, whipping hair into her eyes. She dragged it out of her face. A drizzling mist fell, but that had been pretty standard since she arrived in Scotland. She'd long given up on her flat iron and let her hair run wild. There was no help for it.

She looked to the spot where the bus had been parked. It had sat there, waiting as she and twenty-one other tourists roamed the mist-shrouded hills.

Everything about her surroundings felt magical. As though there really were fairies here like the tour guide had said. She could practically feel their eyes on her now, watching, whispering. She had been sucked in, so caught up in the wonder of this green-dappled land with its moaning winds that she had lingered too long.

Twenty-one tourists had boarded the bus without her. And left. She couldn't get over that fact. She'd been abandoned.

She eyed the sky reproachfully again. It wasn't evening yet, but she had seen very little of the sun on this trip. It would be fully dark soon. She couldn't just stand here in this cold drizzle. Night was coming. She'd freeze to death.

She swung her backpack off her shoulder and dug out her phone along with her itinerary that included all pertinent numbers. Reception was spotty out here. Wi-Fi nonexistent. Even so, she lucked out and managed to get through to the tour group company based out of Glasgow that she'd hired to get her around Scotland. Her luck ended though when an automated message came on stating their office was closed for the day. Fabulous.

At least she knew her group was returning to the Drovers Inn where they had stayed the night before. She just needed to meet up with them there. Somehow.

Heaving a great sigh, she tucked her phone and itinerary away again, slung her pack over her back, and started down the narrow road. Assumedly, it would lead her to a more-traveled motorway where she could flag down a car to take her to the Drovers Inn.

Except after half an hour she began to wonder if this road would ever lead anywhere.

She didn't remember it taking so long to get to the glen, but she had been an awestruck tourist with her face pressed to the window, reveling in the beautiful landscape. Scotland really was everything she had always dreamed. The perfect honeymoon.

Even minus the groom.

The drizzle turned into full-fledged rain. She looked up at the darkening sky as it unleashed torrents of water. Her sodden clothes felt like a hundred pounds weighing her down. It was getting harder to see in front of her. She took cautious steps, concentrating on not straying off the path or hitting a particularly slick spot. She could just imagine it. They'd find her corpse a year from now in some Scottish bog. Her grandmother would tell anyone who would listen that she had told Thea not to take this trip.

Grams always made her opinions very clear. Women should not travel alone. They should not take trips to faraway lands. They should marry and stay home and make babies.

Gina would be sad. She would cry. Maybe even blame herself a little. After all, Gina was a good friend who had encouraged Thea to take this vacation and get herself under the first big, brawny Scot she met. *Best way to get over a man was to get under one.*

Shaking away thoughts of her imminent demise, Thea squinted against the rain and gazed up at the deepening sky—then stopped hard. There was smoke in the distance. Off to her right. A curling trail of pale gray against the curtain of rain and descending night.

Excitement thrummed in her chest. It was the only proof of civilization she'd glimpsed since the bus abandoned her. She glanced down the road and then at the smoke again. She didn't think the source of that smoke could be too far away.

She hugged herself. It was getting colder. What if she kept to the road and no car came along? She could freeze to death while there was a house nearby. Venturing off-road didn't seem so risky when she thought about it in those terms.

Adjusting her grip on the straps of her backpack, she stepped off the path and set out, heading up the grassy-thick hill. She was glad she'd invested in some good tennis shoes for this trip. Even so, they weren't rainproof hiking boots. Those would have been handy. Her shoes were soaked, her socks squishing miserably around her feet. The ground was turning spongy and unstable beneath her, slowing her progress.

She kept a bead on that plume of smoke, convincing herself she was drawing closer to it. Bleating sheep sounded close, too, and she imagined they weren't enjoying the rain any more than she was.

With ugly pants of breath, she made it to the top of the hill, hoping the way down wasn't going to be treacherous. Even as exerted as she was, the cold was having its effect. Her teeth clacked together, and she was positive nothing felt as miserable as the combination of wet and cold. It was steep going down, and she stepped cautiously until she reached level ground.

She looked up through sheets of rain, searching for that plume of smoke again and following it down. *Finally.* The answer to her prayers. Civilization.

The house was nestled on the top of the next hill over. White walls. Shutters at the windows. Dark slate roof. Quintessentially Scottish. A smaller outbuilding sat beside it, along with a fenced pen.

She hurried ahead, minding her steps. Visibility was fast fading. She didn't want to turn an ankle. She slogged through the mud, teeth chattering, bones aching from the wet-cold. Rain sluiced her face, dripping off the numb tip of her nose. She wiped at her face hopelessly. The rain continued its assault.

She almost wept with relief when she reached the house. A small stone path led to the wood door. She staggered over the path, probably looking drunk. Light glowed from the windows. That, coupled with the smoking chimney, told her someone was home.

She pounded on the door with the side of her fist for what felt like minutes. Rain continued to beat down around her. Who didn't have a covered porch? In Scotland of all places where it rained a lot? Her teeth clacked together so hard her jaw ached.

Screw it. Circumstances were dire. With a muttered prayer, she gave up on knocking. Her hand circled the door latch. Turned. Pushed it open.

"Hello!" She stepped tentatively inside the warm interior of the cottage. It was heaven. The cessation of rain on her aching body felt like she'd crossed over into heaven.

A large fireplace crackled on the far side of the room. Her gaze scanned the cottage. No sight of anyone. The door clicked shut behind her, shutting out the biting cold.

"Hello!" she called out again, in case someone lurked somewhere out of her line of vision.

She hovered near the door, shivering, an ever-widening puddle encircling her feet. It didn't take long for awareness to return. She was still cold. Still wet. Still miserable.

The pop of the fire and crumble of charred wood were the only noises. She was alone. There was not a single living person inside the house.

She rotated in a small circle, assessing her surroundings. It was a cozy single room cottage with every amenity as far as she could see. A fully outfitted kitchen. Refrigerator. Oven and range, which even now held a steaming pot of something that smelled delicious. A large couch sat angled before the fire, and a large brass-framed bed covered with a quilt that looked like something from the previous century was pushed against the far wall across from the fireplace.

She strode into the kitchen area, wincing as she left a trail of water behind her. Leaning over the sink, she gathered up her mass of hair and wrung it out into the sink. That done, she turned and moved back toward the fireplace in the main room, holding out her hands for warmth.

As blissful as the heat felt on her hands, she still could not seem to get warm enough. She couldn't stop shivering. Her teeth continued to chatter. She was likely in danger of hypothermia as long as she remained in her wet clothes. She glanced around helplessly, wondering what to do. She was in a strange house. She didn't even know who lived here, but somebody obviously did. Somebody who could not have gone very far if they left the fire burning in the hearth and a pot simmering on the stove.

She couldn't feel her toes inside her shoes anymore. Desperate for more warmth, she stripped off her shoes and socks and flexed her naked toes in the thick fired-warmed rug, hissing in pain as sensation gradually returned in the form of tiny needle pricks.

Hugging herself, she rocked side to side before the fire, talking to herself and hoping that might get her teeth to stop clacking together so violently. Ah, hell. This wasn't cutting it. It had come down to self-preservation. She had to do what she had to do. She'd seen enough documentaries about surviving in the wild to know desperate situations called for desperate measures.

She wouldn't normally break into someone's house and help herself to their property (Gram's would have heart palpitations if she knew), but nothing about this scenario was normal.

Moving away from the fire, she told herself the owner of the house would understand. She stopped before a large bureau and opened the double doors, awarded with the sight of several long-sleeved shirts. She stroked a hand over the array of thick cotton and flannels. Was there ever anything so warm as flannel? She pulled one shirt free of its hanger, eager to wear it.

With a quick glance at the door, she snuck into the bathroom and undressed.

Hanging her wet clothes over the shower rod, she reached behind the curtain and turned the water on, cranking it to hot. Why not? She was freezing, and a hot shower would be the quickest way to warm up.

Naked, she hopped inside the shower, letting the warm water pound over her and praying no one chose this very moment to return home. She availed herself of the shampoo. Sadly, no conditioner was available, but she'd deal with the tangles later. She was warm and clean and not dead of hypothermia. She'd take her blessings.

Shutting off the water, she stepped out onto the well-worn bath rug. Pulling a fresh towel from a nearby shelf, she briskly dried herself. Catching sight of her hair in the small mirror above the sink, she rubbed the towel over it and then attempted to comb it into some semblance of order with her fingers. She didn't spy a brush or comb in the vicinity, but even if she did, using some stranger's brush felt too much of an invasion. She'd already borrowed his shower and shirt.

Fully dry, she slipped on the thick flannel shirt and opened the bathroom door, peering out cautiously. Satisfied no one had arrived home yet, she padded barefoot into the cottage.

The blue shirt hung to her knees, so fortunately she didn't feel too risqué. She flexed her bare toes on the wood floor as she moved warily about the living space. Oddly enough, her naked feet made her feel even more vulnerable than wearing some stranger's shirt. Bare feet seemed to say: *Hey, I'm home!*

Nerves stretched taut, she stared at the door. Imagined it opening. Imagined some grizzled old Scot stepping through it. She didn't know why she thought the man who lived here was old. She just did. The cottage was clearly a single-resident dwelling, and she's always envisioned hermits as old men. There was no sign of technology. No TV or computer or electronic devices of any kind. The guy who lived here definitely wasn't young.

In preparation for when he returned, a sea of explanations tripped through her mind. All the various things she could say the moment his eyes met hers in order to explain her presence in his house.

She hurried to the door and parted the curtains to peer out into the night. Rain and darkness stared back at her; the verdant green she'd come to associate with Scotland was gone, put to rest with the night.

Letting the curtains fall back, she moved into the kitchen, following the savory aroma of whatever was cooking in the pot on the stove. Her stomach growled. The tour bus had provided a sandwich, apple, and water at lunch, but that felt a lifetime ago. She never was one to skip a meal. That had been a bone of contention with both her exes. First Eric and then Charlie. The only boyfriends she ever had. Both guys thought she should eat less and hit the gym more.

Well, at least she could eat whatever she wanted without feeling guilty now. No more pointed glances at her plate. No more of those hated lifted eyebrows when she ordered dessert. And no more spending her money on a gym membership she didn't want. Half the time she lied anyway and didn't go to the gym. She'd tell Eric or Charlie she was going to the gym and then she'd go sit in a coffeehouse with a book and yummy drink.

No more pretending. Period.

No more trying to make herself fit with guys who only ever wanted to change her. For the first time in her life, she acknowledged she'd rather be alone than with a guy who felt all wrong. It was like a great weight lifted off her shoulders with that realization.

She'd tried explaining it to Grams. The funny thing was… Grams had been widowed forever. She'd lived most of her life without a husband. She was a strong, independent woman. No one told her what to do. No one dared criticize her. She ate as much dessert as she wanted.

She'd raised Thea all by herself after her parents died. Thea had been four when she went to live with her. She barely remembered her parents, but Grams had always been there. Every field trip. Every graduation. Every boy that came to the door, Grams was there to grill. Grams would never conform to a man's expectations of her. She was no wilting flower, so Thea didn't understand why she expected Thea to be one and marry a man who wanted her as long as she changed everything about herself.

She lifted the lid and picked up the wooden spoon resting nearby. She stirred the pot, her mouth salivating at the sight of chunks of meat, potatoes, and carrots in a brown gravy broth.

There was enough in the pot to feed an entire family and still leave leftovers. No one would notice if she ate one bowl. When the old man returned she'd offer to pay him back for everything. For borrowing his clothes, eating his food, for a lift to the nearest village.

Decision made, she plucked a bowl out from a cabinet and ladled a healthy portion for herself. She had to hand it to the old man who lived here. He didn't skimp on the meat and vegetables.

Charlie had liked soups and stews, but they'd been broth mostly. Not much else. He cut calories that way. He'd always been focused on their diets. Especially hers. She was a curvy girl: her hips, her ass, her D-size cups. That was how she was built. He had wanted all that to change, however. To shrink.

Hopefully Charlie was enjoying his newfound freedom without her. The thing that smarted the most was *he* had dumped *her* and not the other way around. She wished she'd had the courage to end it first.

At that regret, she made a sound of disgust as she went in search of a spoon, licking the bit of soup that had gotten on her thumb and moaning in appreciation. She could taste the butter. And what else was in there? Sherry? Whoever lived here, he could definitely cook.

Locating a spoon, she sat down at the kitchen table and dug in. She ate with gusto until the bowl was empty. Too bad there wasn't any bread around to mop up the last bit of broth. Sighing contentedly, she rubbed her stomach and stood from the table. Taking her bowl and spoon, she washed them out in the sink and put them away.

Moving back to the fire, she let the warmth sink into her bones. She glanced toward the door again. The rain and wind were really picking up. She felt a stab of concern. What could be keeping the man who lived here? He couldn't have meant to be gone long or he wouldn't have left a pot simmering on the stove. She hoped he was okay.

Yawning, she settled down on the couch and sank into the well-worn cushions. Blinking, she trained her gaze on the door, practicing in her head what she was going to say. She'd begin with an apology and segue into how she had been stranded and had no choice but to take shelter in his house.

Her lids grew heavy and she gave herself a small shake, determined to stay awake, determined that the patter of rain, crackle of fire, and her full belly not lull her to sleep. She refused to be caught in such a vulnerable position.

With her head resting on a couch cushion, she curled on her side. Tucking her knees to her chest, she pulled the delicious flannel shirt down to her ankles. She would lay like this for a few minutes. No more than that. She wouldn't close her eyes.

She wouldn't fall asleep.

Tired and warm, her belly now full from her tasty meal, Goldilocks fell fast asleep, unaware that she had taken shelter in the house of a foul-tempered bear.

T HEA RELEASED A startled gasp as a roar ripped her from sleep.

For a moment she couldn't place where she was. Bewildered, she thought she was back in her apartment in Phoenix and her roommate was playing some kind of trick on her. Gina would do something like that.

But then it all flooded back. She was on a couch. In a strange house in Scotland.

And she wasn't alone.

The man who lived here had returned and walked in on her asleep on his couch—*in his shirt*. Precisely what she had hoped wouldn't happen. She'd wanted to greet him and introduce herself. Explain her situation.

She froze, feeling like prey caught in the sights of a predator. She stared straight ahead. Directly at a pair of denim-clad legs in front of her.

Mortified, she popped up in a sitting position and dropped her feet to the floor. Her blonde hair sprang into her face. She dragged the out-of-control mass back. Her hair had mostly dried, and she could only imagine the bird's nest it looked like. Her gaze shot to the stranger's glowering face.

Not an old man. Not by a long shot. *Crap.* A young man. She processed this with her quickly waking mind.

He was young. Maybe only a few years older than herself, but that was hard to know for certain. The scowl on his face undoubtedly aged him. Too bad it didn't detract from his hotness factor. Gina would call him lickable. His dark hair and close-cropped beard glistened wetly. He wore a slicker that dripped water onto his floor. He hadn't bothered to take it off yet, and he didn't seem to care. He must have spotted her right away when he entered the house.

The longer she stared at him, that scowl of his seemed to deepen.

"Hello," she greeted, wincing when the word slipped out sounding like a question.

Typical this would happen to her. She would have to get stranded in some hot Scot's house when she was at a low point in her life and looking her absolute worst. Gina would think this was hysterical.

She futilely tried to twist her wild hair into a ponytail. It was useless without a hairband to help. The instant she let go of the mass it sprang loose all around her in wild waves.

"I said: who the hell are you?" His words were heavy with a brogue she felt right down to her toes.

He's asked her a question before? It must have been the bellow that woke her.

She moistened her lips. "I'm Thea." She paused for his reaction although she didn't know why. She didn't expect her name to make a difference to him. She was no one to him. "I was on a tour bus and got left behind. I started walking and it started pouring, but I-I found your house and—"

"Let me guess," he snarled. "They took you out to visit some magical faerie glens." He spit out the word *faerie* like it was the ugliest of epithets.

"Y-yes."

He whirled away with a stinging curse. He continued to mutter under his breath as he moved about in such a rage that she eyed the door, wondering if she should take her chances with the cold Scottish night. God knew this strapping, virile man could snap her like a twig if he chose.

Standing, she inched that direction, stopping when he whirled on her, blocking her path.

She yelped and took a hasty step back, craning her neck to look up at him. God, he was tall.

"Did it ever occur to ye that those faerie glens are a bunch of shite? Something drummed up for numpty tourists from America?"

"Numpty?" she echoed blankly. "What is that? A candy bar?"

"Numpty," he repeated, his tone much harsher. Rolling his eyes, he clarified, "Idiotic. Stupid."

"Oh!" Offended, she squared her shoulders. "Tourism is good for the economy, sir. I would think that—"

His blue eyes widened. He looked fit to kill, and she knew she had said the wrong thing. She didn't know what could have been the *right* thing to say, but clearly she had missed it.

"Good for the economy?" He advanced on her.

She retreated until the backs of her legs hit the couch and could go no farther.

He continued, glaring down at her. "Tour buses tearing through my land? Tourists traipsing all over my property with their cameras, dropping their candy wrappers and terrifying my sheep? You call that good for the economy? Whose? No' mine!"

Her stomach bottomed out. "The faerie glens are on your property?"

He nodded once, his blue eyes cutting and deep. "And I can assure you there is nothing magical about them. I've lived my whole life here. It's simply land. Simply my farm that's been in my family for generations."

She nodded again, feeling wretched. "I didn't know that." She moistened her lips. "The tour guide never mentioned we were trespassing—"

"It's no' trespassing. It's called freedom to roam—one of my country's least ingenious ideas. Two years ago a couple hikers happened upon my property. They took some video and posted it on YouTube and proclaimed the glens magical. And there you have it." He snapped his fingers. "My family's farm is invaded nearly every day of the year by you locusts." His top lip lifted in a sneer.

She flinched. Heat burned her face. She was a locust. "I'm sorry. I did not know."

He looked her up and down. "And now I have one of you in my house. The one place I thought myself safe from you people."

He stared at her a long moment, raking his gaze over her as though seeing her for the first time. "And you're wearing my shirt. Is nothing sacred?" he bit out the words, his straight white teeth a striking contrast against his dark beard.

"My clothes were soaking wet."

"So you just helped yourself to my clothes?" He shook his head. "Typical."

"I was on the verge of hypothermia!" she said hotly, finally getting angry. She wasn't to blame for every wrong done to this man. How was she to know her tour bus was one of an army driving through his property?

"Maybe you should have taken a trip to the Bahamas. Can't get hypothermia there."

"Trust me! I'm wishing I had. Just get me to the village and I'll catch the first bus to Glasgow and then hop on a plane home." Because really, this trip wasn't going the way she planned at all. But then, the way she had planned it involved Charlie. The two of them together on a romantic honeymoon. She grimaced. Romantic had never been a word that could be applied to them.

They hardly had sex in their years together, and when they did she was always the initiator. In fact, it always felt as though he were doing her a favor when they did it. That didn't do great things for a girl's ego.

Engaged couples had a hard time keeping their hands off each other—or so she'd been led to believe. Not them though. That should have been her first warning they weren't right for each other.

When Charlie broke off the engagement, she wasn't really surprised. *We're just not a good fit.* His words had stung, but she couldn't disagree with him. They weren't a good fit. Her boyfriend before him hadn't been a good fit either.

She seemed destined for bad fits.

The Scot still glared at her as though she were some unwelcome critter that had crawled beneath the door into his house.

She dug out her composure and took a deep breath. "I'm very sorry. If you would be kind enough to drive me to the nearest village I'll get out of your hair. And please, let me pay you for the use of your shower."

"You used my shower too?" He glanced toward the bathroom. "What is this? A Holiday Inn?"

She winced and exhaled. Might as well confess everything. "And I'll pay you for the soup too."

His gaze whipped toward the stove. "You ate my dinner?"

"There's plenty left," she assured him, offering a weak smile. "It was very good."

He shook his head and inhaled sharply, as though fighting for endurance. "I don't want your money. I want to be left in peace."

She nodded and motioned to the front door. "Then by all means, let's get going—"

"We can't. There is only one road to the village and it's flooded at the moment. It happens when it rains. I'll check on it in the morning."

He stomped away and wrenched open the bathroom door. She flinched at his angry movements.

She stared after him in shock. He could not be serious. She could not stay the night—*maybe longer!*—with this awful bear of a man.

He looked back at her, his blue eyes scathing. "Don't worry. I'm as anxious to see you away from here as you are."

"So what am I supposed to do?" How could a pair of eyes be so piercing?

"I would tell you to make yourself comfortable, but it appears you already have."

She had never felt so thoroughly disliked by a person. She wondered if she would feel this wounded if he wasn't so good-looking. If he didn't have those cutting eyes and strong jawline and deep brogue. If there wasn't that delicious-looking beard, a dark pelt that beckoned her fingers.

She gave herself a mental slap. He was a sheep farmer, for God's sake. He was a broody Scottish hermit farmer, and she could almost hear Gina's voice in her head. *What are you waiting for, Thea? Jump his bones. Get feral with that farmer.*

God. She really needed to get out of her if she was fantasizing about sex with this thoroughly unpleasant man.

"Maybe I should just go," she said quickly, the words a rush.

"Out there?" He laughed roughly. "Didn't you hear me? The road is flooded and it's still raining." He waved toward the door. "You'll freeze to death … if you don't fall into a bog and drown."

She shrugged. She didn't care. She'd take her chances with the storm.

She moved to the door and lifted up her pack. She glanced back at him. His big body blocked the door to the bathroom where her clothes hung to dry. She glanced down at herself in his too-big T-shirt. It would offer little protection against the elements.

"Don't be a fool." As though to illustrate his point, he strode across the house, right past her, and yanked open the front door. Immediately a gust of wet wind swept into the house. Shivering, she stared out the door into that blackest night she had ever seen. The cold reached out to her, grabbed her in its grip and squeezed. "You'll die out there," he announced.

She flinched at the words, knowing them for truth. He might be the rudest man alive, but she was stuck here. Stuck with him.

And he was stuck with her.

He shut and locked the front door. Turning, he disappeared into the bathroom, closing the door between them with a resounding thud. She was grateful for that barrier. It put distance between them and would give her a little time to compose herself … and try not to think about her underwear and bra hanging over the shower he was about to use.

Running water soon carried from the other side of the door and she knew he was doing the same thing she had done—ridding himself of his sodden clothes and stepping beneath the warm spray of water.

Closing her eyes in one weary blink, she rubbed her fingers against her forehead. Of all places she had to get stranded, it was with this surly Scot. Why couldn't he have been a kind old man?

She claimed the blanket draped over the back of the couch, settling in for the night. With a huff, she arranged the afghan around her. Sleep. That's what she would do. Sleep so the night would pass quickly and when she woke she would be able to leave this place.

The shower stopped and she tensed. She couldn't help it. She was stuck in this house all alone with a stranger. Totally at his mercy. For some reason, she didn't think he would harm her. He could have done that already if he was inclined. He didn't want to be bothered with her. Murdering her would be too much of an inconvenience for him.

The bathroom door yanked open and the jerk himself emerged.

Wearing only a towel.

Oh, holy hell. Her gaze traveled over him. She'd known he was big beneath his clothing. He'd towered over her, but she had no idea his body looked like this.

Charlie had worked out and subscribed to *Men's Health* magazine, reading every issue cover to cover. He'd wanted a body like this, but could never quite manage it. Hotty Scotty, on the other hand, was built. Toned and hardbodied. Apparently working a farm and running sheep in the Highlands got you washboard abs, muscular shoulders, toned biceps, and a narrow waist.

And a crappy disposition.

She gulped against the sudden dryness of her throat. He might be a grump, but she was still female and all her girl parts (her long-neglected girl parts) were doing somersaults.

Water beaded his chest and arms and traveled down his happy trail, disappearing beneath his towel. She couldn't help following that line of water with her eyes, and that mortified her. She shouldn't be so affected. He might have a body that belonged on the cover of a romance novel, but that didn't change the fact he was a jerk.

His lips curled in a smirk, and she knew he was aware of how he looked and his impact on her. A man didn't look like him and not know.

He strolled into his room, presenting her with his back as he opened the doors to his bureau. The view of his back was as lovely as the front. Nicely formed, muscles and sinew rippling with his movements.

He pulled out a pair of briefs and glanced over his shoulder at her, one dark eyebrow cocked as his hand came to the edge of the towel knotted at his waist. "You gonna keep watching me?"

She gasped. "You're getting dressed right here?"

His blue eyes glittered, clearly still annoyed with her. "This is *my* house. My space you've invaded. So. Yeah. I'm going to do what I normally do."

Proving that point, he undid the towel. She dropped her face into the couch cushion as the towel dropped. She only caught a flash of skin. No clear visual of his body. For the first time she felt gratitude and regret simultaneously.

His chuckle fell warm and deep, like his voice, and sent goose bumps along her skin.

After a moment, she heard him moving around in the kitchen. A glass clinked and she lifted her head, making certain there wasn't a naked man behind her.

He was wearing boxer briefs. The fabric hugged his ass. An ass that looked like it could bounce quarters.

"Did you enjoy my stew?" He didn't turn around as he asked the question.

"Y-yes. It was delicious. Thank you."

He ladled himself a bowl. "Is it a habit of yers? Breaking into houses and helping yourself to clothes and food and whatever else strikes your whim?"

She bristled. "I told you. I was stranded and freezing. And I'll pay you for any—"

He held up a hand, cutting her off as he sank into his chair at the table. "You've said as much. The point is … it's no' right. You never should have been on my land."

To that, she could only claim ignorance, but she knew he didn't see that as a valid argument so she held silent.

He was arrogant and rude and … why the hell couldn't she stop staring at him? Even as he sat there, bare-chested at the table, feeding himself, he looked like someone who could be on TV. He was that beautiful.

Not perfect, mind you. That would be boring. He had the kind of face you could stare at for hours. Artists would want to paint it. She did, and she was just an art teacher. She hadn't sat in front of a canvas in years. Once upon a time she'd wanted to paint, but Grams and Eric and Charlie had convinced her it wasn't practical. No one made a living painting.

His mouth was fascinating. Her stomach flipped as she gazed at it. Full and broad. The top lip dipped sharply at the center. She wanted to trace the shape. Recreate it with a brushstroke. His nose was slightly crooked at the center. Likely broken at some point. Had he been in a fight? Or was it the result of a farmyard accident? A sheep gone rogue? She giggled at the thought, imagining a sheep kicking him square in his too pretty face.

He glanced up at her, pausing with the spoon near his mouth. "You're a strange bird."

"Me?" She pressed a hand to her chest. "You're the one acting like Shrek because I invaded your precious space."

"Shrek?" He blinked those brilliant blue eyes at her.

"Yeah. The movie."

He stared blankly.

"Wow. You really should get out more." She glanced around again. As already noted, there was no TV. She spotted a bookcase full of books. That must bet he extent of his entertainment. "Shrek is this hermit ogre who lives in a remote swamp. Kinda like you."

He shook his head. "You're a nutter."

She could only infer that to be an insult. Her indignation burned hot again. "And you're rude." She'd never met a more unpleasant man in all her life. Sure. She had basically compared him to an ogre, but he was acting like one.

He scraped his spoon against the inside of his bowl, not even looking at her. "You think it such a good idea to insult your host?"

"You've insulted me. Repeatedly."

"And you've invaded my home." He shrugged one well-formed shoulder and continued to eat. "How is it you came to be here alone? Did you wander off from your family and friends?"

"I'm traveling alone."

He raised his eyes to her, looking at her for the first time in several minutes. Even across the distance the blue of his eyes was vivid and intense and made her feel shivery inside. "You came to Scotland all by yourself?"

"This is the twenty-first century. Women can travel alone. We even get to vote and drive cars too."

He grumbled something under his breath that sounded close to *smart-ass*. "Maybe if you brought someone along with you on this trip, you wouldn't have wandered off and gotten lost."

Why did the question feel like a dig to her intelligence? "I didn't get *lost*. The bus left me."

"If you had been traveling with someone else, that wouldn't have happened."

The words reminded her how alone she was in this world, and she resented the hell out of him for the reminder. Grams lived in a retirement community for active seniors. There was Gina, but she had a boyfriend who was on the verge of proposing. Soon Thea would be living alone.

"I don't need a babysitter. I'm an independent woman. I can take care of myself."

He gave her a pointed look, his gaze skimming her in his too big shirt. "Right."

She glared at him as he finished eating. Really, there was nothing else to look at. Nothing nearly so pretty at least. Too bad he didn't have a personality to match his looks.

Sighing, she stood and fetched her phone from her backpack. Might as well check. Still no signal.

"That won't work out here," he answered. "No' in this storm. Even in good weather it's spotty."

"What kind of place can't get service?" she asked testily.

"The kind of place nature intended. Without unnecessary technology or annoying people checking their Instagram every five seconds or taking selfies."

"Oh, you've heard of Instagram?" She arched an eyebrow. "I figured you've been living out here in the sticks forever, Shrek."

He scowled and got up, bowl in hand as he moved to the sink. "I know things."

Her gaze crawled over that body. She couldn't help it.

She was twenty-five years old and had precisely two *failed* relationships where the sex had been less than stellar, no matter how much she had tried to make it good. She'd tried to satisfy her partners. She'd tried to satisfy herself. It didn't matter. As much as she pretended—and even lied—sex for her had always been … unsatisfying.

After her broken engagement, she figured that was her lot. Eric and Charlie didn't fit. She guessed no man ever would.

I know things.

His words echoed through her and took on an entirely different meaning. She flushed hot. She knew he didn't intend for her to interpret his words in a sexual way, but that was what her overactive imagination and overwrought senses heard.

She had no doubt he knew a few things, all right.

Get your head out of the gutter, Thea.

This guy was out of her league. She never would have even attempted to talk to someone who looked like him back home. Not that she came into contact with men like him working at a middle school. She'd met Charlie in college at a park when her dog peed on his leg. Not the most auspicious start to a relationship, she knew. Somehow they ended up on a date after that.

He washed his bowl in the sink and then moved to the fireplace. He added a few logs and stirred the fire. She watched his back, mesmerized at the play of muscles underneath his smooth skin.

Standing, his gaze came to rest on her. "If the road is clear, I'll take you to the village in the morning."

The morning. Why did that seem so far away?

She nodded jerkily. "Thank you."

He moved about the house, turning off all the lights. The house was saved from complete darkness due to the fire. It cast a deep veil of gold-red over the interior of the house.

"Can I get you another blanket?" he asked gruffly, gesturing to the blanket she'd already covered herself with.

"I'm fine. Thank you."

He stepped up to his bed and removed a pillow from it. Turning, he advanced on her couch. She grimaced inside. Either he was offering the pillow to her or planning to smother her with it. Either way, she preferred he kept his distance.

She shook her head and squeezed the couch pillow tucked beneath her cheek tighter. Still, he kept on coming.

His frowned, extending the pillow. "Take it," he said.

God. He was so close she could smell him. He smelled like the soap she had used. And something else. Something inherently male and primal that made her stomach muscles quiver.

She snatched the pillow from him, wanting him to go away. Desperate for him to go to his own bed and leave her alone, to take himself as far as possible from her inside this house.

She shoved the pillow under her head and watched his easy gait as he walked to his bed and climbed in. The firelight did amazing things to his skin and body. The palms of her hands tingled with the hungry need to touch. To stroke and feel him for herself.

This was insane. She blamed it on Gina. Her friend's parting words rang through her mind. *Get yourself under the first big, brawny Scot you meet.*

Thea knew Gina would heartily approve of this guy for her to work out all her sexual fantasies on, but that wasn't why she came on this trip. She came here to enjoy herself ... to maybe even find herself and think about her future. She'd already figured out she would rather be alone than with douchebags who didn't love or appreciate her. No more guys who didn't *fit*. No more men who wanted to change her. She'd either feel *right*, feel *good*, when she was with a guy or she wouldn't be with a guy at all.

This fixating on a stranger in the bed across from her was wholly unhealthy. She was confident he didn't entertain any sexual thoughts about her.

She listened as he settled into bed, the mattress squeaking slightly under his weight. His movements eventually stilled and there was nothing but the pop of the fire, the howl of the storm outside, and rush of blood in her ears.

She couldn't hear his breathing, but strangely enough ... she thought she *felt* it. As though it matched in rhythm to her own. Inhale. Exhale. Inhale. Exhale.

Sweet Tater Tots. She was losing it. Her grandmother had told her she was crazy when she said she was still going on her honeymoon. Grams insisted Thea needed to stay home and patch things up with Charlie or she was going to end up one of those old ladies living with a bunch of cats. Never mind she was allergic to cats and Grams knew that.

You've messed up two relationships now, Thea. You may never get another chance. You're not getting younger. Or thinner.

Thea rolled onto her side and curled her knees to her chest. She shoved Grams's voice out of her head and closed her eyes.

She could not *feel* his breathing.

She could not feel his stare from the bed. He was not looking at her with those brilliant blue eyes of his and thinking naughty things. No, that was only Thea. It was all in her head. *Her* crazy head.

She hugged herself and tried to make herself as small as possible.

She kept her eyes closed. Even if she couldn't fall asleep, she could at least fake it. The night would pass. She'd lay here and wait for the morning.

Face to face with the bear, Goldilocks had never seen so fierce a creature.
His hungry eyes, his snapping teeth, his dark pelt…

SOMEHOW THEA DID fall asleep. And she dreamed of him.

She dreamed of that hot body over hers, skin to skin. Pushing and pulling. His hands. His mouth. The delicious weight of him driving into her, taking her so close. Right to the brink of shattering.

She opened her eyes to the fire-cast room with a ragged gasp, her body shaking and panting, just shy of orgasm. She released a mewling whimper, her frustration acute. She'd been close. Closer than she ever came with Eric or Charlie, and this had been a mere dream.

She dragged a hand over her face, her skin feverish to the touch. God, she was pathetic. A woman with two long-term relationships under her belt should have more experience with orgasms.

She was curled on her side on the couch, her shirt—or rather his shirt—hiked up around her thighs. Her hand pressed between her legs, her fingers buried in her heat. She was throbbing there, her sex aching. In her sleep, she'd sought to relieve that ache. The base of her palm pushed right against her bare sex, grinding into her clit as she drove her fingers into her clenching channel.

She wrenched her hand away with a soft gasp and buried the treacherous thing under her pillow as though needing to restrain herself.

Immediately she began to rationalize her behavior. Dreaming about him wasn't so unusual. He'd been on her mind before falling asleep, and didn't people usually dream about things that weighed heavily on their minds? She'd been obsessing over him, and why wouldn't she be? She was trapped in a house with him. It was only natural.

Except the nature of her dream wasn't exactly natural. Masturbation wasn't normal. Not for her.

She couldn't remember the last time she'd had an arousing dream. Maybe never. Of course it had been ages since she last had sex. Even months before Charlie broke off their engagement. It hadn't really bothered her because the sex had never been noteworthy. She'd actually convinced herself sex wasn't all that important in a relationship—or in life.

She wished she knew what time it was. Then she would know how long she had to wait until morning.

"Come here."

The deep voice sent a wave of gooseflesh over her. Still, she doubted her ears. Why was he awake? And why would he be speaking to her?

"I said: come here."

Okay, there was no denying it that time. He was definitely talking to her. She lifted her head and looked toward his bed.

He was sitting up, his upper body propped against the headboard of the bed. He looked relaxed and casual, and yet there was something restrained about him that made her body tingle. An animal magnetism. Like a creature of the jungle, watching its prey and biding its time.

Maybe it was that body of his. It was born of labor and sweat. Muscled and ridged and lean as any warrior's. It was like he walked right off the screen of *Braveheart*. He only needed the requisite war paint.

"You want me to come over there?" Still requiring confirmation, she pointed at the bed.

He nodded. Just once. Hard and curt, his expression void of emotion.

She swung her legs over the couch and walked toward his bed with hesitant steps, stopping near the edge, a careful distance from him.

"You're awake," he announced, his deep voice an accusing growl.

"So are you," she countered.

His blue eyes glinted in the dim light cast from the fire. "You were making some verra interesting sounds in yer sleep."

God, that voice. It was too hot. *He* was too hot.

Heat fired her cheeks. "I'm sorry. I didn't mean to disturb you."

"That's what you've done though." He paused a beat and she wondered if this was where she should apologize again. "From the moment you invaded my house, you've disturbed me."

"Was I talking in my sleep? I do that sometimes."

"No. I wouldn't call it talking, but you were making sounds."

Her pulse skittered beneath her skin. She was afraid she knew what kind of sounds she'd made. Her body still hummed with need, so she had a fairly good idea.

"I'll try not to disturb you anymore."

He stared hard at her, unmoving. Silent and taciturn.

She started to turn around, figuring he was done with her.

"Come here."

She figured wrong.

Now this was the point when she should ignore him. She should keep going. Return to the couch and slip beneath her blanket. That would be the safe and logical thing to do. That would be what middle school art teacher Thea Hoover from Phoenix would do—a woman who only ever chose safe men.

Men who didn't work out. Who never worked out. Who ended up being all wrong.

Even though he was commanding her to come closer, he wouldn't stop her if she turned around and went back to the couch. She sensed that about him. He wasn't some sadist out to hurt her. He was your everyday run-of-the-mill sheep farmer hermit.

Who wanted her to come closer.

Holy hell.

Moistening her lips, she walked forward on legs that felt as steady as Jell-O. She stopped when her knees brushed the mattress.

He sat forward. The covers pooled around his waist. He gripped the hem of her shirt where it hung to her knees.

"Those sounds you were making…" His eyes fastened on her face as he spoke. "You sounded like a woman getting fucked."

His outrageous words ran through her like a bolt of lightning, straight to her aching core. "Oh." The single word escaped her, small and useless.

"But how can that be?" His voice was soft and dangerous. She felt it. It moved through her like a curl of heat. He angled his dark head, those vivid eyes of his intent on her face. "You're all alone over there on my couch."

She nodded wildly in agreement, on the verge of saying it was impossible.

But then his hand was under her shirt.

Oh. God. He was touching her. His fingertips grazed the tops of her thighs. She felt like her legs might give out.

"Were you touching yourself over there?" his deep voice husked. "Fucking yourself with your wee hand?"

She was standing with her legs slightly parted. There was just enough room for his hand to find its way between her legs, but even so she adjusted her feet involuntarily, parting her legs wider, granting him access to her throbbing center.

His breathing hitched. "Let's see then."

She wasn't wearing any panties. With no barrier, his fingers slid against her folds. She cried out at the first touch of his fingers on her aching flesh.

His pupils looked darker, larger. "Oh, you're soaking wet," he growled, his fingers brushing over her clit.

This couldn't be real. She was still dreaming.

"Is this for me?" His finger moved on, dipping to her opening.

She bit her lip to stop herself from crying out.

"Answer me," he commanded.

She swallowed back a sob and nodded, broken and bared before him and not caring. "Y-yes."

His thumb moved up, brushing her swollen clit and she shuddered, her hand dropping to the edge of the bed for support. Her head bowed and her hair fell in a tangled curtain, hiding her face. She was grateful for that. Grateful he could not see her eyes rolling back in her head.

"I could hear you from here. All those little moans." He pushed up with his thumb, pressing just a fraction inside her, but it was enough. Enough to make her gasp. Enough to push her right to the brink of orgasm. "I could smell your pussy from across the room. So wet and cock-hungry."

She swallowed back a cry at his filthy words. No one had ever said such dirty things to her. It should horrify her. She should stumble away and slap his face like a good little girl who grew up on casseroles and Sunday church.

Instead, she shook. She was so close.

"You're right there and I've barely done anything to you."

He was wrong. He'd done far more than any man had when it came to getting her off.

Gripping the edge of the bed with both hands now, she closed her eyes and bore down harder on that thumb, riding it and seeking more pressure.

Then, all at once, his hand was gone.

What the hell? She almost fell forward, but her hands on the mattress saved her. She bit back a cry of frustration at the sudden loss and lifted her eyes to him.

His expression had gone dark and feral, and she marveled she had done that to him.

He brought his thumb to his mouth and tasted her. His eyes drifted shut as though savoring her. As though she was something sweet and delicious. Her stomach dipped. Oh. God. Charlie would *never* have done that. He would have thought it disgusting. He wasn't a proponent of cunnilingus in any degree, and he had convinced her she wasn't either.

Clearly she had been lying to herself.

He slid his thumb out of his mouth and leaned forward, bracing his arms on the bed between them, his biceps strained and flexing. "You have two choices."

Her stomach muscles fluttered. She watched him raptly, mesmerized by his face, his beautiful lips as they formed those words in a voice that was the embodiment of sex.

Without tearing his eyes from her, he nodded toward the couch. "You either turn around and go back to that couch and stop touching yourself and making those little come-and-fuck-me sounds."

Everything inside her sank and deflated like a dying balloon at that option. She didn't want to do that.

"Or…" His eyes were blue fire. Heavy-lidded and intense. He leaned forward like he might lunge off the bed at any moment. "You join me on this bed ready to fuck."

A heavy breath pushed out of her lungs. Well, that left no room for vagueness.

He was out of the bed. With two strides he was in front of her. Tall and broad, a veritable wall. An impressive erection tented the front of his briefs, proof of his desire.

He followed her gaze to his cock and then looked up at her.

She opened her mouth and stammered, "I-I…"

"Make a decision. Go run to yer couch or get in my bed. No misunderstandings. No games." His hot gaze crawled over her face, reading God knew what in her expression.

You can do this, Thea. You owe it to yourself. You can have a fling. Take what you want for once in your life with no guilty voice saying you can't.

He reached for her and threaded his fingers through her unruly hair. "What's it gonna be, Goldilocks? You gonna take what you want?"

It wasn't arrogance. Okay, he was arrogant, but it was the truth. She did want this. She wanted him. And he knew it.

She released a shaky breath and nodded jerkily.

In that moment she felt everything crumble away like bits of sediment from a cliff. Her grandmother giving her all kinds antiquated misogynistic advice. Boyfriends who only made her feel bad about herself.

They vanished. They were gone. Things of the past.

There was only now. This. Him. Her.

His big hand flexed in her hair. "Say it. Say the words."

She swallowed and stopped nodding. That was fair. Consent was important. He deserved to hear it from her before they went any further. More than that. He *needed* to hear it. And she needed to say it.

"Yes. I want to join you in the bed." There. That sounded nice. Polite.

"No," he bit out, his gaze hard and demanding. "Say you want to fuck. Because that's what this will be."

Her belly fluttered. She swallowed against the lump in her throat. "I want to fuck you."

He plucked her off her feet. A small yelp escaped her as she flew through the air and landed in the center of his bed. She barely stopped bouncing before he was there, the great lean and muscled length of him over her, one knee sliding unerringly between her thighs, his slight leg hair tickling her skin.

Her pulse hammered wildly at her throat as she looked up at him. She knew her eyes must be enormous in her face. She couldn't even manage a blink.

His hand gripped the neckline of her flannel shirt and paused. His blue eyes looked silvery blue in the firelight as he gazed down at her. "No going back now, Goldilocks. You're mine." That said, he yanked down on her shirt. Buttons popped and flew loose, flying in every direction. She guessed he didn't care about ruining his shirt.

Air flowed over her bare body, but she wasn't cold. Not with his scorching gaze sweeping over her. She felt on fire.

She tried not to fidget beneath his scrutiny, but old insecurities reverberated through her. She hated they were here, intruding now.

Too heavy. Too big. Too plump. Lay off the Dr Pepper, Thea.

She had never been this exposed. The firelight revealed everything, and she longed for darkness. She'd spent junior high and high school flattening her breasts with sports bras, but that had done nothing to stop them from reaching melon-size proportions.

She brought both her hands up to cover herself, but he snatched hold of her wrists and pinned them above her head. "Don't."

His gaze fixed on her breasts. She tried not to squirm under his scrutiny.

"This is what you were hiding under my shirt?" He tsked as he released one of her wrists. She hissed and arched as one of his big hands palmed her breast. "Such pretty tits need to be worshipped."

His touch grew firmer, almost rough as he handled her—and she relished it.

She arched her spine, crying out and thrusting her chest out for more. He fondled the heavy globe, pinching her nipple between thumb and forefinger. His other hand followed suit.

He squeezed and massaged both mounds, lifting them and pushing them together while tweaking the tips. "Beautiful," he growled.

She writhed wildly and cried out, bearing down and riding his thigh, desperate for the pressure on her throbbing sex.

Her breasts had never been lavished such attention. She felt owned. That was the only word for it. Marked and possessed by a man who knew how to manipulate her body.

He added his second knee between her open thighs and forced her legs wide. He still wore his briefs but she felt him, pole-hard, prodding into her bare sex. He started to grind against her and that was amazing. She was ready to fly apart, and he hadn't even penetrated her.

He bent his head and sucked a nipple deep into the cavern of his mouth. He used his tongue and teeth, and just like that she came in a violent burst, shuddering beneath him.

She buried her fingers in his hair and held him close to her breast, content to keep him there forever as she ground his fully erect cock into her pussy.

"That's all it takes to get you off?" he growled around one distended nipple, scoring it with his teeth. "Och, you're going to be a hot fuck."

"That's never happened before," she gasped, still trembling in the aftershocks of her release. For some reason, she wanted him to know that. To know that his hands and mouth and cock were the first to make her shoot off like a rocket before they even had sex.

He resumed sucking her breasts, squeezing and holding them for his feasting mouth, growling with appreciation as she resumed rubbing against his cock, trying to find the perfect angle. "Too…much," she moaned, her head lolling on the bed.

"We haven't even started. I could spend hours on these tits."

He was a miracle. A sex god. She'd already climaxed, but he had her right there at the edge again. She felt like she was on the brink of death.

Her hands dropped between them, diving under the waistband of his briefs to take him in both hands, and she realized she would need both hands.

"There you go," he grunted in approval. "Take my cock out."

He was big. Bigger than anything she ever had inside her. She stroked him in awe, touching the fat crown of him. She traced the slit, rubbing in the pre-cum that leaked out. The head of him swelled and grew tighter under her fingers.

"Stop." He grabbed her wrist. His blue eyes locked on hers. "I need a condom. When I come, it's going to be inside you." He lifted his head and looked around a bit wildly, as though trying to place where he'd stashed his condoms.

He started to pull away and she locked her thighs around his waist, loath to let him go from her for even a second. She needed him inside her now. More than she'd ever needed anything on this earth she needed to feel this man's cock buried deep inside her. "I'm on birth control."

He paused and looked down at her.

She took advantage of his hesitation and brought the head of him to her opening, gliding the bare tip of him over her wetness. "I have an IUD."

She'd gotten it a year ago when she got tired of remembering to take the pill every night. She'd been considering going back to the doctor to have it removed. It seemed unnecessary since her sex life was nil.

She read the hesitation in his eyes and guided the crown of him inside her, just a fraction. She wasn't above manipulating him.

She knew he'd relented when he propped his elbows on either side of her head and framed his hands along either side of her face. "What's your name again, Goldilocks?"

That gave her a start. She was about to have sex with a man and they didn't know each other's names?

It should shame her, but nothing about this moment felt wrong. She was on fire.

"Thea," she breathed.

"Niall," he returned. Tension rippled over his jaw and then he let go. Shoved inside her with one slick thrust, filling her completely, stretching her deliciously.

She wiggled under him with a sob, her hands pushing his corded shoulders as if needing sudden leverage. "Oh, you're big!"

"You can take it," Niall's lips husked against her neck and then bit down on her earlobe, sending a rush of moisture between her legs. "Och, you just got really wet." He thrust again. Harder. "You feel amazing." Another thrust. "Like you were made for my cock."

She cried out at the fullness of him sliding in and out of her, but he was right … the friction shot sparks through her and she lifted her hips for him, greedy for more.

His mouth claimed hers, swallowing her cries. He kissed her senseless, his tongue sweeping against hers, arousing her on a whole new level and sending another rush of moisture to her sex where his giant erection pulsed.

"How are you this tight?" He groaned and pulled back to thrust even deeper inside her again, shoving her higher on the bed.

A small scream escaped her. Her nails dug into her shoulders, hanging on for dear life. She'd never been fucked so hard and it was incredible. She didn't know it could be like this. She didn't know she could want it like this.

"That's right. Scream for me, Thea."

Her body was out of her control. Shaking and wild. He drove into her again and she came in a violent burst. She cried his name and went limp, quivering in the aftershocks. Tears sprang to her eyes from the wonder of it. He'd given her the best orgasm of her life.

He didn't stop though.

He continued riding her, pumping relentlessly. His hands dug into her hips, lifting her for his plunging cock. "Again, Thea," he demanded.

"No. Can't," she gasped, shaking her head. There was no way. It was too much. He could not possibly wring another orgasm from her.

"You can." He was unrelenting, fucking her ruthlessly. His thrusts fell faster, harder, pushing her again to the edge of climax.

She clutched his shoulders, his back. Her hands moved down and gripped his taut ass, reveling in how it flexed as he pumped over her.

He launched her over that edge again. Tears streaming down her face, she shrieked and he lost all restraint. He became a thrusting animal, savage and intense as he plowed into her body, taking it and claiming it and using it for his desire. As she had used his. She'd never felt so desired. So innately female. So powerful.

A few more lunges and he stilled, throwing back his head with a groan as he came inside her, spilling his seed deep.

She couldn't slow her breathing. Her breasts rose and fell in heavy gasps. He lowered his gaze back down to her and she knew she looked shell-shocked. Because that was how she felt.

She fought to regain her breath. "That … was …"

He nodded, looking so grim right then that she didn't know what to make of him.

He was still lodged deep inside her and that only added to the sudden awkwardness. What did one say immediately following sex with a stranger? Should she thank him? At this point Charlie would go brush his teeth and get ready for bed.

He eased out from her body and collapsed on his back beside her, throwing one arm over his forehead. His breathing was still labored and that made her feel better. Maybe he felt shattered too. Maybe he needed some time to compose himself.

Several moments passed, however, as she lay there staring at the dancing shadows on the ceiling, and she was sure she needed to get up. She reached for his shirt, determined to slip it back on even if she had to hold it shut since the buttons were gone, scattered God knew where.

"Where are you going?"

She stopped and looked down at him, clutching the shirt in front of her to shield her nakedness. "Going back to the couch?" Why did that have to come out like a question?

He sat up and tugged his shirt from her hands, tossing it aside. "We had an understanding."

"Yeah. And we…fucked. So…" She gestured lamely to the couch.

"There's a lot I still want to do with you."

"We're not … we're still…" Her voice faded.

"I'll need you again. Soon," he said. "Unless you're too sore?" His expression turned almost sulky at that prospect.

She shook her head dumbly. "No. I'm fine." He could go again? More than once in a night?

"Good," he said, his eyes dropping to her body. "Because I'm not close to done with you." His voice dropped even lower. "Maybe I was wrong. Maybe there is a bit of magic in those glens, after all." His hand trailed between the hollow of her breasts. "Are you even real?" His hand circled round to palm a heavy breast, thumbing the nipple until it strained for more of his touch. "Maybe you're a faerie come to bewitch me, aye?"

Her only response was a whimper as his thumb rolled her nipple.

Then his hand was gone.

She looked around desperately as he climbed out of bed. But then he was back. He wrapped an arm around her waist, lifted her easily from the bed, carrying her into the bathroom. Her head twisted and turned, unsure what he was about until she heard the loud hiss of the shower water.

He deposited her inside the tub. Warm water sluiced down her, plastering her hair to her face. Gasping, she pushed the strands out of the way, slicking the long hair back.

He followed her inside, pulling the curtain shut on them and sealing them in.

She admired him. The water hit him and he angled his neck and head to better wet his hair, turning the dark brown strands black. He looked so at ease, as though showering with a woman was the most natural thing in the world for him. Had she ever known so confident a man? Certainly she had never been with one. He was grumpy, to be sure. And bossy. But Lord was he sexy.

His body towered over her, crowding her in the small space. She stared up at him uncertainly.

He stared back down, eyes narrowing, considering her. "You never took a shower with a man before." A statement, not a question.

She shook her head. She might have two lovers to her credit, but there was a lot she hadn't done. A lot she didn't know. "Am I so transparent?"

Why did she get the impression he could read her mind? Her throat constricted and she looked away. That would be embarrassing if he could.

Then he would know exactly how into him she was, how much power he had over her already.

"Look at me."

She returned her gaze to him. The water beat at her back and ran down her legs. Still watching her, he grabbed a bar of soap and built up a lather with his hands.

Putting the soap aside, he set his soapy hands to her body, washing and massaging her so thoroughly she couldn't help from moaning. It was incredible.

He started at her shoulders and then worked his way down. He spent a lot of time on her breasts, his fingers sliding over the slippery skin, rolling and squeezing her nipples while murmuring, "Such pretty tits."

He let go and stepped closer, his chest flattening against her breasts as his hands worked their way down the slope of her back to massage the rounds of her ass and lift her higher so his erection poked her in the stomach. "And this ass."

She arched her face up into the spray of water, sharp whimpers escaping her.

Nothing had ever felt this good.

"Spread your legs," he commanded.

His fingers slipped down the cleft of her ass. He pushed his cock against her backside, sliding it against the cleft of her cheeks, teasing her with long and deep strokes. Then his fingers were back, skimming lower until he found the entrance to her sex. He brushed there before his soapy fingers drifted to softly circle her oversensitive clit and give it a roll.

A hiss escaped her.

Then his hands vanished from between her legs. She cried out in disappointment. He dropped to his knees in front of her. Her head spun, dizzy with desire and bewilderment at his actions. He lifted one of her legs and draped it over his shoulder. Then his mouth was on her. He devoured her. Licking with his hot tongue, nibbling with his teeth, his beard rasping her most sensitive skin. *Oh. My. God.*

She screeched, one hand gripping his hair while the other one braced along the shower wall. "Niall ... you can't..."

He stopped and looked up at her with hard, glittering eyes. "I'm eating this pussy."

She stared down at him, words she could not bring herself to say on the tip of her tongue. *Men didn't like to do this. It was dirty.*

She licked her lips. "I've never…" Her voice faded as a supremely satisfied look came over his face. Damn it. She just revealed her inexperience.

"Then it's long overdue. Tonight this pussy is mine and my mouth is going to taste all of it."

Shock ripped through her at his words. Then his head was back between her thighs, pushing them wide. He worked her furiously, tasting her like he had promised. Licking long and deep everywhere.

Soon she didn't care. She lost all restraint and rocked against that mouth of his. Lost all ability to speak as she rode his face, driving and seeking her own pleasure. There were only cries and whimpers and pleas as he consumed her with his mouth.

"Fucking come for me," he growled against her sex, his tongue flaying her clit. She trembled, shaking against his mouth.

"I can't." She tossed her head side to side, and then he did the unthinkable. He sucked her clit between his teeth, pulling deep as he pressed one finger slightly against that *other* hole … another first. She screamed and came in a blinding rush.

She gazed wide-eyed at him. Who even was she anymore?

He stood and backed her against the wall, his hands flat on the shower tile, caging her in. Only, he felt more like the wild animal with his huge body pinning hers and his feral gaze dancing all over her face.

"Kiss me," he ordered in that growly brogue. "Taste yourself." And she did, ripe and tangy. She tasted her own need on his lips and tongue.

He gripped her waist and lifted her as though she weighed nothing at all, guiding her legs around him. He pushed inside her, seating himself to the hilt. His lips moved against her drenched hair. "You're so tight. Sure you're not too sore from that last fuck?"

She shouldn't love dirty talk like this, but her stomach dipped and twisted at his words. He woke something inside her. A primal earthiness that demanded release. He made her feel like a goddess. Like the last woman on earth.

"I'm fine." Contrary to her denials, she was a little sore and swollen and he actually felt bigger inside her than the last time, but somehow that made it better, the feeling more intense. Who cared if she couldn't walk tomorrow?

He fucked her into the shower wall, his thrusts long and heavy, grinding deep inside her so he hit that hidden spot, the thick crown of him rubbing where no one had touched before. She cried out, the pleasure white hot and blinding, dancing the fine line of pain.

"Niall!" She lifted higher, away from his cock. Again, it was too much. The sensations overwhelming. She didn't know how to take it.

He grabbed her hips and forced her down, seating her on him. His hard gaze pinned her. "Milk my cock. Come for me, sweetheart."

"Not again—"

"Again," he commanded, his own movements losing rhythm as he grew frantic, his strokes rough and without restraint against her.

She surrendered, sinking onto his member, her inner muscles squeezing like a fist around him, milking him as he commanded.

With a guttural cry, he came, shooting off inside her.

Her thighs clenched around him as her orgasm followed fast and brutal. She flew apart, sharp cries exploding from her lips. Her vision went black for a moment as she hugged him tightly, dragging her nails down his back.

He pulled back and stared at her. For the first time she saw a crack in his stoic mask. The same astonishment she felt was there, peeking out from the fissures.

He turned away, shutting off the water and lifting her out of the shower. He dried her off like she was helpless. Honestly, she was still shaking and probably couldn't have lifted her arms. She wasn't too certain she could manage it.

Once they were both dry, he carried her back to his bed and placed her in the center. She was glad for that. Glad he had answered the question of whether they were done yet and where she would sleep for the night.

He slid in next to her, pulling the covers over them. She gazed at his beautiful face, the lines and hollows all the more stark in firelight. The dark glitter of his blue eyes brought emotions she dared not examine swimming to the surface. This was a fling. That was all it was. That was enough.

Smiling, she reached out and stroked his mouth, tracing those lips she longed to paint. His beard tickled her palm.

He caught her palm and pressed a slow kiss to it. "Promise me you'll be here in the morning," he growled against her skin.

She chuckled. "And where would I go?"

He frowned, his eyes deep and grim. "If yer no' real, you could disappear."

She wasn't so sure, but she thought he might be a touch serious. "I'm real. I won't disappear," she promised. A yawn escaped her.

"Sleep," he ordered.

"Always so bossy." But she closed her eyes and fell asleep anyway.

Goldilocks could only hope that the foul-tempered bear controlled his impulses and didn't devour her during the night…

T HE STORM RAGED through the night.

Thea slept restlessly as it battered against the shutters. At least she told herself it was the storm and not the giant bearded Scot in bed beside her.

She was unaccustomed to sleeping with a man. She and Charlie had never lived together. Even when one of them did stay over at the other's place, they each kept to their own sides of the bed as though some invisible barrier ran down the middle. Not Niall. His body had to be touching hers at all times.

She woke hugging the edge of the mattress to feel his arm wrapping around her waist and hauling her against him. She sighed and snuggled into him, feeling his erection prodding her backside. He was insatiable. She might have rubbed against him. Maybe she was insatiable, too, because she couldn't stop herself from arching her spine and moving into the perfect position so his cock aligned with the lips of her pussy. She rubbed against him until he was sliding slippery against her.

Sore or not, she wanted more.

She'd be gone tomorrow and she wanted her fill.

He must have had a similar thought. He'd grabbed her by the waist and guided her to her knees. "You haven't had enough yet?"

She was still groggy at his first thrust inside her, but that didn't last long. He grabbed a fistful of hair at the back of her head and pulled, arching her throat so he could bite down on her neck. Tears smarted her eyes. The pleasure was so acute, edging pain.

"Say you need more cock," he rasped against her skin, his fingers tightening in her hair as he held his throbbing cock inside her.

"I need more cock."

278

"My cock," he instructed.

"I need more of *your* cock."

He gave it to her then, pulling out and pushing in deep.

He let go of her hair and her head dropped like a limp noodle, unable to support herself. He kept her upright on all fours though. His hands grabbed her hips, fingers digging deep to all her generous flesh, anchoring her for him as he took her from behind, deep and steady, the rhythm building until she was moaning and rocking back into his every lunge. It was a different position, the glide of his cock inside her hitting all new nerves.

She climaxed with soft, shuddering sighs, her hands fisting the bedsheets. He fucked her a little longer, collapsing over her with a groan when he came, his big body crushing her, but she didn't care. She reveled in the delicious weight of him.

She barely remembered him rolling off her or pulling her to his side.

She dozed off for a while.

She remembered the question that came later, however, spoken into her ear and rousing her from sleep when the first gray of dawn started to lighten the room.

"Why are you here? In Scotland?"

She smiled sleepily, rolling over to look at his serious, handsome face. "I'm on my honeymoon."

She felt him stiffen. His next words fell hard and accusing, his eyes cutting. "You said yer alone here."

"I am." She yawned, still sleepy. It had been an exhausting night. "He dumped me."

He didn't respond to that. Frown lines creased his forehead as he stared at her. She traced her fingers over the lines, trying to relax them. "It's okay. I'm glad. You're a much better lover," she teased.

His scowl deepened and he came up on his elbows over her again. "That's verra good to know."

"What about you? Ever been on a honeymoon?" She knew even in her drowsy state she was fishing for information about this man, and she didn't care. It was a one-night stand. She'd already thrown all her rules out the window. She could say anything she wanted.

"Aye. A long time ago."

"Ah. So you're...divorced." God, she hoped he wasn't married. It made her sick to think she had possibly done all the things she had done with a man who belonged to another woman.

"Not divorced. But she's gone now. She and my daughter are gone. I lost them both."

He'd been a family man. He had a wife and child.

And he lost them.

She sat up on an elbow and looked down at him, seeing him fully with his wounds laid bare before her.

She glanced around the cottage, understanding. It was the home of a man cut off from the world. Someone who didn't want to share his life with anyone because he'd loved so much and lost so much and it destroyed him.

She considered that, wondering if anyone would be that wrecked if something happened to her. She honestly didn't think so.

She looked at him and touched his face. For a moment, it seemed he would pull away from her hand, but he allowed it. Tears pricked her eyes. Sadness for the wife and daughter he lost. And for him…for the man left behind.

"They must have loved you very much." She knew that because she would have loved him—a man who loved so completely his heart died right alongside his family.

Maybe she already did love him a little.

He blinked. She didn't know what he expected her to say, but she sensed she had surprised him.

He ended up saying nothing. He kissed her then. It was different than their other kisses. This one was long and deep and tender. She was moaning and aroused as he shoved her legs apart and entered her in one smooth thrust.

She gasped. "You really like to do this a lot."

"It's been a while," he growled against her mouth.

"Me too," she panted as he stroked deep inside her, driving her into the mattress. "My ex wasn't really into sex."

"He's a fucking bampot."

She assumed that was an insult. She couldn't really form the words to ask. He was moving faster and kissing her harder and she was coming again in a violent burst. He climaxed soon after her with that groan she was coming to know well. She'd hear it in her dreams, long after she left this place.

Once finished, they rolled apart. She brought the sheet back over her.

"You really know how to wear a girl out." Smiling, she tucked her hand beneath her cheek, already feeling the pull of sleep again. Her eyes drifted shut.

"I wouldn't want you to leave unsatisfied."

The smile slipped from her face. So he still expected her to leave. Naturally. *Of course.*

She cleared her throat. "Do you think the road is clear yet?"

He was silent for several moments, and she opened one eye to look at him. He wore that surly expression again. "I'll go check in a while."

She nodded, a hollow feeling spreading throughout her chest. She would leave soon. Maybe even in a few hours. She'd be on a tour bus with a group full of Americans by the end of the day, no sexy brogue whispering naughty things in her ear.

She'd have one hell of a story to tell Gina. That gave her a small jolt of pleasure. Until she realized this would soon be reduced to a story. A memory.

One that would only fade and grow dim with time.

Soon the storm passed, and Goldilocks began to wonder if the bear wasn't so foul-tempered after all...if the bear was perhaps a little bit wonderful.

WHEN THEA WOKE again sunlight was streaming into the room and the bed was empty. She sat up, holding the covers close to her chest as she glanced around the house.

"Niall?" she called.

No answer. She could almost believe she dreamed him up if not for the soreness between her legs. Last night had happened. She'd had sex multiple times with a too hot guy and it had felt just right. Nothing had ever felt as right in her life. She released a shuddering breath.

She slipped from the bed and padded barefoot into the bathroom. She reached for her clothes, testing them. Mostly dry.

Turning on the shower, she jumped in and quickly washed herself. Her skin was chafed from his beard in several places. Her neck, breasts. Between her thighs. Heat flamed her face when she recalled those places his beard had been. Finished, she emerged from the shower and was wrapping a towel around herself as the door to the bathroom opened.

Niall stepped inside and the space seemed to shrink. He was dressed, wearing a jacket, sweater, and jeans. The crisp scent of wind clung to him. Clearly, he'd been outdoors.

She felt shy. Dressed and with the bright light of day between them, she remembered she knew next to nothing about this man. "Good morning."

Instead of returning the greeting, his eyes raked her up and down as she stood there dripping with his towel wrapped around her. After some moments, he asked in his taciturn way, "Hungry?"

"Yes, food would be good."

Turning, he left her in the bathroom.

She dressed in her clothes that were fully dry now and emerged as he was pulling toast from a toaster. Eggs cooked in a pan on the stove. She inhaled the delicious aroma. He glanced at her and went back to scrambling eggs.

"Smells yummy. Can I help with anything?" she asked, trying not to feel awkward.

He lifted one shoulder in a shrug.

Okay. She watched him a moment longer and then moved into the kitchen area, opening cabinets until she located the plates. She removed two and moved to stand by him at the stove.

He didn't say anything as she held one out. He glanced at it and then scooped eggs onto the plate. She held out the other one and he followed suit. She reached for the toast, placing one on each plate.

She turned for the table and set them down, each one across from each other. She turned to fetch utensils, but he already had them. He nodded at her and set a fork on the side of each plate. "Sit. Eat."

She obliged, trying not to feel uncomfortable as she watched him move about the kitchen space. He fetched butter and what looked like a jar of jam from the refrigerator. "You drink coffee?" he asked, reaching for the pot that was already made.

"Yes. Thank you." He brought two mugs over and poured the steaming liquid into one for her. She stared at his hands, the tapering fingers and short-nailed blunt tips. Her face warmed remembering their texture, the sensation on her skin. How strong they felt. How safe and worshipped and so very *right* they'd made her feel. No one ever made her feel like that. For one brief, terrifying moment she worried no one ever would again. Then, she shook off the fear. If that were true, then at least she had last night. She'd cherish that memory.

She lifted the mug to her face and inhaled the wonderful aroma, trying to act composed. "It smells great." She took her first savoring sip, letting the caffeine seep into her system.

They ate in silence for a while and she marveled that he had spoken more during sex. There was nothing about this man that smacked of shyness or reticence. Light of day brought reality. If he wasn't talking to her now it was because he didn't want to. He didn't want to talk to her.

She moistened her lips and reached for her slice of toast. "When do you think you'll check on the road?"

"Already did."

She froze as she held a slice of toast to her lips. He'd already checked the road? He'd said nothing about it to her. "You did?"

He drank from his mug, staring at her over the rim. "Aye," he answered as he set his coffee back down on the table. "Water's still too high to cross."

"Oh." The news left her with mixed feelings. She wanted to stay. She didn't want last night to be all there was. But she wanted him to *want* her to stay … with the same desperate hunger she felt, with the same longing. "I'm sorry for putting you out."

He stared at her silently.

She moistened her lips. "I'm sure you have things to do. Please don't let me inconvenience you. Don't let me keep you from what you need to do today."

What else could she say? This man had never wanted her here. He'd made that abundantly clear. They'd had their one-night stand and she couldn't even do him the courtesy of hitting the road after it was done. She'd never had a one-night stand, but she knew how they worked. That's why they were called one-night stands.

And then suddenly it was important she ask. Important she knew. She cleared her throat and lifted her chin. "Do you want me to stay?"

Maybe it was just her ego at work, demanding to hear him say he *wanted* her here. As seconds ticked by, she repeated the question. "Do you want me to stay?"

"There's not really a choice right now, is there?" He stabbed some egg onto his fork. "There's no getting through the road. Maybe tomorrow, but more than likely the day after. It should be passable then."

So another day. Maybe two.

She fought against the excitement that threatened to overwhelm her. This was forced proximity. He wasn't saying he'd like her to stay.

"That's not what I asked you." She held his gaze and spoke slowly, enunciating each word. "Do *you* want me to stay here?"

He stared at her, still frustratingly mute, not offering what she craved to hear, what she *needed* to hear. After last night, she had to know. Was this truly a one-night stand?

Or was something more happening here?

Please, let it be more.

She knew what she wanted him to say, but as they regarded each other in silence, she grew certain she wasn't going to hear what she wanted. He wasn't capable of telling her what he didn't feel.

Of course, something more *wasn't* happening here. She'd shown up here unwanted and unwelcomed and had a surprising night of sex with a too hot guy. *Great* sex. But it was just sex and now it was over.

She knew what she had to do.

Thea pushed up from the table and carried her dishes to the sink. She made quick work of washing them and putting them in the dish rack to drain. She wouldn't leave him with more work because of her. She would clean up after herself, and it would be like she was never here. A pang near her heart accompanied that thought.

She heard his chair scrape back from the table. He carried his dishes to the sink where she worked. "Allow me." She smiled tightly and reached to take them from him. "You cooked, after all. It's the least I can do."

She gripped the plates, and then realized he wasn't giving them up. She looked up at him, angling her head inquiringly.

They shared a long look, full of the heat and the memory of last night. It hovered between them a crackling, palpable thing. She held her breath, hoping he would do something. *Say* something. Touch her. Kiss her. Throw her down on the bed and never let her leave.

That didn't happen. Because that would be crazy. The stuff of movies and romance novels. Not reality.

He released the plates into her hands and turned away. His solid footsteps thudded across the house. He paused near the door and lifted his jacket off a wall hook and slipped it on. "I'll be back later."

He pulled open the front door and stepped outside, closing the door after him.

Turning back around, she finished the dishes, trying not to think how this was the last time she would see him. Drying her hands on a towel, she glanced around and spotted the unmade bed. She tackled that next, making certain it was military neat. She would leave no mess behind. She tidied the couch cushions next, folding the throw and draping it over the back.

Satisfied, she fetched her bag from the floor near the couch. Her shoes waited at the door where she left them the night before. Had that only been a night ago? Not even twenty-four hours had passed. How was that possible? She didn't even feel like the same person.

She slid on her shoes and bent to lace them up, feeling a little sick. Standing, she secured both straps of her backpack over her shoulders and looked around one final time, blinking burning eyes as she imprinted the house in her memory.

She stepped outside. It was still chilly, the sun hidden behind the clouds. She looked around the yard. No sight of Niall anywhere—a fact that both relieved and saddened her. She really would never see him again. She could hear the sheep bleating somewhere in the distance. Maybe he was checking to see how they fared through the night.

Gripping the straps of her backpack, she headed off down the road, admiring the rippling green hills. As much as it hurt to think she was never going to see Niall again, she knew she was doing the right thing.

She walked for almost half an hour. It was uphill, downhill, and then uphill again. Her breathing picked up as she followed the winding road. There had to be a way on foot to get across the road. Just because a car couldn't cross it didn't mean someone on foot couldn't. She'd find a way.

The sound of burbling water reached her ears and she knew she was nearing the stream. She rounded a bend, fully expecting to see the road overrun with water.

But all she saw was a road.

A fully passable road.

She froze as this sank into her brain. A thin layer of water covered the road, no more than an inch high. A car would have no trouble crossing through it.

The road was passable.

She blinked a few times as though her eyes were deceiving her. The blood rushed to her head, roaring in her ears.

He'd lied. Why had he lied to her?

The sound of a car approaching had her whirling back around. Niall's Jeep rounded the bend and braked hard. He flung open the driver's side and hopped out, an anxious look on his usually passive face.

He started toward her and she held out a hand as though to ward him off. "Stop."

He obliged, his gaze darting over her face. "Thea," he began.

"You lied to me," she accused, pointing a damning finger to the road.

His expression turned pained.

"I asked you and you said the road wasn't clear!"

He nodded. "Aye, I lied."

She shook her head. "I can see that! I don't understand—"

"I dinna want you to go," he flung out. "Damn it, I want you to stay longer so I lied."

She stared at him in stunned silence. At this surly, too hot man with a panicked expression on his face that was all because of her. Because … she was leaving.

She glanced back at the road with the barely there current of water trickling over its surface as though needing to see it one more time—the evidence of his deceit.

She faced him again, her heart tumbling headlong at the sight of him, at the incredible words he was saying to her in that delicious brogue of his. They echoed in her head. *I dinna want you to go. Damn it, I want you to stay longer…*

"Why didn't you just say that?" she whispered.

He dragged a hand through his hair. "I don't know. Because I'm an idiot who couldn't find his voice around you. Who felt like a tongue-tied lad because he wants you so damn much. Because I was scared that you would think I was deranged and run screaming for the road. I haven't even known you a full day, but I want you to stay." He flung out both arms. "I want you here. I'm sorry I couldn't say it before." He looked at her bleakly, emotion ripe in his eyes. "Don't go."

Elation swelled inside her chest. She shook her head and tamped down on her joy, fighting for her composure. She didn't want to look like a giddy child on Christmas morning, even if that was how she felt. "I don't think you're deranged."

"No?" He advanced on her slowly, his expression hopeful. "I'm not a rash or reckless man, but you've done something to me. Changed me." He held out both hands, gesturing around them. "I think yer a faerie and those glens are magical. I don't know how else to explain it. How else could I have fallen in love with you the moment I found you in my house, wearing my clothes, eating my dinner? You made me feel again. You made me believe. How can I no' believe those glens are magical anymore? They brought you to me." His hand reached out to caress her hair. "What's it going to be, Goldilocks?"

Her eyes burned, swimming with tears, and this time the tears were not from pain or disappointment. She fought against a tide of joy, trying to not to get swept away in it. She needed to be reasonable now.

He couldn't love her. It was impossible. Too soon. This didn't happen to people.

This didn't happen to *her*.

He took another step, stopping just in front of her. "Stay." He inhaled. "Please. Stay forever."

She opened her mouth and just then she heard another engine. They both looked up as a small car came into view, cresting the hill and zipping down toward them. It crossed over the stream and pulled to a hard brake beside them.

The driver rolled down the window. A man with a grizzled beard stuck his head out the window. "Hello, there. I'm looking for an American." He eyed Thea speculatively. The pocket of his T-shirt bore the logo for the tour company she'd hired. "A tour bus left her behind, and I've been sent to find her. You haven't seen her, have you?"

She lifted her gaze and locked eyes with Niall. He watched her, his blue eyes intent, hungry. Hungry for her. But he volunteered nothing. He waited for her to say something. Waited for her to reach a decision.

She looked back down at the driver, her heart pounding hard in her chest as she reached her decision. The only choice she could make.

"You can go back," she told him, and no words had ever felt so natural, so right coming out of her mouth. "She's not lost. She's right where she wants to be."

Epilogue

Two years later...

THEA SET DOWN her charcoal pencil and pushed up from her stool, arching her spine and stretching against the perpetual ache in her back as she critically evaluated her work. Well, perpetual ache as of eight weeks ago.

Rubbing the small of her back, she glanced at the clock. It was well after twelve and she hadn't stopped for lunch yet. Her stomach grumbled in protest. She removed her smock and hung it on the hook on the wall.

She followed the sounds of hammering outside. Standing on the porch, she held a hand up to shield her eyes. It was a rare sunny day, and she smiled as she caught sight of Niall on the roof of the new house. It should be ready for them to move into next month.

With three bedrooms and two-and-a-half baths, she could invite Gina and her husband to come and stay with them now. Maybe Grams would even pay them a visit, now that she had adjusted to the idea Thea was staying in Scotland forever.

Of course marrying Niall six months after they met had definitely forced Grams to get accustomed to the fact that Thea would only ever be returning home for visits.

That day on the road had changed everything. She had hoped she found something special with him. She had wanted to believe it, had longed to believe in the forever he was offering.

Within the week she knew it for truth.

She was totally, irrevocably in love. And as the days slid to weeks to months, she knew that wasn't going to change. She wanted him in her life forever.

He proposed to her precisely one week after walking in on her asleep on his couch.

Worried that he might regret it later and come to change his mind, she made him wait. Even though she knew she already loved him, caution from the old fears of her failed relationships made her wait.

She didn't want him to change his mind. She couldn't live through that again, not this time with a man who really mattered to her, with a man she really loved. It would be unendurable.

He'd proposed every day for three months until she finally said yes.

He loved her. He wanted her. And he wasn't going to change his mind. They were married three months later in a beautiful spring wedding. The Highland heather was in wild bloom outside the village church. Gina, her grandmother, her cousin, aunt, and a few other close friends flew over for the occasion.

And here she was. Married to a six-foot-four surly Scot who made love to her every night (often in the day too) and whose smiles were reserved for her alone. A year and a half later and still no regrets. Still blissfully happy. Even the worst day here was better than any day she'd had before.

She leaned back against the front door. He was shirtless as he worked. She admired the play of his muscles as he pounded the hammer, and she felt the familiar stirrings. She would never grow tired of that sight. Never *not* feel this arousal, *not* feel this love.

Her stomach growled again, reminding her of the reason she came out here.

"Niall," she called, waving at him. "Want some lunch?"

He looked up. Even across the distance she could make out the grin on his face. He climbed off the roof, swinging down and landing on his feet on the new porch deftly.

He strode across to where she stood, pressing a hard kiss to her lips and tweaking her nose. "You've smudged some charcoal there."

"Oh." She rubbed at it with the back of her hand. She'd been painting local landscapes for the previous year and selling them to shops in the surrounding villages. They were very popular among tourists.

Her landscapes brought in a tidy little sum every month. Her hand drifted to her stomach. Due to recent developments, she'd put aside her acrylic paints for pencil and charcoal. It was a happy sacrifice and only temporary. She was quite enjoying the new medium anyway.

This life was more than she ever hoped for. She was in love and loved in return. And painting again.

And—

"How's our wee one here?" Niall bent down and pressed a kiss to her belly.

Four months ago she had her IUD removed. It hadn't take very long to get pregnant. No surprise, she supposed. They did practice quite a lot.

"Famished," she replied.

He straightened and wrapped an arm around her waist, hauling her against me. "Then we better feed you."

Lifting her off her feet, he carried her into the house. She fanned her fingers against his hard shoulders, damp with sweat. "And perhaps after lunch, you can take a break."

"A break?" His eyes gleamed down at her in amusement. He knew what *break* was code for. Rarely did a day pass without a *break*.

"You know, wife, this house would have probably been finished three months ago if I took less breaks."

She grinned. "Are you sorry? Should I stop suggesting them?"

He claimed her mouth in a slow, searing kiss, his hand drifting down to palm and squeeze her ass. He pulled back to growl against her lips, "Don't you dare. I don't regret a single break. I see a long future ahead of us with many such breaks."

She sighed happily, not doubting that for a moment. She saw their future too. And it was this.

It was beautiful.

THE END

THANK YOU!

I hope all of you loved Thea and Niall's story. It was largely inspired by my trip to Scotland. As I traveled through that beautiful country, I kept imagining an American getting abandoned by a tour bus and ending up at some sexy Scot's cottage. It was so much fun to write this story as a modern-day Goldilocks.

If you enjoyed it, you can read more of my sexy contemporary romances in my Devil's Rock series. Start with ALL CHAINED UP:

"Off-the-charts hot and emotionally charged! Get ready for these sexy-as-sin ex-cons to take you on a wild ride!"

(NYT bestselling author Elle Kennedy, praise for The Devil's Rock series)

"I read the gritty, sexy as hell, addictive story in one sitting!"

(#1 New York Times Bestselling Author Kresley Cole)

There are bad boys and then there are the men of Devil's Rock . . .

Some men come with a built-in warning label. Knox Callaghan is one of them. Danger radiates from every lean, muscled inch of him, and his deep blue eyes seem to see right through to Briar Davis's most secret fantasies. But there's one major problem: Briar is a nurse volunteering at the local prison, and Knox is an inmate who should be off-limits in every way.

Knox feels it too—a shocking animal magnetism that drives him to risk his own life to protect Briar's. Paroled at last, he tries to resist her. She's too innocent, too sweet, and she has no idea what Knox is capable of. But a single touch can lead to a kiss—and a taste . . . until the only crime is denying what feels so right . . .

And sign up for my newsletter to find out about my new books and giveaways:

www.sophiejordan.net/newadult/contact.html

BROKEN HARP

A Jack and the Beanstalk Retelling

Nora Flite

CHAPTER ONE

JACK

When I was sixteen, I met an angel.
On that same night, I met the devil himself.

TOWERING OVER ME in a way my father never had and never would, Mister Big watched me from the nexus of his private, aging booth. The Copper Tub was an opulent jazz club full of glass chandeliers and drink menus that didn't bother to list the prices. I was smart enough to know he was making a point by holding our meeting here.

Places like this screamed money.

Money was more important to me than my soul.

"Here," he said, sliding the pile of paperwork towards me. The corners of the pristine sheets touched a small beer puddle; they turned a rusty color. "It's all in order. A quick signature, then you and I will be the majority owners of the club I plan to buy."

I brushed my fingertips over the ink. There were two men sitting beside Mister Big, neither had spoken a word to me. They just watched and waited and *expected.* "It's really that simple?" I asked, shifting in the plush booth.

His lips pulled back in a smile so thin I waited for it to split open and show all of his teeth and gums. "It's as simple as you want it to be, Jack. Selling your property to me is *much* smoother than trying to go on the market. One shady auctioneer, and your home… your mother's jewelry… well." His shoulders rocked upwards. "You'd get nothing. Not a dime, not what any of it's worth."

What it's worth, I thought, my fingertips digging into my thighs under the table. Mister Big had listed everything I'd been sent to sell at the bottom of the paperwork: my childhood home, my dead father's fading farm, and my mother's most prized possession. The printed words called them *jewels,* but they were so much more than that. I'd watched from the hallway as my mother sat at her cracked vanity, stroking the necklace with its three kidney-bean sized emeralds. She did it often, she did it without thought—and she'd done it up until she'd handed the necklace to me in a box while her tired eyes turned puffy with tears.

Behind me, there was a noise. It was mild; the slight rustling of the club waking up. Speakers squeaked with feedback. On impulse, I looked up and away from the paperwork that would change my life.

And I saw her.

Dressed in gold sequins that hugged her young, budding curves, she swept across the small stage on the opposite end of the club. Luscious strands of thick hair—thicker than molasses, surely smelling as sweet—framed her face and drew out the rich blue of her eyes.

She was a stranger to me, but low in my gut, I knew her the way only young love knows itself.

"Jack?"

I twisted back to face Mister Big and his associates. His face was placid, his huge hands resting over each other in a sign of immense patience. "Sorry," I said, scanning the pages again. "This is all new for me." The men chuckled—my insides twisted. "How long do I have to wait before you sell everything and invest it into your new club?"

"Oh, not long. I've got interested buyers already."

Already? But I'd only spoke with him on the phone yesterday. It had been a chance meeting with one of his representatives who'd put us in touch. Originally, I'd wandered into the town's marketplace, searching for a local realtor to help me place my home for sale, as my mother had asked. She was too ill to make the trip and we'd been without a car for some time. I was used to walking the five miles, I didn't even mind.

On the road with the blue sky above, I could forget how fucked up my life was.

Mister Big leaned closer. "You're not getting nervous, are you?" His thick beard made his frown look even more severe. "I'm sure I can find another man interested in investing with me. Another *man* who wants to sit as my partner and rake in the passive cash of a hot new club."

Sweat collected between my shoulder blades. No one had called me a man before. When he did, it skirted the edge of an insult. I was messing up the biggest deal in my life. My mother would be furious, my mother would...

"Silent waters," a voice crooned through the air. Instantly the club went dead silent.

The woman on the stage was singing.

A pen dropped heavily onto the table, startling me. One of the other men—a lanky guy who still managed to fill out his gray suit—leaned backwards. I realized he'd dropped the pen, reading all the cues from his boss to hurry this forward.

I was hesitating… but why? What was I worried about? If I didn't sell everything, my mother and I would be out on the street. The bank wanted to foreclose; I'd been unable to find work in this shithole of a town, or at least, nothing that could afford the high-rate escalating payments the bank wanted so suddenly.

My mother had begged me to find an answer.

Wouldn't I be a fool to walk away from the first sliver of good luck I'd been blessed with?

"Alright," I said, gripping the pen and scrawling my signature. The ink smeared onto the side of my hand—Mister Big had snatched it up before it had dried. Sitting back, I looked him straight in the face, fighting to breathe. Fighting to get a hold on my emotions. And all the while, just behind me, that beautiful woman sang her song. I ached to look. "Now what?"

"Now?" he chuckled dryly. Lifting his hand, he motioned sharply; from the shadows came a woman with a tray of drinks. Had she been waiting there for our deal to end? "Now we drink!"

Squeezing the glass of whiskey that was poured for me, I joined them in a toast. Their joy should have been contagious. Five glasses later—each more pushed on me than the last—it finally was. Somewhere between my anxiety and my uncertainty, hope had blossomed.

Mom is going to be so happy.

When she heard what I'd done, she'd probably even hug me. How would that feel?

"Silent waters…" that voice again; wobbly this time, struggling to reach me through my alcohol haze. Time had warped, the night eroding away until I only vaguely noticed the club had gone empty. Arms pulled at me, familiar voices laughing as I was pulled out a door and towards the alley.

"Where are we going?" I asked, finding it hard to stand.

The man holding me was the lanky fellow from earlier; a friend of Mister

Big. "A smoke, we're just getting some fresh air and a smoke. Celebrations can't end without that."

I didn't smoke; it was a luxury, but also, I'd never been fond of the stuff. "I'll just stand and listen," I said, trying to break free. "If it's all the same to you gentlemen."

"Gentlemen," someone snorted. One man had become two, their bodies crowding me in the low light of the back-alley's single lamp. The edge in his voice set my brain on fire—my intuition kicking in a second too late. Or maybe it was days late, at this point.

Hard knuckles drove into my gut, forcing out air and whiskey and bile. Coughing, I fell hard enough that my temple thudded on the rough ground. Gravity held me there, disorientation making my mind swim. I was too drunk for a fistfight. Even on my best days, I couldn't have taken two men at once.

"Can you believe this kid, Hector?" The man who'd hit me did it again. I scrambled to grab his ankles; he just laughed and jammed his heel into my gut, then my spine. My vision was red stars and nothing more.

Tobacco filled the air. I tasted it around the blood in my mouth. "Mister Big knows how to spot a sucker, that's for fucking sure. Hit him again, Tino. Get his face real good."

Spitting out whatever was in my mouth, I shielded myself as Hector railed on me. The ringing in my ears got louder, muffling everything until I could have been suffocating under a pile of mattresses. "Why?" I coughed.

"Shit, he speaks." Gravel scraped by my cheek; Hector had knelt, his fingers knotting in my short hair and ripping me upwards so that I had to face his grim smile. "The answer is obvious, kid. Mister Big wanted your money. But anyone as stupid as you doesn't deserve to work with him."

Stupid? I wasn't stupid.

I was *hopeful.*

I'd believed, just for a bit, that life couldn't be cruel 24/7. That somewhere, eventually, a break would come and people like me... people like my mother... would get our due. We'd be given enough room to just take a full breath for once.

Now I knew better.

"The contract," I moaned.

Sighing, Hector released me. My chin dropped heavily to the ground.

"Did you even read that thing? All it did was give ownership of your stuff to Callum. Fuck, I wonder if you can even read."

Callum, is that Mister Big's real name? The ruse was obvious now. I hadn't known who I was dealing with. Smoke and mirrors, that was all this was. But the danger wasn't an illusion. I tried to draw in air—my ribs crunched like rusty pipes. "Not… not fair. It's not fair."

"Welcome to the world, kid." Hector drove one more kick into my kidney. I screamed, my throat full of blood and rage. "Wanna finish him off?"

"Nah," Tino said. "Look at him. He's got broken ribs, probably a punctured lung. He won't last the night. Let him die in the alley."

My eyes were shut… or perhaps I was already dead. I saw only blackness, heard nothing. The pain was still there but I was numb, as if the injuries had happened to another person. In another life.

They were right, I thought bitterly. *I'm so stupid.* I was a reckless fool who didn't deserve a break. There would be no second chances for me. I'd lost everything.

Hope had never been more than a dream.

"Hello?"

A flutter moved through me at the sound of that sweet voice. It caused my pain to brighten; I coughed, shaking with each tiny movement. Living was worse than death.

"Oh god! What happened to you?" She touched my hair; rolled me gently, so that I was looking upwards at the empty sky above. I knew there'd be stars, but I saw none of them. How could a whole galaxy compare to the face of an angel?

She still wore her sequin dress, but a thick, black coat was hiding most of it. Once more she cupped my cheek, her hand bringing me warmth. "I'm calling an ambulance," she said, never once looking away. "Stay with me. Okay? Are you listening? Help is coming!"

She'd saved me, but she'd done so much more.

This wonderful woman… this graceful angel…

She'd given me a second chance.

I was going to use it.

CHAPTER TWO

HARPER

"**C**LIMB! CLIMB! CLIMB!"

Seven years ago, I'd used these hands to stroke the keys of a piano. Back then they'd been graceful, part of me, a tool that enhanced my songs. These days I still performed on a stage. But now my hands were strong from climbing a metal pole; they were pretty with pink nails and glitter.

It's funny how our lives can change in an instant.

"Climb, bitch!" a man shouted. His words were blunt, but bravado had lost its effect on me. Men showing off for their friends isn't personal. No, it's only when you're alone with them that you learn what they really think. In a private booth, they spill their guts… the most perverted thoughts swimming in the corners of their minds.

People laugh and say that strippers are therapists to their customers.

That's wrong.

To these men… we're less than human.

Being insulted in public is cake next to that fun fact. I could hear "bitch" a million times and still fake a smile. Hoisting myself up the pole, I twisted my body, making the bikini shimmer with my movements. Not every girl in the Golden Goose could pull herself all the way to the top balcony. I could, and the muscle burn was one of the few exquisite things left in my life.

On the top row of private booths, a group of men in midnight suits watched me. Only one of them *truly* watched me, though. Mister Big had spent years staring at my body. I was sure he hoped he could see into my soul and scoop up my heart if he stared hard enough.

He was wrong. He'd always be wrong.

Reaching the tip of the stripper pole, I bent backwards, thighs crushing the metal while I did a slow spin. Money rained down; my boss's associates cheered, the balcony only an arm's length away. For a second, Mister Big met my eyes. I so badly wanted to spit in his face.

Instead, I dropped like a stone.

People squealed and screamed—I caught myself before my body smashed into the stage. As a torrent of cash flitted through the air, I twisted on my ankle-breaking heels, doing a little hip-wiggle.

No matter how my life had changed, I'd always been one hell of a performer.

There were whistles and claps. Scooping up my money, I noticed someone watching me. Well, lots of people were watching me, but this man was hovering by the short steps that led off the stage. His face was a scraggly mess of beard; his hairline receded into nothingness.

But what concerned me was how he kept fidgeting. He'd glance at me, then away, his hands in his pockets—out of his pants and clenching—then in again as he swayed. This was more than nerves; I wondered if he'd taken some kind of drug.

Deciding to avoid him asking me for a private dance, I scooted to the other end of the stage and hopped off it. "Excuse me, boys," I said, weaving through the crowd.

I could afford to avoid him. I didn't work here because I needed the money; I did it because it was the only way Callum would allow me to see my little sister.

I'd do anything for her.

✧ ✧ ✧

THE PARKING LOT was silent. I was the last to leave, I usually was. Some of the girls had a habit of drinking too much. I'd taken it upon myself to call rides for them; I wasn't about to let anyone drive drunk.

My old but faithful green Ford Taurus was waiting for me in the lot. I'd had it for years—when Callum tried to buy me something nicer, I always turned him down. This car had life in it. It was an heirloom, one of the last pieces of my mother that I could still touch.

Sometimes, if I shut my eyes and tried hard enough, I could still smell her sandalwood perfume on the seats.

Shouldering my purse, I hummed under my breath. It was a bad habit— one that came out whenever my mother entered my mind. I promised myself I'd never sing for anyone ever again, especially not Mister Big, but humming didn't count. No one cared if you could hum nicely.

I was reaching for my keys when the hand closed on my wrist. "Hey hun, where you off to?"

It was the man from earlier—the one who'd eyeballed me from the stage. His sour breath poured over me, his grip tightened as I retreated. "Nowhere with you. Let go. Now."

His scowl showed me how uneven his bottom teeth were; little rotten gravestones in a cemetery assaulted by a tornado. "Come on, sweetie-cakes. I jus' wanted to get your number. Maybe a drink or two. Wanted a dance, but you kept running off in there."

"That's because I was politely avoiding you." I yanked hard, and when he held tight, I shoved forward, trying to throw him off balance.

"Bitch!" he snarled, stumbling—and for a second I was free. Like a manic bird of prey, he snatched at my purse, grappling until he had his arms around my waist.

"Let go of me!" My lungs burned with the crisp night air. I inhaled deeper; screamed harder. "*Let go you piece of shit!*"

"You heard her."

It was a new voice. Fierce, all gravel and dark whispers, it softly threatened pain for anyone who didn't obey. Together, my attacker and I paused, turning to look at the man who approached. He was wearing a faded leather jacket, the front open to display how his chest strained beneath his tight v-neck.

This stranger was all muscle. All beast. I wasn't surprised when my attacker released me, hastily backing up in the lot towards the main street. "Fuck off, man," he said. "I ain't doin' shit to her." That was all the bravery he managed; my savior flexed his hands, and the sour-breathed man sped off into the night.

Hugging myself, I looked the stranger up and down. "Thank you. That was getting out of hand."

The way he swept his stare over my body, I had to fight back a shiver. I was used to men who didn't give free handouts—especially when they went out of their way to save your life. What kind of payment was this intimidating man going to ask for?

He stopped in front of me. "That song you were humming earlier, what was it?"

Cold prickles swept up my back. *He heard that? Was he just standing in the shadows this whole time?* "I wasn't humming. You must have imagined the sound."

Tension moved between his eyebrows. "Didn't know I was blessed with such a beautiful imagination." My mouth went slack from his surprising compliment. No one but Cena had appreciated my voice in years. I'd stopped singing for the public the day all of my dreams were ripped out by their roots.

I considered him with new eyes. "I'm Harper, do you have a name?"

His grin turned him from gruff ravager to warm ruffian. "That your real name? Lotta girls in that club over there go by something else than what their mamas named them."

"Guess I respect my mom too much to go by anything else."

"Risky move for a stripper."

"Wait, how do you know I'm a stripper and not a waitress or a bartender?" I wasn't wearing anything that gave me away—my coat and jeans and flats didn't mark me as a dancer of any kind. My stomach tightened. He must have seen me *inside* the club tonight.

How did I not notice him? Very few of the male customers were what I'd call attractive; this guy was beyond handsome. Everything about this encounter felt… strange.

He tucked his thumbs in his pockets. "Call me observant."

"I'd rather call you by your actual name."

"How about hero? It has a nice ring to it."

"Listen," I said, pulling out my car keys. "I'm too tired to play games. This whole Mister Mysterious thing you're trying isn't as cute as you think, so if you don't mind, I need to get home and—"

"It's Jack."

I paused, turning to watch him again. His smile went up at the corner. It made him even more attractive, and I didn't like that one bit. In the flickering parking lot lights, his eyes became more gold than chocolate.

For a second I was drawn into the past. To a time when I was young and free and alive with vibrant music in my heart. To a memory of a performance where a young man kept looking my way with enraptured interest.

It was a weird memory; I shook it off and wet my dry lips. "Do I… know you?"

Jack's grin shifted into a hard frown. "No one knows me here." Pushing his muscular shoulders upwards, he turned away, speaking as he moved. "Watch out for crazy stalkers. You never know who's waiting in the shadows."

His subtle threat had me crushing my purse strap. I almost told him to come back, but instead, I slid into my car and turned it on. Whoever Jack was, I didn't know him and never would. I was grateful he'd stepped in to help, but I'd had my share of encounters with eager men; I could have gotten away if things went ugly. I knew how to take care of myself.

Speaking of taking care of things…

I pushed on the gas and hurried out of the parking lot.

✧   ✧   ✧

"HAP," CENA SAID, using the nickname she'd had for me since she was only a baby, "Is everything alright?"

"Of course."

She squinted at me. "You're lying."

"I've never lied to you."

"Now you're gaslighting me!"

I made myself laugh. "Where did you even *learn* about that word?"

With the brand of pride reserved only for eight year-olds, she grinned at me. "Internet."

"I shouldn't be surprised. You spend way too much time on there."

"Now you're changing the subject!"

Tossing my bag of stripper gear into the top shelf in the hallway closet—the one place I hoped Cena couldn't reach—I faced her and crouched down to eye level. "Everything is fine, really. But even if it wasn't, I'd still know how to fix it."

Her nearly invisible blonde eyebrows inched up. "How's that?"

Pulling her close, I pointed at the kitchen. "Gigantic bowls of ice cream before bed. Deal?"

"Deal!" she laughed, squirming free and racing towards the fridge.

A few scoops of strawberry in a bowl later, and my sister was scrubbing her eyes as she yawned. I gave her a nudge to get her into the shower. Playing mom wasn't natural for me. I did my best, though. I helped with homework and I made lunches, always slipping the extra cash Mr. Big handed over for Cena's school expenses into my secret bank box.

I was an okay cook, but nothing compared to Mom. Cena never really got to know our mother so my mistakes went unnoticed. That, or she was too sweet to point them out.

She came out of the bathroom wrapped in a giant robe, a towel covering most of her head. "How do I look?"

"Gorgeous," I said, taking the chance to rub the towel over her hair until her blonde strands were wet instead of soaking. "Pajamas and bed, come on."

Cena rushed to change, diving under her blankets and shooting me a wicked little smile. "Sing me a bedtime song, please?"

She was my light, my soul—I couldn't deny her any more than I could tell my heart to stop beating. Settling on the edge of the bed, I brushed a curl from her forehead. "Just don't tell anyone."

"Never. I promise."

There are no promises more sacred than those uttered between siblings. "Sweet moon," I sang. "My moon, yours… hanging over the silent waters…" Singing calmed me to my core. It was a power that required focus, I had to center myself to make it flow. Mostly, I had to grasp for control because if I didn't, I'd remember all the times Mom had sung with me as we made pancakes.

Crying is a great way to ruin a bedtime routine.

The last note of my song faded into the air. Cena fluttered her eyes, fingers wrapped in the top of her down comforter. "Will you walk me to school tomorrow?"

This was an odd request. Cena—determined to grasp independence—always demanded she walk alone. I hadn't minded; the school was close by, and the street was busy with people. "Sure, but why?"

"Can I tell you a secret?" she asked in a hushed tone.

"Always."

She chomped down on her pink bottom lip. "Sometimes, I think there's someone watching me."

Fear rippled in my blood. "Who?"

Her shrug was pure sadness, like she felt guilty answering. "I dunno. It's just a feeling… like a ghost or something spooky. But I'm too old to believe in monsters, you know?"

I wanted to tell her that monsters don't stop existing just because you quit believing in them. Instead I smiled fondly, kissing her on each eyelid and tucking her in. "I'll walk with you tomorrow. But listen, no one can get you while I'm here. Monsters or otherwise."

She had one eye on me, sleep starting to steal her away. "And you'll always be here," she said, yawning. "Always and forever."

"Always and forever," I replied.

I headed for her door, flicking off the light. Something moved the hair on the back of my neck. Thinking about Cena's cryptic admission about feeling watched, I glanced sharply over my shoulder.

A breeze swirled through her cracked window. Had it been open all day? Shutting it, I peered out into the dark. The street below was quiet; the city didn't allow cars to park overnight in such a nice area. Anyone living in this luxury condo kept their expensive vehicles in the lot beneath the building.

Nothing moved out there.

Get a grip, I scolded myself. My encounter outside the club was still fresh in my head. I'd been attacked; wasn't it normal to feel some lingering paranoia? *I'm safe here.*

This building was a castle in the clouds. Some days, if I looked down from my step-dad's penthouse roof, I could swear the city was invisible beneath the white haze. No one could hurt us up here... no one but the enemy already behind our gates.

Except for the maid service that came early in the morning, and the security that kept watch in the lobby, it was private. Callum paid for all of it. But even if he lived an elevator ride away, he rarely visited us. He preferred his own sort of privacy; it meant he didn't have his eight year-old daughter cramping his style. He was free to bring woman after woman into his bed.

Honestly, I didn't care. If he was busy with them, he was leaving me alone.

Just ten more years. Then she'll be eighteen and we can leave together.

Turning away, I moved around Cena's bed. My fingers lingered on the door-frame. The light from the hallway lit up her profile; her soft cheeks, her button nose.

She was innocent.

I'd do anything to keep her that way.

CHAPTER THREE

HARPER

T HE CLUB WAS alive tonight.

Hard, violent drum beats punctuated every swing of my hips. Many of the women here called themselves exotic dancers, but I was one of the few that *really* danced. I could bury my voice, but I could never hide how the music flowed in my blood. I was a slave to the rhythm.

Purple lights glowed along the edge of the stage. There were two other girls up here with me, both of them lazily swinging around the pole. Customers shouted as they threw dollar bills. Strippers who knew how to work the floor scooped the excited men up, pulling them into the booths hidden in the shadows of the club.

Bending backwards, I scanned the men who waited at the tip rail around the stage. They were all ugly grins—animals who saw me as meat. Every one of them was faceless. Forgettable.

Except for him.

Jack was waiting just on the edge of my vision, the purple club lights turning his dark eyes into wild comets. He was dressed just as he'd been last night; a leather jacket, open at the front to show off his tight, moss-green shirt and how it clung to his broad chest.

The sight of him stole my breath. It was a miracle that I didn't stumble on my heels; his slight grin made me wonder if he could tell he'd thrown me off. He approached the stage, settling into the chair with his legs spread wide. Never breaking eye contact, he slid his elbows forward and onto the tip rail. Large hands fanned out a stack of ten dollar bills in front of him.

His offer was clear… but I think, even if he hadn't put down any cash, I'd have approached him. I was curious about this guy. He'd rescued me last night, had I made an impression? Enough of one to lure him back here?

Or was he after something else?

Gathering myself, I swayed slowly towards him. There was another pole here, just a few feet in front of Jack. Keeping my eyes locked on his, I curled my fingers around the cool metal and did a meticulous twirl. When I came back around, my ass was facing him.

Men loved that—it drove them crazy.

I wanted Jack to go *insane.*

Casting a look over my shoulder, I rocked my hips in a lazy circle. He rewarded me by leaning closer, still unblinking, as if he didn't dare to miss a second of my show. His eyebrows hung low over his eyes—made them fiercer. Jack didn't hide his simmering hunger.

I bent low; his gaze followed me. Sinking to my knees, I arched my back, turned so he had a view of me from the side. With my chest jutting out, ass on my heels, I was confident I looked good. But if I'd had any sliver of doubt, all it took was one peek at Jack's hands on the stage.

His knuckles glowed in the black lights; pure white from crushing the tip rail. He was barely holding himself back from pulling me into his lap. That rush of power was intoxicating—it jolted in my veins, it made my blood rush until my lower lips swelled in my thong.

Then he crooked a finger at me and I forgot my routine.

Hesitating, I bit back my instant desire to crawl within reach of him. *It's okay to get close,* I told myself, moving on hands and knees across the wooden boards. *It's fine to tease him with some contact... all the other girls do.* They did that and much worse, honestly.

Before I knew it, I was crouched in front of him. The tip rail—a foot high expanse of flat metal to rest drinks and cash—was all that was between us. The stage was raised, and still, Jack was eye-level sitting down as he was.

He raked his gaze from my face, to my chest, then back again. His smile was subtle; it stole the strength from my legs.

The club music rolled in my ears. I blanked out—I was fixated on his fucking mouth, his thick hair, how the lights bounced off his exposed collar bone. "Hi," I blurted.

Jack grinned slyly. "Hi? Shouldn't it be 'Hey, Sexy?' or something similar?"

Breathing in, I gave a quick, relieved laugh. It was so *good* to have him ease the tension. "That's bold."

"I don't know," he said, crossing his arms. "With the way you were looking at me, I think it's spot on."

Heat swam in my skull. I was too warm, too full of mixed emotions. I didn't know the last time I'd bantered with anyone, never mind a painfully hot man like Jack.

A waitress jumped between us, interrupting our moment and giving me a second to gather myself. "Want a drink, handsome?" she asked.

Slipping a few bills off his stack on the rail, he handed them over. "Gin and tonic, then whatever she likes."

The waitress gave me a look; she knew I was one of the dancers who didn't drink on the job. Alcohol made it too easy to make dumb mistakes… or to let men get away with more than they should. "Tequila sunrise," I said, hoping she'd get the hint and bring me a virgin drink.

It only took a few seconds for her to get our order, hand it over, and then Jack and I were back to our little corner of the stage—alone as you could be in a busy club.

"Cheers," he said, clinking his glass on mine. I took a small sip; definitely alcohol. "So, what were we talking about?" he asked playfully.

I set the tequila sunrise on the stage, then I rose up, perching next to him so that my chest was inches from his face. "I think we were discussing how you should talk *less* during my stage set."

His lips pulled to the side. With patience, he took a slow sip from the glass, then put it out of reach. "Fine. I'll sit here all pretty and let you do your thing. I was enjoying it, anyway."

The music went all bass, the rich, textured rhythm mirroring my heartbeat. Jack was disarmingly charismatic. That definitely explained a lot of my drive to get closer to him. Of course… as I brushed my fingers over his jacket, pulling it open further, I got a good look at some parts of him that certainly didn't *hurt* his likability.

Jack's shoulders were like multiple lush valleys; lines of muscle covered in black and green tattoos. Before I could shut myself down, I traced my fingerpads over his skin. It was warm, mostly smooth with the occasional interesting ridge of a scar here or there.

My hair hung around us, creating a shield from the world. It did nothing to muffle his sharp intake of air, then the following low, hot groan. I locked up; he looked up at me and whispered, "Oh no, baby girl, don't stop there. I've wanted to feel your hands on me for longer than I've had any right to."

The DJ's voice boomed overhead. "Thank you, gentlemen! Get ready for the next round of beautiful ladies… Frangelico, Lulu, and Sensual!"

"My set is finished," I said, breathing heavily.

"I'm not." He sat up, looking around the room. His attention narrowed in on the far staircase. "Let's go have a private dance."

It was good that he pulled me off the stage; I wasn't confident I could follow him without losing my balance. Were we really going to do this? Could I be alone with him and behave myself?

Did I *want* to?

As we climbed the steps, we rose high enough that the second floor balcony came into view. Across the way, I caught someone watching us. Callum was smoking, the thick curls half covering his face like some shifting mask.

Making me work here was his way of controlling me, but deep down, he clearly hated seeing me with other men. I didn't do many private dances; was he wondering how rich Jack had to be to lure me away?

One final push of smoke through his thick lips… and my boss strolled away from the edge.

Jack had stopped yanking me up the stairs. He was staring in the same direction I had been.

Is he wondering who Mister Big is?

Quick as a whip he glanced down at me, frowned, and then we were off again.

Reaching the top floor, Jack thumbed a stack of cash over to the man standing by the private booths. The rooms were curtained off, allowing for the people who used them to get up to all sorts of trouble. Jack had paid enough that the guard purposefully walked away.

No one was going to bother us.

"In," he said, the word more of a guttural sound than any sort of English language. I did as he asked. The heavy curtain fell around us, the black light on the wall above the single, over-stuffed chair making our eyes and teeth blue.

Shrugging out of his jacket, he dropped into the seat. His knees spread wide, hands resting on the arms like a king on a throne. His demeanor demanded I come forward—come to him—without having to say it out loud.

Just do your job. Clinging to that, I reached behind me as I sought out the soft beat of the music. It was quieter in here, but it still existed. I rode on the waves as I danced in place. Jack watched me like he had at the stage.

Like he had last night.

I had the oddest feeling he'd always been watching me.

My top fell from my grip, the gold glitter sparkling where it landed on the floor. Stepping over it, I kept my palms over my breasts. Jack hadn't seen me naked yet. The private dances lasted fifteen minutes, I could do what I always did; strip tease until the very end. The customers *hated* that—they expected physical contact for their hundred dollars—but I'd never cared.

But now… the idea of not filling the empty air with Jack's body was depressing. I wanted to touch him, to be touched, so why was I hesitating?

He shifted on the chair. "Fuck, you're turning me on like mad. Come here."

I peered at him through my lowered eyelashes. "Ask me nicely."

"You want me to beg?" he chuckled. Then he spread his legs further, showing off his massive erection. Palming it, Jack hissed through his teeth. "Look at this. Isn't it obvious I'm dying without you? I won't bite, not much."

My tongue ran over my bottom lip. "And if I ask you to bite?"

His eyes locked on me, his jaw falling open. Then he smirked so sharply I felt it cut through the last of my resistance. "You're something else. Something special, for sure. Get over here."

It took so few steps on my too-tall shoes to reach him. I swung a leg over, straddling his thighs. Between us, his cock was hard as stone. I gasped; he moaned, eyes rolling back at the gentle pressure of my weight on him.

One of his arms moved behind me, stroking along my naked back. On impulse I bent forward, thrusting my breasts into his face. He grabbed my hair, holding me there, looking from my cleavage to my eyes. "It's taking all I've got not to lick these perfect nipples."

My tongue was stuck to my teeth; I made it work. "You can't."

"No?" he asked softly. His other hand slid onto my hip, guiding me over his hard-on as he rolled his pelvis. I whimpered at the sensation of his firm cock bumping my pussy over and over. I didn't give lap dances like this—not to anyone.

Jack squeezed my ass, forcing me to rock faster along his erection. The thin strip of cotton over my pussy might as well have been a figment of my imagination. It did nothing to protect me from the pressure of his denim on my swelling clit. Had I ever been so turned on?

"I don't have sex with customers," I said quickly, like I was trying to talk myself out of a bad decision.

His smile was thin. "I'm not a customer."

"Coming here to buy lap dances makes you a customer."

"That's not why I came here."

Intrigued, I tried to focus on his words instead of how soft his lips looked. "Then what are you doing at the Golden Goose?"

Sweeping his fingers up my throat, he made my hairs stand on end. The tightness on my skin swirled down to my belly, then right between my thighs when he curled his grip in my scalp. It was a firm hold that caused no pain but trapped me against him.

In my ear, he whispered, "I came here for revenge."

"What?" I breathed out the question; his lips scooped it up, kissing me so suddenly that I forgot what gravity was. I was falling and floating and everything in between. His tongue slid over my bottom lip, tasting the deep indent—the marker that cruder men used to comment on how good I must be at sucking dick.

Jack made no such observations. He kissed me like he needed me to live.

And I forgot that we were two people completing a transaction.

Money didn't matter.

Rules didn't matter.

All I wanted was relief from the knots in my lower belly. I hadn't had sex in forever, it wasn't something I sought out. But now... now, it was all I could think about.

One of his hands abandoned me, reaching between us to unclip his belt. Panting, I hurried to help him slide his jeans down his thighs. Jack pressed me down; I was grinding on his cock where it strained in his boxers. The cotton material was damp, his pre-come saturating the inside.

Knowing I'd turned him on this much was making me dizzy. It couldn't be the alcohol—I'd had one sip, or was it two? No, this was pure arousal in my blood and pretending otherwise was foolish.

I stroked my hand down his chest, across his firm abdominals. When I reached the elastic band of his boxers he grabbed my wrist. "You sure?" he asked, his mouth in a pained grimace. "You grab my cock, baby doll, and I'm not leaving here without fucking you. I don't want you to get in any trouble with this place."

"It's fine." Looking down at his cock, I saw it flex in the cloth. The cotton couldn't hide the fat ridge of his head. "My boss won't fire me."

"No? You get special treatment around here?"

My laugh was as dry as an overcooked chicken bone. "I could probably set this place on fire and he'd keep me around."

Jack tensed up—so suddenly that I focused back on his face. He didn't give me a chance to read his expression, he kissed me again, his hand no longer holding mine back. He forced my palm onto his erection, the two of us groaning around the swirling tongues that teased in our mouths.

Gripping his warm shaft, I pumped him experimentally. Each movement had him panting on my skin. He nipped my bottom lip, then my earlobe, then he laughed. "That's incredible. I want to feel that sweet pussy, though. You're dripping on my lap. I'm going to slide into you so *easily,* no matter how fat my cock is." His filthy mouth made my clit twitch. "Grab the condom in my back pocket."

I scooted down his legs enough to bend back and dig into his jeans where they'd pooled at his ankles. The foil square was easy to find.

Peeling it open, I stared through the latex like it was a monocle; the room went all funky yellow. It was an unappetizing color, so how did Jack *still* look so damn delicious? In one smooth motion I sheathed his cock in the condom.

"Jesus," he growled. Clamping his palms around my waist he lifted me easily into the air.

"Wait, my bikini bottoms!" Was he going to shred the material?

Without straining, like I weighed nothing, Jack hooked his left thumb into the crotch of my glittery outfit. He didn't snap anything, he simply slid it out of the way, exposing my very wet pussy to the air.

Flaring his nostrils, he spread my lower lips, pushing the tip of his thick shaft against me. "Fuck," I gasped. Inch by inch he spread me open, no longer holding me up; he let my own weight help sink me down onto his cock. I was being speared like an animal he'd hunted down. The deeper he went, the more my vision blurred.

Then he thrust once; hard, quick, and I threw my head back with a desperate shout that had been growing in my belly. "Holy hell, holy fuck, Jack—Jack!"

"I love your voice," he growled. "Louder. Scream louder for me."

"Please, I'm not sure—"

"You can handle it." Gritting his teeth, he curled me against him. His shirt was warm with his sweat, my own running down my back. I was being wrung out like a damp towel. My insides shrank and expanded, heat blossoming as pleasure overtook any memory of pain. "You've got it, baby doll. That's it, rock your hips."

His fingertips came between us, circling over my swollen clit with clear intention. He knew how to touch me—I was relieved, I didn't think I could speak well enough to instruct him. Round and round he teased me until I was fucking him without any care for how loud I was getting.

I burned with an insane need to have him *deeper*. His hands played with my hair, lips brushing my temple as he whispered to me. "Feel me stretching you out?" he asked, filling me to the brim. "You're milking the hell out of me, Harper. Your pussy is fucking astounding."

And there it was; he'd gone so deep he was having sex with my brain.

Closing my eyes, I moaned as a hot spike of tension rocked down and made me squeeze his cock harder. I was right there, on the edge as my body vibrated between his seeking fingers and thrusting shaft.

His breathing went raspy. "Your moans are almost as good as your singing."

My singing? How could he... Blanking out as I came, I saw purple and glitter and the whole damn milky way. "I'm coming," I sobbed. "Fuck, I'm..."

"Me too," he hissed, embracing me as if I could escape him during my convulsions. Through the condom he twitched, expanding bigger; his orgasm was a second behind mine.

This stranger cradled me against him as we languished in a pleasure that I knew, for me, had been absent for years. But what about him? Did he go to clubs and screw strippers often? The idea was enough to cool me; I found my eyesight, my clarity beneath my bitter suspicion.

Carefully I pulled my body off of his. He chuckled, the noise rich and satisfying. "That was amazing."

My lips pressed up into an uncontrollable smile. "I'm glad." I wanted to say *That was beyond stellar! Best of the year, of the decade!* But I said no such things and instead straightened out my bikini bottoms.

Jack eyeballed me, not moving from his seat. Then he peeled the condom off, knotting the top. "We should hide this."

"It's fine, there's a garbage can behind the chair. Toss it there."

His eyebrows furrowed drastically. "Guess your boss really doesn't care what you girls do."

I stood up taller, trying to gauge his new tone. "If he gets his cut, he's happy."

Violently, he threw the condom into the can and turned to face me. His eyes reminded me of the center of a volcano. I waited for him to burn me into ash. "How could you work for a man like him?"

"Maybe I like working for him," I said quickly, not wanting to go down this road.

"Please. You're better than this."

I was wrong; he wasn't a strip club regular, he was a wannabe white knight. That was almost worse. "How would you even *know* that?"

He didn't flinch as he said, "Because I've heard your beautiful voice." If there was any hesitation in his eyes, it vanished as he looked me over with renewed determination. "I've heard you sing before."

"When?" Feeling exposed, I circled my arms over my chest. "The last time I sang was over seven years ago."

He stood up from the chair, his jeans still undone—why had I gone so far? "It was long ago, yes, but I'll never forget that night. You've got music in your veins, Harper. You could shake the world, bring it to its knees." His warm hands clasped my shoulders, then cupped my jaw like we were old friends—older lovers. "A voice like yours belongs on a stage."

"I've got a stage," I whispered. Shrugging him off of me, I backed up until the curtains hiding us from the rest of the club tickled my spine. "I belong up there on the pole with the other forgotten girls." *I don't want to sing. Never again.*

Jack stayed where he was. He was vibrating with a barely controlled energy; a single drop of sweat, a reminder of our bodies' heat, rolled down his chest. He breathed in thickly; I had to resist reaching out to touch his massive muscles. "I can tell when someone is hiding. I'm familiar with that world."

"Fine," I said, scooping my top up, rushing to tie it on. "Use your *familiarity* to recognize it's not your business if I'm hiding or not. Stay out of my life. You don't know me, Jack. And you shouldn't want to."

His voice was somber. "It's not the knowing that's the problem. It's the forgetting."

We faced off, both hiding secrets and, perhaps, wondering if revealing them would make the static energy in the air worse. A knock came on the wood outside the booth. "Harper?" a girl asked sweetly. "It's Sensual, you almost done in there? Maurice said you only had fifteen minutes and it's been twenty, so…"

Jack moved around me. He didn't look back, not once, as he opened the curtain. He stared straight ahead as he handed me a stack of money from his wallet. "We're done in here," he said to Sensual and the man beside her. "All yours."

The other customer peered at me, probably smelling the tang of sweat in the booth. I felt bad that I'd set Sensual up for trouble; this guy definitely assumed he was about to get some stripper-vag action.

The dancer was squinting at me with a half-smile. "Girl," she whispered, "You okay?"

"Yeah. Yeah, all good." Running my hands through my hair, I stared around the club. Jack was gone, lost in the crowd, maybe even out the front door by now. All I had was the stack of bills he'd given me for the dance.

It was the first time I wished I hadn't been paid.

The stairs rocked under me—I could have been on a ship at sea. *Jack knew me when I used to sing. He remembered me.* That part of my past was a wound so raw and open, any mention of it was pure salt and vinegar in my cells. Jack had taken me high only to drop me so hard I was shattered through my middle.

In my hand, the money was heavy.

Forget him. Who cares if he knew you. He's just a guy who got a dance… way more than a dance. If he wants to storm off, acting like a child, fine. Everything was fine.

It had to be.

"Harper?"

Mister Big was standing along the edge of the hallway, blocking me from the stairwell that led to the girls' dressing room. He looked at me closely. When he focused on the cash in my hand, I slid my arm behind my back on reflex. His smile was sickening. "Nice haul, all that for one dance?"

I was confused until I lifted the money back into view. Jack was supposed to pay me a hundred bucks, but this was more; way more. *Five hundred damn dollars?* Blinking, I offered my boss a quick shrug. "He… really liked me."

"Well," Callum chuckled, leaning in close. We weren't alone, but I felt like I might as well have been. No one would interrupt this man… no one was that stupid. "You're a beautiful girl. Any man would fall for you, if you gave them a chance. Your mother had that same natural gift." He stroked my cheek; I pulled away, not hiding the disgust on my face.

This was why I avoided him. I couldn't fake niceness when he pressed me.

The next time he spoke, he was seething. "Hate me all you like, but I should remind you that the only reason you and your sister are together is because of me."

I didn't need him to remind me of anything. "Did you want something, or can I go?"

He adjusted his black jacket, looking over my head, then back to me. "Give me my cut of your dance money, then you can go back to work."

Not arguing, I peeled off his share of the cost; twenty bucks.

His fingers curled in his open palm. "No, dear. Twenty percent would be one hundred dollars."

I recoiled, gripping the cash tight. "But I did *one* private dance!"

"And you were paid five hundred for that. I still get twenty percent, Harper. Understand?"

Furious at his attempt to bully me, I debated my options. It was a waste of time; as long as I insisted on staying in Cena's life, I had to obey Callum's rules. Curling my lips over my teeth, I slapped the money into his hand. "Fine. Here, now can I go?"

Shoving the bills into his jacket's inner pocket, he nodded. "Yes. Get back out there," he mumbled, strolling around me. "And don't do anything stupid."

He didn't know it was too late.

I mean, I'd already screwed Jack.

How much stupider could I get?

CHAPTER FOUR

JACK

AFTER YEARS OF plotting my revenge, I'd made my first mistake.

My grim face looked back at me in my car's mirror. Red veins slithered through the edges of my eyeballs—reminding me how little I'd slept. After leaving the Golden Goose, I'd driven around for hours, trying to shake Harper from my brain.

It was a pointless effort.

I shouldn't have spoken to her. That much was obvious, but I'd never been great at ignoring people in trouble. I'd thought she was just another dancer. Then I'd heard her humming... and that sound had burrowed into my memory. Suddenly I was back on that alley ground. Suddenly, the angel who'd shown me mercy was hovering over my broken body.

I couldn't have predicted that I'd find her again.

Least of all, I wouldn't have guessed she'd be in *that* filthy club.

She belonged on a stage meant for goddesses. Instead, she spent her nights twirling around a greasy metal pole for the lowest scum around. *You're no better,* I reprimanded myself. *You bought her body the same as the rest.*

Harper had smelled like a sweet dream and tasted like glory. She'd reminded me of who I'd been before years on the street had hardened me.

That girl... my past... none of it belonged to me any longer. I had a mission. My second chance was all about revenge. I reminded myself of that as I scanned the sidewalk outside of my car, watching the condo for signs of my target.

If I did this right, I wouldn't need to go back to the Golden Goose. I wouldn't see Harper again. I'd make Mister Big pay. Then my conscience would be clear.

Thinking of the look on that man's face when I ruined his world had my heart racing. Squeezing the steering wheel, I squinted at the condo doors.

They were glass but the morning sun was reflecting in such a way you couldn't see inside.

Movement; the doorman in his coat stepped aside to let a small girl out into the sunlight. Cena was tall for eight years old, her hair in a short bowl-cut that enhanced her round face. Cute. Sweet.

Would she cry when I kidnapped her?

"Slow down," Harper laughed, chasing Cena out onto the sidewalk. The sight of the woman I'd screwed under black lights just last night filled my lungs with cement. She was wearing plain jeans and a loose pink sweater, her hair that had tickled my bare shoulders thrown up in a loose bun.

She was more beautiful than ever.

Why the *fuck* was she here with Cena Blunderbore?

Leaning back in the car, paranoid she'd see me, I ran through all the options in my head. I'd witnessed Harper entering the condo a few times since I'd been scouting the building. My guess was that she was screwing her boss, a fact that turned my insides into sour-mash once I'd realized who she was.

Mister Big had everything; even things he didn't know belonged to me.

Sitting there, I watched Harper as she scooped up Cena's hand and guided her down the street. The young girl attended an elementary school nearby. Normally, she walked alone. What had changed about today? Whatever it was, it was messing my plan up.

They were at the corner across from me when I made a snap decision.

Pushing my car door open, I stepped out, shielding my eyes from the early sun. *Act natural. No one knows what you were going to do.* "Hey!" I called, waving, dodging through the light traffic and over the double yellow lines.

Harper's eyes went so wide I expected them to fall to the ground.

Good. We both got to enjoy some shock today.

As I grew closer, I noticed Harper had her hands clasped on Cena's shoulders. They were closer than I suspected, which meant her and Mister Big were close, too. She *had* hinted last night that he'd never fire her.

He's her sugar daddy. The realization made it hard for me to fake a smile. "Hi," I said. "Funny running into you."

"Funny?" she asked, arching one eyebrow. "That's not the word I'd pick. What are you doing here?"

Before I could answer, Cena broke away from Harper, standing on her tip-toes to look closely at me. "I've never seen you before! Are you Hap's secret boyfriend or something?"

Harper's cheeks burned red. I fought down my urge to reach out and test how hot they felt. Crouching down so I was face to face with Cena, I whispered loud enough for Harper to hear. "You mean she didn't tell you? That's not very nice of her."

"No!" she agreed, glaring playfully up at the older woman. "It's not! Hap, why'd you keep him a secret? It's not like he's an ugly troll or something."

Laughing heartily, I reconsidered Cena. "That's nice of you to say."

"I have good taste," she chirped. "Are you walking your kids to school?"

That question threw me off, and I caught Harper grinning behind her hand. She liked seeing me on off footing... but that made two of us. "No kids for me yet, maybe one day."

"Well, Hap doesn't have *any* babies either, so maybe—"

"Cena!" Harper grimaced, lightly nudging the girl along the sidewalk. "Let's get going."

Grabbing my belly, I followed close by. "I'll walk with you."

"No," she said softly, "You won't. We're safe."

"But Hap! He can help keep us safe! Want to be our knight, Sir...?"

"Jack," I chuckled. "I'll be Sir Jack. It's an honor to guard you."

Cena beamed, but Harper looked unimpressed. The small girl was almost skipping around us both as we walked. "Sir Jack," she asked, giggling, "Did you bring anything for Hap? Good guys always bring things to pretty girls, like flowers, or fancy cars."

"Would you like those things?" I asked, talking to Cena, though I was watching Harper with a wry smile.

Shaking her blonde bob of hair, she said quite matter-of-factly, "Nope! I want a ride to the moon!"

At my blank expression, Harper shrugged one shoulder. "She loves space. Wants to be an astronaut someday."

"I can't take you to space," I said to Cena, sighing. "Does that make me a bad man?"

She stopped on a dime, peering up at me with her nose all scrunched. "You only look a *little* like a bad man. Kind of like James Dean in *Rebel Without a Cause*."

Harper didn't bite back her laugh that time. The longer we walked, the more she seemed to relax. "Cena adores old movies."

"Okay, we're here!" Cena squealed, hugging Harper tight. She waved at me frantically. "Bring me to space next time! Bye, bye! See you later!"

"So," I said, watching Cena jog into the school building, "Your boss pay you extra to play babysitter, or is that just written in the fine details of your contract?"

Instead of answering me, she snatched my forearm, digging her nails in. "What the hell are you up to?" she hissed.

I laughed uneasily. "Good grip you have there."

"I'm not joking around." Her grip didn't loosen; she rose up, speaking an inch away from my mouth. "Why were you waiting for me in your car?" A flash of something passed across her wild expression. "If you're being paid to make sure I don't run off with Cena, you can tell Callum I know better than that."

Firmly, I grabbed her hand and pried her fingers off of me one by one. She didn't fight back. "Now why would he think you'd do something like that?"

"Answer me: do you work for him?"

The suggestion curdled my guts. "He didn't hire me to do shit."

Harper searched my eyes for a long minute. Whatever she saw satisfied her, because she breathed in deep, hands hanging at her hips loosely. "Then why are you here? We had *one* dance, Jack. You shouldn't be so hooked on me."

Her suggestion hit too close to home. Grinning so wide my cheeks hurt, I rustled my hair. "Yeah, well, it was a really good dance."

Harper laughed, the sound so clean I wanted to bottle it up and save it for my darker days. "I see what's happening here. But just because you saved me from one stalker doesn't give you a free pass to become one yourself."

"Do you really think I'm a creep?"

"It's possible. The part of me that's supposed to give off warning bells if someone is dangerous has never worked."

"I believe it," I said, following her as she started to walk back towards the condo. "I'm definitely a terrible person and you've clearly got the hots for me." She covered her mouth to muffle her giggle. My ears ate up every sound she made, the vibrations swimming in my heart until it thrummed like a live wire. "I know I keep saying it, but your voice is beautiful."

There was a hiccup in her pace. Harper shot me a furtive look, then stared straight ahead. "You said last night that you heard me perform. Where?"

Here it was—a direct question that would reveal our connection. Would she remember that night, and if she did, would that help or hurt my plans? "There was a place back in Sommersville, the Copper Tub. You performed that night... first and only time I heard you sing."

She pulled up short. We were alone on the street, so it struck me as odd how she darted her eyes around before settling on me again. Why did any talk about her singing make her so edgy? "I hated that place. What were you doing there? That club was known for dirty deeds."

I looked down my nose at her. "You're right," I whispered. "You can make an educated guess why I was there. Dirty business."

We faced off; her, staring up at me with what I kept expecting to be disgust. Instead, her features softened, the edge of her ruby lips creating a curious smile. "Huh."

"What's up?"

"It's just funny," she said, half turning away from me. "You're set on trying to make yourself sound awful. I don't believe any of it."

Unsure what to do with her observation, I followed at her side as she walked. "You said it yourself, you can't read people."

"Maybe," she mused. We approached the condo, the doors reflecting our images back at us. In the glass, we were all stretched out and wobbly, our hands warping, almost touching in their imperfection. I loved it. "This is my stop," she said, jerking her thumb at the building.

"Wait, you live here?"

She made a face. "Of course I do."

This was a new twist. Did it mean Callum paid for her rent, or did she get a discount because he owned the place? Maybe stripping really did pay the bills. "Are you chasing me off? Cena told you, I'm not a bad guy."

Harper's eyes moved to the doorman, then back to me. "Give me one reason to invite you up to my place."

Cocking my hip, I chuckled warmly. "We could play twenty questions."

I'd meant it as a light joke, but her expression said I'd intrigued her. Perhaps telling her that I'd heard her sing would actually turn out to be a good thing. "If you come up," she said slowly, "You'll behave."

"What did you say last night?" I asked, so softly she had to strain to hear me over the cars driving by. "Something about… not biting unless asked?"

Harper's lips parted; I ached to fill the gap with my mouth. Whirling, she pressed a key card to the door, motioning for me to go inside. The lobby was wide; bright from all the windows. A large elevator reached up from the middle of the room, gold and crystal. The stripper poles at the Golden Goose kept entering my mind.

Callum owns all of this. It was impossible not to think of this place like a stone tower. And at the top was Mister Big, ready to crash and burn once I toppled him down.

"This way," she said, leading me towards the elevator. We passed by the security desk as we went. There was a man there, his face jagged, too thin in all the wrong ways. His hands were harmlessly holding a phone to his ear. But I knew exactly what cruelty they were capable of.

He watched me as I walked by, but no recognition flashed in his face. Between us both, the only reaction was my ribs straining with the memory of old injuries.

"You okay?"

Blinking, I stood next to Harper in the elevator. "Fine. Just thinking about how small of a space we're in."

Her cheeks turned a dusky pink. "I said behave."

"I am." Purposefully, I set my hand on the smooth wall right above her head; she flinched, breathing deeply. "I'm just riding up with you. That's tame. I'm definitely not thinking about how much time I have to kiss you and get your clothes off before we… ah." The doors dinged. "Never mind."

Harper gave me a slight shove. "You're something else."

"Flattery is always appreciated."

The walk down the hallway to her condo was short. She clicked a key in the lock; the entryway opened straight into a wide, brightly lit room. A chunk of speckled marble formed the island in the kitchen; I could see it from the door thanks to the open floor plan. No question, these condo arrangements had to run a high five figures a month.

"Your boss pay for you to live here, or do you take care of that with your dance money?"

She didn't bristle, though she did look away from me. "He pays for it."

The knife of jealousy cut deeper into my heart. I was right; sugar daddy arrangement.

Harper went into the kitchen, draping her purse onto the back of the chair. "Callum paid for everything. It started slow, but soon, everything was in his name."

My mouth went dry. "Why would you let him have that much control over you?"

Running water from the sink, she snorted loudly. "Sorry. It's not like I had a choice. Mom wasn't exactly old fashioned, but what wife turns down her husband's gifts?"

I grabbed the island to balance myself. There was no way I'd heard her right. "Husband?"

"Yeah. My mom was married to him before she passed away."

Impossible. Callum is her dad? But... when I researched Mister Big, I'd learned he only had one daughter: Cena. How was this possible?

"Here," she said, setting a glass of water on the island. She'd poured one for each of us. When I didn't immediately take it, she squinted at me. "Jack, you okay?"

Regarding the room... Harper... everything with more distrust, I sat on a stool next to her. "I didn't know your boss was your dad."

"Stepdad. He married my mom when she got pregnant with Cena. I kept her last name, I'd had it my whole life, why change it when I was nearly sixteen?"

Then Cena is her half sister. I was reeling, absorbing all this information at hyper-speed. Everything made more sense; Harper coming here at night wasn't to fuck her boss, it was to be with her sister. Walking her to school wasn't a job. They were flesh and blood.

Fuck.

This will mess up my plans, won't it? I dug my fingers into my knees. *No, it won't. It can't. I can still go through with everything. I have to, I...*

"Jack? Jack!" Harper grabbed the front of my shirt, holding my shoulders tight. "What's wrong, you're so pale."

I circled my hands on her forearms. I'd zoned out, but when I zeroed back into the moment, I saw how close her and I were. I could count her eyelashes, see the fine lines in her plump bottom lip. The fear in her eyes made her blue irises glint with silver.

Her shirt was loose enough that my angle gave me a view of her lavender bra inside. She was breathing quicker; she'd noticed our proximity, her body's signals giving her anticipation away. It was exactly how she'd reacted when she was giving me a lap dance.

The memory made my jeans too tight.

She started to back up; my hands became a vice. "Wait."

"Okay," she said nervously, "Just tell me what's wrong."

Closing my eyes, I took a slow breath. The particles in the air were all her. "What's wrong," I said, my voice thick with need, "Is that I haven't felt your lips in over ten hours."

We came together like a wave on a beach. I wanted to kiss her until she eroded my fears. I needed her wetness, her warmth, the sweetness of her taste buds on my own… and I needed it more for my heart than for my body.

Kissing Harper the first time was a mistake. This? This was suicide.

Cupping her cheeks, I rubbed my nose on hers. "Dammit," I hissed. "How can you be this perfect?" Catching her hip, I lifted her knee and pressed it against my ribs. She was standing; I was still sitting. I'd rooted myself to the spot, as if I was sure, if I rose to my feet, duty would force me to end everything.

I wasn't ready for an ending. For years, I'd been sure I was; the end was the only thing that gave me meaning. I fell asleep each night thinking about how I'd crush Mister Big. It was my drive, nothing had threatened that.

Cena is her sister.

Fuck.

"Jack," she said as I pulled out of the kiss. Her nails cut through my hair; each motion created tingles in my bones. My muscles went taut, cock raging in my boxers.

Nearly panting, I released her leg. "I can't," I said. "We can't."

"What?" My rejection shocked her almost as badly as it did me. Harper stroked my bicep and I stepped off the stool. Both of us saw me adjusting my painful hard-on, her confusion making my heart ache. "Did I do something wrong?"

"No, of course not. I just… I just need a minute." My neck twinged as I looked around the room. Behind me was the exit to the main hall, in front of me was Harper, and to the side was the bathroom. *Go out the front door, leave her. This won't work—you can't have her. Fuck, you're going to kidnap her sister*

---

to use as blackmail.

She's Mister Big's daughter. Maybe not by blood, but... for all it counts... family.

You can't get Cena today, but there's always tomorrow. Unless you chicken out.

Harper is your enemy.

The angel who'd saved me was looking at me like I'd cut out her lungs. I'd had plans to do so much worse. "I'll be right back," I mumbled, dodging around her and into the bathroom. Closed away there, I could still *feel* her with me. The walls, the door, they did nothing to separate me from Harper.

The room was pure white marble and silver fixtures. Bending over the sink, I ran the water, cupping it in my palms. It slid between the gaps in my fingers. *That's my resolve,* I thought, fighting the urge to laugh. How could I possibly go through with kidnapping Cena now that I knew she was Harper's half sister?

Splashing my face, I gripped the edges of the basin and stared at my reflection. The sight of my own uncertain features strangled my heart. Flaring with anger at my own weakness, I filled the sink to the brim. I shoved my whole head under.

Idiot.

I let the water fill my nose.

You've forgotten everything you struggled for.

The sensation of drowning cleared my head. When my chest seared like I'd filled it with tar, I ripped myself upwards, drawing in oxygen with pained gasps. Palming soaked strands of hair off of my forehead, I smoothed my hands over my scalp. My eyes throbbed, but I could see clearly, think sharply.

When I'd been left to die in that alley, I'd learned the only time we're capable of awareness is when we're balanced on the frayed wire of death.

And that was the only reason I spotted what I did above the mirror.

Freezing, I squinted in disbelief at the spot between the two large light bulbs in their silver casings. What I saw made my veins run with acid. It infuriated me in a way few things could.

I knew exactly what I had to do.

CHAPTER FIVE
HARPER

H E CAME BACK out, his face a map of turmoil. I didn't know Jack well and I had to keep reminding myself of that. Our connection was all in my head, and I was great at making poor decisions. But I wanted to know what was going on... why he was acting so weird... so I sat there, perched on the stool, and waited.

Jack paused in front of me, stiff as a statue of armor. "Your stepdad, do you love him?"

Again and again, Jack left me guessing. "Why does that matter?"

"Just tell me."

I leaned away, scrunching up my nose. "No. I don't love the man."

"Then why the hell do you work for him?"

"Jack, if you're about to try and pull some 'Save the poor stripper' bit on me, I don't need it."

"I'm not trying to save you. I'm trying to understand you."

Jack sought me out with a raw, genuine expression of concern. Only Cena looked at me that way. My guard cracked, every reason I had not to tell this man about my situation falling into the shadow cast by my heart. "It's not a happy story."

He smiled, but it didn't reach his eyes. "Few of them are."

I closed my eyes and breathed. In my ears was the low ring of white noise, the stuff that filled the gaps between memories. I scooped it out of the way and let myself talk. "Callum wanted me to be a singer. He always wanted that... he said I was special, knew I'd make him rich. When he discovered me, I felt blessed. But that meeting was what linked him to my mother." Wincing, I uncurled my fingers; my nails had dug into my own flesh. "When I realized that singing had ruined any happiness my family could have had, even if we remained poor... I decided I no longer wanted to sing. I convinced

Callum I'd lost my ability due to… grief." I glanced away, not ready to expand on that part of the story. "It infuriated him. But he wasn't going to let me off free of charge. If I wanted to see my sister, I had—have—to work for him."

"He doesn't know you can still sing?"

"Only you and Cena know."

Jack blinked. "It's hard for me to wrap my brain around, choosing stripping over singing."

My laugh was hollow in my chest. I wondered if that meant my heart had shrunk, and all I had inside of me was useless air. "I'd choose it over and over, and then I'd choose it again."

"But you're voice… it's amazing."

"This *amazing* voice ruined my life, Jack. Stripping my clothes off for strange men isn't torture. Callum can't hurt me by making me get on that stage. If anything… I relish it."

He scooped my hands up where I'd folded them in my lap. His fingers brushed the sensitive undersides of my wrists. "Explain that for me."

I hated this story. I wished we could just go back to kissing, to forgetting. *This is better,* I told myself. *If he knows everything, there's nothing left to hide. He can accept my messed up life or walk away before I'm too attached.* Part of me knew it was too late. "Every night that Callum sees me up there, twirling on his damn pole, dollar bills showering over me? It's a reminder to him that he'll never, *ever* get what he wants from me."

I waited for him to tell me I was insane; because I certainly was. Or maybe he'd say I was stupid. I sometimes felt that way, too. I waited for him to cut me open and see that I was full of dust inside. His lips made a "y" shape and I rapidly prepared for his sentence to be: *"You're wasting your life."*

"You're a fool."

"You're worthless."

Jack said, "You're the strongest person I've ever met."

My ribs hurt; my heart wasn't small, it couldn't be with how much it made my chest strain to keep it from bursting. "What?"

"How else could you spend all of this time throwing his loss in his face? That's powerful stuff, Harper. There's just one thing I'm wondering about."

I swallowed, noticing how I'd leaned closer to him. "What?"

"Why did you stop singing in the first place?"

My voice came out flat. "I can't answer that. I don't know you well enough."

Jack didn't press it. Letting go of my wrists, he took my chin, gazing down at me like he could read the grooves in my brain. "Has Callum ever hurt you?"

"Not physically, but I'd let him make me suffer as long as he left Cena alone."

His touch vanished. Jack paced the kitchen, his hands knotted at his sides. They were coiled springs, waiting to unleash their power on anyone who dared to get in his way. I watched with fascination, but not fear—angry men didn't frighten me. More than that... Jack didn't frighten me.

When he came back my way, I heard he was whispering. I caught none of it, just that he was talking to himself in a rapid, disgust filled tone. Words were chewed up, spit out, forgotten so he could make room for more.

Finally, he whirled on me. The ferocity in his eyes paled next to his hard-set jaw. "No more of this. I can't let a monster like him hurt anyone else. You deserve better, Harper. Someone as kind as you deserves the damn world."

My head began to float away, my voice distant to my ears. "You can't know that. You don't know me, Jack. Deep down I'm horrible. I've ruined lives."

"No," he snapped, standing over me, but never touching me. It was like he feared I'd shatter in his grip. "You're an angel. You saved my life... you gave me a second chance."

I was definitely floating away now. My skin felt too tight over my skull. "What are you talking about? A second chance at what?" I wished I could read his mind the way he seemed to be able to with mine. *I never saved him... we just met a few days ago.* I chased my memory for any tail-end hints of what he was speaking about. Then I locked up, recalling something with vibrant unease. "Jack, last night, you said you were at the club for revenge."

Jack didn't stir. He watched me expectantly.

My lungs struggled, my breath getting quicker. "You want revenge on Mister Big. I'm right, aren't I?" It made sense, all these questions about my boss... about if I loved him, if he'd hurt me. I was right and I knew it before Jack said a word.

Bending closer, he took my hands, spreading my fingertips on his face. Slowly, he brushed them over his jaw and forehead. There were fine, raised lines; old scars. "Do you remember a young man lying in an alley?" he asked softly. "A fool who thought life would reward him just because he'd known nothing but suffering?"

A trumpet wailed in my head. Sound waves hammered on my memory until they molded it into something diamond-clear. Someone was brutally beaten and lying in an alley. His face was swollen, more crimson than tan-skin—nothing like the hardened jaw of Jack now. Yet I knew them to be one and the same.

In my memory, sirens screamed. I'd hung around just long enough to make sure the ambulance got to him. The last I'd seen of the young man was his body strapped to a gurney.

Until now.

At some point I'd yanked my hands away from him and moved them over my lips; I whispered through them in desperate fear. "What did my step father *do* to you?"

Every line in his face told a story with the same tragic ending. This was a man who'd been unquestionably wounded. How had I not recognized our kinship? "He stole *everything* from me. But that's fine, because I'm going to return the favor tenfold." The way he smiled made my heart stop. "Mister Big has lots to hide. I've got a plan to make him admit to the worst shit. All I need is some leverage."

Sparks of paranoia went off in me, traveling along my spine until I was lit up from within. I needed to know his plan, because as intriguing as this was, as *tempting* as hearing him muse over destroying a man I hated was, I suspected his plan was dangerous.

He considered me, watching for my reactions. "I was going to kidnap the one person that I thought meant something to him. His only daughter."

I choked on a wave of bile. The room swam, but only for a second. "No," I said flatly, stepping towards him. "You need to leave."

"What's wrong?"

"Leave. Or I'm calling the police."

The confusion in his eyes hurt me more than I expected. "Don't you hate Callum as much as I do?"

Marching to the front door, I grabbed the knob, yanking it open. The air that swirled inside caught my hair so that it blinded me. It was brief, and I wished it lasted forever. Seeing Jack so... betrayed... it was too much. "I do hate him. But I love Cena more."

Jack's face went slack. "I wouldn't hurt her. It'd be an act, and with you in on it, she'd—"

"She'd be terrified. And what if your plan failed? What if Callum's vengeance is worse than yours? Jack, I'm not going to put her through that."

He drew himself up. "She doesn't have a clue who he is, does she?"

"She's eight fucking years old, Jack. Of course she doesn't know. And if I get my way… she never will." I couldn't imagine the way Cena would change if she got a whiff of how corrupt her own father was. The guilt would sweep over her, staining her soul. She deserved better.

On long legs he came my way. I readied myself for fight or flight, his approach setting my heart into hyper-mode. "I get it. Your grand plan is to sit here and suffer until she's old enough to legally leave with you. How fucking long is that, ten years? Until she's eighteen?"

My shrug was heavy. "I'll take the misery now if it means I get the future I want."

"You're wrong, weren't you listening to me?" He slapped his chest with an open palm. "I suffered, *I* lost everything… my home, my own mother… that's what suffering gets you. Life doesn't care if you put in your dues, Harper. Hoping for a happy ending just because you went through hell to get it is a fool's dream."

His words smothered me, pulling at my confidence until I wondered if my path was the wrong one. Jack took another step; when he did, I saw past him, spotting Cena's room. She'd covered the outside of it with music notes and pink flowers.

I thought about the mother she'd never known.

How that was all of my fault.

Calmly, I said, "I'm never going to put my sister in danger."

"Not even if it gets you both away from that giant monster?"

I narrowed my eyes, staring at his stoic expression. "Tell me what happens if your plan works."

Jack perked up, his arms flexing as he gestured over his head. "I'll bring that bastard to his knees. I'll chop everything out from under him until he's got nothing to stand on, nothing to keep him above our heads. Then when he realizes he has to do as I say or he'll lose more than his reputation, I'll make him sign the Golden Goose over to me."

"The club? Why do you want that place?"

"Because it belongs to me." His fists balled up, knuckles straining, blood-less. "He promised it would be ours together. Then he betrayed me. After everything else, I'm getting what's owed to me."

"And then?"

Jack's eyes were foggy, like he was somewhere else. His tone was pure acid. "Death is too good for him. He'll go to prison, and with any luck, be tortured by people who learn how evil he is."

The man in front of me wasn't the one I'd tangled with in the club. Certainly not the man who'd emerged from the darkness to rescue me in the parking lot. Jack's aura burned the color of death; there was no way he'd consider Cena's safety or my own on his path towards vengeance.

I thought about the mantra Mister Big had spit at me since I began work-ing for his club. *No court will award custody of an eight year old to a dirty stripper. Just try me. I've got friends in high places.*

"It won't work. If anything happens to him, Cena will get put into the system. I won't see her for years, I won't be able to keep her safe. Leave," I whispered. "Just leave."

For a minute I thought he wouldn't. He shot one quick look over his shoulder, towards the hallway bathroom. The wrinkles around his forehead deepened. Jack stood so still he could have stopped breathing, and I wondered what he was thinking about.

Finally he brushed passed me. "I'll go, but if you think I'm done, you're wrong. The only way this ends is with him in a broken pile at my feet." He looked at everything in the hallway but my face. "You're willing to let yourself be hurt in order to save her. But she's not as safe as you assume. As long as he can reach her... she never will be."

Then he was gone.

CHAPTER SIX
HARPER

*J*ACK WAS GOING *to kidnap my sister.*

No—past tense was wrong. Why would he call off his plan? The guy was single minded; just thinking about him reliving his past as he told me it had my adrenaline racing. He'd been so passionate about destroying my stepfather. He'd made it sound *easy.* I was too smart to think taking down Mister Big was anything close to the word "easy."

In the elevator, I tapped my hand on the metal wall. I'd never forgive myself if I assumed Jack would change his plan. *Did Callum really take everything from him?* Remembering Jack's bloody body in the alley seven years ago, I shivered.

I understood his desire.

I really, truly did.

But Cena… she was my heart. I couldn't put her in danger. Besides, I'd lasted this long, I knew what Callum could do to me. The devil you know is better than the devil you don't.

And I didn't know Jack.

The elevator dinged; I jumped out, scanning the lobby. The security desk was empty—that wasn't strange, Hector was usually lax in his duties. What mattered to me was that Jack was nowhere in sight. Good, I wanted him gone. Even if I wanted to grab his hands and talk him out of his suicidal mission, to tell him to give up on revenge and just waste time with me… I knew it was foolish.

Breathing faster by the second, I stormed down the sidewalk in the warm air. I didn't breathe easier until an hour later when, as I stood sentry outside her school, my sister walked outside. Her eyes lit up at the sight of me. "Hap! Look what I made!" She ran to me, lifting some sort of paper bag with hearts on it. "It's a homemade kaleidoscope—oh!" Cena couldn't finish because I'd crouched down, scooping her up and squeezing her tight.

She's safe. For now, she's safe.

"Hap?" she asked, muffled in my chest.

"Sorry!" I set her down, but my hand stayed on her shoulder. "Just happy to see you."

She searched my face. The perfect pink bow of her mouth became a thin line. "Something's wrong."

"No, no, I'm just having a weird day."

"Hm."

Pulling her with me, I eyeballed every person on the street as we walked back towards the condo. "Tell me about school."

"Wait, where's lover boy?"

A tiny flutter corrupted my heart. "Jack is busy. Don't worry about him."

"I like him. He seems nice, even if he *does* have a lot of tattoos."

A smile escaped me. The sickness in my stomach overwhelmed the small burst of joy. "Hey, how about we do some errands together?"

"Sounds boring."

"Drat. I didn't know ice cream at the Dairy Queen near the bank was boring. Guess I'll have to think of something else."

Whatever distrust she'd wielded faded away. "Wait! I take it back!"

Laughing, I hoisted her onto my shoulders. It was a quick jog to the condo, and as I passed the doors, I couldn't keep myself from looking inside at the lobby desk. *Is Hector STILL gone?* The lack of security, in my current state, infuriated me.

"Can I get whipped cream?"

"Huh?" I asked, pulled from my thoughts.

"And chocolate syrup," Cena said, buckling herself in. "I've been very good lately. I probably deserve it."

Pursing my lips, I turned the engine over and drove my Taurus out of the lot. "You're right, Cena. You deserve whatever you want."

I meant it.

WHEN I FINISHED handing over my envelopes of cash to the scrutinizing bank clerk, I headed back to Cena. She was sitting in one of the fluffy chairs along the wall, trying to wrap two lollipop sticks together. Her tongue was blue when she smiled. "Was it still there?"

I knew she was talking about more than the money I was stowing away for our future. "Of course it was. As pretty as ever."

"I can't wait until I can wear it." She hopped down, following me out the doors into the sun. "But I'm not supposed to until I'm older, right?"

"Right," I said seriously. "It's a necklace for adults." Frankly, the emerald necklace wasn't meant for anyone. Mom had worn it only twice that I'd seen. I was shocked to find it buried deep in her dresser, beneath her old pregnancy clothes. It had to be worth a fortune. I'd been uncertain about Cena's future and my own back then, so stashing the necklace in a secret bank box was my only solution.

One day, Cena found a photo of mom wearing the necklace and cuddling a newborn version of her. Cena's chubby hand was grasping an emerald. She'd thought it was beautiful, magical... so I'd taken her to the bank. When I saw how huge her eyes had gotten at the sight of the necklace... I'd promised it would be hers.

But she had to keep it a secret.

We had a lot of secrets.

Outside, the picnic table's red umbrella turned everything pinkish from the sunlight. It made our vanilla ice cream look like it was really strawberry. Cena's face was sticky; her smile gigantic. If anything hammered home how I'd made the right choice not to work with Jack, this was it.

I wanted to stay with her as the sun set. But I knew I couldn't. "Come on, time to go."

Cena wiped her hands on her napkin. Her voice was low, which wasn't normal. "Work tonight?"

Standing, I watched her closely. "That's right."

The napkin twisted in her fingers, just like the lollipop sticks earlier. "Hap... what do you do for work?"

A spider of fear crawled through my chest. "I'm a waitress, you know that."

"Mn." She tossed the napkin in the trash.

"Cena... why are you asking this?"

There's nothing sadder than a small child's defeated shrug. "Daddy was talking to Manina." That was our weekly maid. "She was cleaning the kitchen, and I heard him say to her that he could get her a job where you work. That didn't make her happy."

"Oh, that…"

"Are *you* happy there?"

I was lost for words. Kneeling, I brushed her hair from her face. "Cena," I said, waiting until she looked at me. "Work is work. You do what you have to, it's okay if you're not happy. Lots of people don't like their jobs."

Resting her hands on my shoulders, she said solemnly, "But you should always be happy. I want you to be happy."

Inside of me, the storm that had been boiling for hours broke apart. Cena was in my arms, crushed in a hug, before I thought it over. But why even think? Loving her was an instinct, and of all the things out there, I trusted it the most. "I love you," I whispered. "You make me happy. Did you know that?"

"I love you, too." Usually she struggled to get free. Not this time.

As we drove back home, my mind was a wreck. Cena wanted me to be happy, but did she know what that meant? Did she suspect my job wasn't waitressing, but something more sordid? Her innocence was something I'd taken for granted. She was only eight, and I did my best to shield her, but the condo we lived in was frequented by people all touched in various degrees by my stepfather. Security, the maids, the women he took home, business associates…

How much longer could I keep Cena from seeing the dirty truth?

Chapter Seven
Harper

"CENA," I SAID, knocking on the bathroom door. "You all done?"

"Just plucking my eyebrows!"

"What?" I sputtered, bursting into the room. Steam from the shower had turned everything hazy; she stood in front of the mirror, grinning at me. Her eyebrows were intact. "Don't scare me like that!"

Giggling, she tipped her head upside down, drying her hair with a towel. She'd slipped into her long blue night-shirt, the length exposing her knees. She was going to be taller than me, at this rate.

Chasing her into her bedroom, I tucked her under the blankets. "Tomorrow is Saturday," I said, killing the lights. "Maybe we'll go to the zoo or something."

"Can Jack come?"

I went stiff. "I don't know. Why do you want him there?"

"He makes me feel safe. Like you do, Hap."

Hovering in the doorway, I watched my little sister thoughtfully. Her eyes were wide; luminous in the night sky that drifted through her window. "Cena… is something making you worried?" An idea struck me. "Do you still feel like you're being watched?"

She rolled onto her side. "Just ask Jack to come with us. Please."

Her shoulder rose and fell. I wasn't sure if she was already asleep or not, so I whispered, "Alright." Something was plucking at me; what was making Cena so scared? Why did she think someone was watching her?

Shutting the door, I stared at it and the flowers taped there. It was impossible not to think about my encounter with Jack earlier today. He'd revealed so much to me, I'd done the same for him. No one knew I was keeping my voice a secret from Callum except for Cena, and she didn't really get the why of it. I was lucky she respected the sanctity of sister secrets.

Moving to the kitchen, I looked at the island. The water glasses from Jack and I still sat there. *He kissed me,* I remembered, brushing my lips. He'd gotten so worked up, then he'd run away. *It was only when he came out of the bathroom that he revealed his plan.*

Staring at that room, a creeping sensation of unease moved up my body. On soft steps I entered the bathroom. The shower steam was long gone, but there were streaks on the mirror where Cena had written "I <3 Ice Cream."

Grabbing a towel, I started to wipe it clean. My gaze wandered upwards. I saw my own tired eyes—knew I'd have to pack on the makeup thick for work tonight. Guys didn't like when you looked exhausted.

Something glinted between the light bulbs. I spotted it in my reflection, squinting as I drew closer. On tiptoe I peeled the almost invisible black device off of the vanity. In my fingers it was cold; my heart grew colder as I studied it.

A camera?

Someone was watching this room... someone was looking at me in the shower. *No, not just me.* I nearly vomited; I gripped the sink, hunkering down as I fought a wave of nausea. *Someone was able to see Cena showering, too.*

And who did I know that could have put this here? Who had spent such a long time in my bathroom today?

I didn't want to believe it; I didn't know what else the answer could be. Jack had placed a camera here, and the best case was he was hoping to find... what? Evidence against Callum?

Something was making my ears hurt—I was grinding my teeth. Squeezing the camera, I looked at it closely. It was simple enough; it probably broadcast with a wi-fi signal, the photos uploading somewhere. It had a small on and off button, and to my surprise, I realized it was already off. *Jack forgot to turn it on, I guess.* But I had to know for sure. Deep down, I didn't want to believe the man I'd kissed... the man I'd let myself get wrapped up in... was a perverted creep.

It didn't make sense. I needed answers.

Checking on Cena once more, I grabbed my work bag from the closet. It was early enough that I knew I could do some searching and still get to the club on time. Locking the doors behind me, I took the elevator, bursting with a mix of anxiety and anger as I entered the lobby.

Hector was actually at the desk. He'd worked for Callum for years, was known for being a bit shady. I definitely wouldn't trust him with my life. *But maybe he knows something about remote video recordings.* "Hector," I said, moving his way.

His eyes shot up to spot me. "Harper, hey. Off to work?"

I ignored the way he grinned knowingly. "You ever seen one of these before?" Gently, I set the camera on the desk between us. Hector showed no reaction.

"Where'd you find it?" Frowning, he pinched the camera between two fingers and made a noise.

Abruptly, the idea of mentioning that there might be nude photos of myself floating around gave me cold feet. Biting my tongue, I reached to take the camera back. Hector let me have it, his thick eyebrows lowering an inch. "Never mind that, do you know much about how they work?"

"Usually they send pictures or video to some online server." His fingers brushed over mine, his voice falling. "Listen, if something is going on, you know you can tell me."

I knew the look of a man who was willing to trade favors. *This was a bad idea.* Putting on a sweet smile, I backed up. "You know, I realized I've got to get to work. See you."

Hector nodded. He didn't take his eyes off of me, not until I turned my back on him, and then I had to just guess. *If I can't find out about the camera from him... the only person to talk to is Jack himself. But he left, where would be go?* It was hard to picture him fleeing, not after his admission about wanting revenge on Mister Big.

I didn't have a clue where to begin. Blind with the peaks and valleys of feeling like a fool for letting Jack close to my sister and I, as well as the desire to want to think he did nothing wrong, I drove around the city. I checked everywhere I could in a two-hour span. I even scouted out the airport, thinking it wasn't entirely impossible for him to be abandoning his plan and vanishing to another country.

Jack was a ghost.

I can't keep this up, I decided, noticing I was going to be late to work. I wasn't a damn bloodhound; if Jack was still in this city I'd find him. It didn't have to be tonight.

I was a zombie at the club. I moved through the motions, but I was too busy panicking in my head to focus. Most guys don't care if you're dead inside, though; they tossed money my way regardless of if I remembered their face or their name.

I didn't notice my shift was over until the lights flashed on inside the empty club. "Come on," Spider, the DJ, shouted at me. "Grab your damn ones and go clean up. I'm heading home."

Nodding, I scooped up the crumpled bills and hurried downstairs. The dressing room was abandoned. Something crunched under my heel; a compact case of blush. The deep rouge looked like blood, I hurried to clean it off the floor.

Rubbing alcohol wipes over my body, I removed every trace of sweat and strange men. Looking in the mirrors reminded me about the bathroom camera. I'd never felt so sick before.

Changing into my jeans and a sweater, I wedged my sore feet into my sneakers and headed upstairs. In the dark hallway, my brain a giant knot, I barely heard him at first.

"Harper."

Turning, I spotted Mister Big behind me. He was standing by the door to his office, and one small move of his wide jaw told me he wanted to see me in private. Fuck, had he noticed me come in late?

"Hey," I said, following him inside. It was so quiet; had everyone else left? This was becoming a weird habit of mine. "Everything okay?"

His office was all sharp edges and hard colors; black trim, rich red rug, a desk bigger than some people's beds. He stood in front of it, hands behind his back and his smile rather coy. "You tell me."

Shit, he did notice. "Listen, Callum—"

"Call me Mister Big."

I stopped short. He only asked for that when he was genuinely furious. "Okay. Mister Big, I didn't mean to show up late. I'm always on time, surely you can overlook this." The club had a penalty system; being tardy cost two hundred dollars. It was a steep price, I'd never faced it before.

"What were you so busy doing that you lost track of time?"

Unsure how to answer that, I hesitated. That was my first mistake. "Cena had trouble going to sleep."

"Liar," he spit. "Try again."

Sweat warmed between my shoulder blades. He was acting strange; what was going on? "I'm not lying. It's what happened." And there was my second

340

mistake.

Sighing, my boss swayed closer. He was fast for such a large man. "Then we're going this route."

"What route? Callum—"

The back of his hand landed solidly on my cheek. I didn't fall, but only because he caught me by the throat with a meaty palm. Each finger sank in, holding on as I scraped at his wrist in surprise. "It's *Mister Big,* you lying bitch," he snarled. "I know what you did today. I know you went to the bank to take out money, I *know* you went to the airport to buy tickets for you and Cena."

The cells in my brain had to be dying, because otherwise, what he said made no sense. "Wrong... that's wrong."

His smile was so sweet it was cloying. "Thought you'd take your sister and run. As if it wouldn't be as simple as me calling the police on you. We've been over this before."

"No," I wheezed. "I wasn't..."

"You're as stupid as your mom. She thought she could leave me, too."

My brain jump started—hot sickness invaded my guts. She'd tried to leave him? I'd never heard that before. I'd never even guessed she was unhappy until I'd found her body. It was then that I'd readjusted my understanding of the world.

I'd seen her growing silence... her fading health... and known it was because Mister Big was in charge of her life. I'd blamed myself for introducing them. I'd blamed myself for her suicide.

His grip constricted on my throat. Thin lines of black began to crawl into my vision. In one swing, he knocked me into his desk, sending everything on top tumbling to the ground along with me.

"She thought she could take you and Cena away. But I had men following her, just like you. Watching. I knew the second she looked up plane tickets for you girls on her fucking laptop. She'd even sent herself copies of the photos I had of you from the dressing rooms, trying to blackmail me."

Like a terrible dream you remember after you wake up, everything he said began to flow together. I'd met Callum when I was at a middle school pageant. He'd "discovered" me, given me his card, and I'd brought him to meet my mother. I mistook his hungry eyes for excitement at my skill. Not attraction to my teen body. I was young and innocent.

Like Cena.

"No one seems to understand me," he said against my scalp. His fist knotted there, holding me still. "No one gets the *thrill* of being so much bigger than those young girls. I feel like a giant. How can that be so terrible? And Cena." Fuck, when he said her name, my heart broke in two. "She's starting to look just how you did when you were fourteen. She's maturing so quickly."

The flickering defeat inside of me found a waft of air. My terror... my righteous disgust for my little sister... it gave me strength.

Callum forced me to the floor. My cheek was crushed into the maroon rug of his office; the fibers burned my skin, then I suddenly didn't feel it. All I felt was the way my shoulder was stretching to its limit, reaching for one of the pens that had rolled off his desk.

He whispered, "I can't stop thinking about you, how I never got to have my way. Photos... all I was allowed was to look. So I looked, Harper. I watched you so long I didn't see your mother watching what I was doing."

My mother had known. She'd tried to save us.

It wasn't suicide. He murdered her.

"Harper," he said thickly. His cracked lips stroked my earlobe. "Stay like this, let me—*FUCK!*"

In a great thrust of my body I'd stabbed the pen into his cheek. Callum roared, pulling away, giving me enough room to scramble backwards towards the wall. He was between me and the door.

Standing tall, he threw the once silver but now red pen onto the rug. "You stupid slut," he snarled. His palm clasped his face; blood dripped between his fingers, across his teeth and chin. "You're going to die now. Understand that? It won't be nice or quick, either."

The click of a gun came from behind him. I stared over his head, my face morphing into surprise. Jack was in the doorway, his frame so wide he blocked the hallway out. The handgun he gripped was aimed calmly on Mister Big. "Move," Jack said. "Back up."

Callum did as he was asked, shifting so his back was to the desk, facing his attacker. He swiped at his own hair; blood smeared on his forehead, sticking in the brown strands. "Who are you?"

"A dead man," Jack said, shutting the door behind him. "One that you buried long ago."

Screwing up his face, he studied Jack, the gun, then he glanced at me. Mister Big saw my triumphant smile, and it amazed me that his voice came out so smoothly. "I buried a lot of men. You'll have to be more clear."

Jack laughed, the sound like an old house falling to the ground. It gave me goosebumps. He placed the tip of the gun to Callum's bloody cheek. "I'll remind you with a story. One that begins with a cruel giant taking advantage of a small boy."

His eyes shot wide. "Jack?" he whispered.

"The very same."

I swallowed, slowing rising to my feet as my stepfather watched me. "I'm glad to see you're whole. I always wondered what happened to you."

"Bullshit." Lifting his shirt with his free hand, he displayed some scars that were worse than the small ones he'd made me feel on his face. "Your guys did a number on me. Guess you didn't count on me being saved by an angel."

That went over Callum's head. Or at least, he didn't seem to connect that I'd been the one to save Jack so long ago. He was busy giving his attention to the gun in his face. "Jack," he said, and the bastard smiled wide. "Let's talk. You're here because you want something, right? What is it, money? I'll happily give you that."

"I don't want you to happily give me anything." Reaching into his back pocket, he pulled out a few thick squares of paper. He dropped the photos onto the desk; all of us looked. I rocked to one side when I spotted myself in one of them.

Mister Big's chest rose as he began to panic. "What are those?"

"You *know* what they are," Jack growled. "Your little camera set up was pretty slick. Running the feed to your *unlocked* laptop was bold, though."

"It was in my penthouse, how did you…" His mouth snapped shut, he was glowing a furious red.

"Hector might throw a mean kick, but he sucks at his job." Jack's head swung side to side. "Left his station more than long enough for me to snatch a master key card to your place. I'd say you should fire him, but when we're done here, you won't have that kind of power anymore."

I couldn't find him because he was right above me in the penthouse. I picked up some of the photos. Each had a time stamp on them; most were from the last week, a couple were from months ago. Way before I'd met Jack… and before he'd entered my home. The camera really didn't belong to him.

"It was off when I found it," I said, looking at Jack. "You turned it off. Why didn't you tell me? You could have said Callum was filming us, I would have..."

"Believed me?" He adjusted his grip on the gun. "Maybe. But I didn't have proof, not until I accessed the server and downloaded the photos from that camera's feed."

My foot touched the bloody pen; it rolled away from me. "You were coming here tonight to confront him. Jack, if you hadn't, I'd be dead."

"Tsk," he said, ending my dark ramble. His attention went back to the oddly silent owner of the club. "It's pretty obvious that these photos will ruin you, Callum. I didn't bring the worst, but thousands of pictures of your own underage daughter exist. Pictures you took. You own that server, you placed that camera."

Mister Big waited, his eyes closed now. "Get to what you're after."

"Sign over the club to me. Then you're going to quietly accept jail time for creating child porn. Don't lawyer your way into a smaller penalty, don't fight it. You're going to bow your head and take the title of fucking pedophile with *pride,*" he spat. The tendon in Jack's neck bulged. His grip on the pistol tightened, then loosened; he was struggling with an urge that deeply wanted to murder this man.

Jack said, "You're also going to stay out of the custody situation between Harper and her sister. No cruel words or mud-slinging, she's the best person to care for Cena, and you know it." He inhaled sharply, bending near Callum so I almost couldn't hear his next words. "If you don't do this exactly as instructed, your fate is simple: I'll shred you up bit by screaming bit. You see, I'm not scared of jail *or* death. I'm going to hell just like you are, and if I have to drag us down together, arm in arm, I will." He watched me from the corner of one eye. "I'd just prefer to wait a bit before I cross those gates."

The gravity of his admission kept my feet stuck to the rug. He'd bluntly said that he expected to be welcomed to Hell with open arms. But somewhere between our fated meeting in an alley and our kiss in my home, he'd made a decision. He wanted more time—with me.

Mister Big finally opened his eyes. "I don't have much choice. I'll sign whatever you want."

Jack didn't remove the pistol. "One more question. I know who bought the house and the farm, but who did you sell my mother's necklace to? The one with the three bean shaped emeralds?"

My stepfather stared, apparently searching his brain. "I don't know what happened to that." His attention slid my way. "I gave it to her mother long ago. I looked for it after she died, but..."

"Think harder," Jack said. He fingered the trigger.

"Wait." One of my feet glided over the rug; a half-step, enough so I could rest my fingers on Jack's shoulder. The man was all steel, but under my touch, he started to melt. "He really doesn't know. But I do."

Nodding, Jack kept his weapon on Callum and tossed me a roll of tape. "Tie him to his chair. We'll call the police so he can make his confession."

I moved quickly, rolling the thick tape around my stepfather's wrists. He didn't struggle, he just stared straight ahead, his skin a sallow cheese color. "Harper," he said under his breath. I didn't slow down, the tape squeaking. "Harper... listen closely. That man's insane. I didn't take those pictures. I—"

Slapping a chunk of tape over his mouth, I turned the chair so he was facing me. "She was beautiful, amazing, she risked everything to try and save Cena and I from your twisted shit. This whole time, I blamed myself for her death. How could you kill her?"

With his mouth sealed he couldn't answer. That was fine; nothing he could say would satisfy me.

Jack was talking on his phone in the doorway. I caught the words, "Child molester." And also, "Ready to confess, tied him up so he won't change his mind."

There was blood on my hand from where I'd stabbed Callum. Scrubbing my skin on my jeans, I gestured for Jack to come with me. "The police on their way?"

"Yeah. Said they're sending a car now."

The second we entered the hallway, the door cracked just so it lit up the dark walls, he pounced on me. Fingers grasped madly for my face, my hair, my hips; Jack kissed me with such heat I forgot my own name.

This is real. This isn't a dream.

"You almost *died*," he gasped out. I saw my reflection in his glistening stare. "When I saw you on the rug in there, the bruises on your throat..." I touched my tender skin as he mentioned it; how bad did it look? "Harper, I had all these plans. Clear, factual pieces on a map. But the second I saw how he'd hurt you… fuck, I nearly shot him. It would have ruined everything but I came *so fucking close.*"

"But you didn't." Holding his head steady, I made him look at me. His eyes were rabid. "You didn't kill anyone. Jack, you got your revenge. Beyond that, you saved me and Cena. I can't thank you enough."

"I'm the one who needs to thank you." His fingers flexed in my hair; open and shut. "I nearly kidnapped a kid. How the fuck could I be such a broken monster?" His head hung low, voice stirring the air between us as my chin rested on his scalp. "Harper… I hate that man in there for so many reasons. But I almost became just like him."

"You're nothing like him, Jack."

"I said almost." When I tried to pull him up, he fought me. "I nearly hurt a kid. Just like that piece of shit."

"Jack!" Grappling with his jaw, I forced him upwards. He let me this time, or maybe I was finally strong enough. There was a shine in his eyes. I worried he'd cry, because my heart would surely crumble from the pain. "Callum did something unforgivable. There's *no* reason to do what he does." *Those damn photos.* I had the urge to go back inside and kick him in the teeth. "Kidnapping Cena would have been wrong, but you had a reason, and what matters is you didn't go through with it."

"It was because of you that I stopped myself." His arms circled me until I lost all the air in my lungs. His kiss was the only source of oxygen. The only beam of life-giving light. "I love you," he whispered, the words tattooing on my soul. "I've loved you since the day you saved my life."

Then there were tears. The salt burned my eyes, it tasted bitter as we kissed, somehow savory and addictive. If this was what love tasted like… felt like… I was content to become a glutton. "I love you too, Jack. It's not been long, it makes no sense—"

"Love never has to make sense."

"—But it's true. I love you with everything I have, all my broken bits." I imagined if you took all our pieces, you could glue enough of the good ones together and make something whole… maybe something beautiful.

We held each other as the sirens grew in the distance. "Promise me something," he whispered.

"Anything."

"Callum is gone. There's no reason not to sing again."

I tightened up like a cannon ready to fire. "It feels strange. Wrong, to think I could do it out in the open again."

"It's not like before." He brushed the new tears from my eyes. "Hell, it wasn't ever like it seemed. It wasn't your fault that your mother met Callum. Your talent isn't a curse, but not using it surely is."

Thinking it through brought me pain. Old scars split open, spitting out memories I'd stowed away to make it easier to live each day. Singing with my mother when I was just four… learning the words to Christmas songs… harmonizing with the most stunning woman I'd ever had the pleasure of knowing, and who Cena reminded me of each day.

I linked my fingers with his. "You have to promise me something, too."

"The world, the moon, all the treasure in existence."

My smile felt like I'd never worn it before. "I'll sing, but you'll have to be there to listen."

Jack's laughter rumbled through his chest and into mine. It created buttery heat, a sensation in my mouth like I'd eaten too much cream. It was addicting. "I've waited seven years to hear you sing again, Harper." His lips tickled across mine until I shivered. "I won't miss another musical note if it means I have to tie myself to you by the hip."

And I knew he meant it.

EPILOGUE
HARPER

"DO YOU THINK this will grow into anything?" Cena asked, gently pouring dirt over the hole.

Jack scrubbed sweat from his brow. "What do you want it to become?"

My sister tapped her chin, eyeballing the clouds. "Hm. A rose bush. Or a huge beanstalk! Or... some moon flowers. Did you know those *only* bloom at night?"

I laughed into the back of my hand, spreading more soil and patting it down. "Jewels don't normally grow like seeds."

"True," Jack said seriously, "But this necklace is special."

"Special how?" she gasped.

He crouched next to her, his wide, strong hand gently brushing over the gravestone beside us. "The woman who wore this had a dream about prosperity. She wanted nothing more than to keep her son happy and alive. That emotion went into the necklace. Emotion can create magic."

Cena was caught up in his tale. Sitting on her heels, she took extra care when scraping her small shovel over the dirt mound. When it was finished, she ran towards our car to get paper towels to wash herself off.

I watched her go, loving how light she moved—how her hair flipped in the sun. "Do you really believe that?" I asked.

Standing up, he stretched with a groan. "That emotion can create magic? Of course I believe it. I've experienced it in person."

He looked at me intently. Blushing, I darted my eyes back to the ground. "Your mom would be very proud of you."

"Yours, too," he said, circling a forearm around my middle. It fit perfectly. "Do you need to do anything tonight before your show at the Golden Goose?"

Biting the inside of my lip, I watched Cena running back towards us. "It feels weird to invite her to my first real performance."

"It shouldn't. That place isn't the same anymore. Plus, she's excited."

I hadn't fully wrapped my brain around taking my sister to the former strip club. But Jack was right; after all the renovations, the new club was family friendly. It even served as a singing school during the day. I taught there, a fact I delighted in.

But nothing compared to the exhilaration of walking down the street in broad daylight and just *singing* again. It was as if a boulder had been removed from my gut. Without Jack around, some days, I might just float away into the sky like a kite.

Cena slammed into my legs. "Let's go! It's hot and I'm thinking we deserve a treat for our hard work!"

"We, or you?" I teased, messing up her hair.

She stuck out her tongue, then giggled wildly when Jack snatched her up and spun her in the air. "Come on," he said, "Ice cream is calling. Us bad men have to do *some* nice things to keep you girls around." He winked at me, but I just smiled fondly.

Jack could call himself bad all he wanted. He'd done enough good for our lifetime and a thousand more. And… I had a feeling he wasn't done yet.

Hand in hand, swinging Cena between us, we left together.

THE END

THANK YOU!

Thanks for reading this wicked little romp! If you're looking for something that's got a similar edge, and a whole lot of happily ever after, check out my newest release, Royally Bad!

You can also sign up for my newsletter here and get a free, smoking hot book!

RED HOT PURSUIT

A Little Red Riding Hood Story

AL Jackson

Chapter One

Broderick

I'm not sure how you handle things where you come from, Mr. Wolfe, but I can assure you it is not how we handle things in Gingham Lakes. Mrs. Tindall has been a value to our small community since the fifties, and her family long before then, and I have every intention of securing that legacy for many years to come. Why don't you make things easier on yourself and remain in your high-rise office, which I'm sure affords you quite the dramatic view of Manhattan. You seem better suited for that than our 'provincial' town.

I didn't even fight the satisfied smile that pulled at my lips as I let my eyes retrace her latest email.

God, this woman was a handful.

Determined and feisty.

A challenge I couldn't wait to take on.

For the last five months, we'd been going back and forth via email. My interactions with this tough-as-nails attorney, who was working pro bono for a tiny company in an even tinier city in Alabama, had escalated with each click of *send*.

Maybe it was a little sick that I'd come to crave this game.

Cat and mouse.

Round and round.

She was sharp and obviously loyal. I'd never even seen her. But apparently, I didn't have to. Just sitting there and reading the fight in her words made my dick hard.

There was nothing like a strong woman who knew what she wanted.

The best part was I wanted it more.

My laptop screen burned through the dim light of my high-rise office, which did indeed offer the most spectacular view of Manhattan. With a smirk, I leaned forward and let my fingers fly across the keyboard.

That is where you're mistaken, Ms. Redd. I'm sure you're well aware of our company's reputation. The Wolfe name is the very definition of success. It's the cornerstone on which our company has been built, and I will not let that name be tarnished. I will have that building, and in the end, my hotel will stand in its place. I'm trying to be fair, but make no mistake, if you force me into a corner, I will come out, teeth bared. I've been told they're sharp.

A shock of lust curled in my gut as I sent the email. Why did I get the feeling I would love sinking my teeth into this woman?

It took only a few moments before my inbox pinged with a new message.

Is that a threat, Mr. Wolfe? Because if it is, I can assure you, my nails are equally as long, and I never hesitate to fight back.

Visions assaulted me. Ones of her nails clawing at my shoulders and raking down my back. Her body straining beneath mine as I ravaged her.

My breaths turned shallow as I typed out a response.

Is that a promise or your own threat, Ms. Redd? I'm *up* for either.

God. What the fuck did I think I was doing? I'd always been about the job. But this woman…this fiery woman had me stepping out of bounds. Saying things I knew I should never say.

Her response was almost immediate.

Don't flatter yourself. You're clearly compensating, and I definitely don't need that kind of disappointment. Save yourself the trip. You wouldn't want to embarrass yourself with that kind of *failure*.

"Oh, you went there, did you?" I murmured beneath my breath. I fucking loved that she didn't hold back. My teeth scraped my lower lip, my mouth watering as I gave into the chase.

Failure is not a part of my vocabulary, Ms. Redd. I think we've already established that. But don't worry, at the end of all of this, you will be thanking me.

I pressed send a little too eagerly, becoming even more excited when I clicked into her quick response.

Only in your lofty, lofty dreams, Mr. Wolfe. I will see to it those dreams are crushed.

A chuckle rumbled free, and I rubbed at my jaw. She had no idea just how much pleasure I would take in crushing her.

This could have been an easy acquisition.

We'd made a more than generous offer, after all. Instead of accepting it and moving on, they let nostalgia taint their decision and rejected the small fortune.

Some people didn't seem to understand when it was best to take the path of least resistance.

But you wouldn't see me complaining. They had no clue just how much I relished the battle.

My cell bleeped and lit up where it rested on the glass desk, and I subdued the irritation that fought to work its way up my throat. I cleared it as I rocked forward and accepted the call.

"Father," I said by way of hello as I stood and shrugged into my suit jacket before closing down my laptop and sliding it into its leather case.

"Son. Tell me you've taken care of the issue."

"I'm working on it."

"Working on it isn't good enough. I needed this finished yesterday."

I gritted my teeth in an attempt to keep from spitting the words at him. "I told you, I would handle this one my way."

He huffed. "Haven't you figured out yet that *your* way doesn't work?"

A jolt of bitter laughter tripped from my tongue. "I think I've cleaned up enough of your messes that you would have realized by now that it does."

If it were up to my father, he would have gone in there and basically stolen that building right out from under that old lady. His men had no qualms about making a threat or two to get what he wanted, bending people to his will by cowardly shows of force.

Silence traveled the line, the two of us at odds, the constant contention that had churned between us since I was a little boy so close to reaching its boiling point.

"Two weeks, Broderick. Two weeks," he finally said. There was no missing the threat.

"I won't need them." My voice lowered. "And I'm warning you—do not interfere in this. I *will* do this my way."

"We'll see." That was the last thing he said before the line went dead.

Fuck. I squeezed the phone in my hand. It took every ounce of willpower I had not to send my phone sailing through the air.

Broderick Wolfe Sr. thought he was the epitome of success.

Believed his efforts were what Wolfe Industries was built upon.

When in truth, the man was nothing but underhanded deals and greed.

Those were footsteps I refused to walk in.

I worked relentlessly for what I wanted.

Chased it.

Hunted it until I had it in my clutches.

And when I won? It was because I was actually the best at what I did.

I buttoned a single button on my jacket and shook out the cuffs. Lifting my chin, I grabbed my case and strode out the door.

I had work to do.

And I was going to love every second of it.

CHAPTER TWO

LILLITH

"**S**O HELP ME God, if he even looks at me wrong, I will snap. I think there's a legitimate chance someone will have to keep me from strangling him, Nikki. Gah…he's so infuriating." With my phone pressed to my ear, I tipped my face toward the sky and sucked in a few breaths of cold air as if it might stand the chance of cooling some of the anger still boiling in my blood.

Never had I hated a man as much as I hated Broderick Wolfe. That snarky, arrogant voice made my skin crawl. Of course, it was a voice I'd never actually heard. What was most frustrating was the fact that even in its silence it skated my skin like sex and sin.

No question, that was what this man was.

Sin.

Wicked and immoral.

Ten minutes ago, I'd left a meeting where we were planning exactly what strategy we'd take tomorrow when the big dogs from Wolfe Industries descended on our city.

I needed a few moments to vent.

My best friend Nicole laughed through the line. At least someone found some humor in the situation. "Oh, I seriously doubt you're going to actually strangle him. You might have spent the last five months fantasizing about it, but I know you, Lily Pad, and you are the pillar of self-restraint. But if the stories are true and he's as gorgeous as everyone says he is, you have been fantasizing about all the wrong things."

The winter air was chilly, and I tightened the belt of my coat, my black patent heels clicking on the gray-bricked sidewalk that ran the quaint downtown street. I strode beneath the trees, their barren branches stretched over my head like a shield of protection. Rays of sunlight darted through the

357

spindly limbs, creating a pattern of warmth on the ground.

Gorgeous old buildings rose up on each side of the street. Most of them were one-to-three stories high, the upper floors apartments and the bottom floors family-run and independent stores.

Many had been there since long before I was born.

So yes.

I could admit many were run down and in dire need of repair.

But that didn't make the histories held within their walls any less important.

Our city had always stood for something—family and community and coming together when things got rough.

There were parades on almost every holiday, and our parks and lakes were meticulously maintained—a safe place where children could run and play—all thanks to the residents who devoted their time and efforts to make sure the public areas were cared for. And when someone was in need? Those same residents came together with fundraisers and food drives to help ease the burden.

That was something I would do everything in my power to protect.

"Believe me, Nikki. There is absolutely no fantasizing on my part other than imagining his complete demise. The man is an arrogant slime ball. I don't care if he looks like Charlie Hunnam—I'm talking SOA here—I don't want anything to do with him other than to run him out of town as quickly as I can."

Nikki gasped as if it were the most horrific statement I'd ever made. "That is some serious hate, Lily. SOA? Are you sure you're really going there?"

I sighed, and a tumble of nerves rolled in my stomach as I approached the storefront at the heart of it all. My gaze traced the plate glass windows with the store's name and logo printed in white.

Tindall's Thimbles.

"You think that hate is undeserved?"

Nikki hesitated, and I could almost see her chewing furiously at the tip of her thumbnail, as if she weren't sure what to say. Her voice dropped. "Is there really anything wrong with revitalization? The city could use the jobs."

A sigh filtered free. "Of course we could use the jobs. But you know this is different. They're forcing this without consideration of the people who have been here all along. They're steamrolling people out of their homes and out of business without a second thought other than the number of dollars that will line their pockets. It's not as if they actually care about Gingham Lakes. You know the second they sign on the dotted line, they're out of here."

"You're probably right."

"If you were to read the emails I've shared with them, especially *him*, you'd understand, Nikki. This is all about the money. Any bullshit they're feeding us about pumping fresh blood into the community is just that—bullshit."

A tease made its way into her tone. "And we all know the bullshit stops with Lillith Redd."

Memories of when I couldn't see through people's bullshit barreled through me, and I pushed out the words on a whisper. "God, I hope so." I shook them off before I got too lost to them. "All right, I need to get inside."

"Okay, but I'll see you tonight at seven, right?"

Shit.

I'd forgotten about that.

"Of course," I muttered noncommittally.

I could almost see Nikki raising her eyebrow at me. "Do not bail on me, Lily Pad. You need to unwind. I don't care how busy you are or what you need to prepare for, you are getting a night out. Do you understand me?"

I puffed out a breath. "Fine. I'll be there."

"Promise?"

"Promise."

"Okay, see you then. Don't make me show up at your office to drag your ass out."

A short laugh rumbled free. "I wouldn't dream of it. I'll see you then."

"Bye."

I ended the call and slipped my cell into my bag. Sucking in a breath, I reached out and pulled open the door. A bell dinged from above, the light tinkle ushering in a thousand more memories.

The overwhelming relief I'd felt every time I'd stepped through this door.

The warmth and the comfort.

The hope when the only thing I'd felt was fear and defeat.

Movement pulled my attention to the far corner where an arch led to the back room filled with sewing machines and fabrics and tools. On the opposite side of the sewing machines were racks full of hanging garment bags waiting to be picked up by their brand new owners or to be reunited after a repair or tailor.

Addelaine all but floated out, the old woman willowy and thin. Hair long and silver. Grayed, blue eyes keen.

"Lillith, child," she murmured through a tender, wrinkled smile. "It's so wonderful to see you."

Immediately, I went to her, wrapped my arms around her frail body, and hugged her close. She smelled like baby powder and cotton, the way she always had.

"Addelaine," I whispered.

For a long moment, I clung to her before I forced myself to untangle from her familiar warmth. Even still, I reached out for one of her weathered hands. "Tell me how you're holding up? Has anyone been harassing you? Have you received any more letters?"

Softly, she smiled. "I couldn't be better."

A frown pulled at my brow. "You don't have to pretend for me, Addelaine. I can't imagine the type of stress this has put you under."

She touched my cheek. "Hmm…child…why do I get the feeling it's you who is the one who is stressed? I told you before, whatever will be, will be."

"And what will be is you staying put, right here, where you belong." The words were out, strength behind them. I wouldn't allow myself to fathom another outcome.

Her chuckle was slow as she worked her way back around the counter and began to sift through the orders she would start that day. "With you on my side? I have no doubt about that."

"They come in tomorrow." I glanced around the space. "The people who are trying to steal this building from you."

I knew she wanted to hide it, but I saw the resigned fear that flashed through her features. "It's going to be a fight."

"A fight we will win." I took an emphatic step forward. "We're fighting for what's right."

Her smile was sad. "I'm the one who got myself in this mess, Lillith. How many years am I behind on my taxes? And now the mortgage has gone late? I'm the one who hasn't been holding up to my end of the bargain. I took out that second mortgage thinking I'd be able to repay it, and you and I both know I just can't. Sometimes it's better to admit it's time to let things go."

If I had enough liquid cash, I would pay it off myself. But between the second mortgage and back taxes, the total was much more than I'd been able to get together. So, I'd settled on the one thing I could do—fight the battle through legal channels.

"Your family has been in this building for eighty years. You grew up here," I told her.

Meaningfully, she looked across at me. "And so did you."

I gulped around the emotion that threatened to seize my heart. "Yes." I took a pleading step forward. "You saved me, Addelaine. You took me in when I had nowhere else to go. And I won't stand for someone taking your home away from you, too."

I fumbled over the counter and took hold of her hand again. "I promise you, I will do whatever it takes to ensure that doesn't happen."

She squeezed back, her eyes raking my clothing, my dress pants and heels. But most of her attention was on the coat I wore. The thick, red material sewn to become something solid.

A patchwork of healing.

I could still feel the pain in my fingertips as I'd struggled to work a needle into the coarse, heavy material when I was fifteen. I could still hear Addelaine's voice in my ear as she'd coaxed me through it. Telling me all goals were achieved through some amount of pain.

When she'd whispered about growth and strength and had slowly but steadily helped to mold me into the woman I'd become.

She patted the back of my hand. "You're a good girl, Lillith. You will always be the granddaughter I never had. Whatever happens, know you have made me proud."

And that was exactly why I would do absolutely anything to make sure I didn't let her down.

Chapter Three
Broderick

"WHAT DO YOU think?" James asked. He was my partner and my closest friend, and truly the only person in the world who I trusted wholly and without question.

"It looks solid to me."

"You're still confident?"

"Of course I'm still confident," I returned without hesitation. I was sure he already knew the answer. I was always confident.

"Your father is going to be pissed."

I scoffed. "When isn't he pissed?"

"Touché." James laughed quietly, and I could almost see him nodding. "All right then. Keep me posted after the meeting tomorrow. Good luck and let me know if you need anything."

"I will." After ending the call, I stuffed my cell in my jean's pocket and slowly ambled down the bustling street of downtown. Fairy lights were strung between the buildings, crisscrossing the busy road in the downtown area that ran the edge of the lake.

It was an area that had been reinvigorated over the last ten years. Life pumped back into its veins after the mill and cannery had shut down in the eighties.

A new kind of energy thrummed the street.

Vigorous and buzzing.

This was exactly what I hoped to achieve with the revitalization project just three miles away in the old town square that had once been the focal point of this city. The one mile radius was downtrodden but bursting with possibility.

And I was a guy who was all about possibility.

Pair it with opportunity, and my visions were unstoppable.

Earlier today, I'd driven through the area, checking out the exteriors of the building we still needed to acquire.

Excitement had burned like a fucking flame as I'd taken in the untapped potential.

Then I'd checked into my suite up the block, shed my suit, and redressed before I'd headed out into the approaching night. I wanted to take in the vibe of the locals out casting aside their day-to-day cares or maybe grumbling about them.

Sit back and watch. Get a read on exactly what we were working with.

I checked my phone again, a little disappointed that I hadn't gotten a reply from Ms. Redd after I'd invited her to meet me for drinks and whatever other activities that may arise.

Not that I'd expected her to accept.

I'd just been hoping she'd tell me to go to hell.

Maybe spar with me some more.

Amp me up to go toe to toe with her tomorrow afternoon.

My stomach tightened in anticipation. Fuck. I couldn't wait to be in a room with her. I'd forced myself not to look her up and, instead, let my imagination run wild, envisioning everything from a ditzy Elle Woods to an older hard-assed Diane Lockhart.

I just couldn't help myself. Sue me.

Just as I was approaching the intersection, my attention caught on a busy bar sitting on the corner. It was two stories high with an upstairs terrace. People leaned on the railing as they chatted and laughed, taking swigs of their beers and sipping their cocktails.

It was exactly what I was looking for.

Roughing an easy hand through my hair, I pulled open the door and stepped inside, gaze quick to scan the area.

Edison lights, which were strung from the high ceilings, hung down to add a glow to the dusky space. The floors were reclaimed wood, and the walls were old brick. It all added a comforting charm to the modern furniture and decorations that gave the vibe this was the place everyone wanted to be.

That was the ambiance I wanted to achieve for the whole town. A slice of exactly what I wanted to accomplish here—a merging of old and new.

It was a shame so many people were afraid of change.

Small groups sat around high-topped round tables, and more crowded the marble-topped bar. Muted laughter tumbled down from the staircase that led to the second floor and mingled with the mild chatter that echoed on the walls of the bottom floor.

I headed directly for the bar at the back and slid onto a free stool. I raised a hand to grab the bartender's attention.

He lifted his bearded chin at me. "What can I get you, man?"

I scanned the top shelf.

"Knob Creek. Neat."

"You sound like a man who needs to unwind. Bad day?"

I rubbed at my chin. "Not bad at all, actually."

He reached a tattooed arm to the top shelf. The guy had a tough, intimidating look about him, even though he was wearing a button-up with the sleeves rolled to his forearms, dress pants, and suspenders.

"Ah," he said with a grin. "Now you sound like a man who's ready to celebrate."

He poured a tumbler a third full and slid it across the bar top toward me.

Clasping the glass, I tipped it toward him. "Soon, my friend, soon. Right now, I'm just prepping for the hunt."

With a lift of his brow, he said, "A sportsman."

There was no missing the sarcasm behind it.

A smirk pulled at the edge of my mouth. "I guess you could say I'm a sportsman of sorts."

Amusement had him shaking his head, and he tapped the bar top with the knuckles of one hand. "Just let me know if you need anything else."

"Will do."

He turned his attention to three women who'd sidled up to the bar, and I heaved a satisfied breath as I lifted the glass to my lips and took a sip. I was rolling it over my tongue, savoring the flavor, when a sound touched my ears.

It was laughter.

It was the kind of loud, messy laughter that typically would have annoyed the hell out of me. I had little patience for foolishness or nonsense.

Yet, there was something intriguing about it that snagged my attention, pulling at some place inside I didn't wholly recognize. There was absolutely nothing I could do but swivel on my stool, needing to see exactly from where and from whom it was coming.

Propping my elbows on the bar with the glass still clutched in my hand, I let my gaze hunt the room.

Landing on its mark.

It took a whole lot to stop me in my tracks.

Even more to impress me.

It wasn't that I was an asshole.

Okay, fine. Maybe it was exactly the fact that I was an asshole.

But I lived in New York City and had a place in Los Angeles. I traveled the world and wooed and entertained wherever I went. Half the time, women threw themselves at me in some kind of vain attempt to sweeten a deal.

Beautiful people were just a way of life.

So, how the fuck was it possible that the most gorgeous woman I'd ever seen was sitting across the room?

Her face was some kind of mesmerizing masterpiece. High, defined cheeks that tapered down to a narrow jaw and chin, sharp and distinct.

Unforgettable.

But her lips. Fuck, those lips.

They were red and full and delicious, so goddamned appealing that I had the urge to walk across the room and demand a taste.

Her full attention was trained on the single woman sitting across from her, who was clearly goading her into debauchery.

The sex kitten of a woman pressed both her hands to the high-top table, as if she were searching for strength. Lush locks cascaded around her shoulders like a black river shimmering in the moonlight as she shook her head at whatever her friend had said.

My ear tuned in, keen and far too curious.

I didn't have time for distractions.

But here I was.

Distracted.

"I have work to do tomorrow," she said in a voice that struck me like a straight shot of lust. Low and deep and seductive. "You know I can't afford to mess this up. There's too much riding on it."

The other woman, who had short, messy brown hair, nudged a shot glass her direction. "Do it. I told you tonight was about unwinding. I'm not letting you leave here until you've forgotten all about the bullshit you're dealing with. Think of it this way…it will help you relax so you can get some good sleep tonight so you're ready and raring to go tomorrow."

A needy groan rumbled in my chest. I could think of a few better ways to leave her relaxed.

Satiated and satisfied.

All of them involved my tongue and my fingers and most definitely my cock.

The woman who was somehow making me lose a little bit of my head hesitated, working her lip with her teeth as she contemplated just how far she was going to allow herself to cut loose.

Then, as if she felt me staring at her, her gaze suddenly slanted my way.

I sucked in a stunned breath.

Vivid green eyes blinked back at me.

Emerald and ice.

Piercing.

Stunned.

As if she were just as affected by me.

Good God.

This woman.

I let my mouth tip up at the corner, relishing in the way those eyes went wide in surprise before they slid down my body. Just as quickly, she ducked her head and turned back to her friend, nodded, and tossed back the shot with a trembling hand.

Her pretty face pinched, that mouth puckering as she shook all over as she swallowed it.

I let loose a low chuckle, bringing my drink in for a sip as I pushed to my feet and headed in her direction.

I was a man who went after what I wanted.

And what I wanted right then was her. Even though she seemed resistant to look my way, I knew she felt it.

Knew she felt me.

That instinctual sixth sense that raised the hairs at the back of your neck and made your heart leap into action, thundering hard and low, your stomach quivering in awareness.

Run or freeze.

This girl?

She froze.

I came to a stop at the side of their table. "Is this seat taken?" I tossed out the most ridiculous cliché I could find as I gestured to the empty stool with my index finger of the hand still curled around my glass.

Another thing?

People loved clichés.

They really did.

It didn't matter how much they rolled their eyes and complained about it. They still flocked toward them. You know, that whole people don't like change mentality. It applied to all things.

The brown-haired pixie beamed up at me before she widened her eyes at the woman currently knotting my guts with a need unlike anything I'd felt in a long, long time.

"Why no," the pixie said as she waved a hand at the stool. "It just so happens it is not. I guess I was saving it for you. I'm Nikki."

I pulled out the stool and slipped onto the padded seat. "Ah, it seems a thank you is in order."

She angled her head. "This is the South. We're all about the hospitality." Her eyes made a pass over me. "You don't look like you're from around here."

I hefted a shoulder. "Just passing through."

I felt the movement to the right of me. The disturbance in the air as the woman who'd hooked me shifted in her seat. Her scent wrapped around me like ribbons, this rosy sweetness that made me itch to turn my head and bury my nose in her neck.

Inhale.

My gaze moved that way, a smirk already on my face when she tipped her chin so she was meeting my eye.

A tremble ripped down my spine.

Fuck.

One of the things that made me most successful? I could almost immediately get a read on people.

I instantly knew who was shady, keeping secrets and harboring ulterior motives, and who could be trusted, their cards laid on the table because they had everything to lose or everything to win.

Sitting a foot from me was a strong woman. Convicted. Fucking gorgeous, but I already knew that.

But the alcohol coursing her system had chipped away a few of the bricks that lined her defenses. Exposing a bit of something vulnerable in the depths of those emerald eyes that sparked as I met her gaze.

"Hi," I murmured, so low I was sure it was a growl.

I watched the thick bob of her throat.

Fear and attraction.

"Hi," she whispered.

"This is my Lily Pad, who was in dire need of a little fun," Nikki suddenly said as she leaned farther across the table.

I forced myself to look at her.

The girl admittedly was gorgeous, too, but in an entirely different way, not even close to being able to hold my attention the same way as this raven-haired beauty.

But with the way she was clearly trying to have a silent conversation with her friend, I knew she had as little interest in me as I did with her.

She was definitely playing fairy matchmaker for her friend.

With a flourish, she touched her chest. "And I am the Nikki Walters. We welcome you to Gingham Lakes. The bestest, smallest, coolest city in all the South."

"It's nice to meet you, Nikki."

I shot her a knowing wink before I slowly edged back to look at her friend.

The movement was weighted, igniting a crackle and a spark in the atmosphere.

Her lips parted.

"I'm Brody."

She seemed to hesitate before she finally let a smile ridge her perfect, delectable mouth.

God.

I wanted to eat her up.

"It's nice to meet you, Brody. I'm Lily…only that crazy thing over there"—she lifted her hand, palm out as she pushed it in her friend's direction—"gets away with calling me Lily Pad. And it seems she has me at a disadvantage tonight."

"Disadvantage?" I asked, playing it coy.

She rolled those fucking stunning eyes, and a tiny giggle slipped from her lips. "I'm not normally this loose."

The second she realized what she said, she slammed a hand over her mouth. "Oh my God," she cried against it. "I did not just say that." Her eyes squeezed tight as she shook her head.

Totally mortified.

And totally adorable.

Maybe that was the issue. The way she was dressed, she exuded power and strength, which I'd always thought of as the single quality required to get me hard.

But there was something soft about her, too. Something intriguing and equally charming, this attribute that had me wanting to shift forward so I could get a better look.

"God…your shoulders…" She caught me off guard by blinking at me when she suddenly uttered the words.

"What?" I prodded, my voice deepening as I erased another inch of space between us.

"They're…" Her head barely shook as she struggled to find the words. "So big," she breathed.

A chuckle rumbled free as my brow arched. "You think it's my shoulders that are big."

She suddenly reached out, fingertips tracing my knuckles, sending a spiral of lust shooting through my veins.

"Like these hands?" she murmured with the shiver that took her whole.

I leaned forward, my mouth at her ear. "Among other things."

"I think that's my cue," Nikki suddenly said. Her stool skidded on the floor as she pushed it back, hopped to her feet, and grabbed her cocktail. "I'm actually over here getting hot and bothered watching the two of you." She waved her drink toward the same bartender who'd poured mine. "I'm going to flirt with Ollie over there and see if I can finally get that man to crack."

Lily giggled. Again. And again, I fucking liked it.

What the hell was wrong with me?

"Good luck with that," Lily said.

"With that man? God knows I'm going to need it," Nikki said before she spun and skipped toward the bar.

We both watched her go, saying nothing as a silence built in the space between us, growing thicker when I returned my hungry gaze back to her.

"So, Lily…tell me about you."

She wrapped both hands around her half-empty cocktail sitting in the midst of three empty shot glasses. She took a slow sip. "What would you like to know?"

"Everything." It was out before I could think better of it.

She shook her head. "Don't lie to me, Mr…"

"Brody," I instantly supplied.

"Brody," she settled on, as if maybe it too sounded as odd in her mouth as it did in mine. But there was something about sitting there that made me not want to be that guy who was here in her town to turn things upside down.

"Okay then, *Brody*, no lies. What do you really want to know about me?"

I reached out and wound a piece of her hair around my finger, moving in close, my nose just touching hers. "You really want the answer to this?"

"Yes." It was a wisp of a word that filled my senses.

Intoxicating.

"What I really want to know is if you taste as good as you look."

A soft gasp pulled into her lungs, and she edged back, watching me with those eyes. "Why do I get the feeling that, given the chance, you would swallow me whole?"

My mouth brushed the very corner of hers, the words a low promise where they grated from my tongue. "Believe me, baby, I might devour you, but you'll enjoy every second of it."

Her head rocked back a fraction, her lips parted, her breaths shallow. "I…" She blinked, as if she were searching for herself. "I…think I need to go."

"I think you should stay." She scooted back her stool and stood. She swayed as if she were struck with a wave of dizziness, her hands darting out to grip the table to keep her standing.

"Lily…why don't you let me take you home. I'll make sure you won't regret it."

She huffed a tiny laugh. "That's funny…because you have regret written all over you."

She leaned forward, and with a throaty murmur, her next words sank into me like a hook. "You stick around, Brody, come find me. Because I might be loose, but I'm not easy."

My mouth watered, and I gulped around the hunger, watching slack-jawed as she grabbed her red coat and purse and wound toward her friend at the bar.

She barely cast me a glance when they both headed for the door.

My fingers twitched.

The hunt was on.

Chapter Four

Lillith

Drinks? You are truly delusional, aren't you, Mr. Wolfe?

I banged my fingers on the keyboard a little more aggressively than necessary before I directed the cursor to *send* and fired off the message with a nice, hard click.

Shots fired, asshole.

So maybe I shouldn't be returning messages at one in the morning when I was drunk and still a swoony mess over the gorgeous guy back at the bar.

Believe me, baby, I might devour you, but you'll enjoy every second of it.

Chills lifted as the memory of the man's words back at the bar skated across my skin like temptation and sex. My stomach twisted in a needy knot of want, desire rushing free as I thought of the magic that man would surely bring with his hands and that mouth and the *among other things*.

That sweet spot between my thighs sizzled and tingled.

I covered a giggle with my hand, and a hiccup followed it.

Okay.

I most definitely did not need to be messaging the asshole at one o'clock in the morning.

But I just couldn't help myself.

Not when I'd climbed into bed and pulled my laptop onto my lap after the relaxing night, so thankful that for a few moments I'd been able to shed the stress and the worry that had haunted me for the last five months.

Nikki was right.

I'd needed the break.

To unwind and let loose.

And God...oh God, had meeting Brody been exactly what the doctor prescribed. I'd known exactly where we were headed, and it had taken all I had to resist, to stand and force myself from the table.

A few flirty moments more, and the two of us would have been a tangle of limbs and needy hands.

Which in my book was nothing but a recipe for heartache and regret.

But that didn't mean I hadn't needed the attention. That I hadn't needed the bolstering. Someone to remind me I was beautiful and strong and appealing. Everyone needed encouragement before they set out for war.

So, I couldn't stop myself when I'd seen Wolfe had emailed me. With the audacity to ask me out for drinks, nonetheless.

I huffed and started to close down the lid when my inbox pinged.

"I bet you don't even need to sleep, do you, Mr. Wolfe. You aren't even human." It was all a mumble under my breath as I opened his message, hating the way my heart sped an extra notch.

Delusional? I think not, Ms. Redd. I'm merely giving you one last chance to come to your senses before you become an embarrassment. I am a gentleman, after all.

An embarrassment?

How dare he?

And a gentleman?

Hardly.

My fingers flew across the keys.

An embarrassment? Who me? I think you've forgotten who you're talking to. You are going to be the most embarrassed, embarrassed, embarrassed man to ever walk the earth. You just think you're so big and bad, don't you? Well guess what, I'm not afraid of you. Not at all. Because guess what? You're STUPID and arrogant and, just because you're supposed to be some gorgeous rich guy and everyone kisses your ass, it doesn't mean you always are going to get your way. The buck stops here, buddy. So, you can just turn around and go back from where you came, because you won't be blowing down any houses around here. Assholes like you are nothing but hot air.

I tacked on a nice, "Ha," when I hit send.

With a victorious grin, I quickly reread my words.

Dread curled in my stomach.

Oh God.

Shit.

No.

What did I do? What did I do?

Panicked, I looked around my bedroom as if I might find the message still floating in cyberspace. The only thing I wanted right then was the chance to put a stake in it.

Kill it dead.

I sounded like a blubbering fool.

I groaned in misery when my inbox pinged. Why did he still have to be awake?

Oh, Ms. Redd, I'm afraid it's you who is again confused. You seem to be lost in the wrong fairy tale. In the original story of Wolfe and Redd, I win. And did you just imply I'm gorgeous? Hmm...perhaps you do have a few things right, after all.

Grrr. I wanted to scream.

Like I said. Arrogant.

Apparently, I just couldn't resist. I needed an intervention. But there I was, all by myself with no one to rein in the disaster I was galloping straight for.

Almost immediately, my inbox pinged.

I think you're confusing arrogance with confidence. I'll be packing plenty of it when I meet you tomorrow. And I promise you, at the end of it, I won't be the one who is embarrassed. Get your rest, Ms. Redd. You're going to need it.

I banged my head back on my pillow.

Shit. Shit. Shit.

What did I do?

✧ ✧ ✧

"How do I look?"

I smoothed out my crisp, white blouse and straightened my pristine black pencil skirt that landed just below my knees. The uber professional outfit was set off with my hair up in an intricate but flowy twist so I could show off the emerald and diamond necklace I'd bought when I'd passed the bar.

It was my power piece.

It and the pair of super high black pumps that made me feel as if I held the keys to my own little kingdom.

That didn't mean I wasn't shaking in my boots.

"You look fabulous, as always," my assistant, Tina, said as she plucked a stray hair from my shoulder. "Nervous, though. You do look nervous."

I scowled at her. "Thanks for the vote of confidence."

"Hey, I didn't say you weren't going to slay this meeting. All I'm saying is you look a little nervous. You aren't even getting paid for this one. I don't get what the big deal is."

Maybe that was half the problem. No one really understood what the big deal was. Businesses came and went all the time.

"This is important to me," I told her.

"Obviously."

I glanced at my watch. "Two minutes."

"If he's as prompt as you."

I sucked in a steeling breath. "Something tells me he's every bit as prompt as I am."

"I'd better get out there then. Wouldn't want to keep the Big Bad Wolfe waiting, now would I?"

"Not helping," I told her.

"Just getting your blood pumpin'."

Exasperation widened my eyes, but Tina just grinned before she flounced from my office, leaving me with my nerves and the worry spinning through my mind.

Needing something to busy myself, I moved to where I had Addelaine's file opened on my desk. Nervously, I shifted through the papers while I was still standing, reciting the presentation and offer I'd memorized under my breath.

"You've got this," I whispered nearly silently right before my head jerked up when I heard the door click open.

My eyes went wide as my mouth dropped open, and I swore my damned heart came to a full stop, stuttered, and then tumbled before it took off at breakneck speed.

Anger bristled just under the surface of my skin as stunned disbelief shook my head.

In sauntered the most attractive man to ever take up my space. There wasn't any hesitation in his step when his head cocked to the side, and he sent me the most presumptuous, cheeky smirk as his eyes dragged over me from head to toe.

Arrogant.

Cocky.

Confident.

My hands trembled.

"You."

Chapter Five

Broderick

*Y*OU HAVE TO *be shitting me.*

A low rumble of disbelieving laughter filled my chest, and I bit it down, refusing to show Ms. Redd just how dumbfounded she had me. So maybe I stumbled a minor step at finding her standing in the office. Totally floored Ms. Redd and the fucking gorgeous woman who'd kept my dick hard all last night were one and the same.

Figured.

There had already been something about her that had me intrigued. Something that had me wired and excited at finally coming face to face with the woman who'd worked to cut me off at every turn, thwarting plans and throwing up roadblocks.

And somehow…I'd liked it.

It took my walking into her office for me to fully understand why.

"You…Brody…Broderick Wolfe," she sputtered through her own shock as that unmistakable attraction from last night lit up like the Las Vegas Strip between us, powered by the circuit of contention that had already been well-established.

I straightened my tie. "Ah, Ms. Redd, it's so very nice to see you again."

She heaved out an incredulous breath, her tiny hands fisted in little balls of indignation. "Did you…did you seek me out last night? Did you already know who I was? Were you following me?"

It was all a fiery demand that burned in all the right places.

God.

I liked this woman about just as much as I hated her.

I shot her a mocking smirk. "Who me?"

Her jaw tightened.

Damn, she was easy to rile.

Her attention fell to her desk, as if she were gathering herself, before she returned that emerald gaze to me, her chin lifted. "I'll have you arrested for stalking."

I almost laughed as I moved farther across the room. "Don't you think you're getting a little carried away, Ms. Redd? I find it presumptuous of you to assume it was me who searched for you to gain the upper hand. You were the one who knew I'd asked you for drinks. Perhaps you were the one stalking me."

Aghast, her pretty lips parted in a gust of fury, and her fists clenched tighter. "How dare you imply I would do anything outside of the law. I'll have you know, Mr. Wolfe, I take my position and all it entails very seriously."

"As do I."

"I doubt that." Her tone was a sarcastic blade.

My chuckle was low, laced with more amusement than it should have. "Then perhaps you should have done more homework, and you'd know full well how seriously I take my position and the ethical business policies and practices I demand."

A disbelieving huff jetted from between that goddamned, lust-inciting mouth that I wanted nothing more than to devour.

"You're going to stand there and pretend as if Wolfe Industries doesn't have a reputation for shady deals? Broderick Wolfe Sr. is infamous for infringements and wrongdoings. It's the platform on which your company was established."

The second she said it, anger rushed in to erase the lust, and the rigid, powerful exterior I always wore dropped for the barest moment as I grated the words. "This is my deal...not my father's, and I'd appreciate you not comparing me to him."

"It's all in the name, *Mr. Wolfe*."

Rage bloomed in my blood, and I strode forward and pressed my hands to the top of the desk. I leaned over it in her direction just as she leaned mine. The two of us nose to nose. Breath to breath.

My heart hammered harder in the confines of my chest, and something more severe than the anger twisted through my nerves as I inhaled her sweet, rosy scent.

Her breaths became shallow, her eyes growing wide, and I swore I could smell her. Her need. Her want.

The need to consume her slicked across my skin like a slow, demanding burn.

"I. Am. Not. My. Father." It was a growl. He was the last thing I wanted her to see me as.

"No?" she challenged.

"No."

She lifted her chin, her face so close to mine my mouth was watering again. "Then prove it by not screwing over Mrs. Tindall."

My tone lowered. "Believe me, Ms. Redd, I will finalize this deal. And when I do, there will be absolutely nothing shady about it. I've been more than generous…more than fair to your client. It's you who is making unreasonable demands."

I leaned forward, my mouth at the tender lobe of her ear. "*Lily Pad.*" The last slipped from my tongue like a slow, promised threat.

Edging back a fraction, I reached out and ran my fingertip along the sharp, defined curve of her jaw, my eyes keen on the movement as I did. Her mouth dropped open just as I began to murmur deeply, "Mark my words…I will have that building, and then I will have you." I edged even closer. "Or maybe I'll have you first."

A shiver tumbled through her delicious body.

Blood still burning with an irresistible hunger, I forced myself away from her, adjusting the cuffs of my jacket as I tamped down the need that raged in my body, my dick hard and my determination at its height.

"What do you say we get started here, Ms. Redd? It seems we have work to do."

I ROCKED BACK in the chair where I sat in the office area of my penthouse suite that overlooked the twinkling lights that glittered and gleamed on the blackened waters of the river that ran through the middle of the city, fed by the two lakes at the base of the mountain that sat as a darkened silhouette on the near horizon.

Of course I was staying in the nicest hotel in the city which afforded an awe-inspiring view of the area.

That was at least until mine stood tall and proud in what would be the reclaimed city square.

Bigger and better than ever before.

Resolve settled into my bones, and I leaned forward to where I had my laptop sitting open at the end of the long conference table. I let my fingertips move across the keys.

Confidently.

Precisely.

Without question or hesitation.

Ms. Redd,

My offer is the best Ms. Tindall will receive. She can sell to me for more than double the value of the building, or I will simply bide my time until I can buy it from the bank once the property has been repossessed.

I'm not entirely sure what your end intentions are here, but it seems you're denying the inevitable, whether I'm involved in the equation or not.

But make no mistake. I am a part of this equation.

I never have been, nor will I ever be, a quitter, and I'm more than eager to enlighten you on that fact. I've been told I'm a great teacher.

I always get what I want. *Always*. You'd do best not to forget it. Actually, I think there's little worry in you forgetting who I am. When I'm finished with you, the only thing you'll see when you close your eyes is *me*.

I pressed *send* while a thrill built up inside of me. God, I wanted that building if for no other reason than to prove to my father my approach was better than his. But I was beginning to wonder if I might want Ms. Redd more.

CHAPTER SIX

LILLITH

"**N**OT A CHANCE, Nikki. There is no way I'm going back to that bar."

Nikki spun around and started walking backward so she could face me as we strolled along the sidewalk. "And why on earth not?"

The newer buildings on Macaber Street towered on either side of us, and deep gray clouds grew with the threat of a storm where they glowed against the twilight.

That was exactly what I felt.

A storm coming.

Unsettled.

Unsure.

My brow lifted beneath my bangs. "Um…you do realize I basically told that bastard last night, if he wanted me, he would have to come hunt me down? If I show up there, he will actually think he has the chance of catching me. Ugh," I groaned. "I can't believe I didn't realize it was him. I mean…how many gorgeous strangers suddenly show up in Gingham Lakes? I must have sucker written all over my face."

She frowned at me. "He looked harmless, Lily Pad. Don't beat yourself up. There was no way you would have known. He was wearing jeans for crying out loud."

If it were possible, my brow lifted even higher.

She giggled. "Okay, he so didn't look harmless. He basically looked like he was ready to tear you to pieces in the best of ways. I think you're due for a little *shredding*."

I swatted at her, my voice lowered so the elderly couple walking by wouldn't be subjected to our conversation. "Shredding? What is wrong with you? You're so disgusting. How are we even friends?" I muttered.

"Because you love me." She sang the words as she reached out and grabbed my forearm. "Come on, Lil-Lil. When's the last time you got laid?" It was almost a whine. Apparently my lack of sex life caused her physical pain.

"You know the answer to that."

So long ago I could barely remember. Or maybe it was because the sex was hardly memorable. Either way, it was completely pathetic.

She groaned as she spun back around, came to my side, and hooked her arm around mine. "See. That right there is a shame. Look at you. You're gorgeous and successful and probably the nicest, most genuine person I know, and you let UFF fuck up your mind and your heart. That is so not cool."

My eyes narrowed in confusion. "UFF?"

"Um…Unfortunate Fucker Frederick?" By her expression, I was sure she thought I'd lost my mind that I didn't know exactly what she was talking about.

"Unfortunate Fucker Frederick?"

She released an insufferable sigh. "Come on, Lily Pad. That dude didn't know up from down, if you know what I mean. Now, that shit is *unfortunate*."

"Oh my God, why did I ever tell you that story?"

My skin crawled just thinking about my last boyfriend—Frederick. Gross. I'd broken up with his lying, cheating, stealing ass more than a year ago. I knew better than to trust the guy, or any guy, for that matter. I'd just gotten so….lonely. But lonely was a hundred times better than vulnerable and weak.

Nikki was right. The whole experience was *unfortunate*.

Luckily, I'd learned my lesson.

Nikki feigned a horrified gasp. "Because that's what best friends are for, which means you owe me all the stories. Plus, I warned you the second I saw that guy he was no good and up to no good, didn't I?"

"Yet, you're trying to drag me back to that bar?"

"Uh…yeah. You did see the man in question? Sometimes we luck out, and reality is even better than the rumors. And Broderick Wolfe is definitely all the rumors and more. Much, much more. And besides, that's *our* bar."

"He's the enemy."

"Who wants to do dirty, dirty things to you."

My stomach fluttered, and my heart beat faster. "You don't know that."

"Psh." She waved her free hand and steered us left so we cut across the street, rambling the whole way, "You know I have this sixth sense, and there are things I just know. And just like I knew Frederick would be all limpy and gimpy, I know Broderick or Brody or whatever you want to call him will blow your mind."

My belly lurched, thoughts of his promise from earlier today spinning through my mind, planting seeds of temptation I could never give in to.

"Even if he was the best lover on the face of the planet, you know there's no chance I'm letting that man touch me. He's trying to take Addelaine's building, for God's sake."

Even wanting him felt like a betrayal.

"What if he's not as bad as you think he is?"

"Oh, believe me, Nikki. Broderick Wolfe is the villain in this story."

She took another sharp right until we were standing in front of the very bar where I'd unwittingly met Mr. Wolfe last night.

She slanted me a wide, victorious grin. "Then maybe you need to show him exactly who the heroine is in this story."

Nervous energy skittered through my veins when I glanced at the signage above the bar. "He probably won't even be here."

God. Why did I feel disappointed at the thought?

Nikki pulled open the door. "There's only one way to find out."

✧　✧　✧

HE WAS THERE.

Of course, he was there.

Oh my God, he was there.

This was such a bad idea.

But there was no backing down when he swiveled in the stool and locked eyes with me.

A slow, predatory smile spread across his gorgeous face.

All teeth.

Tonight, he was wearing the same dark gray suit he'd worn to my office, but he'd lost the jacket and tie. The cuffs of his pink button-up were rolled to his elbows and the top two buttons were undone.

One ankle was hitched casually across his opposite knee, a tumbler full of amber liquid swishing in the crystal as he rocked back so casually in the stool.

But there was something so dominating in his blasé posture.

My knees weakened and my insides shook.

"Come on, let's get a drink," Nikki urged as she started toward the opposite end of the bar.

And there was absolutely nothing I could do but lift my chin as I started after her, my stride strong and purposed as I slowly untied the belt of my favorite red jacket.

He didn't even pretend as if he weren't watching me.

Didn't try to conceal the fact that he watched my every move.

Savored them.

Memorized them.

Hunting without moving an inch, his presence so big it was enough.

Because I already felt captured.

Entangled in his gaze.

"Ollie!" Nikki squealed.

God, the girl had it bad.

Ollie smiled his unreadable smile as he tossed two napkins down on the bar. The man was an enigma. Gorgeous in a tough, unattainable way. Quiet. Mysterious. And somehow, so utterly soft beneath the brute and tattoos and beard. "Your regulars? Or are you here to do it up big the way you did last night?"

A groan slipped free. "Don't ever let me drink that much again, Ollie, or I'm never coming back. My regular is perfect."

He chuckled. "Well, we can't have that now, can we?"

"Um, no, we definitely can't have that," Nikki added a bit too enthusiastically.

Ollie turned away and began making our drinks. I chanced peeking over at Mr. Wolfe, who'd swiveled a fraction so he was entirely facing my direction.

No shame.

He made a gesture, saying something silently to Ollie. Ollie returned whatever interaction they shared with a nod of his head.

Two minutes later, Ollie was passing Nikki her bright pink cosmo and me a glass of chardonnay. "Compliments of the gentleman at the end of the bar."

Oh no he didn't.

I scowled in Mr. Wolfe's direction, angling my head and pursing my lips as I pushed the stemmed glass away as if it were tainted. "No, thank you, Ollie. I'd prefer to pay for my own drink. If you'd return this to him."

Confusion passed through Ollie's expression before he shrugged. "Suit yourself."

He headed that way, passing the glass to Mr. Wolfe, who had never turned away and had witnessed the whole exchange. I shouldn't have been surprised when the arrogant man was already pushing to his feet the second he had the rejected wine glass in his hand.

Turning away, I tried to pretend I was in deep conversation with Nikki, searching for any subject to launch into. "Um…so it's supposed to rain, yeah?"

But it was no use.

There was no running.

A shiver flashed across my skin. Hot and cold as it raced and sped, tingling in all the places I couldn't afford to recognize this man. I tried to hold my breath, tried not to breathe in the faint scent of a spicy mandarin and sweet nutmeg.

His cologne dizzying.

Or maybe it was just him.

I felt the ominous presence eclipse me from behind. Because suddenly he was right there, his breath on my cheek and neck and ear. "I believe this belongs to you, Ms. Redd."

He reached around and set the glass down in front of me.

I struggled to rein in the mix of emotions that stampeded within me, this confusing dichotomy of hate and the crushing demand of my body.

Remember.

Remember why you're doing this.

Finding solid ground, I forced myself to look over my shoulder and meet his eye. "I can't be bought, Mr. Wolfe. I have no interest in you or your drink unless it will send you running out of town. So, why don't you go back to your seat, or more preferably, back to New York." The words grated from my tongue. God, this man brought out the worst in me. Made me crazy and angry and confused.

That penetrating gaze glinted and danced to a dark, dark beat, the hint of a smile twitching at his mouth.

He was laughing at me.

Of course he was.

"It's a drink, Ms. Redd. A peace offering. Not a goddamned bomb and certainly not a bribe. I was simply being nice."

Guilt tried to mix with the confusion he incited. I forced a dubious laugh. "Nice?"

He angled to the side and leaned his elbow on the bar so he could meet my eyes. He was so close he stole my breath. My sanity. "I could be...if that's what you wanted me to be. If you want, I'll promise not to bite." He angled closer, the words a low, guttural whisper. "But I'm pretty sure you want me to."

I jerked back, my breaths too shallow and my heart a wild thrum. I blinked through the daze. "You have a lot of nerve, Mr. Wolfe, waltzing in here thinking you can just take anything you want."

A smirk climbed to his ridiculously gorgeous face. "Since when is it a bad thing to go after what you want?"

God, I had to get out of there before he mixed me up any more. I grabbed the glass he offered and tossed it back, draining the entire thing in one gulp before I slammed it back down.

If anything, the bastard looked satisfied.

My attention turned to Nikki, who was sitting there biting her lip as if she were watching some kind of ridiculous teen drama.

"I'm going to use the restroom and then head home," I told her.

Concern washed her features. "Are you sure?"

"I'm fine. I promise."

She hesitated, wary, before she nodded and waved her drink in the air. "I'm just going to finish this." There was no missing the longing in her voice, the undercurrent of why she was really there.

"I'll talk to you tomorrow."

I spun on my heels, took a single step, and then stalled, backing up to meet Mr. Wolfe's face, putting every ounce of strength I had into the warning. "The petition for historic landmark will be filed tomorrow. I will win this fight."

Then I strode away with as much poise as I could muster before I rounded into the hall and then nearly broke into a sprint when I knew I was out of eyeshot. I pushed open the restroom door, panting as I tried to regain my composure.

This was so not like me.

Needy and wanting things I could never have.

My willpower weak.

Why had I always gravitated to the people who would hurt me?

Addelaine had been the exception, which was why I couldn't let her down.

Finding my purpose, I moved to the sink, washed my hands, and dabbed a towel beneath my eyes as I studied myself in the mirror. My pupils dilated. My cheeks flushed.

God.

This was so stupid.

But that foolishness seemed to matter none when I swung open the door and stepped out into the darkened hall. Halfway down, my feet stopped short when I ran straight into the big body towering over me.

"Whoa, there, Lil' Redd." His words were as soft as silk.

A gasp rocked free, and my chest constricted, my thrumming heart going *whoosh, whoosh, whoosh* as I took a fumbled step back. He followed, angling around and backing me into the wall.

"Ms. Redd," he whispered, his glorious, ravaging face in shadows, those unmistakable eyes burning with fire and something deep. Something I couldn't quite recognize. He reached out and wound a lock of my hair around his big hand. "Lil' Redd. Who the fuck do you think you are?"

He inched closer, fingers fluttering along the edging of my coat, as if he were mesmerized by the color. It ignited the air in a furor of severity, his breaths mingling with mine, something alive. "Who do you think you are, driving me out of my damned mind? For months, I've been fantasizing about you, wondering why every time I opened one of your messages, my cock grew hard. Desperate for a taste of the unseen."

His mouth was at the shell of my ear, eliciting chills. "And now I know."

Oh God. What was he doing to me? And why did I like it so much?

"I can't do this," I mumbled, attempting to push him away. He captured my hands in his, brought them to his mouth, and kissed across the knuckles.

Shivers slipped down my spine, and oh my God, I was going to lose all control.

He leaned in closer, his mouth a whisper at my jaw. "You want me to chase you, Lil' Redd? *Run.*"

He suddenly stepped back, the expression on his face so severe I had the instinctual feeling that he needed me to run before he snapped.

I sucked in a shocked breath, turned on my heels, and propelled myself forward and away.

Fled.

I ran out the door and into the night.

Rain poured from the raging heavens, streetlamps shone down through the haze. It created a kaleidoscope of light that glimmered all around me. I leaned over, sucking in breath after breath, knowing I needed to escape.

Run.

But I didn't get far.

Because he was suddenly there, his presence unmistakable where he appeared behind me.

Slowly, I turned around.

He stood there, looking like sin.

Drenched by the rain.

It only emphasized his beauty.

His strength.

I stood frozen while that attraction blazed between us. Zapping and demanding. Pulling and pulling and pulling.

I resisted all I could, the tension growing tight. It took all of five seconds before it was me who snapped.

I rushed his direction.

Hating the pull and loving it all the same.

I moaned when he twisted his hands in my soaked hair and spun me, pulling us into the alley before he had me against the wall and his mouth on mine.

Overpowering.

Overwhelming.

So fucking wrong.

So damned right.

His tongue licked out, tangling with mine.

His body hard.

Every. Inch.

"Oh God…you're so…big."

He rocked against me. "So much better to fuck you with."

I gripped his shirt. "There will be no fucking."

"No?" he challenged as he snaked a hand beneath my jacket and pushed my skirt up high enough that he was able to hitch my leg around his waist.

He angled me perfectly.

His hard cock against my lace-covered clit.

Pleasure pulsed. I gasped for a breath.

"Do you like that, Ms. Redd? Do you like the way you know I'm gonna feel?"

"Yes." It was a whimper when he rocked again.

His mouth moved along my throat, nipping at my chin, my lips. Nibbling and biting. I swore the man was eating me alive. The hand on my thigh roamed higher, scraping my skin.

His fingers slipped beneath the lace of my panties as the storm raged on around us. He edged back just as lightning flashed, his chiseled face vicious in the impact, dark, dark hair dripping across his forehead and his eyes…his eyes black with lust.

"I told you that when you closed your eyes I'd be the only thing you'd see." He drove three fingers inside of me.

A moan burst from my throat, and I rocked back against the hard brick wall. "Oh."

He fucked them in and out, his cock pressed into my thigh as a reminder of who he was, his fingers steadily driving me to a place I couldn't go.

His voice was grit as he uttered the words ferociously at my ear. "Your pussy is perfection. I can feel it, Lillith. How perfect it is. How tight and sweet. I can't wait until I make you mine. Mark my words. I will make you mine."

I wanted to fight and struggle and push him away.

Instead, my knees buckled when he rubbed his thumb in a demanding circle around my clit.

I clung to his shoulders, no longer able to stand.

His fingers drove deeper, his thumb magic as he circled and rubbed and coaxed.

Pleasure built.

Steadily.

Magnificently.

Destructively.

It split.

I swore I could feel the earth tremble around me as bliss rocketed through my being.

So good.

So good.

So good.

I couldn't see.

Couldn't think.

Couldn't stand.

I soared while I remained prisoner to the rain. Prisoner to the man.

Slowly, he eased his fingers out of me and took a step back while I stood there shaking. Shaking and shaking as I came down.

Way, way down where realization and ramifications set in.

Horror took hold of my spirit.

What did I do?

Oh my God, what did I do?

"You." It was a quiet, trembled accusation

He sucked his fingers into his mouth. "I warned you to run. And you ran directly to me."

Before I could stop it, my hand cocked back, and I slapped him across the face. Then I turned and stormed through the driving rain.

I just couldn't tell if I was angrier with him or myself.

CHAPTER SEVEN
BRODERICK

A GRIN CLIMBED to my face as I watched her as she strode out of the alley, the tail of that red coat whipping in the wind as freezing cold rain continued to beat down from above.

"That's right, Lil' Redd. Run. Because I'm really going to enjoy the chase," I murmured so quietly into the howling wind, forcing myself to remain standing as she raged down the sidewalk with her chin held high.

Hot waves of lust rippled through my muscles that strained with the effort of restraint. I wanted to chase her down. Push her a little further.

There was something about this woman that had me hanging on by a thread.

I wanted to get deep inside her.

I'd made that much clear.

But there was something more. Something dangerous about the way she forced me to slow down and listen. Take note. The intrigue and respect she commanded with the clear passion that burned through her spirit was never so clear than when we'd sat through the meeting this afternoon.

She'd stood there so sure and defiant, threatening to file the property with the National Register of Historic Places to stall our purchase of the building. Stating it was a historical landmark and citing all the reasons we should leave it standing.

As is.

Clearly, she was no fool, and she knew as well as I did there was little she could do to hinder or halt our plans. Instead, she'd appealed to our better natures with the thinly veiled promise of legal recourse.

She knew she had little grounds. Still, every word had been delivered with strength and an undercurrent of her base faith in humanity.

Somehow, it'd made me crave her all the more.

It was sheer strength that had forced me from her office.

Biding my time.

All too eager to show up at the bar this evening, knowing she would do the same, the lure too much for her to resist.

Shaking myself off, I turned the opposite direction and headed to my hotel, the luscious taste of her still on my tongue, my cock hard as stone as I rode the elevator to the top floor. Entering my suite, I went straight for my laptop still open on the conference table.

You are delicious. I knew you'd be. I can't wait for the full meal.

It took all of five seconds for a message to show in my inbox—just like I knew one would.

I'd rather starve.

I chuckled beneath my breath. God, there was nothing I liked more than a feisty woman. And I was beginning to think I liked this one best.

✧　✧　✧

"YOUR FATHER IS pushing to close this deal by whatever means it needs to be done. So far, he hasn't sent anyone down there, but you know what will happen if he does."

Anger ratcheted up in my chest as I stared out the window from the backseat of the Lincoln, my attention hooked on the old building that had seen far better days. "I told him this was my deal and to stay out of it. I'm tired of him making a mess of things. There are protocols that need to be followed."

James sighed. "He's not exactly a man who listens to reason. What's the end goal here?"

I swallowed hard. "The same as it always is."

"Then I'll try to hold him off."

I nodded, even though I knew he couldn't see it. "Thank you for giving me the heads up."

"You know I always have your back."

"I do."

"Keep me posted."

"Okay," I said as I killed the call, giving myself a few moments to study my surroundings. Finally, I sucked in a breath, pushed open the door to the car, stood, and straightened my jacket as I headed straight for the door.

I didn't hesitate.

I just swung it open and strode inside as if I owned the place.

It was only a matter of time before I did.

My entrance didn't seem to faze the elderly woman who stood hunch-back behind the counter. She just tilted her head a fraction to reveal her knowing, gray gaze.

Ah. No doubt, this was a woman who had seen many things. Made wise through the wounds of life.

"Addelaine Tindall," I said, my voice low but somehow soft.

She gave a slight nod. "Mr. Wolfe."

"I take it no introductions are necessary?"

A deep, short laugh echoed from her as she shook her head and went back to organizing the papers she had strewn across the counter. "That fancy suit you're wearing is really what gives it away. Considering I'm the only one in these parts who could make something so fine, I know you must be from out of town."

I began to wander the small storefront on the bottom floor, taking in the old pictures on the walls. The vast majority of them featured beaming brides in their custom wedding gowns. Others were family portraits that served as thank yous and endorsements. Proof of the talent that resided within these walls.

"Besides, men who look like you don't typically walk through that door, Mr. Wolfe."

I barely glanced back at her. "And what do I look like, Mrs. Tindall?"

"You look like a broken heart."

I hummed in question. "Do I really look that dangerous?"

The small sound she made was somehow both disbelieving and affection-ate. Catching me off guard, it made me pause and shift so I could read her expression.

"Wasn't talking about you breakin' the hearts, young man. I was refer-ring to your own."

I started to correct her ridiculous assumption but before I could, she winked.

A smile threatened, but I bit back my amusement. How was this woman making jokes when I was the one dragging her right up to the line?

I turned back to wandering the store, studying the pictures, my eyes going wide and my feet faltering when my sight landed on a cluster of pictures arranged on the wall near the counter.

Image after image of a raven-haired girl.

Young.

Beautiful then.

But different.

Broken.

Timid.

Not the bold woman who'd captured my thoughts and stoked my desire.

"She's something, isn't she?" Addelaine said from right behind me, startling me.

A lump suddenly felt prominent in my throat. I forced the heavy words around it. "I didn't realize she'd worked here."

Mrs. Tindall tsked. "Men like you often don't take the time to realize a lot of things. Look closer. You'll see she didn't just work here. She found herself here. I'd reckon this place was more like a home. A safe haven, if you will."

Realization settled into my bones. "Which is why she wants to save your store?"

She shrugged a thin shoulder. "Women like Lillith fight for what they believe is right. For what they believe is fair." She eyed me without fear. "So, why don't you tell me what you're doing here, Mr. Wolfe."

I fully turned around. "I came here to find out what it is you think is right."

CHAPTER EIGHT

LILLITH

I POUNDED ON one side of the double doors. A frenzy of fury sped through my veins. It was the only thing that made me stupid enough to show up here. Of course he would be staying at the nicest hotel in town in the best suite. One call and I knew exactly where to find him.

I pounded harder.

Finally, the door to the penthouse suite flew open. My breath caught, and I swallowed around the awe that suddenly thickened my throat as a startling jolt of attraction flashed in the air.

God, how could I find this man so attractive?

He was so gorgeous. So appealing and big and bad.

I hated him, didn't I?

I took a deep breath and found my resolve. Yes, I hated every single perfectly sculpted inch of him. I fisted the reason for my hate in my hand and charged passed him through the door. I spun around and shoved the paperwork his direction. "What is this?"

He widened his eyes as he let the door fall closed. "Please, Ms. Redd, *do* come inside."

"I asked you what this is." My voice was gravel as my gaze flashed down his body.

Desire burning me from the inside out.

I tried to stop them, I did, but I was assaulted by the memories of the alleyway from last night.

His fingers.

His mouth.

Heat swept across my flesh.

I looked away, as if I were suddenly interested in taking in the luxury of his suite. The area was dim, only a spray of light that tumbled in from the attached bedroom to my right cut across the floor. A living area was at the front and a long conference table was set up in the back near the floor-to-ceiling windows. It offered an awe-inspiring view of the city I loved.

The reason for my visit.

I turned my attention back to him and refused myself the pleasure of taking in his glorious face or his irresistible body. It was close to impossible to do, considering his shirt was unbuttoned, showing off a hint of the toned, olive skin of his chest and abdomen.

Oh God. This was so very bad.

I struggled to keep my mouth from trembling when I spat the words again. "What is this?"

He looked at me as if he couldn't believe I could be so dense. "A contract of sale."

"I know it's a contract of sale. What I want to know is how you already have it and why Addelaine Tindall signed it."

He stood a mere ten feet from me, the lines of his face playing in the shadows.

He slowly stalked forward. "I warned you, I always get what I want."

"Not this time, you don't. I told you I would see to it that building remained intact. I know her signature was coerced, and I intend to prove it."

In a flash, he was in my face, his stance fierce and bristling as he backed me deeper into the space. "I would suggest you get your facts straight before you barge in here making accusations."

My teeth grated. "She would never sign this of her own free will. I *know* her."

He pried my fingers from the papers I fisted and tossed them onto the table I hadn't even realized he had me backed against. "Ms. Redd, maybe you think you have it all figured out, or maybe you know absolutely nothing at all."

"I know you're an asshole." It was a whisper against his lips. His lips that were suddenly crushing mine.

It was a tyranny. The way his mouth moved over mine and his hand fisted in my hair, jerking my head back as he commanded the kiss.

Aggressively.

Precisely.

Air shot from my lungs when he hoisted me onto the table, a massive hand gliding up my backside as he pushed up my skirt. He greedily gripped my ass. "I bet this ass will feel just as good as that sweet cunt."

"Fuck you." I hissed the words as I tore his shirt free from the wide, foreboding strength of his shoulders, exposing the raw beauty of this overpowering man.

Desire spiraled, pulsed, and ached.

He wedged his hips between my thighs as the demand of his kiss intensified.

Devouring.

Provoking.

His hands were at the belt of my jacket, tugging at the loop, setting it free. "Red drives me wild. Did you know that, Lillith? Did you know finding you standing in my doorway in it was nothing less than a provocation. A bull set to charge."

"I hate you," I barely managed.

"Are you sure about that?" he crooned. "Maybe you're wrong about all of that, too. I think you want me just as badly as I want you."

A moan rolled from my tongue when he yanked my coat down my arms and peeled it from my body. The movement forced me back. His mouth was instantly on my neck, licking and biting, building a frenzy of need in my belly.

My fingernails dug into his shoulders as he rocked against my center.

Need lit up like a torch behind my eyes, and my full focus turned to the button and zipper of his pants, tugging them loose.

"What am I doing?" It was all a delirious jumble of words as he gripped my breasts in both of his enormous hands before sliding them against my belly and rushing them up beneath the satiny material of my blouse, stoking flames across my skin.

He tore the fabric over my head.

"You're getting ready to find out just what it's like to have a man you'll never forget."

He released the clasp of my bra. The cool air that blew across my nipples beaded them into tight, hard peaks. He leaned down, flattened his tongue across one in the same second he was twisting out of his pants and his underwear.

My fingers drove into his hair. Tiny sparks of pleasure shocked through my body. Tightening my belly and throbbing between my thighs. Teeth scraped my chin. My neck. "Asshole," I whimpered.

"Bitch," he grated before my skirt and underwear were gone, casualties of this man who laid every reservation to waste with every hungry touch.

God, how badly I needed this.

And how badly I hated I did.

I gulped when I realized we both were bare, my eyes wide as I took him in where he towered over me.

Everything about him was compelling.

Formidable.

Unstoppable.

Irresistible.

Every sculpted inch of his body was perfection.

But his eyes...his dark, dark eyes were demanding something I couldn't read.

"You won't win this," I somehow managed as I stared up at him, my chin rigid.

He gripped it between his thumb and forefinger, his words a breath against my lips. "I already have."

That was right in the same second a frenzy of movement ignited between us. The man covered his cock with a condom in the flash of a second before he fisted himself at the base, his dick just parting my slit.

My head spun, dizzy with desire and a hint of pain as he spread me.

"Oh...oh..." I panted for coherency. "You're...too big."

He gripped my thigh, and his teeth clenched as he worked himself inside. "Big is better, baby. I thought we already established that."

"I'm more a 'how you use it' kind of girl." Where that came from, I had no idea. But with him, I couldn't stop. The hostility that raged against this attraction I didn't understand. An attraction too great. Something beyond reason.

Because this was insanity.

He gripped my knees, spreading me wide. Wider and wider. My hands barely clung to the edge of the table as he rocked, thrusting deeper with each pass. Deeper and deeper.

The clutch of my walls taking him. Needing him.

He groaned a guttural sound when he finally seated himself fully. It was something animalistic. Primal. "I knew it. I knew your pussy would be perfection. Sheer, utter perfection."

His fucks grew harder, a demanding concoction that escalated with each deadly stroke. His hands slid from my knees to under the inside of my thighs, lifting me so he could get a better angle.

"Tight and sweet. I told you I'd make you mine. I told you. You're mine, Lil' Redd. Fucking mine."

His fingertips evoked some kind of madness where he ran them along the crease of where we were joined, brushing all the way back to the pucker of my ass, before his thumb came insistent against my clit.

My head flailed as I fought the mounting pleasure. My nails raked across his magnificent chest and down his stomach.

"Stop fighting it. Stop fighting me. Trust me," he growled.

"I don't trust you at all." I raged against the drive of his body that nearly sent me over the edge with each deep, decadent stroke.

A buzz bloomed in the deepest well of my body.

Physical.

Spiritual.

I no longer knew.

Building and building. Tingles shimmered and danced. Growing in intensity.

"Trust me," he demanded as he pressed down on the base of my belly with a palm, his thumb magic where it stroked me into bliss.

Shattering, all-consuming bliss. A torrent that flowed and lifted and spun.

I cried out, gripping his shoulders as he thrust harder and faster and deeper until he roared, his teeth flashing in the night before they sank into the flesh of my shoulder.

It sent another shot of pleasure to my clit.

Aftershocks.

Quake after quake.

My foundation shattered.

He threaded his fingers in my hair, panting at my cheek. "Trust me. I promise you I won't hurt her."

Chapter Nine

Lillith

THROAT DRY, I gaped out my doorway in shock at the man standing there, not sure if I wanted to slam the door shut or go running through it.

"What are you doing here?" I managed with a pull of my brow, my thoughts just catching up to my heart that was racing ahead of me. "How did you even know where I live?"

Broderick tsked. "Come now, Ms. Redd. It's a small city where the dirt doesn't run all that deep. It took nothing more than asking about you at the restaurant in my hotel to gain that information. And don't tell me you weren't missing me." He was dressed in worn jeans and a casual button-up like he had been the first night I'd met him. Only this time, the morning light cast him in a kind of warmth I didn't think I'd ever associated with him before, his eyes softer than they'd ever been.

That didn't mean there wasn't a smirk twitching at the corner of his gorgeous mouth, something powerful and threatening beneath the informal disguise.

Heat flashed across my skin as my thoughts roared back to last night, and I sucked my bottom lip between my teeth as I looked at the ground for a beat while I gathered my courage and thoughts.

I still couldn't believe what I'd done. How I'd let myself go. And how much I'd liked it.

I forced myself to look back at him. "So, now you really are stalking me. And does the fact you showed up here mean you were missing me?"

Now I was teasing him.

I'd lost all control.

A grin danced across his full lips. "Maybe."

He took a step forward, his voice suddenly a low rumble that shivered across my skin. "You were quite unforgettable last night. I have to admit that after you left, my bed had never felt so cold."

"You don't need to play me. You already got what you wanted."

He wound a finger in my hair, his head cocked to the side, those dark eyes ablaze. "That's where you're wrong. I've only started."

I swallowed around the attraction, trying to find footing beneath his striking severity.

He stepped back, giving me space. "Come with me. I want to show you something."

Hesitation warred with the want that tumbled through my belly. "I have work to do. I need to get to the office."

"I think this will be well worth your time."

Doubt hovered in the air between us before he reached out and tugged at my hand as he took another step backward. "Come on, Lil' Redd. There's no need to be afraid."

A scowl climbed to my brow, though somehow a tease slid out with the words. "Really…I think I already bear the proof that you bite."

He laughed. Straight belly laughed. Confusion twisted through my spirit, an inkling of something I didn't quite understand—something sweet and hopeful—before he tugged me closer, his mouth at my temple. "Do you know how much I like you, Lily Pad?"

I blinked into his shirt, wondering how it was possible that I was starting to like him, too. "You don't even know me."

"Oh, I think I know you well enough, don't you?" He pulled back to shoot me a wink before he was threading his fingers through mine and leading me to the car parked at the curb in front of my house. "Come."

And I had no idea if it was distrust or excitement that flapped in my belly when I let him lead me to his car.

Ten minutes later, Broderick made a left in his rented Audi. The realization of where we were going injected a dose of anxiety into my system, and I leaned forward in my seat, my voice riddled with doubt. "Why are you bringing me here?"

My gaze traveled the line of old buildings that sat like a beacon. A harbor. My safe haven.

He slowed when he came to the shabby three-story building that housed Tindall's Thimbles. Easing up next to the curb, he put the car in park but left the engine idling.

He shifted in his seat to face me. "Because I want you to understand my goals. My vision. I want you to know why Addelaine Tindall signed those papers."

Unease stirred through my senses. Along with a shot of hope. I met his gaze. Fully and without restraint. "Tell me."

I watched the thick bob of his throat, his voice hoarse. "I am not the bad guy, Lillith. Evil might run through my veins, my blood my father's, but I have fought his brand of corrupt morals my entire life. I'm not here to ruin people's lives. I'm here to make them better. And if stamping my father's name on a project makes me the bad guy, too, then so be it. I love winning, Lillith. I won't lie. But my wins are on my own merit, and they are always, always fair."

I shook my head. I wanted to believe him, but all my reservations warned me to remember exactly who I was dealing with. "But you pushed this purchase without concern for Mrs. Tindall. Just like the rest of the buildings your company acquired."

A scowl marred his face. "How could you say without concern? Every financial offer I've made has far surpassed the current value of any of these holdings."

Frustration bubbled inside of me. "But that's it, right there. There is no dollar value that can compensate for memories. For heritage."

His gaze slid to the plate glass of Addelaine's store. "Is that what you're trying to protect, Lillith? Your memories? Is all of this about you?"

Somehow, the words that fell from his mouth were as soft as they were sharp.

As if there was a chance he might understand and he was accusing me of an agenda at the same time.

Old wounds flared. I attempted to stuff them down where they belonged. Apparently, I didn't succeed because my voice cracked as I pressed my palm over my heart. "I'm fighting for the woman who gave me everything. I'm fighting for her legacy. I'm fighting for her family and her friends and all the people who have stories like hers."

His arm suddenly shot out, his hand fisting in my hair, his tone emphatic. "What if financial compensation is the only thing I have to offer them? What if it's the only thing I can do to save what they've created? The only way I can help preserve what they've made of themselves?"

My heart thrummed in the confines of my chest, my eyes darting across his face, desperate to read the truth in his expression. "What are you saying?"

He grimaced. "I'm saying my father has already made his decision. This street will bear the Wolfe name. Our hotel will stand here, in this spot, one way or another. His way or my way. And I promise you, my way is best."

Awareness settled over me, like a rock sinking to the pit of my stomach.

His thumb brushed over my cheek. "Addelaine signed that contract because when I went to see her, I asked her what *she* wanted. I asked her what she believed was fair in this situation. She felt the purchase offer was more than fair, and additionally, she asked for six months to find a new location before the sale closed. I agreed, and she signed. She and I? We made a deal. There was no coercion."

Regret twisted through my consciousness.

Had I pegged him wrong all along?

"Then why isn't that six month promise in the contract?"

"Because my father is pushing for a closed deal. I give that to him, and he moves on to his next acquisition. It's an easy distraction."

I wanted to believe it. In him.

A wry grin pulled at his mouth as his gaze traveled to the storefront. "She's an incredible woman. Smart. But she's also flexible." He moved his other hand to my face, framing both sides when he looked back at me. "And that's what I'm asking you to be. Flexible."

There was no missing the innuendo behind it.

God, he had me tied up in knots. Because there I was with butterflies in my stomach and a blush on my face. The man made me vulnerable in a way I hadn't allowed myself to be in so many years.

Broderick Wolfe brought out the best and the worst in me.

"What do you want from me?" I finally whispered.

His hands tightened. "First…I want you to say you trust me and to drop that silly application to make the building a historic monument. You and I both know it won't stick."

Fire glinted in his dark, dark gaze. "Then, I want to take you back to my suite so I can fuck you again, and then from there, you and I can see where this goes."

"Where this goes?" It came off as incredulous.

"Yeah, Ms. Redd. We'll see where it goes. I loved the taste I got last night. Something tells me I won't ever get enough."

My spirit lurched. Reaching toward something that should be impossible. Because I was supposed to hate him.

He smiled that magnetic smile.

And I realized that was what terrified me the most about him.

I didn't hate him at all.

"And you'll give Mrs. Tindall six months?"

"Six months."

"Promise me this isn't some kind of trick." A plea slipped into my tone because I'd opened myself to him in a way that gave him the complete upper hand, every advantage in his corner.

God, the last thing I needed was to be lured into a trap by this mesmerizing man. Let my guard down so he could rush in for the kill.

"Trust me," he said again.

"I'm not sure I know how."

"Then let me prove to you that you can." His fingertips trailed down the hollow of my throat, a dark promise coating the words, "Do you trust me with this body?"

"Yes." A shiver raced down my spine, settling low, igniting a throb between my thighs.

Broderick sat back, that arrogance setting like stone on every line of his magnificent face. "Good. Then let's find out where this goes."

Chapter Ten

Broderick

"**D**O YOU TRUST me?" I whispered close to her ear where she was bent over the side of my bed, her hands pressed to the mattress.

Shivering, she nodded, locks of raven hair cascading around her shoulders. Her back was bare and just as gorgeous as the rest of her, and I slowly trailed my fingertips down the length of her spine, all the way down to the only thing she wore.

A red, lacy thong.

That and a pair of red high, high heels.

Lust tightened my balls and hardened my dick.

Yes.

"I love red," I murmured as I dipped my fingertips between her cheeks and glided them over the fabric. "So fucking much."

She whined, her ass jutting out, asking for more.

"Did you wear these for me?" The question rumbled from deep in my throat. "Did you know I would come for you? Find you? Take you?"

A whimper slipped from her mouth.

"Tell me," I demanded.

"Yes." It was a breath. "Please."

Hunger ricocheted through my body.

Something primal.

Fueling the obsession she'd incited in me since the first time my eyes had scanned across her impassioned words.

But standing there, a different kind of emotion rushed me. Something bigger. Something more.

I swallowed around it as I dropped to my knees behind her, forcing her legs apart and situating myself between them. My palms cupped her cheeks, spreading her. "Your ass is as perfect as your pussy, Lillith. Did you know

405

that? Did you know every inch of you drives me wild?"

I pressed my nose to the fabric of her underwear, which did nothing to cover her, and inhaled deeply. "You smell delicious."

No. Not like flowers or sugar or chocolate.

She smelled like a woman. She smelled like sex. She smelled like *me*.

A growl pulled from my lungs, and I licked the wet, glistening flesh that peeked out from the fabric before I nudged the lace aside so I could go deeper. Fucking my tongue into her tight heat and running my fingers along the crease of her ass.

She moaned. "Broderick."

I bit the inside of her thigh.

She yelped.

"I'm going to devour you, Lillith. Every inch."

Her legs shook. "Yes," she whispered.

I edged back a fraction so I could pull her thong from her waist and drag it down her legs, sitting back on my heels so I could appreciate the view as I unwound them from her feet.

The lights were off in my room, and only sheer drapes shaded the windows from the winter day.

It cast her as a silhouette.

Sleek and sexy.

"You are so damned beautiful," I murmured when I gripped her by the outside of the legs. I edged forward, tongue gliding into her folds.

"Brody." Her saying my name that way had me close to coming unhinged, and I angled so I could lave attention on her clit. I flicked and circled while she writhed and moaned. "Please...more...don't stop."

My hands explored. Greedily. Skating her soft skin, her legs, her round bottom, and the small of her back.

God, she was a miracle.

Appealing in a way that had hit me like a flash flood. Unaware and unprepared.

I swept my fingertips through the desire that coated her, teasing before I plunged them inside.

"Like this?" I demanded.

I drove them deep, making her jerk with the sudden pleasure.

"Yes," she begged then cried out in frustration when I pulled them free before she was squirming and panting and flailing again when I brushed them up the sensitive flesh at the back of her pussy and to the tight pucker of her ass.

"Trust me," I whispered against her skin, kissing along her inner thigh as I continued to touch her. Tease her. Taunt her. "Tell me you trust me."

She warred, her words a wisp of concession. "I...I trust you."

I had to suck in a breath to steady myself.

Because I could feel something wanting to give.

Something rigid and hard wanting to go soft.

She whimpered and gave, her legs shaking as she struggled to relax as I slowly eased two fingers inside. "You're mine, Ms. Redd. Do you hear me? I told you I'd make you mine."

Her low moan echoed from the walls as I slowly drove my fingers deeper, her knees weakening as she clawed at the bed.

"I...I can't...please."

"Please what?"

"I need you," she pleaded.

Swiftly I stood and pulled my fingers free before I sank the fingers of both hands into her ass cheeks, my cock catching on her pussy as I nudged in an inch. "Is this what you need?"

Desire blazed.

"Yes. Please...don't tease me. I'm yours."

I'm yours.

I was consumed by the confession of her words, and I drove my cock deep inside her body. Her walls spasmed with the intrusion, clutching my dick in needy desperation.

"Fuck...you feel amazing, Ms. Redd. So fucking good. Tell me how good my cock feels. This is why you won't ever get away from me."

The words spilled out without thought or reason.

The only thing I knew was their truth.

I would never let this woman get away from me.

I would hunt her. Find her. Keep her.

"I...oh my...fuck." It was all an incoherent jumble of words from her gorgeous mouth as she struggled to keep standing as I began to fuck her—hard and fast.

Unbridled.

Wild.

Claiming.

Her flesh stretched around me, gripping me in its satiny welcome.

Offering it all.

So, I took it.

With each fierce thrust, she cried out, her fingers digging into the comforter of the bed. I ran my thumb around her slickness, gathering it as I dragged it upward and pushing it into her hole. My other fingers wound around to her front, grabbing her tit, her throat, before I forced two fingers into her mouth.

She sucked me with her hot, wet tongue while her hot, wet body clutched and begged and moaned.

Completely unhinged.

As unhinged as I was.

My head spun and her body bowed and I was suddenly overcome.

Staggered in a way I wasn't sure I could afford to be.

A surprise gasp flew from her when I pulled out, picked her up, and tossed her onto her back on the bed.

And there she was. All spread out, raven hair and milky skin and red high heels.

I was quick to crawl over her, caging her for a heated moment, staring down at her gorgeous face as I felt something shatter inside me.

I drove back into her, pleasure spiking as I filled her.

And she watched me with those emerald eyes. Her lips parted. Her heart clear.

"Redd," I whispered, "what have you done to me?"

"It's you who's taken me." Her words were a wispy admission.

I edged back so I could run my knuckle over her clit.

That single touch was all it took.

She arched from the bed as she slammed into ecstasy. Her head rocked back and those perfect tits jutted toward my face.

My mouth grazed a rosy nipple as I eased my hand away before both my hands were on either side of her head as I conquered her with each erratic thrust.

Pleasure rushed down my spine. Tightening my balls. Constricting to a pinpoint.

Exploding and blowing through my body on a fiery circuit.

Every nerve.

Every cell.

I poured into her, my body bowing and my head dipping down to the soft flesh of her shoulder.

My teeth sank in.

Making my mark.

Sated, I collapsed onto her sweat-drenched body before I pushed up onto my elbow and brushed my fingers through her hair. "I think I like where this is going."

Lillith giggled. "I think I do, too."

She sobered, touched my face, vulnerability slipping into her tone. "I shouldn't fall for you."

I edged down and nipped at her bottom lip. "Yes, you should."

CHAPTER ELEVEN
LILLITH

"THAT WAS AMAZING," the deep voice grumbled from beside me, his rugged pants rising into the air as night took hold of the hotel room.

I struggled to find my own breath. My body blissfully spent.

But it was my heart pulsing full of an overwhelming satisfaction and joy that shivered through my senses. The feelings pressed and pulsed and thrummed, demanding to make themselves known.

Affection.

Fondness.

Care.

Stripped of my anger, they were right there, taunting me with the fact I'd rather be in his arms than anywhere else.

I knew those feelings put me in greater danger with this man than I'd ever been.

I rolled onto my side and propped up on my elbow. "What is happening here?" I whispered.

Broderick lay on his back in the middle of the massive bed we'd spent the entire day utilizing to its fullest potential.

I couldn't resist tracing a fingertip down the sheer strength of his bare chest and over his ripped abdomen. As if I hadn't spent the last eight hours exploring every inch of him while he'd consumed every inch of me.

No place in me had been left unattended. He'd taken me hard and fast and rough, again and again. Until the last time when his touch had turned tender and slow as he'd stared down at me through the descending night.

He grinned. "I thought we were seeing where this goes."

"But now that you have things settled here, you'll be going back to New York."

"Will I be?"

Quickly, I shifted up farther so I could get a better look at him. "What?"

He raised a hand and threaded his fingers through my hair. "Maybe you were entirely wrong about my view back in Manhattan, Lillith. Maybe I have the best view right here."

Tingles spread like sparking matches to my spirit.

Stunned, I blinked down at him. "You want to stay here...because of me?" It almost came across as an accusation.

"You think I wouldn't?"

My head shook. "You don't even know me."

His smile was easy. "You keep saying that."

He seemed completely unperturbed by my sudden questioning, while my whole world felt as if it'd spun off its axis.

I was a realist.

A planner.

Cautious to the ninth degree.

I didn't carelessly fall in love. To me, love was a decision that was made only by choice, given after every consequence had been taken into consideration.

Otherwise, you were left stung. Bitten. Broken.

I also didn't fall recklessly into someone's bed.

Yet, there I was.

"I keep saying that because it's true."

"What are you so afraid of?" he asked as he ran gentle fingers through my hair, a frown denting between his eyes.

I had the sudden urge to slip from his bed and cover myself, hide, the impulse stronger than it'd been in a long, long time.

His brow furrowed, the man so intent as he ran the knuckles of one hand down my cheek and under my jaw. Tingles lifted. Warmth and comfort and a stroke of that fire. "Who hurt you, Lillith?"

"The people who were supposed to love me most."

I had no idea what had come over me, because the urge to tell him was suddenly so much greater than the need to run. The pain I'd kept hidden for so long begging to be released. He watched me, silently coaxing me to continue.

I swallowed around the lump in my throat before I forced out the confession. "I was fifteen..."

I blinked through the memory, my voice going soft as I got lost in it. "It was just like any other day. I went to school. My momma had been more scattered…flustered. Depressed maybe, I don't know."

My tongue felt as if it might freeze up, but the words kept flooding out when Broderick tightened his hold in my hair. "I let myself into the house after school that day, and they just…were gone. She and her boyfriend. I kept calling for her, thinking it was some kind of joke. I ran to her room and all the drawers were open. Empty. She'd left me this letter…telling me she was sorry and that everything would be okay. That I was a *big girl*."

Something that looked like anger took hold of his expression before awareness settled into its place. Slowly, he nodded in understanding. "And Addelaine took you in."

"Yeah. I answered a call for a help wanted ad, naïve enough to think I'd make enough money to keep paying rent on the house. But Addelaine and that store…they became my home. I lived with her until I graduated from college."

He smiled. "I knew she was an amazing woman."

"She is."

"Like you," he murmured, brushing his lips across mine.

Butterflies tumbled. My heart full. The rigid pieces splintering beneath the weight of his care. And suddenly I was wanting things I hadn't dreamed of wanting in so long. Maybe Nikki was right. I needed a little shredding. But it was my distrust and skepticism that this man was shaving away.

Silence hovered in the air. "I should probably go."

"Oh no, Ms. Redd. You aren't going anywhere."

My brows lifted as my mouth pulled into a smile. "Is that so?"

He grinned. "I thought we already established you don't need to be afraid."

My fingertips raked across the strength of his chest, and I peeked up at him. "But I am. I'm afraid of this. It's insane that I'm here. You're the last person I should fall for."

His big hand cupped the side of my face. "Don't you know all great love stories never should have been? That's what makes them great."

"Is that what you think this is…the start to a great love story?"

"Do you want it to be?" There was a tease behind his words, but a softness, too.

Heat flashed across my skin, warming me inside and out. "That's...crazy. Just last night, I hated you."

But there I was, smiling down at him like a lovestruck fool while I said it with something powerful and wonderful threatening to burst, the weight inside of me so much lighter since I'd admitted to him the root of so many of my fears.

A low chuckle rumbled from his chest. "You didn't hate me, Lillith. You were afraid of me because I made you feel things you didn't want to let yourself feel. You wanted me, and you hated that I had that effect on you."

His hand cinched down tighter. He yanked my face down close to his. "You hated that you couldn't say no."

It was a tease.

It was the truth.

That attraction flashed.

A wildfire.

Broderick guided me over him, his cock already hard as he aligned himself with me. "I told you that I always get what I want. And what I want is you, and that's not ever going to change."

What I couldn't comprehend was how this man who'd been my enemy for five months had made me want him in less than three days.

Because there was nothing I could do when I slid down onto his length but give him all of me.

My body. My heart. My trust.

✧   ✧   ✧

DISORIENTED, I BLINKED into the shadows of the darkened room. Slowly, I came to awareness. Broderick's big, warm body was next to mine where he was lost in the contentment of sleep, his breaths deep and slow.

I sank back into the comfort of him, nestling closer as I let my eyes drift closed. Seconds later, they popped back open when I realized what had originally pulled me from sleep.

His phone lit up on the nightstand on his side of the bed and vibrated against the glass.

Telling myself to ignore it, I forced myself to close my eyes and go back to sleep, only for the offending noise to recur.

Leave it, I silently told myself. But I couldn't escape the tingle of worry that buzzed at the back of my brain.

Apprehension twisted through my nerves. Prodding and pinching and warning.

I sucked in a breath, trying to convince myself I was only this way because this relationship was new and it'd started on bad terms. I'd just come to recognize the side of the man that was good and honest.

We'd been a whirlwind.

Caught up. Shot to the highest high before I'd even realized I'd been swept off my feet.

That was why I felt unsettled.

It had to be.

I heard the vibration of his phone again.

Would it be so wrong to peek? Maybe it was an emergency. It was the middle of the night, after all.

I sat up, holding a decadent sheet to my bare chest, feeling like such an asshole for doing this but unable to stop as I peered through the darkness to the nightstand. I hesitated and then finally gave in.

I reached over him and glided a shaking finger over the screen to find the series of texts that screamed back from Broderick's phone.

All of them from Rex Gunner, the owner of the most successful construction company in Gingham Lakes. A man I knew well. A man I trusted and admired.

A heavy lump grew in my throat as I skimmed through his words.

If you think I'm going to bulldoze those buildings two weeks from tomorrow, you are insane.

Do you think I don't know it's impossible to get permits that quickly? Someone got paid off to make that happen.

I told you I work on the up and up.

Gut told me something was off the second you walked into my office.

Deal is off.

Dread slicked my skin in a hot sheen of sweat and nausea rolled in my stomach.

I pressed my hand to my chest to try to stop the ache blossoming there as tears sprang to my eyes.

I should have known. I should have known.

You fool. You stupid fool. He played you. He played you just like they all do.

Knees weak, I slipped off the bed, trying to stand. Moisture blurred by sight as I fumbled with my clothing, trying to be as quiet as possible as I slipped out of the bedroom and into the main area of the suite.

I dressed in the dark, piecing my exterior back together while everything inside shattered.

I grabbed my purse from where I'd left it on the entryway table, fumbled with the knob, and slipped out into the hall. My breaths were shallow, my mind racing with how I could possibly fix this. Panic took hold of my spirit, and my feet moved faster and faster as I made my way down the hall and to the elevator.

I didn't even have my car.

But I didn't care.

I would do whatever it took to fix my mistake.

✧   ✧   ✧

I JERKED TO a stop in front of the modest house on the outskirts of town. A light blazed from the porch, Rex Gunner visible through the sheer curtains as he ambled around his kitchen, obviously a prisoner to his own woes.

Or maybe tonight our worries were one in the same.

I'd taken a cab the two miles back to my house, grabbed my car, and drove straight here.

I figured if anyone had the down-low on the details, it was Rex Gunner. He had connections in this town.

I'd also known him my whole life and trusted him implicitly. It was no secret he hadn't been the same since his wife had left two years ago, but the one thing that hadn't changed was his company's character. He saw to it that it stayed that way. And judging by the texts I saw, that hadn't changed.

I clicked open the door to my car and stumbled out, still reeling from my foolishness, barely able to stand beneath the crack in my heart. I'd allowed myself to be played. Hunted down like prey and ripped to shreds.

And God, those wounds burned and hurt and ached.

Because when I opened up, I opened all the way.

Reservations incinerated.

And that vile monster had gone straight for the kill.

I rushed up the walkway and quietly knocked at Rex's door so I wouldn't wake his daughter. It took only a second for me to hear heavy footsteps thudding on the other side, the twist of the lock, and the squeak of his door.

Rex jerked back when he saw me, blinking through his shock. "Lily. What are you doing here?" He widened the door. "Come inside where it's warm."

"Thank you," I managed, not realizing I was freezing, my bones chilled, my skin brittle as I rubbed my hands together.

"What's going on?"

Rex Gunner was every bit as powerful as Broderick Wolfe. But where Broderick went straight for what he wanted, disregarding anyone who got in his way, Rex kept himself barricaded by the hard scowl on his blatantly beautiful face, life hardening him to sharp edges and bitterness.

"I...were you working with Wolfe Industries on the Fairview Street project?"

Awareness dawned on his expression. "'Was' is the key word."

"I saw the texts you sent to Broderick," I admitted, lifting my chin, knowing full well what I was revealing. How else would I have seen them in the middle of the night? But I'd suffer any humiliation to gain the proof I needed to set my mistake right.

He looked to his feet, before forcing himself to look back at me. "You get yourself in some trouble, Lillith?"

"Only my heart."

With his hands on his hips, he gave me a tight nod, fully understanding.

"I need to know what you know so I can stop this. Addelaine Tindall was promised six months to relocate and one hundred and twenty-five thousand dollars to compensate her for the transition."

He huffed in anger. "I was told the same until I got word Addelaine signed a contract agreeing to a quick sale. Premises are to be vacated by the thirtieth and demolition begins on the first. RG Construction was supposed to have the bid, but I pulled it as soon as I got word. No question they have the city big dogs in their pocket because things just don't move that fast. Someone got paid off, and as soon as those types of dealings start goin' down, I'm out."

Anger and hurt billowed in my chest. "I can't believe he'd do this."

Rex eyed me. "Can't you?"

I pressed my hand to my mouth, trying to quiet the cry that slipped up my throat without my permission.

"Lillith," Rex murmured in sympathy.

I shook my head at him. "Just...tell me everything you know."

Chapter Twelve
Broderick

SUNLIGHT POURED THROUGH the sheer drapes that covered the windows. I groaned as I stretched where I lay flat on my stomach, my muscles flexing as my cock stirred back to life, my body bristling with this desire I had a hunch wasn't ever going to lessen.

Just like I told Lillith.

Once I tasted her, I wasn't ever going to get my fill.

A satisfied grin stretched across my mouth, and I slid my hand along the mattress. Seeking her. Already ravenous. Ready for another bite. The only softness I found was the cool bottom sheet.

I jerked my head up from the pillow to look at the spot where I'd watched her fall asleep. The top sheet was gone.

So was she.

Anxiety twisted in my gut. "Lillith," I called, voice turned in the direction of the attached en suite bathroom.

Silence rained down, ominous in the still, quiet morning.

Dread seeped into my skin and settled in my bones. My gaze swept the room.

Her clothing, which we'd left strewn across the floor, was no longer there.

My teeth gritted. *What the fuck?*

I thought we were passed this.

I reached for my phone to call her, gripping it in my hand as I swiped my thumb across the glass.

The alarm I felt ratcheted up a thousand notches when I saw the messages that had already been read. My chest tightened in rage at what they implied. At the suspicions they confirmed.

Motherfucker.

Lillith had seen these texts.

God. I couldn't even imagine what she was thinking.

Panic spiraled through my body. My mind raced. Flipping through every detail James had fed me.

I flicked into recent calls listed on my phone until I found the name I was looking for.

He answered on the second ring.

"I warned you," I seethed.

Mocking laughter filtered in from the other end of the line, his disappointment thick. I shouldn't have been surprised. After all, that was the only thing I'd ever been.

"And I warned you. You had two weeks to get her out of there, not six months, and you sure as hell didn't have the authority to pay her what you promised. So I had my men fix it."

Anger rippled through my straining muscles. "I promise you, I won't let you get away with this," I said, crushing my phone to my mouth where I spat the words.

He laughed. "It's already done."

CHAPTER THIRTEEN
LILLITH

MY HEAD JERKED up when the bell above the door chimed, flaming the indignant anger that burned through my body and trembled all the way to my core.

"Don't you dare walk through that door." The words shook and grated as I forced them through gritted teeth. Broderick Wolfe froze halfway through the door of Tindall's Thimbles. He was back to wearing his suit that made him appear every bit the villain he was.

Dark and dominant.

Last night, Rex Gunner had given me enough information so I knew where to begin digging. The proof I'd found in the few hours I'd spent combing through files on my computer was insubstantial, but hopefully it was enough that the complaint I filed to order a hold on the sale until the claims could be investigated would stick.

All night and morning I'd focused solely on this task. Refusing to give into the nagging thoughts of him. Thoughts of his touch and his kiss and the promise of something more. Refusing to let myself dwell on the fact that I'd been nothing more than a game.

A pawn used to bring down the final obstacle standing in his way.

The sickest part of it all was that obstacle was me.

He'd pitted me against myself.

He took the final step inside, and I narrowed my eyes at him. I guess I shouldn't have been surprised, should have I?

His throat bobbed heavily. "Lillith...I can explain."

Nervousness seemed to line his demeanor for the first time, but I knew better than to fall for his tactics. The man managed to switch from one disguise to another flawlessly.

That didn't mean I couldn't see his razor-sharp teeth.

"I don't want to hear anything you have to say." I lifted the short stack of papers. "I have everything I need to know right here. I know your company bribed the county commissioner. I know your company signed off on pushing the permits through. And I know your company had no intention of honoring the deal *you* made with Addelaine."

He rubbed a big hand over his jaw, which today was unshaven and coarse with thick, dark hair.

A beast.

A beautiful, terrible, lying, betraying beast.

Hate flared, that emotion mixed with the cutting grief.

"My father—"

Biting laughter broke through the air. "I don't give a damn about your father, Broderick. I give a damn about what you promised. What I care about is the fact you're nothing but a disgusting manipulator. A liar driven by greed."

I sucked in a sharp breath when he suddenly flew across the floor. He was in my face, nostrils flaring as he stared me down. Yet, when I expected to find anger in his eyes, I found nothing but desperation. His next words a hoarse plea. "You told me you trusted me. I demand a little of it now."

I refused the instinct to soften, and instead I scoffed as I tipped my head back so I could meet his penetrating gaze. "You *demand* it? You don't get to demand anything of me. You don't own me, and you can't have me. I promised you before you came here that I would stop you...but now? Now I promise I will destroy you. I won't stop until there's absolutely nothing left of Wolfe Industries. I trusted you, and you lied to me. Used me. And I fell for it."

The worst part was that I'd fallen for him.

Bile rose in my throat. "You disgust me, and I don't ever want to see you again unless it's in court and I'm taking everything important to you away."

He sank back, shoulders straightening as something like hurt flashed across his face. It was gone before I could decipher it, his jaw going rigid. "You really think so little of me?"

The words dripped like venom as they slid from my tongue. "I think even less."

What hurt so badly was I didn't want to. I'd wanted to think the best of him. Wanted him to be the man he'd shown me he was yesterday.

His lips pursed, and he nodded twice, as if he needed to accept what I'd said. Then he turned on his heels, strode toward the door, and pulled it open. He paused halfway out, looking at me from over his shoulder, his expression like a straight kick to the gut.

Pain.

"That's too bad, Lillith, because it only took three days for you to mean the most to me."

Then he tossed the door open wide and disappeared out into the glinting sun that shone through the frigid winter air.

I stood there gasping for air as I watched him go, trying to hold on to reason. To my senses and resolutions and the reality of who he was, all the while my spirit burning and aching, my insides twisting in two.

How had I let him hurt me so badly?

Off to the side, movement caught my attention, and I turned to find Addelaine wringing her hands where she stood in the archway to the sewing room in the back. "Child," she whispered like a loving reprimand.

Angrily, I swiped at the tears that started to fall when I saw her standing there. "He's a bad man, Addelaine. A big, bad man."

She shuffled forward, her head angling to the side as she did. "You didn't tell me."

I looked to the papers in front of me, pretending as if I could actually make out the words printed on the page through the bleariness that suddenly clouded my eyes. "There was nothing to tell," I said as offhandedly as I could muster.

She clucked in disapproval. "Lily, child. Come now. Do you think I don't know you better than that? That right there had nothing to do with this old building and everything to do with the expression you're wearing right now."

I jerked my attention back to her. "I made a mistake, Addelaine. A foolish, rash, horrible mistake, and because of it, I let you down. But I promise you, I won't fail you."

Addelaine peered up at me with her weathered face, and my breath caught somewhere in my lungs, my heart a tangle of pain and devotion.

This woman meant everything to me, and I'd let someone threaten that.

"Maybe it's a sign that we need to let this go. You've been fightin' a good fight, but maybe it's not the right fight. Maybe winnin' this one just isn't meant to be."

"How can you say that? You belong here. This is your home," I pleaded, pushing the papers that held the complaint across the counter toward her in a bid for her to sign them.

Her attention danced around her store like a loving caress. She turned back to me with a soft smile. "Yes, it's been my home." She tapped a finger at her temple. "But I hold the memories right here. And more importantly"— she tapped her fingertips over her heart—"I hold them here. And even if it scares us, sometimes change is okay."

She angled her head to the side as she reached out and set her hand on top of mine. "It's time you asked yourself why you're fighting so hard for this. You're no longer that girl who walked through my door lookin' for a place to hide. That girl needed walls to keep her safe. Are you going to continue to make her a prisoner to them?"

Tears clouded my eyes. I blinked, setting them free. "You know that girl was someone I never wanted to be."

She tenderly cupped my face, and even though I was much taller than she was, somehow I felt as if I was a little girl as I stared up at her motherly face.

"Yet, that girl is still a part of you, and she's always gonna be. She's important. She taught you the lessons you needed to know. She became the smart, successful, caring woman you are today. But she's also holdin' you back. Refusing to let you trust, even when the truth is right in front of you."

A frown twisted my brow, and I blinked rapidly. "What do you mean?"

A shot of air puffed from her nose. "You really think that man walked in here wearing his heart on his sleeve because he wanted to gloat about winnin'? If he did what you think he did, then he already won. That man came in here wearing remorse, plain as day."

My head shook, wanting to believe her so badly it vibrated in my spirit. But when I trusted, it only led to pain. "He's been foolin' us, Addelaine."

My words slipped into the casual tongue of my childhood, the hours I'd spent in this place sewing at her side, listening to her talk, strength growing each day as she instilled hope and belief in me.

"He's nothin' but a wolf in sheep's clothing."

She almost smiled. "Child, that man doesn't look nothin' like a sheep. Think he's wolf through and through. But I think he just might be your wolf."

"How...how could I ever believe him after everything?" I tossed the papers across the counter, the stack of them sliding and separating. "After I found all of this?"

Addelaine sighed before she began to shuffle through the stack of papers, pulling out the two different contracts she'd signed that were hidden beneath the stack of evidence I'd printed.

She pointed at the two signatures. "Look at this, child. Look closely."

Confusion knitted my brow while heartbreak trembled my lip.

She jabbed her index finger between the two of them. "Those signatures aren't close to bein' the same."

She looked up at me with a flash of fear in her grayed eyes. "And the men who came in here...they were...mean. Cruel and without compassion. I recognized it the second they stepped through my door. Just the same as I recognized the compassion in him when he first came here, too."

I blinked as I studied the signatures that were clearly different even though they both bore Brody's name. Broderick Wolfe III. A fact I had missed in my quest to find him guilty. In my mission to prove his betrayal, I'd overlooked the obvious.

Guilt built up inside me.

She lifted her chin. "You feel something for him?"

That feeling bubbled again. The affection and warmth I'd felt in his arms. The *possibility* that had become something tangible. I tried to resist it. Refute it. But it didn't matter. My own truth came flying out. "Yes. I feel so much, Addelaine. More than I should. It shouldn't be possible, but I do."

She smiled. "Then you need to ask him why you should trust him yourself. Give him a chance to explain and see where the heart leads. It's time for you to let it run. You've been holding it hostage for a long, long time. See what happens when you decide to *trust*."

The tears came unchecked, and I pressed my fingers beneath my eyes and wiped the moisture as I struggled for a breath.

"Oh God...I think I messed up."

In such a different way than I'd been accusing myself of all day. Because the thought of hurting him ripped me in two.

"What do you want?" she asked with a knowing smile threatening on her mouth.

Realization settled over me. Something powerful. Overcoming and overwhelming.

Unmistakable.

"Him. I want him."

Her smile bloomed into a full-blown grin. "Then go." Addelaine lifted my red coat. "Go, child, before it's too late."

I sat there stunned as I came to acceptance before I shot into action. Skidding around the counter, I darted for her, taking the jacket and dropping a kiss to her wrinkled cheek. "Thank you, Addelaine. For everything. I hope you know you mean everything to me."

She clutched my hand. "Same way as you mean everything to me. You're a good girl. Always have been. Now it's time for you to go get what you deserve."

Nodding furiously, I shoved my arms into my coat, wrapped the belt around my waist, and tied it as I flew outside. Cold air slapped me in the face, the sky an icy sort of blue. I didn't even slow. I just rushed down the sidewalk, winding through people who were on their lunch breaks, my heels clicking on the concrete as I stumbled along as fast as I could.

My heart thundered.

Heavy in my chest.

A pound, pound, pound as I let myself fully feel for the first time since I was fifteen. Without reservation. Without question.

Trust.

It was terrifying.

But freeing in the most miraculous of ways.

I moved faster, rushing across the street and heading in the direction of his hotel, praying he would be there.

That I wasn't too late.

That he'd give me the consideration I'd refused him minutes before. That he'd stop. Listen. Let me apologize. A frantic need built up, propelling me forward.

Faster.

Needier.

Filled with a hope unlike anything I'd ever felt before.

I gasped when I collided with a big body rushing my direction.

A stunning, powerful, strong body. Those big hands went straight to my face, gripping me tight, his eyes so intense and mesmerizing.

I clutched his jacket lapels. "Broderick...oh my God...I'm so sorry. I..." I forced myself to meet his steely intensity. "I told you back there that I fell for it, when in truth, I fell for *you*. That terrifies me, and the second something seemed to go wrong, I immediately thought the worst of you. And I don't want to be that person anymore. I don't want to be cynical and filled with doubt, always searching for the worst in people. Please...forgive me."

His thick throat bobbed. "Do you trust me, Lil' Redd?"

I swallowed hard, clutching his jacket tighter as I offered the words. "I told you I don't trust easily. I'm the one always waiting for the other shoe to drop. Just waiting on someone to let me down, because no matter how good things might be, they're bound to go bad. But it's time I realized I'm not that same girl who stood abandoned in that empty house. I'm not her. I've found love. A family. I don't have to be her anymore."

His hands cinched down on either side of my face. "I made both you and Addelaine a promise, and I intend to keep it. My father sent in his men to force this deal through and make it look like Addelaine agreed, threatening her into going along with it, and forging my signature to make me look like I was the one who was responsible. It's not the first time this has happened, but I promise you it will be the last. Tell me you trust me. That you believe I wasn't responsible."

My chin trembled when I nodded. "I do. Completely."

It was the truth.

Standing there with him, I'd never trusted anyone more in all my life.

Not with my heart. Not with my body. Not with *my* Addelaine and everything she represented.

He wrapped me in his warmth, pressing a bunch of kisses to my forehead, to my temple, to my lips, while my spirit soared. For the first time, freed.

He leaned back to meet my stare, his expression firm and unyielding. "I told you I always get what I want, Ms. Redd. I was already coming back for you. Because I'm not leaving this town without you."

I gazed up at him, my soul completely bared. "Then why don't you stay?"

A chuckle spilled from his mouth, and he hugged me tighter. "I think I like where this is going."

I breathed him in. At ease. Wholly. Completely. "I think I do, too."

He brushed back a stray lock of hair that whipped in the cold gusts of wind then threaded his fingers through mine. He lifted our entwined hands and grazed his lips across my knuckles. "Let's go, Ms. Redd. It's time to set things straight." He squeezed my hand. "Together."

EPILOGUE

BRODERICK

"DO YOU THINK she's going to like it?" Her hopeful whisper tickled my ears as my Lillith stared out the window of Pepper's, a dingy old diner that just so happened to have the best pie in the entire town with a direct view of where Addelaine's building once stood.

Her raven hair cascaded over her shoulder. Her delicious, delicious shoulder. Fuck, I loved her skin. I loved her body.

And God, how much I loved the woman.

Finding someone like her hadn't been in the cards.

But we were never in control of the hand we'd been dealt.

I'd been dealt a straight flush.

Lucky me.

I couldn't stop the grumble of possessiveness that filled my chest when I looked at my fiancé, who was wearing that expression of careful tenderness that was at the true root of who she was.

I reached across the table and took her hand, brushing my thumb along the back of the silky flesh, wondering how that simple action managed to stir the hunger inside me. "How could she not like it? She's going to have primo space."

Tindall's Thimbles would be located on the first floor of the brand new hotel going up across the street.

She turned to look at me with a tiny smile. "You wouldn't have it any other way."

"Of course not. You love her."

Her teeth clamped down on her bottom lip.

So damned enticing. I wanted nothing more to be the one delivering that bite.

"And you love me," she murmured.

"More than anything."

I toyed with the huge diamond that glinted from her ring finger, the ring I'd given her just two weeks ago. The day we'd broken ground on the new hotel.

This woman had been instrumental in seeing to it that my father was stopped. His corrupt practices silenced in the evidence Lillith had worked nonstop to prove.

My father had resigned from the company, and I'd taken his place as CEO.

But I sure as hell wasn't walking in his shoes.

"Did you ever think when you came here that you'd stay?" she whispered.

I leaned her direction, inhaling her distinct scent, words a growl. "Not until the first time I tasted you."

She shifted in her seat, and a heated flush skimmed her flesh.

Affected.

Needy.

Ready.

Just the way I wanted her.

"Are you wet?" I murmured casually.

She not so casually nodded her head, a tremble raking through her body.

After pulling my money clip from the inside pocket of my suit jacket, I tossed a stack of bills onto the table.

Then I sat back with the challenge.

She clutched the table, a harsh breath parting her lips.

"Run, Ms. Redd. Because I'm going to chase you. And where I catch you? That's where I'm going to fuck you."

She inhaled a sharp breath before she slid out of the booth, her knees clearly weak as she made her way through the restaurant. Today she wore a red summer dress, which she knew that color always drove me out of my mind, and a pair of sexy black heels. Her hair a black avalanche down her back.

She pulled open the door, only looking back at me to give me a smirk from her red, red lips.

Then she stepped out into the day and disappeared down the sidewalk.

I stood from the booth and straightened my tie.

The hunt was on.

And with her? It was never going to end.

THE END

THANK YOU

Did you enjoy the small taste of Gingham Lakes? Don't miss the passionate, unforgettable stand-alone novels in the FIGHT FOR ME series, including the stories of Rex Gunner and Ollie Preston. Get full details at http://smarturl.it/FightforMeSeries

Never miss out on the latest news from A.L. Jackson. Subscribe to http://smarturl.it/NewsFromALJackson

KNOT

A Rapunzel Story

Lili St Germain

PROLOGUE

.

S TEALING FROM IGNACIO *Garcia Hernandez was risky at best. At worst, it was your death, but first, things worse than death. Maria de la Cruz knew this, and yet she had stolen from her boss. Just a little of the crude opium that grew wild in his fields. Just a few bulbs at a time. Without the opium, Maria thought she might die.*

But now, with a machine gun aimed at her head, it seemed that even with the opium, death was certain.

"Take her up to the tower," Ignacio ordered his men. "It's almost dark."

At his feet, a heavily pregnant Maria pressed her hands together, her knees squashing precious poppy bulbs that grew all around them. Ignacio tried not to think about how much her bony kneecaps were costing him right now, what with the groveling and the trampling and the blood that was tainting his precious opiate flowers. Hector and Rico made quick work of dragging the laboring woman to her feet and up toward the disused water tower in the middle of his poppy fields.

"Watch the fucking flowers!" he barked at their suit-clad backs.

"Please," she begged, screaming as another contraction overtook her. Ignacio held up a hand and his two burly guards dropped her arms, letting her writhe on hands and knees in the dirt this time. Ignacio waited patiently as she crested the peak of her pain and breathed back down the mountain of it, her pupils giant in the weak light of dusk, her hands covered in the blood of the dead husband who lay a few feet away. Ignacio glanced at him, the man whose name he couldn't remember, the man who had stolen from him, the man who would never again step foot onto his property, because he was about to be buried beneath it. The skeletons in these fields could tell all kinds of secrets if they were ever exhumed — but here, in the most remote pocket of Mexico's mountain valleys, there was nobody to dig.

In the tower, Hector and Rico set Maria on the ground. She was bearing down, the life inside her demanding a swift exit. That was good. Ignacio was a terrible man, but he preferred not to murder babies unless absolutely necessary. Ignacio loved babies. He desired the innocence they possessed. He coveted the malleable nature of their youth, the ability to bend them according to his whims.

He imagined his supper at home, cold, as Rico headed back down the steep flights of stairs to bury Maria's thieving husband.

"Ignacio, please!" Maria screamed, clutching her swollen belly. The waves were so close there was barely pause between contractions now.

"Please what?" Ignacio asked, in a voice that was far too calm.

"Please let me g-go!" the woman begged. "I promise I won't t-tell anyone. I swear!"

Ignacio crouched before Maria, careful not to get dirty. Nobody had been in this tower for years. It was filthy and barren and the perfect place for what he had planned. "You stole from me, Maria. You took drugs that were not yours and probably hurt this poor child." He placed a hand on her belly. "And you think I am the bad man here?"

Maria continued to sob. "I'm sorry," she said, strings of saliva hanging from her lips as she tried to beg for her life while giving birth at the same time. Not an easy feat, by any means. Ignacio wrinkled his nose up at her animalistic grunts and screams, so primal, so Neanderthal. His first wife – before he'd stabbed her to death after learning of her infidelity, God bless her soul – had birthed all of their ten children at home, in the bathtub, in silence. Ignacio had caught more than his share of children in his lifetime; such was the wonder of holding a child in it's very first moment, of whispering in their ear your plans for their destiny, for Ignacio was a maker of destiny and fate. To hold a brand new being in the palms of your hands and begin shaping them to your will as they took their first breath; new life was exquisite, something to be revered.

Ignacio checked his watch again; he had to hurry this up. "Give me your jacket," he said to Rico, who obliged immediately, shrugging his meaty arms out of his suit jacket and handing the pile of material to his boss. Ignacio folded the jacket lengthways, sitting it on the ground on front of the spot where Maria was laboring. He rolled up his sleeves, mindful not to get any blood on the starched white linen he preferred to wear in the summer heat, and got down to business.

Maria screamed when he used two fingers to check her dilation. She was barely awake, though, so depleted of strength that the pain was the only thing stopping her from passing out.

"Come on now, Maria, you're completely open in there. Open like a beautiful flower. You have to push," Ignacio said, shaking his head as if they were talking

over dinner and not holed up in the dark in an abandoned water tower, surrounded by poppy fields in the Sierra Madre Mountains.

Maria, carried by her body's urges rather than Ignacio's, bore down, screaming as she pushed, and a baby's head appeared. She leant against the wall in between contractions, her breath ragged, the fields absolutely silent on this balmy spring night.

The desolation only added to Ignacio's feeling of excitement, of wonder – right now, the rest of the world didn't exist. His men melted into the background, dutiful soldiers who were there merely for their muscle and ability to fire a gun, nothing more. No, right now it was Ignacio Garcia Hernandez and Maria de la Cruz and – one more push! – now they were three, Daddy Bear, Mommy Bear, Baby Bear. Maria reached for the baby as it slithered out from her body, but Ignacio was faster. He took the child, still attached by reams of umbilical cord much like a bungee jumper to a bridge. Ignacio didn't cut the cord right away. He'd read somewhere – or was it his wife who had told him? – that the best way to ensure a healthy baby at birth was to wait until the cord stopped pulsating before cutting it.

This was also the reason he had not simply killed Maria and cut the baby from her flesh, though he was hardly about to tell her that. Mothers tended to get violently hysterical when confronted with their own mortality.

The baby was still. He turned it over and gave a great slap on the back – a sharp intake of breath, the very first air to touch its lungs, and then the baby cried, strong and sharp.

Ignacio Garcia Hernandez held the wet, screaming bundle in his palms and smiled. A healthy child, with a thick head of blonde hair. Bright blue eyes and the most adorable little fists that were currently clenched as it wailed. Ignacio moved the umbilical cord to the side and confirmed what he'd already suspected.

His newest possession was a girl.

Of course. He smiled, bringing the tiny infant to his chest, bundling her into the space between his shirt and bare skin to keep her warm.

She quieted immediately, her little eyes wide, her clumsy head rooting around for mother's milk that would never come.

"Milk," he ordered, and as if by magic, a bottle of formula appeared in front of him in Rico's outstretched hand. Ignacio took the bottle and teased it around the baby's mouth, a surge of affection running through him when she attached and started suckling greedily.

Maria de la Cruz was watching all of this from the floor, her eyes already full of the knowledge that the rest of her life was now measured in seconds, not years.

"Let me feed her," she whispered, holding out her arms. "Let me hold her, Ignacio, please—"

She never quite got to finish the "s" in please, because Ignacio, multi-tasker that he was, balancing baby and bottle in one thick arm, withdrew the Gold-plated pistol from his shoulder holster with his spare hand and shot Maria de la Cruz right between the eyes. She died instantly, sagging to the side as the bullet's exit path through the back of her head painted a bright red line of blood down the wall.

The baby girl in his arms stiffened at the sudden explosive sound; her back arched, she spat the bottle teat out and scrunched up her face, wailing as her mother had wailed only moments earlier. "Shhh," Ignacio murmured, rocking the tiny thing gently as he holstered his gun. "Come on, my girl. Everything will be okay."

She quieted, finding the bottle teat again, pulling milk by sheer instinct and the ravenous hunger of being born.

"My beautiful girl," Ignacio murmured, gazing down at the child whose mother and father he had just murdered in cold blood. She was falling asleep already, her thick lashes fluttering as she dreamed earth side for the first time. She was so pretty already, but more importantly, just like her mother, she would be an exquisite beauty. A beauty that Ignacio would shape and mold like a potter sitting behind his wheel, wet clay skimming against his hands, forming a masterpiece.

"All of this was meant to be, little one," he whispered, rubbing his thumb along his baby's forehead. "All of this was fate."

He smiled. Fate had always been kind to Ignacio.

SERAPHINA

Eighteen Years Later

IT'S ALMOST NIGHT. Anticipation bubbles up in my belly; he'll be here soon.

I have to be ready. Everything has to be ready. Everything has to be perfect. My skin is soft and creamy from the moisturizer he brought me; my pussy bare from where he shaved me last night. Every inch of me is silky and smooth and smelling of coconut.

I would usually be ravenous by now; my days have a very particular routine. I wake up with a sliver of the sun, peeking through the tiny crack in the boards that cover my windows to keep me safe. I read; I drink water by the gallon to quell the hunger pangs in my belly; I paint with the watercolors he left for me. I sleep, because I'm so weak from the lack of food. When I sleep, I dream of the same angel; the man made of midnight, with the kind eyes and the wide smile. I think about my small hand tucked in to his, his earthy smell, the way I am so sure he is real. The first time I saw him, his tender words. "I'll get you out of here, sweetheart."

He can't be real, because he never came back. Not after I fell out of the window, fresh blood still running down my thighs from what Ignacio had done to me. "You're a woman, now," he had whispered, and then he had turned from my father to a monster, right before my eyes.

But mostly, I wait.

My pulse quickens as I hear his car pull up. I've never been in a car before. I wonder if it feels like flying along the dirt roads, engine purring. Not that I can fly, either.

I hurry to my spot on the bed that takes up the center of my circular room; on my hands and knees, facing away from the door, trying to still my breathing.

I hear the hard soles of his shoes as he ascends the stairs: clackclackclack. His keychain jangles. The key inserts into the locking mechanism and turns.

I break out into a cold sweat, which is so unlike me. I am always full of anticipation, excitement to see him after a long day by myself. But this night, something is wrong. My skin is clammy, oscillating between hot and cold, and I want to throw up.

The door closes again, locked tight to keep me safe. Those same shoes clack across concrete floors to the bed, to where I wait, ass in the air, naked as the day I was born into Ignacio's arms in this exact spot.

He stops at the end of the bed. I feel the mattress dip as he climbs on to the bed behind me, already hard as he takes my hips in cold, rough palms and pulls me in to him. He plants a single kiss on my tailbone. "Did you miss me, Seraphina?"

My eyes fill with tears. "Yes, papi." It's true, I always miss him so much. He's my entire world. Without him, this room stays dark and it's just me, touching myself under my panties until my skin is raw and my fingers are soaked.

"Your hair is wrong," he growls. Fear spikes in my belly, alongside the dull ache that has been in my side all day. I've never forgotten to arrange my hair just the way he likes it. He prefers it loose, so he can wrap it around his hands while he drives himself into me. Today I forgot. It's the pain. The pain in my side. It's been plaguing me for days; making me forget things.

I open my mouth to apologize, but my platitudes are drowned out by a sharp smack to my rear. And another. And another. It hurts. I grip handfuls of the snow-white sheets in front of me, barely visible in the fading light. Sometimes I think he visits me at dusk so that he doesn't have to see me properly.

He stops striking me; my skin stings from the sudden assault. But it's nothing compared to the sharp throb in my right side.

"Let down your hair," Ignacio snaps over the sound of a zipper, and I sit back on my heels, fumbling with the long braid that reaches almost to my knees, combing the weaves out so that it hangs loose. "I'm sorry," I whisper. "I'm – oh…"

Without any warning, he's pushing inside me. I make small noises as he fills me up with himself, feeling myself contract around him. He brings one hand around to my front and strokes the tiny bundle of nerves between my legs that makes me arch my back like a cat in heat.

"Baby likes that?" he asks, nibbling on my ear. He never stays angry for more than a moment. He says it's because he's besotted by me. I think it's because my pussy is clenching around his cock and making his mind blurry with lust.

He is not my father, but he is like a father to me, sometimes. And other times, like now, he is my lover. Like his lust-filled mind, sometimes the lines of what we are to each other blur until they run into one another.

My legs start to shake as his finger moves faster between my legs, circling me to the brink and then backing off. My stomach drops as he takes his fingers from my pussy and slides them into my mouth. "Suck."

I open my mouth and taste myself on his skin. But my mind is somewhere else. It's wondering if this pain in my side might kill me. It feels like it might. I feel as if somebody has taken the fire poker from the corner, the one I use to stoke the coals on cold winter nights, and rammed it into my stomach.

I start to shake harder. It's no longer pleasure driving me to such dizzying heights; it's knowing that I will pass out. Black bites at the edges of my vision as I struggle to breathe. I gasp as Ignacio pulls on my hair, pulling himself deeper inside me, swelling inside me as he lets go and I feel his warm seed spurt deep inside me.

He lets go of my hips and I collapse on my front. He will be angry. I'm supposed to turn around and lick him clean. This is our routine, the same thing, every night.

"Seraphina?" he says quietly, in a tone that suggests he knows something is not right. He pulls out of me, sticky semen seeping out of me, quickly growing cold on my thighs. He gets off the end of the bed and circles around to the head, kneeling beside my face.

It's the first time I have seen him all day; his short stubble, his dark eyes, soothe me. I am not alone. "Bambina, what's wrong?" he asks.

"My stomach hurts," I whisper.

"I would feed you more," he says, stroking my cheek affectionately, "but we need to keep you small. You understand?"

I nod through the hunger that pulses in me; it is always there, an omnipotent beast that eats me from the inside out. I am always starving. I am always weak.

But this feeling isn't hunger.

Ignacio senses it, too, I think. I feel his body tense under me as he brings the back of his hand up to my forehead. It is like ice to my fire; he sucks in a breath.

"You're burning up, little bird," he says, concern thick in his voice. He gets back on to the bed, pulling me into his lap so that my back is against his chest. On reflex I part my legs, and his fingers find the spot where they fit so well.

"Let me make you feel better, precious girl," he says, his tongue on my neck, his fingers bringing me ever closer to the edge. I raise my hips greedily, wanting more, wanting relief and release. He starts to fuck me with his other hand, two fingers inside me, then three, the other hand circling my bud until I'm moaning loudly.

There are times I could almost believe that he is my father, except for times like this, the way I'm naked in his lap, my legs spread wide, my head resting back against his shoulder as his rough fingers stroke the wet spot between my legs. In the books I read, stained with mildew and covered in layers of dust, fathers do not do these things. He kisses my neck tenderly, rubbing me between my legs until they start to shake. "This will help you forget," he breathes, his words warm on my neck.

Stars burst behind my eyelids as my orgasm finally arrives; and for a precious moment, with Ignacio's fingers buried deep inside me, with his teeth biting softly at my neck, the pain goes away and everything is pure white light inside me.

But then he takes his fingers away, pushes me to the edge of the bed, to my feet, cold fluid running down the insides of my legs as he guides me gently to the small bathroom. "Clean yourself," he says, turning on the faucet and filling the tiny shower cubicle with steam. "I'll get you food, and some medicine." I nod, not bothering to twist my hair up onto the top of my head like I normally would. I put my palms on the tiled wall and shuffle underneath the water.

"Phina?" Ignacio's voice sounds like it is a million miles away. That's impossible; I've never left this tower since the day I was born, unless you count the time I accidentally fell out of the window when I was a child. No, I could never be a million miles away from my dark love; he's never more than a few feet away.

"Seraphina?!" More insistent this time. I open my mouth to respond, but nothing comes out. I can't see. I can't hear. There is a brief pain in my temple as my head hits hard tile, and then nothing.

XAVIER

I'M ELBOW-DEEP IN Italian mafia blood and internal sutures when my cellphone vibrates in my pocket.

"Bro," I hiss, catching my brother's attention as he monitors the levels of anesthesia being pumped into the criminal on the table between us, the guy whose intestines I'm currently digging in for stray pieces of shrapnel. Liam raises his eyebrows. "My phone. Can you get it?"

Liam rolls his eyes, but he circles the table and our unconscious patient, Anthony No-Last-Name, never once taking his eyes off the vital signs his portable monitor is blinking out in red and green Technicolor. "You expecting a call?" he asks, reaching in to my jeans pocket and pulling out my iPhone.

"Holy *shit*," he says, his expression grave. I never thought I'd describe a black man as *pale*, but I can see the blood disappear from my brother's dark brown skin as he looks at the phone screen.

"What?" I ask, peering over. "I can't read upside down, you know."

"It's The Florist," Liam says. He's seemingly forgotten all about the guy who he's meant to be keeping sedated while I finish my treasure hunt inside his stomach.

"THE Florist?" I ask, glancing at the patient monitor. "Liam, Jesus, your guy's blood pressure is—"

"Falling down into hell," he finishes, rushing around to his spot at the head of the industrial kitchen table we're using as a makeshift surgical bed. I've operated in some pretty crazy places, but I've never before had the aroma of frying oil stuck to the inside of my nostrils as I try to dig pieces of a special-issue 9mm bullet out of somebody.

"Fuck, I've got a bleeder here," I snap, grabbing a pair of clamps from my tray of sterile instruments and fishing around in this guy's fatty stomach cavity for the source of the blood loss. I find the artery and clamp it off, sweat beading on my forehead as a hulkishly tall dude in a custom-made Armani suit strolls into my sterile area, a string of red licorice hanging from between his teeth.

"Hey, Kanye, Jay-Z," Sal Barbieri says to Liam and I, loosening his tie as he bites a chunk of the blood-red licorice. "Let's get this shit tied up. We've got dinner service starting in an hour."

As if on cue, his slightly shorter, equally annoying brother appears beside him, sporting the same cut of Armani suit, a plastic butcher's apron over the top. He's holding a stack of raw rib eye fillets in his arms, and out of the corner of my eye, I watch Liam's face twitch.

"What part of sterile do you idiots not understand?" I say, gently suctioning the excess blood from my patient's abdomen and spotting another piece of bullet. Jesus, this shot is so messy. "What kind of bullets do you guys use?" I ask, holding the latest piece of shrapnel up to show them. "This bullet is in a thousand tiny fucking fragments."

Sal, the taller one, chews on his candy thoughtfully. "They're home-made," he replies, glancing at his brother.

"Awesome," I mutter under my breath.

"What'd you say?" Sal asks, his tone pissed.

I grind my teeth in my jaw and try not to lose my shit; I literally have this guy's life in my hands, and I don't have time to argue with this mafia sociopath. "I said, how did you accidentally shoot your associate here?"

"Oh," he replies. "We were playing Italian Roulette."

Theo, whose arms must be getting tired holding all that beef, clears his throat pointedly. "That's not Italian Roulette. Look it up on Urban Dictionary."

Sal totally ignores his brother's correction.

"Dude, don't bring food into a fucking operating room," Theo adds.

Sal's mouth drops open as he stares at the ribeye fillets stacked ten tall in Theo's arms. "*Dude,*" he replies, raising his eyebrows as he stares pointedly at the steaks. Theo just glares up at his brother, crossing the kitchen to the giant refrigerator unit and opening it with his foot.

My phone starts to vibrate again in Liam's hand, but he's too busy making sure our patient's blood pressure comes back up. The Florist only calls when something is seriously wrong; I haven't heard from him in what, nine, ten years? And it's been a good nine or ten years without that crazy fucker in my business. Then again, I am standing in an Italian restaurant in the middle of Hell's Kitchen, New York City, pulling bullet fragments out of a dude who was playing roulette with his fucking handgun.

"Hey, Sal," I say to the tall one. He flicks his hair out of his eyes, a new piece of liquorice in his mouth. "Yeah?"

"I need you to answer that phone and hold it up to my ear," I say, finding a fresh bleeder in my patient's stomach and sealing it off; this guy is cut to ribbons inside. He'll probably be shitting into a bag for the rest of his life, assuming he survives the teeming bacteria of the Barbieri kitchen and this casual operation that nobody seems particularly worried about.

"Oh, sure, man," Sal says, chewing loudly as he reaches over the patient and grabs the phone from Liam's palm. Liam and I both open our mouths to say something as the phone starts to slide from Sal's hand, right into the bloody gape of Anthony's open stomach. In slow motion, he catches it, grinning like a fucking psycho as he studies the screen.

"I meant to do that," he muses, reading the iPhone screen. "The Florist, huh? You must've really fucked up if you need to order flowers for your girlfriend while you're finger-fucking my buddy's bullet wound here."

"THE Florist?" Theo interrupts.

"THE Florist," I confirm. "And he's onto his third call. So unless you fuckers want him to come here and kill all of us, please, for the love of God, answer the fucking phone for me, will you, Sal?"

Sal rolls his eyes, but slaps the green "answer" icon and holds the phone to my ear. It's really fucking hard to focus on two things at once, when those two things are performing surgery and trying to play nice with the most brutal man in all of Mexico.

"Is this The Doctor?" A Spanish accent comes down the line.

"This is The Doctor," I reply. "How can I help?"

I'm at the suturing stage now. I replace my blood-soaked gloves with a fresh pair and start stitching Anthony's skin back together, at the same time trying to listen to The Florist and not to the sound of Sal's massive jaw moving back and forth as he grinds licorice like a fucking cow grinds grass.

"Patient is eighteen years old, female, unconscious," The Florist says, totally emotionless. "Pain radiating from the right side of her stomach."

"Probably fucking period pain," Sal deadpans in a voice barely above a whisper. I fix him with a pointed stare. "Nausea? Fever?"

"Both," The Florist confirms.

"Appendicitis is my guess," I say, checking Anthony's sutures are straight and in line. "If you can take her to the ER, they'll confirm with some tests." I shouldn't fucking care about whether Anthony has a straight scar or not, but I'm a perfectionist when it comes to my work. Really, I should have just let him bleed out and rid the world of one more moronic person.

"An ER is out of the question, Mr. Bishop," The Florist says, dispensing with formality. "As is guessing. I will arrange a jet for you. You are presently in New York operating on one Anthony Barbieri, yes?"

He's a Barbieri? Jesus. I assumed he was just an associate, not a family member. I'm suddenly very fucking happy that I didn't let him bleed out in the kitchen prep section of *Cucina Diavolo*. The Barbieris would have my balls sliced off and served as entree before the end of the night, and I've heard what they use that fucking deep fryer for.

"How do you know where I am?" I ask slowly, looking around the kitchen.

"I always know where you are, Xavier," The Florist says.

"Is that right, Ignacio?" Fuck pleasantries. Fuck code. This asshole knows I don't want anything to do with the sick shit he orchestrates in Mexico, and he's just made damn sure to put me somewhere where the only weapon I have is the surgical scalpel at my side.

I look at Sal, at Theo. "Please don't tell me you shot a member of your family just to get me here," I say solemnly. Theo looks away. Sal blinks several times. "Well, we could tell you we didn't, but that would be a lie."

I grab the scalpel before anyone can go for their gun. "You people are fucking crazy," I hiss, rage pumping in my veins, Liam looking like he's going to kill everyone in the room just with the force of his hateful glare.

Sal looks down at Anthony, giving him an affectionate slap on the cheek. "We hear that a lot."

Ignacio *The Florist* Hernandez is talking again; I rip one of my surgical gloves off and snatch the phone from Sal's giant palm. "I couldn't risk you disappearing into the belly of Chicago with your friends," Ignacio says. "I decided to get you to a place where I have more associates of my own. It's just business. You understand?"

"Why can't you take her to the ER?" I ask, wiping sweat from my head with my arm. "Answer me properly."

"That's simple," Ignacio says. "I cannot take her to the ER because on

444

paper, this girl does not exist."

"You're trafficking her," I concede grimly.

"If I were trafficking her, do you think I would spend fifty thousand dollars on a private fucking flight for you? Another fifty thousand for your services? Have you ever met a woman that Ignacio Garcia Hernandez would spend one hundred thousand dollars on for a *fucking* appendectomy?"

"You love her," I realize. "I didn't know you had a heart, Ignacio."

"Get your black ass to that airstrip, boy, or you'll be dead and hanging from a hook in the Barbieris' industrial freezer by the time Anthony wakes up from his little surgery."

He ends the call abruptly. I pocket my phone and stare at the collective faces around me: Liam, Sal, Theo. "You two are fucking assholes," I say to the Barbieri brothers.

Theo shrugs. "We get that a lot, too."

SERAPHINA

A N ANGEL IS here to save me.

Skin dark as midnight, kind eyes that are laced with concern; it's almost like he melted out of the walls and picked me up off the ground.

The light above me is too bright. I'm freezing cold, my teeth chattering even as I feel my skin on fire. Feverish. A thousand hot pokers being stabbed into my side. Ignacio pressed a hot poker into my thigh once, when I asked to go outside to see the flowers. This pain is so much worse than that, and that was horrific.

I've never seen a man with skin like his before. Ignacio is Mexican, his skin bronzed from his ancestry, turned a richer brown by the sun. But the man standing over me, shining that horridly bright light that makes me recoil back into the pillow my head rests upon; he is the color of midnight, and I don't think I've ever seen somebody more magnificent. I hear crying and realize it's my own, as I lie sweat-slicked and writhing from the pain. I feel a pinch in the crook of my arm, something cold snaking into my veins, and a few moments later, blessed relief. My eyes grow heavy; limbs loose and soft, my fists finally uncurling. I suck in a breath, the warmth that flows through me similar to the feeling when Ignacio puts his tongue on me and I raise my hips involuntarily to the rhythm of his fingers. I look down at myself, still naked, covered in a white sheet, the middle section cut out to reveal my midsection, my arm resting on top with a tube running into it.

I stare in wonder, my brain addled, my thoughts slow.

There is a new person in my tower.

"Papi?" I say breathlessly, looking around the room as panic grips me. I can't see Ignacio. There is a new man here and *where is Ignacio?* I turn my terrified gaze to the new man, the angel with the kind eyes, and wonder if I was wrong. Maybe he's not here to help me.

Maybe he's here to steal me. Ignacio always warns me that this could happen. If anyone ever comes into the tower I am to hide. If they find me, I must fight. If they take me away, I will surely die.

The world outside is a terribly place. A dangerous place. All these things I have been told, the very reason for me being locked away: *for my own good.* Ignacio saved me from certain death the day I was born. I owe everything to him. My life, my submission, my body, my soul. It is all his.

It makes sense, then, that I should fear the man standing over me, a sharp silver knife in his hand. *Scalpel.* That's what it's called. I read that once in a book. I have read so many books in my life, they all merge together into white pages, black words, stories pieced together in the dull cracks of sunlight that seep into my dungeon.

"Hey," The Man says. His voice is like velvet, but low, commanding at the same time. I stop looking for Ignacio and settle my eyes back on my Dark Knight as he peers back at me, the scalpel now lowered, his expression grim.

I try to sit up. And… I can't.

"My legs," I gasp. I try to rise up onto my elbows to see what's wrong with me. Something *has* to be terribly wrong, doesn't it, because I can't feel anything from my waist down. It's like somebody has sawn me in half; cleaved me through the middle and stolen the rest of me away.

The Man puts a large hand on my chest, high enough to avoid my breasts, firm enough to glue my back to the—what am I laying on? It's not my bed, that much I know. It's hard and smooth. The table. I'm lying on the dining table, and I don't have legs anymore.

"I gave you a spinal block," he says, that rich voice curling around me like smoke. I'm terrified, yes, but something else, as well.

I'm intrigued. I've never seen another person before, not since I was a child. I wasn't even sure they existed, to be completely honest. And, more than anything, I want him to keep talking.

"Who are you?" I breathe.

He takes his hand away, the slightest hint of a smirk tugging at one corner of his wide mouth. "I'm The Doctor," he says.

Whatever stuff he's given me; it starts to really seep into my brain. I'm feeling foggy, now. I'm floating. I'm falling. I can still faintly feel the pain in my side, but I'm oddly detached from it, like it's someone else's body, not mine.

"Am I dying?" I ask him. It would be sad to die now; when I'm on the cusp of adulthood, when Ignacio promised I would be able to leave this tower, when it will finally be safe enough for me to be without him, away from here. The Doctor shakes his head. "No. You might have, if you'd been like this much longer, but I'm going to take out your appendix. You'll be fine."

"Oh."

He busies himself with different metal instruments; I don't know any of their names. I watch his face, searching for some kind of relief, finding none.

"What's your real name?" I ask, wincing as I feel the pressure of something pressing down over my torso. "The one your mother gave you?"

There's no pain; but that doesn't mean I don't feel everything he's doing to me. It's an odd sensation. The world spins around me and I feel my eyes flicker toward the back of my skull. He's so much more focused now.

"Are you cutting me?" I panic.

"Xavier," the man says, probably trying to distract me. "My name is Xavier."

"You're cutting me. Where is Ignacio?" I whisper, my eyes full of tears. He would hold my hand and tell me everything is okay. He would lean down and blow warm air on my face to soothe me, like he did when I was a little girl. He would make me feel that everything was going to be okay but he's not here.

"I'm not cutting you yet," the man called Xavier says. "And I think he's taking a call."

Of course. *A call.* I bite down on my lip, trying to focus somewhere else, trying to pretend the rejection blooming under my skin isn't really there. Ignacio would call me insolent if I dared to question him. He would pull my hair until chunks came out of my scalp, he would smack my thighs with his leather belt until blisters formed, he would push into my ass with no lubrication until I bled. His love is a cruel love, and I daren't ask him to sit by me while this strange Doctor puts things in my spine and takes the feeling in my legs away and washes things into my veins that taste like an orgasm.

"What name did your mother give you?" Xavier asks me, flashing his teeth in what I think is supposed to be an attempt at a comforting smile. That's what they would call it, in the books I've read. An attempt to put me at ease. But Xavier doesn't understand that I was raised in the dark. I am the property of a man who does not give comforting smiles. I was raised by a man who gave teeth-bared smiles only before he sank those teeth into my pale flesh.

I blink rapidly; there are tiny beads of moisture stuck to my eyelashes, from my tears. "My mother didn't give me a name," I say. "Ignacio named me. My mother was dead before she could give me a name."

"I'm sorry," Xavier says, his smile gone, replaced by pity. He still doesn't understand. I wasn't raised on pity, either, and I don't need his.

"It's okay," I whisper, staring at the ceiling, the only ceiling I've seen since the day I was born on this very floor. "I've never known any different. Ignacio named me Seraphina."

"That's a beautiful name, Seraphina," Xavier says, as if testing it out on his tongue.

"It means fiery," I say, as another wave of dizziness slams into me. "And Ignacio means ignite. He's always saying it'll be us who burn the world down together."

"Huh," Xavier says, apparently intrigued by my silly little life. "And do you want to burn the world down, Seraphina?"

I shake my head, my heartbeat picking up to a rattle as I hear Ignacio's shoes on the steps outside. "I don't want to burn the world down," I reply, hoping Ignacio can't hear me. "But I would like to see it."

He nods, his face looking... sympathetic. I don't need that, either. His emotions are useless to me, but I can't pretend that I don't like watching him as he tries to fit his expressions to my words. I'm about to open my mouth and ask him another question when a plastic mask appears in his hand, sweet-smelling air wafting from it as he places it over my mouth and nose.

"First things first," he says, and I almost believe the kindness in his eyes is real and not a trick of the blinding light. "I want you to count back from one hundred. Let me fix you up. Then we can talk about seeing the world."

I want to ask him if he'll show it to me, but the world goes black. I don't even get to 99 before I'm weighted down, a heavy stone at the bottom of a raging river.

XAVIER

I T WAS WHEN I saw her hip bones that I decided I wasn't leaving without her.

She was unconscious, when I arrived. Tucked up in her bed, a cold cloth on her forehead that was rapidly turning as hot as the fever that raged within her veins. Her hair was impossible; hanging loose, it ran across her pillow, over the edge of the bed, and pooled on the floor as if it had been spun from gold right then and there.

The girl with the golden hair. The girl I fixed when she fell from a window.

The girl Ignacio told me was *dead*, all those years ago.

She wasn't dead. She's been here, in this tower, now a woman but still trapped in the body of a child. Malnourished, barely five foot tall by my quick estimations, her cheekbones almost as severe as her hips. This girl has been starved. This girl has been held prisoner. This girl has been in my nightmares since the day I flew out of the Sierra Madre mountains ten years ago, thinking I'd saved her life after her horrific fall, only to get a call when I landed in Chicago telling me she had died, and that it was my fault.

Ignacio enters the room just as Seraphina's eyes are fluttering shut, the gas doing its job of sending her off into a twilight sleep so I can operate on her. I'm so used to working as a duo with my brother, that I'm noticing Liam's absence acutely. It's a juggle, making sure she doesn't feel pain while I take out her dangerously inflamed appendix.

"Did she wake up?" Ignacio asks. I shake my head. "No." I don't want to give him any information. For some selfish, strange reason, I want to keep the conversation I had with Seraphina all to myself. High on pain and drugs and the cusp of death, she somehow managed to bare her soul to me in what probably amounted to three or four sentences we exchanged.

"I heard talking," he says, his eyes narrowed at me. *You were on the fucking phone,* I want to say, but I don't. Ignacio Garcia Hernandez is a cruel

450

man, a vicious man, and just being in his presence dials up the danger that I might earn myself a bullet or two. Of course, if I had a weapon, and he didn't have two machine-gun-toting thugs following his every move, we'd be able to try to kill each other like civilized men.

But here, I have been stripped of all my weapons—literally, those fuckers took my gun and my knife as soon as I strolled my ass onto the private jet Ignacio chartered from New York. In this apparently disused water tower among fields of illegal opium poppies, I wield nothing mightier than a scalpel.

"I tried to wake her," I confirm. "You heard me talking to her. She's out for now."

Apparently satisfied, Ignacio nods, thrusting his hands into his pant pockets as he paces on the other side of my makeshift operating table. I make the first incision into her flesh, clearing my throat as I suction blood from around Seraphina's angry, swollen appendix. She's lucky it hasn't ruptured already; in a place like this, I doubt very much that I could save her. A ruptured appendix requires a higher level of surgical prowess than I can possess alone, in the dark, without so much as a second pair of eyes to monitor my patient's vital signs.

Then again, looking at where we are; in the possession of a homicidal drug cultivator, a cartel lackey, a man who purposely locked a girl away for most of her life – I don't need to draw conclusions about where Seraphina has spent her days; I can see, in the hollows of her cheeks, in her small stature, the way her pupils are permanently inky-black and wide, like a cat's, and the paleness on her skin.

This girl has lived her life in this tower, a prisoner. Ignacio's prisoner.

It takes every ounce of strength and self-preservation that I possess to stop myself from launching across this table and embedding my scalpel in Ignacio's jugular. I'd give anything to watch him bleed out on the dirty floor of this room and take this poor girl away from what must be a living hell.

First, though, I have to make sure she survives this surgery.

Again, I wish for Liam. My constant off-sider, we work in synchronicity. When we were kids, we were a team, protecting our little sister from the procession of step daddies who liked her a little too much; one of us hiding her away while the other fought the latest guy who was obviously not in our house because he enjoyed our mother's company; and when our mother would slip, it'd be Liam holding her hand, calling an ambulance and prying her eyes open while I found a half-decent vein to inject the Narcan.

Yeah, I'm not a solo operator, that's for damn sure. *Fucking Ignacio.*

As if reading my mind, Seraphina stirs momentarily. Ignacio appears at her side like a fucking ninja, all concern and fatherly care, a great charade for a man who kept a child for his own deviant pleasure for God knows how long.

"What's happening?" Ignacio barks, taking her hand in his.

"She's fine," I say quietly, making no attempts to soothe the crazy bastard. "She's probably having a dream. It's twilight sedation. She's not entirely under like she would be with a general."

"Are you sure you know what you're doing, boy?" Ignacio says, clearly hating that I'm encroaching on his space, touching his property, knowing his dirty secret. He's itching to shoot me. I glimpse the gold-plated pistol on his hip and have to force my eyes not to roll back in my head at the ludicrousness of this man. Yeah, looking back at his dark, determined eyes, I have no doubt that if it's up to him, I won't be leaving this water tower alive.

"I've been doing this a long time, old man," I say, even though Ignacio isn't that old. He's probably fifty, wiry and fit, and I doubt he's ever so much as tasted the drug that he supplies to thousands upon thousands of desperate addicts each and every month. He's a smart man, a businessman.

A depraved man.

I continue to work, finally freeing the appendix from Seraphina's abdominal cavity. Once it's gone, sealed in a sterile plastic bag for disposal, I clean up the surrounds and can finally start to suture the wound closed.

"You told me she died," I say, surprised at the hard edge of emotion that rattles in my words. It's barely discernible, and my voice holds steady, but there is so much rage in my chest when I think about the past ten years. Rage for all of the nightmares, of the flaxen-haired girl who was one of my first patients outside of a hospital, back when people like Ignacio started to understand what an asset an off-the-books surgical resident could be to the sprawling arteries of the criminal underworld.

I look up, meeting Ignacio's fiery gaze, remembering what Seraphina told me about him. *He's always saying it'll be us who burn the world down together.*

"What?"

I had to wait until now, until the sutures were almost complete, before broaching the subject with him. Because his fingers are already twitching at his side, and that usually means bullets, and bloodshed.

"This girl," I say. "Seraphina. I treated her when she fell from the window ten years ago. You told me she died."

I'd been back in Chicago with Liam and our sister, Moira, to get the right drugs and equipment to treat such a severe injury. The girl—*this girl*—couldn't have been more than eight or nine years old at the time. Ignacio had fed me a lie about how she was playing in the window when she fell, that her mother was working out in the fields. But now, seeing the thick boards across the windows, the ones that weren't there ten years ago; I know. He lied. She lived.

I've been torturing myself about the way she died for ten fucking years; the crack in her skull, the pressure on her traumatized brain, but death probably would have been kinder than surviving. There are chains on the walls with black leather wrist straps, the girl is covered in bruises, and the windows are boarded up permanently. The fucking *windows*.

"Are you calling me a liar, Mr. Bishop?" Ignacio asks slowly.

"She has the fucking scar on her head where I stitched her up," I snap, my eyes stuck to that spot just below her temple, the spot where she hit the earth below the window I'm working in front of, where her skull cracked and she fell into a coma.

I slide the last suture into place and snip off the excess, making a neat knot. Ignacio doesn't reply. He knows I know. And that's basically my death sentence, in his eyes; I can already see the decision made in his cool stare.

Do you want to burn the world down?

No, but I would like to see it.

"I'm a criminal just like you, Ignacio," I say. "I break the law. I do bad shit, terrible shit. I've killed people, same as you. But *this* is some next-level shit. You kept a girl in a fucking water tower in the dark as your plaything for *how long?*"

Ignacio blinks, his face like stone. Unreadable. Fucking poker-faced asshole. Me, I'm struggling to tamp down the rage that builds inside me like a funeral pyre set alight. His funeral pyre, if I had it my way. My funeral pyre, if he had his.

"I suggest you pack your supplies up and leave, Mr. Bishop," Ignacio says. His voice is like a razor blade across coals. They say you never feel more alive than when you're in danger of dying, and they'd be on the fucking money. I'm going to die here if I don't do something.

"First I need to tell you about her aftercare," I say, making a show of placing my scalpel down and taking my gloves off. "See this here?" I point at the sutures holding Seraphina's wound closed. "This yellow thread?"

He peers closer, looking for a thread that doesn't exist. Idiot.

I've always got a few spare blades somewhere. These little scalpels might be small, but they're sharp for a fucking reason. To slice a person open like a hot knife in butter. I slide my extra scalpel out of my surgical scrubs and sink it into Ignacio's neck, up to the hilt, going for the jugular and praying I don't miss. His eyes bulge as he reaches for his neck with one hand, the other going for his gun. And all this time his neck is spurting streams of dark blood on to Seraphina's bare torso.

Fuck.

I wrench the scalpel from his neck and strike again, this time getting the meaty bit at the top of his arm. I'm most worried about what happens if he gets his hand on that gun. We'll all be dead, and I refuse to be killed by a bullet that comes from a fucking gold-plated gun that looks like it belongs in some B-grade Steven Seagal movie.

Ignacio howls in pain when I get his arm. It's deep, and no doubt it hurt like a motherfucker when I severed the tendon that runs from his shoulder all the way down his arm and into his hand. I hope it's the hand he uses to jerk off. That's not going to be pleasant from now on.

I round the table, Seraphina still oblivious to what's happening, and crash-tackle Ignacio. I can hear footsteps on the stairs, and I've got to get to his gun before his guards get to me. I lunge like a fucking panther, flying through the air, knocking Ignacio to the ground where we land in a bloody pile. His head hits the hard ground with a sickening crunch. I hope the blow to his skull fucking kills him. It'd be karma, that's for sure.

My life is measured in milliseconds; my fingers curl around Ignacio's stupid gun as the door bursts open, hinges groaning as the wood splinters from the sudden force. Two guys, both brandishing AK's I raise Ignacio's gun, squeezing the trigger in rapid succession, two bullets for each of them, and they're dead before they can focus their eyes long enough to pick out who shot them.

SERAPHINA

*H*E'S STOLEN ME. *He's really done it.*
A dark nothingness.

A terrifying void.

A soothing calm.

I was born into nothing and nowhere, and that's where I stayed, for eighteen years. Now I'm out, reborn into the light ... and I don't like it one bit.

The sun is like a burning ball of fire, aimed right at me. Even in the back of the car, with a knitted cap over my head to both conceal my hair and cover my eyes... all I want to do is scream.

The little edges of light below my eyes hurt more than the cattle prod Ignacio used on me once, when I'd broken down and begged him for more food. Water streams from my eyes, sticking the thick wool cap to my eyelashes, sticky salt and blinding pain my first entry into this foreign world.

So, maybe not so different to being born.

All I've ever wanted is to see the sun. Now that I'm out, I can't bear it. It hurts. Is this the world outside? I always imagined it to be... softer. More like the watercolors I paint with while I wait for Ignacio. *The ones I used to paint with*, I correct myself. I'm not there anymore. I'm...

"Where are we?" I ask blindly, my stomach doing somersaults. I've never been in a car before. I've never been *anywhere* before. I don't like it. My body isn't used to anticipating the roll of the car around corners, the need to brace when we slow down suddenly. My legs are only just now starting to wake up; for a time, I was convinced they would never work again. My side is still numb. I want so badly to look at the spot where Xavier cut me open and put his fingers inside me. Part of me is terrified. Part of me is fascinated. Only time will tell which feeling is justified.

"We're on the Interstate, sweetheart," Xavier says. *Sweetheart.* I don't think I've ever heard that word before. I like it. It sounds gentle. It does not sound like a word somebody would use on a person they intended to hurt.

"You okay back there?"

I nod. Then I realize he probably can't see me. "Yes."

"Really? You don't sound okay. You need something?"

I am starving. I haven't eaten in – hours? Days? I have no reference to time, no way to know how many hours have passed since I fell in the shower, doubled over from the pain in my side, the pain that Xavier Bishop fixed by sawing me open and taking something out.

"Are you going to kill me?" I ask. Point blank. I am not a girl of the world; I do not know such things as subtleties.

Ahead of me, I hear Xavier make a choking sound. "Why would I want to kill you?" he asks.

I wiggle my toes, thankful to be able to feel them a little. "You'd want to kill me because I belong to Ignacio," I say dully.

"Jesus Christ," Xavier mutters. "Girl, I just almost got shot getting you out of there. I had to ride in a chopper. I hate those damn things. Believe me when I say if I wanted to kill you, you'd be dead in Mexico right now."

Adrenalin spikes in my belly, and something else, too. I don't know the word for it. It spreads through my stomach, and lower. He risked death to smuggle me away.

"We're not in Mexico?"

"No."

I wait for more information, but he's silent.

"What happened to Ignacio?" I ask, swallowing down nausea from all the turns he's making. "Is he alright? Is he dead?"

"I don't know if he's dead, but he's definitely not alright," Xavier answers.

I feel the car come to a stop, and put my hands out to stop from sliding off the seat. The leather under me is warm, contoured to my body after so many hours on the road.

"We're here."

✧　✧　✧

HERE IS A place Xavier tells me is called a motel. I've never heard this word before, but it's not dissimilar to my circular room in the tower. It has more light though, light that Xavier tries to minimize after he carries me inside. I sit in the center of a soft bed, the sheets smelling of chemical flowers and talc, and follow Xavier's movements with my ears as he closes every curtain and switches off every light.

"Okay," he says. "You want to try and take that thing off?"

Gingerly, I reach up and push the scratchy fabric up and away from my eyes. More tears roll down my cheeks, not from sadness but a physical response to the air, the damp outside, the crack of light underneath the door and framing the edges of the windows.

It hurts. A sob lodges in my throat, and I fold the material back over my face again. I've felt plenty helpless before, hungry and alone in my tower, but I've never felt like this. Despondent. Lost. I don't know who I am, what I look like, or how to open my eyes in this cruel, radioactive-bright world.

"It's still too much, huh?" His voice is kind. My body instinctively wants to lean into whichever direction he's speaking from. He stole me, it's true, but maybe that's not such a bad thing. I nod. It's still too bright.

"I have an idea," he says. I feel him next to me, and then he's looping an arm under my arms, another arm behind my knees, and I'm being lifted.

"Don't be scared," he says quietly.

I curl into his warm body. I am *terrified.*

XAVIER

S HE STARTED SCREAMING in the back of the car when the sun rose. I'm such an idiot, I hadn't even thought about how bright it would be for her, a girl who'd spent her life feeling around in the dark.

I had to pull over on the edge of the Interstate, praying a cop wouldn't fucking stop and check on us, and find the girl I'd just kidnapped after giving her a spinal block and cutting her abdomen open. I'd be in cuffs before they even read me my Miranda rights.

At least she didn't flip out in the helicopter; there's not enough room to freak out in one of those tiny chopper cabins without kicking the equipment and sending everyone to a fiery death down below. Small mercies and all that.

"What is this place?" She had said with wonder, when I carried her into the motel and deposited her onto the bed. I took her hand; she was trembling violently. What an assault on her senses, for a girl who's spent her entire life locked in a tower.

Now, she's calm, but her heart is going so fast it's about to beat out of her fucking ribcage and land on the floor. I hope not, because this isn't exactly the Bellagio, and I don't think the floors have been cleaned recently.

I've chosen a nondescript, boring-looking Motel on the outskirts of Las Vegas. Ground floor, all one level, and we're on the end of a row of rooms, with a parking spot out front and a clear view of any approaching traffic from the front and the back. I'm fairly certain nobody followed our flight path for now, but it's only a matter of time. Assuming Ignacio survived the scalpel attack, he'll be looking for me. And the first place he'll go is Chicago, my stomping grounds. I know he's going to try to fuck with my family, and I just have to hope that they're smart enough to heed my warnings and take cover until I can figure this shit out. I've just spent the chopper ride into Mexico City, a private jet flight over to Los Angeles and a couple hours in a rental car trying to think of a solution to the dilemma I've just taken upon myself to fix: the real-life Rapunzel in my back seat, a girl whose value is seemingly immeasurable to Ignacio.

I mean, apart from blowing Ignacio's brains out. I'm really regretting not doing that the first time around.

And this brings us to my bright idea at the motel. More than anything, I want to give this girl a full medical checkup, apart from the basic history I got from the ever-helpful Ignacio in Mexico, I've got no idea how old she is, where she came from, if her parents are still looking for her.

The sun shimmers across the mountains in the distance, the heat making everything look washed-out, dream-like. I've been travelling and performing surgery and stabbing and shooting for like, thirty hours without a break; I haven't let myself close my eyes for more than a moment since I arrived in New York. I don't even remember what day that was. All I know is that I need to get this girl somewhere away from prying eyes, my sole mission. *Get her somewhere safe.*

Nowhere will be safe for very long. This is the reality of our cruel world. Everybody will sell you out for the right price. Every code of loyalty is only as strong as the will of the people who enforce it. Every lock can be broken, every door can be rammed down, every traffic and security camera can be hacked.

Nowhere is safe in this world for more than a day or two.

I try to make the Spartan-style Motel room as comfortable as possible for her, but it's obvious Seraphina isn't used to light of any kind. Underneath the knitted ski cap I found at a Gas Station for her to cover her eyes with, tears are streaming down her cheeks like twin tributaries, carving rivers of sorrow along her pale cheeks. I remember when my sister used to get migraines when we were younger, how even the smallest crack of light under her door was unbearable to her. I gather Seraphina up in my arms and use my boot to kick open the closet door.

"Here," I say, sitting her against the wall in this tiny square space, no bigger than my refrigerator. I've already arranged pillows and towels on the floor to make her comfortable; soon, the wound from her surgery is going to start hurting like a motherfucker. I set her down and stand, our connection broken.

She starts to panic, her chest rising and falling with small sobs as she hyperventilates.

"Are you leaving me here?" she whispers in the dark, searching the air with her hands. "Are you going to kill me?"

She looks pitifully small, her hands coming to rest on top of her knees. She's wearing a spare pair of my green surgical scrubs that swim on her slight frame. I couldn't find anything to dress her in in that fucking tower Ignacio kept her locked in that was more substantial than a tiny nightgown made for a twelve-year-old. I push the thought of that away for now, knowing that I can't get angry and flip the fuck out until Seraphina is okay.

I mean, I'm not sure she'll ever be *okay*.

"Hey, Seraphina," I say softly, kneeling in front of her, taking both of her hands in mine. She's shaking violently. The spinal block wearing off makes you shake sometimes, and layered on top of her terror it's like she's caught in the middle of an invisible storm only she can see. "Seraphina. I'm not doing either of those things. This is a closet. You know what that is?"

She nods.

"This is the darkest place I can find in here, sweetheart. I know the light hurts your eyes. I promise I'm not going to hurt you, okay?"

She nods again, her breath hitching in her throat as she starts to calm down.

I might not be a legitimate doctor in a hospital, but my motherfucking bedside manner is one of my best attributes. I can talk anyone into believing they're going to be okay, whether they've just been peppered with bullets, or stabbed, or tortured, or had all their teeth removed with a pair of pliers by a crazy fucking Russian. Yes, that really happened once.

"Please don't go," she begs. My heart fucking shatters. I nod, even though she can't see me, as I squeeze her hands. "I'm right here. I'm right here with you."

On instinct, I wipe the tears from her cheeks, her skin warm and wet beneath the spot where the ski cap rests under her eyes.

"Thank you," she whispers.

"It's okay, Seraphina."

"You can call me Phina," she whispers.

"It's okay, Phina. Everything is going to be okay."

It's a lie, but I hope she believes me. I wedge myself in the spot on the opposite wall of the small built-in closet and pull the door shut with my finger, our legs pressed together in the tiny space. When I arrange a towel under the bottom of the door, the world is plunged into pitch black, and I heave a sigh of relief. It's like trying to keep a vampire from burning to ash in the sun. If vampires were real. *I need some fucking sleep.*

"There you go," I murmur, pulling one hand away from her death-grip and taking the ski cap between my thumb and forefinger.

"You ready to try taking this off?"

She nods.

I pull the whole thing from her head in one movement. I almost forgot about her hair, the way she had it tucked up in the cap, but now it unfurls from the loose knot that had been coiled out of sight. I can't see it—I can't see a damn thing—but I feel it. Ignacio must've supplied some good goddamn hair product, because there's silken strands running over my knees, across my hands as they hold hers, even in my lap, where I've dropped the ski cap for now. It's like satin, and it's literally *everywhere.*

I'd say it was suffocating to have so much of her hair in here, but it feels so soft, so lustrous, a faint tickle on my skin wherever it brushes against me, that it's anything but suffocating. It's... fucking mesmerizing. I haven't focused on anything except her survival (and mine) until this point. Haven't had a second to think. So now, in this moment, shame rises along my skin as I welcome her touch. Disgust rises in my throat as I savor the caress of her flaxen hair on my skin. Rage pulses in my temples as I try not to fall under the spell of being in the dark with a girl who needs anything except the things I want to give her right now. I think about cold showers, about that time I got shot in the shoulder and the pain that came from that. I think about treating that FBI agent in San Francisco after some Russian bastard had pulled every one of her adult teeth out trying to get information out of her. In the end, it's only that image that voids whatever terrible things I was picturing about Seraphina....

I don't even know her last name.

Maybe she doesn't have one.

For now, she's safe, and we can rest. So that's how we fall asleep, together, a tangle of limbs and her impossibly long hair everywhere, like the softest vines, curling around me until I'm pulled under.

SERAPHINA

THE FIRST DAY, I am fearful.

The second day, after Xavier has gradually exposed me to little bits of light, I can actually sit in the Motel room he's brought me to and open my eyes without crying. The curtains are still drawn tightly shut, but he opens the door in increasing intervals until I tell him to stop.

The third day, I can have the curtains open for small stretches of time.

I still can't believe I am out, rescued, the girl in the tower now removed. I feel... odd. Empty. *Terrified*. It's not that I miss Ignacio, but I kind of do, at the same time. I miss the familiarity of his visits, the predictability of his torture. At least when he hurt me, I could brace myself because I expected it. Every time I choked on him, every time he put his hands around my neck and squeezed, I knew exactly how many seconds it would be until he let go, until he finished, until I had to swallow like a good girl and then scuttle off to the shower. I knew when to eat—once a day, so my clothes would fit—and I knew what to say, and where to kneel, and when to open my mouth and stick my tongue out.

Now, I don't know anything. I don't know how to choose something to wear from the plastic bags of clothes Xavier has somehow acquired during the long stretches when I sleep sitting up in the closet. I like it in there; it feels safe, and warm, like a mother's womb probably feels. I am the helpless fawn, falling over herself, trying to stand steady and failing. I don't even know how to exist in this strange new world, full of unbearable light and mind-numbing noise. The food smells different. The sheets feel odd. Everything is *wrong*.

I eat little mouthfuls of things, the feeling of fullness from this strange new food a strange and tiring sensation. Ignacio likes me small, my hips prominent, my breasts pubescent. He has kept me trapped inside a child-sized body, even as I grew into a woman. And now Xavier sits across from me in the kitchen he calls tiny but I find spacious and looming, watching me as I try to eat—sometimes three times in one day! I feel sick from the constant food. I prefer it in the closet, where it is cool and dark and I float atop a stack of pillows and blankets, suspended between realities. If I could live in the closet for the rest of my life, my hands pressed against the thin walls, I surely would.

The fourth day, everything changes again.

Because suddenly, we have to leave. It isn't safe anymore. Xavier is pacing, he is on the phone, he is methodically packing things in bags that he takes out to his truck, one by one, until all that's left is me, and the food in the refrigerator. He comes back in one last time, closing the door behind him with a finality that has every nerve in my body on edge, waiting to react. He's going to kill me, now. No he's not. Yes, he is!

"Phina," Xavier says to me, a pair of scissors in one hand, a rectangular package in the other. "Before we go. I have to cut your hair off."

I instinctively grab at the long braid draped over my shoulder.

Xavier's eyes are kind, even as he holds the scissors at his side like a weapon. He told me that he used a scalpel to stab Ignacio. What will he do to me?

"No," I whisper. "No!"

"I'm so sorry," he says, setting the rectangular package down and taking something from the back pocket of his jeans. A smaller rectangle, this one is flat, and stamped with the word PASSPORT. He flips it open to a page and holds it in front of me. It's a girl with dark brown hair, almost black, that falls to her shoulders in a blunt line.

"I don't understand," I say. "Who is this?"

He takes the passport back, pocketing it as he gestures toward the bathroom. "It's about to be you," he says.

In the bathroom, there is a mirror. I have done everything I can to avoid this mirror—another thing to add to the list of things that terrify me. My own reflection.

Xavier stands behind me, a foot taller than me at least, and I marvel for the first time at the way we look together. Like a painting, like a dream—a tiny pale girl, wearing a braid for a crown, and the angel who visits her in that same dream.

I stare down into the basin as Xavier busies himself behind me. He sets up a towel under my feet, several plastic ziplock bags next to the sink. "We can't leave anything behind," he says. "Especially not your hair. They'll be onto us like lightning."

I saw lightning once, when I was a girl and the windows still opened. I don't want anything to be on me like lightning. I stare at my toes, at the basin, at the dirt in the cracks between the glossy powder-blue tiles I'm standing on.

"Are you okay?" Xavier asks. I nod tightly, unable to look up. Suddenly, I feel him freeze behind me. *He knows.*

"You've never seen yourself in the mirror," he says.

I shake my head tightly. Never. Never, ever. I've seen myself in the back of a dull spoon, in the reflection of Ignacio's reading glasses, but those were so fleeting, so small. No, I have never seen myself.

"Seraphina," Xavier says, his voice low, insistent. He uses a single finger to tip my chin up. I close my eyes. I don't know why I'm so scared.

He's closer. I can feel the heat between our bodies, my back melting into his chest, his bare arms brushing against mine. "I-I can't," I stammer.

"Yes, you can," he says. "You are beautiful, Phina. You deserve to know that. Look."

Tears pooling in my eyes, I finally risk a glance. It's so strange. My eyes are so blue. My pupils are much bigger than Xavier's or even Ignacio's, even though they both have dark brown eyes that merge into black pupils. I have a thin ring of blue that the black almost entirely consumes. I look demonic.

"My pupils—" I say. I can't look at the rest of me, not yet. I'd rather have the cattle prod burned into my skin than study my flaws. And I can hardly bear to look at my hair, knowing it will be destroyed momentarily.

"Your eyes are like that because of the dark," Xavier says quickly. "They've never had to adjust. I bet you can see everything when it's dark, can't you? While the rest of us are stumbling around blind."

I nod. I can see perfectly in the dark. It's the light that blots everything out.

"I dreamed about you," I blurt out, meeting his eyes in the mirror. Isn't that absolutely impossible? He's standing behind me, his breath warm on my ear, but I can look into his eyes as he looks back into mine in the mirror. And isn't it impossible that I dreamed of him before I ever knew him? Xavier responds by reaching around and pulling my hair back off my face, running a warm finger down the scar near my temple, the spot that impacted the ground when I fell from the tower. It was the first time Ignacio had turned from loving father figure to something terrible, a horrific monster who wanted to hold me down and split me in half while I screamed. I was just a girl, and in my panic had thought it better to leap out of the window than stay for any more of the pain. Blood running down my thighs, tears blurring my vision, and he laughed at me, told me *I was a foolish girl,* that *I'd never jump.*

I woke up in the tower days later, my head bandaged heavily, my eye swollen shut, and new boards nailed over the windows. That was the last time I ever saw the sun, or the moon, or the stars. That was the day I went from a girl in a tower to something much worse.

"You don't remember, do you?" Xavier asks.

"Remember what?"

"When you fell. When you were a girl. That was the first time Ignacio had me work for him."

My eyebrows shoot up in disbelief. "You're the one who fixed me when I fell."

He nods. There's so much sadness in his eyes. I can't bear it. I look away, finding my own eyes, and there's just as much pain there. Everything hurts in this cruel world, whether you're in a tower or with the prince who rescued you, as he tries to convince you to remove a part of yourself.

I don't want to cut off my hair.

I've spent the better part of my life tending to this hair. Brushing. Braiding. Wrapping like a plaited crown piled on top of my head. When I was a little girl, I used to play with my hair for comfort, and pretend it was my mother. I still do that now. It's so long, that it's easy for me to run my fingers through it and imagine it's somebody else's touch.

"I didn't know," Xavier says, his eyes suddenly watery, his voice thick. "Seraphina, I am so sorry. That first time I was there… he wouldn't tell me your name. He held a gun to my head while I stitched you up and checked you over. And then, when I'd gotten away and was putting together a plan to come back for you—"

His fingers come to rest on my shoulder, squeezing me almost to the point of pain. "He told me you had died," Xavier finishes. "And me, fucking idiot that I was, I *believed* him."

I'm crying, too. The grief in his words pierces my very soul, right down to the core; somebody cared about me, once. Somebody wanted to rescue me from Ignacio.

"I have carried you with me for ten years," Xavier says, poking his chest with a rigid finger, "in here. I thought about you every day. I still think about you every day."

I run my finger down my thick braid, remembering exactly how much Ignacio used to love using my hair for his pleasure, for my discipline. My hair is like this because Ignacio decided it. Because, until four days ago, I was his little fuck doll, his stolen prize, his dirty secret hidden away in the dark.

Suddenly, it's as if I can feel every hair follicle on my head, the weight of this impossibly long braid, the way he used to pull it so hard pieces would come out in his fingers as he forced me back onto him.

"Cut it all off," I say, my voice sounding like it belongs to somebody else, the meek edge gone. It's as if I have been possessed. The hair that was my security blanket is now the weighted chain that will drag me to the bottom of the ocean if I don't get it off.

Xavier opens his mouth to say something, but he must have heard the edge in my voice, because he takes the scissors from the counter, and with three agonizing cuts, he's placing my braid on the counter in front of me.

I look at myself. I've never seen myself to know if I always had that hard glint of determination in my eyes, but I know inside of me that it wasn't there a moment ago. I reach up to run my fingernails through my scalp. I feel light. So impossibly light, as if I could just hold my breath and float away on the breeze.

He colors my hair next, first wetting it as I lean into the sink, and then massaging dark goo into my scalp that smells horrific. My skin burns and my eyes water from the smell, but I bear the time patiently. I am a girl who is used to waiting, used to pain and discomfort. This is my default mode. I am most comfortable when I am held in the predictability of unpleasant things. We don't talk. We've both taken our shirts off for this part, to avoid getting any of the dye on them, and so Xavier is bare chested, his dark skin in start contrast to the ivory sports bra I'm wearing, not to mention my pallid skin. The room heats up considerably when Xavier starts to apply the dye to my roots. I would say it's the chemicals, but it is definitely because we are now both half-naked in a small enclosed space where we are constantly brushing up against each other by necessity. My cheeks burn, two red circles in a pale white face, as I remember all the times Ignacio would be behind me, all the times when I would close my eyes and pretend it was the mysterious angel

466

from my dreams pushing into me instead.

Xavier. It's been him all along. And now that I know, I can barely look him in the eye without a deep warmth spreading across my womb, almost painful in its intensity. My nipples stiffen to hard peaks under the thin bra Xavier bought for me and helped me put on earlier, a purely platonic gesture, but one that I'm now imagining in all different sorts of ways. There is no padding in this bra, and my nipples are clear as day, jutting out like tiny bullets on my chest.

I notice Xavier glance at me a couple of times, almost furtively. Can he read my mind? He doesn't need to, I guess. He can feel it, like ripples of heat between us. I want to be this close to him for the foreseeable future.

Finally, the black goo is washed out of my hair and dried off with a towel. Xavier motions for me to stand, pointing in the mirror at the new Seraphina, the one with the dark hair and the new voice. I look into my reflection and see a stranger.

"How does that feel?" he asks. He looks worried. I smile. I look at my face; at the way my nearly black hair frames it. "Different," I reply, my eyes wide in wonder. "Good."

Xavier grins so wide, his face looks like it might shatter. His teeth are beautiful, his eyes crinkled at the edges from the force of his smile. His joy hits me in the chest like a heavy blow, and my knees go weak.

"Whoa," he says, catching me before I sink to the floor in a heap. If my long hair was anchoring me to the ground, now I feel like I barely exist. It's a heady feeling, like lust. Braced against the counter, I turn my body to face his. I tuck my hair behind my shoulders and look Xavier right in the eyes. He's got that worried look again, and he tries to leave the room. I've already anticipated his move, though, and I sidestep so my back is against the closed bathroom door, the whole room a dizzying mix of pheromones and peroxide.

"What are you doing?" he asks uneasily. I reach for the waistband of his jeans, pulling him toward me. He follows the movement of my insistent tug—to a point. But he freezes shy of our bodies touching, placing his arms on the wall on either side of my head. I'm caged in by him, but it's not like being trapped in a tower; it's like being consumed by a fire than burns *so damn good*.

I'm breathing heavily, the feeling inside my chest dizzying. There's a fine sheen of sweat gathering on Xavier's chest. He looks afraid.

I stand on my tiptoes, curling a hand around his neck. Our lips barely graze, but it's like being slapped across the face, like seeing stars. I know Xavier feels it, too, because he jerks his head away.

Without my hair weighing me down, I am a new person. Meek, subservient Seraphina is gone now, her fate braided into the long plait of hair that sits on the counter, dead. I am another Seraphina now.

Seraphina means fiery, and I am burning up inside.

Xavier tries to grasp the door handle. I don't let him. I am small, but I am fast. And apparently, insistent as well.

"Phina," he protests.

"Xavier," I reply.

I unclasp the bra he bought for me, letting it slide off my shoulders and onto the floor, forgotten. In the past four days I have broken myself open, spilled my dirty soul onto the floor, showed Xavier Bishop all of my secrets... and now I want to show him this. I take his large hand and place it on my left breast, shivering as his rough palms scratch my soft skin. Underneath my jeans, my underwear is drenched. Whoever thought something as innocent as a haircut could cause such a raging desire to be unleashed?

"We can't," he breathes, tipping his head forward so our foreheads are touching.

I unbutton my jeans and slide them down my legs, kicking them off onto the floor so that I am completely naked.

"Says who?" I challenge him. I want to kiss him. More than anything in the world, I want to kiss him. I take the hand that's still on my breast and guide it between my legs, into the warm wetness that's appeared just now, just for him.

"Oh, fuck," Xavier mutters, sliding his finger through my slick folds. He pulls away, though, putting his hand on my shoulder and stepping back to create the illusion of distance between us.

"You don't have to do this," he says urgently, his dark eyes searching mine. "You understand? Whatever he made you do, it was wrong, and it was sick, and you don't ever have to feel like you have to give me that, Phina. I'll do anything to keep you safe. You don't need to do this with me."

I sag against the door, throbbing and empty and light-headed with need.

"You don't want me," I say, looking down at the floor. "It's okay. *I understand.*"

468

XAVIER

O H FUCK. OH fucking fuck. I was just cutting her hair, and then she was taking off her bra, and putting my fingers between her legs. Oh, fuck! She's so wet. My cock is so hard it's going to kill me. *This is where I die.* Not with a bullet, or a knife, but from a brain aneurysm after the impossible pressure in my dick backs up all the way to my skull.

My balls are so heavy, it's like I'm packing a pair of lead weights underneath my jeans.

"You don't want me," Phina says, naked against the door, her wet pussy all over my fingers.

"I fucking want you," I groan, still holding her at arm's length. "But it doesn't matter. It's not *right.*"

She narrows her eyes. "You would rather I live with the memory of Ignacio as the only man who's ever touched me," she responds. Almost like it's a *dare.*

"Just show me," she whispers urgently, her eyes on the spot where my cock is trying to split my pants open. I can't. I shouldn't. But my hands have a mind of their own, unbuttoning my fly, pushing my pants down my locked thighs, gripping my cock in my hand as I stare down the impossibility in front of me.

Seraphina steps forward, her hand reaching for me. She wraps her fingers around my cock and squeezes.

"I want to kiss you," she whispers. I lick my lips. A kiss, my conscience can handle. I wait for her to tilt her head to me, but she sinks to her knees instead. She presses her lips to me, precum smearing across her lips as she plants a kiss on the blunt end of my cock, and my conscience no longer matters. A growl starts deep in my chest as I pull her back up to her feet, my hands grabbing her ass, lifting her into the air. I turn her, from the door to the bathroom counter, the scissors clattering to the ground as I perch her on the edge of the counter and grip her knees, spreading them wide. I'm going to burn in Hell for this, but an eternity of suffering is easily worth every thrust I can get into her wet cunt before I explode.

"I want to kiss you, too," I breathe, my heart hammering as I bury one finger in her tight pussy. Oh, God. My cock throbs with raw need.

"Hurry," she begs, squirming on the counter. I don't waste another second. I drive my hips forward, my cock finding the wet heat of her core, and I just stay there, barely breaching her tightness. I just want to see the spot where we join, the way my dark cock looks against her pale skin. I rock my hips forward slightly, dipping my lips to hers and kissing her. She tastes like me, salt and sex on her lips, and like something else, as well. She tastes like a cold glass of water to a man dying in the desert. My chest tightens at the relief; she didn't die. She survived. And she's here, flesh and blood. And she's fucking *beautiful*.

"Do it," she whimpers, raising her hips toward me. I hold her chest to mine, her nipples warm on my bare skin, and enter her slowly. I savor every inch, every damn second, every wet kiss, every tiny moan. I fuck her on the bathroom counter until she tightens around me, throwing her head back so hard it smacks against the mirror, and then I can't hold back, moaning as my balls tighten and I empty myself into her.

"You're safe now," I grind out, my forehead tipped to hers again as we catch our breath, sweat-slicked and spent. "You're never going back there. You understand?"

Seraphina nods, sagging into me. We stay there like that until our skin grows cold, until the light starts to dim outside, and then we finally untangle ourselves from each other. No way in hell did I expect this to happen, but it feels right, even though I said it was wrong. We dress, I slide Seraphina's severed braid into a bag, and then we're leaving, moving forward to the next hiding place. She stops on the threshold, gasping, her hands to her mouth as she takes in the sky. It's sunset, and the world is awash with dusky pink and purple, slashes of yellow and orange in between. "What is this?" she asks, her eyes wide with wonder. My throat burns. We did it. She's in the light, no matter how fast the sun might be fading.

"That's a sunset, sweetheart," I say, smiling so wide it almost hurts. "I'm going to make sure you see that every single night from now on."

She smiles back at me, tucking her hand into mine. We get into the car. We drive all night. Every mile that we press north is like another weight off, like another length of chain cast into the desert, forgotten.

I get a text from my brother on my burner phone, just as we're entering San Francisco and the safe haven of people I trust. *Ignacio survived.* I was kind of expecting this news, but it still punches me in the gut. I don't tell Seraphina, not yet. She looks too relaxed for me to ruin her life all over again with the knowledge that her captor is alive and most likely looking for her right now.

Seraphina will never go near that fucking tower again, if I have to spend my whole life running with her.

I don't know what tomorrow will bring. But tonight, we are just two people, driving on the interstate, heading toward refuge.

And the knot in my stomach is finally gone.

THE END

THANK YOU!

Thank you for reading Knot! I hope you enjoyed getting to know Xavier and Seraphina. You can read more of their story in their upcoming series, slated to release at the end on 2017.

Lili St. Germain is the *USA Today* bestselling author of the *Gypsy Brothers* series and the *Cartel* trilogy.

Her next series is called **CALIFORNIA BLOOD**, a trilogy set in the criminal underbelly of San Francisco, which follows two warring families who are ruled by blood, power and twisted desire.

Verona Blood is the first book in the series, and will be released mid-2007. Please read on for a short description of the series and links!

✧   ✧   ✧

VERONA BLOOD

Avery Capulet is missing.
Taken by a madman. Kept in the dark.
She might not survive.
He'll use her body. Destroy her mind.
All before he even lays a hand on her.

Rome Montague is a drug dealer. A criminal. A thief.
Rome Montague is missing – but nobody will miss him.
Not that it matters; after the things he's done to this girl, *he doesn't deserve to be found.*

For CALIFORNIA BLOOD pre-order links, release dates and more, visit www.lilisaintgermain.com/CaliforniaBlood

✧ ✧ ✧

If you can't wait that long for Lili's new books to release, check out her GYPSY BROTHERS series, and meet Dornan Ross, the villain readers LOVE to hate! The Gypsy Brothers series centers on a young woman and her quest for revenge, as she infiltrates the biker club who murdered her father and left her for dead. Love, lust and vengeance all collide when Juliette Portland sets out to destroy those who wronged her.

CALIFORNIA BLOOD is available now!

THANK YOU!

Thank you for reading GLAMOUR! You have our immense appreciation for your support of our work. It would be a huge help if you told a friend about this set, especially since it will only be available for a limited time. We'd love for readers to find it before it's gone.

Cover Art by Inkstain Design Studio
Formatting by BB eBooks

Made in the USA
Middletown, DE
31 May 2018